The Man Watching
Anson Dorrance and the
University of North Carolina
Women's Soccer Dynasty

Tim Crothers

Thomas Dunne Books
St. Martin's Griffin
New York

For my wife, Dana,
and anyone else who has ever
chosen to be extraordinary

THOMAS DUNNE BOOKS.
An imprint of St. Martin's Press.

THE MAN WATCHING. Copyright © 2006 by Tim Crothers. All rights reserved. Printed in the United States of America. For information, address St. Martin's Press, 175 Fifth Avenue, New York, N.Y. 10010.

www.thomasdunnebooks.com
www.stmartins.com

Library of Congress Cataloging-in-Publication Data

Crothers, Tim.
    The man watching : Anson Dorrance and the University of North Carolina women's soccer dynasty / Tim Crothers.—1st ed.
        p. cm.
    Includes index.
    ISBN 978-0-312-61609-0
    1. University of North Carolina at Chapel Hill—Soccer. 2. Soccer for women—North Carolina—Chapel Hill. 3. Dorrance, Anson. 4. Soccer coaches—United States. I. Title.
    GV943.7.U55C76 2010
    796.334'6209756565—dc22
                                                            2010030190

Originally published in the United States by Sports Media Group, an imprint of Ann Arbor Media Group LLC

First St. Martin's Griffin Edition: October 2010

10 9 8 7 6 5 4 3 2 1

Contents

Preface

As a Father's Day present in 1997, Anson Dorrance's eldest daughter, Michelle, bought her dad a pocket-sized blue spiral notebook. She titled it *Dad's Quote Book*, and to further personalize her gift she scissored out a photograph from a magazine and pasted it to the book's cover. The photo features a lonely road sign on an anonymous prairie, against a wide blue sky. The sign is directional, a bending arrow pointing the way, and it is peppered with bullet holes. Asked to explain the symbolism of the image, Michelle says, "It's what I've taken from what my dad taught me."

The idea for the gift sprang from Michelle's realization that her father, the University of North Carolina women's soccer coach, had always been a quote collector. He was constantly underlining profound excerpts in books, but then he was never able to retrieve a specific quote when he wanted it. She also admits to a selfish craving for easy access to the motivational words that her father regularly shares with his players. Now, whenever Dorrance stumbles upon a quote that moves him, he scribbles it into his quote book, which is always situated within arm's reach on his cluttered office desk. *Dad's Quote Book*, which contains more than one hundred quotes and counting, is Dorrance's only possession that he can always locate at a moment's notice, and he faithfully remembers to stuff it into his briefcase before every road trip so that he has these inspirational words at his fingertips. Quotes borrowed from that notebook, which also serve as an outline for the core values of the UNC women's soccer program, introduce each chapter in this book.

When Dorrance initially agreed to be interviewed for this project in the summer of 2001, he didn't do it for the notoriety. He didn't do it for the legacy. He did it for the potential recruiting value, and also to satisfy his curiosity. He was interested in how his players as well as his opposition perceive the UNC program. Dorrance presumed that he already knew what he would say, but he discovered that his own responses were more intriguing than he'd anticipated. One evening he suddenly interrupted himself mid-interview and said, "You know, the great thing about this book is that it's become a self-exploration. It's allowed me to answer a lot of questions that I'd never asked myself about why I do what I do."

For forty-eight months this book was my job, and I imagine it's the most rewarding occupation I will ever have. After twelve years of covering both professional and college sports at *Sports Illustrated*, this experience has refreshed my faith in athletics. The book captures a lot of what is good about sports, along with some of what is not. My objective has been to write about the reality of women's athletics, without any sugarcoating, and about how the struggle for excellence can be both humbling and empowering.

I considered it a privilege to be permitted inside the normally forbidden sanctums of the practice huddle, the team bus, and the team meeting room for Dorrance's speeches before, during, and after every game. Nothing was off the record. In the interest of research, I took a position as a volunteer assistant coach in the spring of 2002, which allowed me to scrimmage in UNC's legendary 3-4-3 system alongside U.S. national team defender Catherine Reddick. There I felt firsthand the sting of Dorrance's editorial commentary. I have also risked life and limb by regularly skating in Dorrance's pickup roller hockey game, and by riding shotgun in a van driven by assistant coach Bill Palladino. I have also been thrashed repeatedly by Dorrance in foosball and have endured a long night of his cacophonous snoring as his roommate on a road trip.

To his credit, after four years of living with a writer in his shadow, Dorrance still conjured up fresh stories during each of our frequent interviews, which can best be described as fluid. I recall once walking into Dorrance's office with a few questions about recruiting and instead chatting with him for two hours about Winston Churchill. Whenever I was around Dorrance I could never stop reporting, because he's always on the verge of an anecdote. I've written notes on napkins, matchbooks, forearms, and hockey sticks. We once conducted an interview while driving a UNC player to the emergency room.

Throughout this book, there will be extended quotes and even full speeches from Dorrance, because he is an old-school orator who thoughtfully measures rhythm and cadence and vocabulary as well as the attention span of his audience. To truly understand his power it is necessary to experience a speech or a story in its entirety.

I have interviewed more than 120 Tar Heel players during the writing of this book, and while many of them are married now, with names changed, for purposes of simplicity they will all be referred to in these pages by the names they used at UNC. During my time following the program, witnessing more women's soccer than I would have expected in six lifetimes, I learned that Dorrance is a coach shaped by his players as much as the other way around. This book is about how a man took a group of women and built the greatest dynasty in college sports . . . and about how they built him.

Tim Crothers
August 2006

Infancy

1 Roses

"Here is my secret. It's quite simple: One sees clearly only with the heart. Anything essential is invisible to the eyes."

"Anything essential is invisible to the eyes," the Little Prince repeated, in order to remember.

"It's the time you've spent on your rose that makes your rose so important."

"It's the time I've spent on my rose . . .," the Little Prince repeated, in order to remember.

"People have forgotten this truth," the fox said. "But you mustn't forget it. You become responsible forever for what you've nurtured. You're responsible for your rose . . ."

"I'm responsible for my rose . . .," the Little Prince repeated, in order to remember.

—Antoine de Saint-Exupéry

*A*llllllrightthen, here we go. I'll tell you, I loved last year's Final Four because of the position we were in. I loved coming in as an underdog. Guess what? I think the same thing is happening again at this Final Four. In the press conference yesterday all the questions I got this year were about how well Portland is playing and about how we're struggling. Well, I can play that tune. I went right along with them. But I was thinking that if you people had seen the second half of our quarterfinal game against Penn State, you pinheads!, you'd have known that we outshot them 9–1. Where the hell have you been? I didn't deliver any of that to the media because I know what we can do, and if right now they have written us off, then I want us to show everyone what this team can do out there on the field tonight because I tell you, when you guys play your best you are devastating. You are frigging inspirational. You play through your hearts with extraordinary passion, and our opponents know that if they don't bring it, you guys are going to humiliate them.

In the press conference I thought one of Portland's players talked about their confidence with a little too much confidence. You know what I mean? They think they're on a roll and they think that we're collapsing. They think we're toast. They think they can grind it out. Let them try to grind it out with us for ninety minutes. We are professional grinders. Everybody's talking about all of their great players, but do they have our personalities all over the field? I don't think so. I think we have great weapons and we need to bring them to bear. We have something to *prove. The media doesn't think we're going to play. Portland doesn't think we're going to play. I think we're going to play. Are you with me?*

The man delivers this speech before an audience of women. Coach Anson Dorrance conveys this message to a specific team inside a specific locker room during a specific season, but these are words he could have said at any Final Four in any season in the history of the University of North Carolina women's soccer program, because, like so many of Dorrance's speeches, this one is timeless.

On this day Dorrance will not talk about the past. He will not talk about the ludicrous number of national titles won by women wearing the same distinctive blue uniforms as the women gathered around him. He will not talk about all of those championship trophies back in Chapel Hill that are stuffed into the display case like a set of encyclopedias, or about the fact that runner-up trophies are traditionally utilized as doorstops because anything less than a national title is considered a failure. He will certainly not remind these players that they are the caretakers of the greatest dynasty in the history of collegiate sports. Because, this being college athletics, every season, every team, is totally different, and the women in this room are not even the same women they were at the Final Four last year or the year before that. Far from it. So Dorrance will not mention anything won in the past. Or anything not won. In fact, he will not mention winning or losing at all. Everybody present already understands the one quest that binds them all. Shared expectations. Shared destinies. The roses.

As Dorrance concludes a brief synopsis of the game plan, the team's manager, Tom Sander, carefully removes the roses from a duffel bag in the corner of the room. And thus begins a ceremony that ushers the Tar Heel senior class out of the locker room. Each of the seniors is handed a bouquet of roses. Most of them wipe tears from their eyes. The underclassmen, many also crying, applaud and cheer each senior as she walks a receiving line, stopping for a hug and a few encouraging words from Dorrance and then from assistant coach Bill Palladino, goalkeeper coach Chris Ducar, and finally the team's trainer, Bill Prentice. During these moments, there is a collective flashback to three weeks earlier, when Dorrance walked into the team meeting room back in Chapel Hill before the opening game of the NCAA Tournament carrying a vase of flowers, and told them all about the roses. He had explained then that each red rose in the vase represented a national championship won by the current senior class, and he had read them a passage from Antoine de Saint-Exupéry's *The Little Prince* about caring for a rose. Then he had summed up what it all meant to him. "The rose is symbolic of wherever each of you are athletically, and it's symbolic of championships because you're all responsible for them," Dorrance had said. "What I like about the symbolic use of flowers is that we're celebrating our past, but after a while, the flower shrivels and dies. That glory is dead. Athletics is about renewal, and you guys are sitting in the places of all the previous classes who have tried to send their seniors out as champions. If we lose a game in this tournament, there's no tomorrow for them. Their careers have died. So we play for them."

As the locker room door closes behind the final exiting senior, Dorrance pulls several photocopied sheets of paper out of the breast pocket of his jacket. As is his custom, he has worked through much of the previous night in his hotel room, writing and rewriting a personal letter to each of his seniors in his barely legible longhand. Then he has awakened early this morning to polish his words, editing until the last possible moment, because that is the only way the letters can be genuine, the only way they can express what he sincerely feels at that instant. Then he has delivered the original letters to each of the seniors a few hours before the pregame talk.

He knows that he's only got a moment with these letters, and that this could be his last chance to make sure each senior knows how much he cares about them. He wants each young woman to know that even though he has spent four years telling her this isn't good enough, that isn't good enough, she isn't good enough, that what he's been secretly searching for all along is what really is good enough in her. When he recounts a personal story or two about her that she'd never expect him to remember, he wants her to know what he thinks is her finest quality—and this is never a soccer quality, but a human quality—because he believes that's what his women appreciate most. When he reads the copies of the senior letters to the underclassmen left behind in the locker room, he wants his admiration to resonate. As he shares the words he has written to each senior, no matter how large or small her role on the team, Dorrance wants everyone inside that room to be in awe of her.

We're all familiar with our tradition here, and part of it is that I get to share my memories of the kids we're going to lose. These are the letters I wrote to our senior reserves. It's always hard. Obviously you guys think you've got all the time in the world. You think you're going to be in college forever. At least that's what I thought when I was there. Then all of a sudden it's gone and we'll never play with these kids again . . .

Dear Katie,

There are many great memories that I will treasure from this year, and one that will stand out was after the conference championship game when you were jogging off the field smiling from one ear to the other after playing in just the second game of your career. I heard someone's voice calling my name, and I turned to see your father. Reaching down to extend his hand from above the rail at the Wake Forest soccer stadium, a tear was rolling down his cheek. He was so proud of you. I told him that you were going to take a piece of history with you. Until the end of recorded time in the pantheon of great goalkeepers that this program has had who have won world championships, Olympic medals, national championships, no one will beat the goals against average of his sweet and humble daughter, Katie. Please take that history with you, Katie, and one day brag to your grandchildren that, yeah, Tracy Noonan,

Siri Mullinix, Jenni Branam were all pretty good goalkeepers at UNC, but how about 0.00 goals against? . . . How about that? . . .

So we play for Katie.

Dear Whit,

You are a triumph of the human spirit. Every image I have of you is a catalog of your guts and your indefatigable will. My first image of you was seeing you sprint and dive across the finish line your freshman year to pass your first fitness test. My second image is when we were desperate that first week of games your freshman year, and we asked if anyone wanted to play up front to make up for the lackluster effort of our starters, and you volunteered and with sheer effort turned the game for us. The next image was you as a sophomore on a stretcher after they put those rods in to repair your broken back. And where are you? You're not in the hospital. You're on the sidelines with us. Part of our team. The most recent image brings it all back together. It was this year, and like your freshman year, we were wondering out loud if any of our starting forwards would take any kind of risk to help us win. We asked you if you would take a risk. You survived Lyme disease as a child, a broken back on the soccer field as a young college kid, and a medical dismissal as an old college kid when doctors told you you could never play again. So if you did not want to take the risk anymore, it was OK. You earned the right to quietly decline, but you said yes, you'd take a risk to help the team win. To this day, that goalkeeper does not know what hit her. When she discovered you lying next to her and the ball in the back of her net behind her, she learned how hard and courageous someone's heart could be. You are my inspiration.

So we play for Whit.

Dear Kristin,

I want you to know I think you are an example of everything that is good in athletics. Athletics does not necessarily build character, but it definitely exposes it, and what it exposed in you is uniquely powerful and positive. We won't find your name on any collegiate All-American list or your face on a highlight reel, but your moral fabric and work ethic is pervasive here. Your concerns were for an environment that transcended self-interest, and you supported your teammates and coaches in our mission to be the best we could be even when the playing time and glory went to the goalkeepers you played behind. For four years in a row I have brought you into my office to tell you that someone else is going to play in your place in the NCAA Tournament. And in this, your final year, it is most painful. Your nobility in the face of this disappointment will always set you apart. Please know this. You are finishing at your best, following your greatest performances in a development that's ascending still. We will all miss you on the field, but we will also know that your mark was always made on a higher plane.

So we play for Kristin.

Dear Johanna,

There's a part of me that will forever burn with the idealism that I envy in you. There's another part that wanted you to serve yourself and let West Africa be, but I admire that you had to go there last summer to help any way you could. In the swirl of glitz and glory in the numbers of our tradition, and in the interviews of our stars and goal scorers and me-dia darlings, the stories miss their mark because the values of everything we really treasure are preserved in you. You kept alive the tradition of running fitness with the ones who can't. You gave back to your local community to fight for the construction of fields that you will never play on as an example to the ones who won't. You passed the most excruciat-ing fitness test in the game with only the rarest possibility of ever play-ing as a standard for those who have none, baffling the ones that try to cut every corner. You leave no margin for the ones who whine about the conspiracy of their human condition. When you go, some of the things I like best will go with you. You'll be missed, more than you'll ever know.

So we play for Johanna.

Dorrance's voice cracks with emotion several times throughout the reading of the letters. Twice he stops to compose himself. There is much sniffling among the players, a few are openly sobbing, dabbing at their faces with their uniform sleeves. When Dorrance finishes reading the final letter, everyone in the room, including the coach and all of his staff, have their heads bowed, fighting back tears.

Let me tell you this. I'm watching practice yesterday and we're wrapping it up, doing our set pieces at the end, and I'm watching Catherine Reddick practice free kicks. All season she's so afraid to hit anyone in the wall that most of her shots are skying over the crossbar or going wide. Well, Catherine knows now that it's time to go after it. All of a sudden she smacks one, and it almost tore a couple of ribs off Johanna. I wanted to set Johanna free so I said, "All right Johanna, that's it. You're outta the wall." And she didn't move. She didn't move. It looked like a tear started to well up in Jo's eye, and I know she was in pain. But I was wondering, what was she in pain from? That the ball hit her? Or that this was all she could do to help us win, and she did not feel complete or satisfied, and would anyone even notice or care? So remember this. When you're out there tonight, playing out the last minutes of someone else's career, don't waste a second. Don't avoid a physical risk. Don't not make a run. Don't dishonor the wonderful nobil-ity of the reserves you are playing before. You will never eliminate the quiet pain they are all suffering, but you will make it a bit more bearable, and if you are truly valiant it might even feel inside that all of their sacrifice is worthwhile.

All right. Here we go.

Here We Go

Life is either a daring adventure, or nothing.

–Helen Keller

Albert Anson Dorrance IV was born in an earthquake. Peggy Dorrance felt the tremors as the car barreled through the narrow streets of Bombay in the middle of the night on the way to the hospital. First she thought it was just the rumbling in her belly, but these were Mother Nature's contractions.

As Nathan Dorrance awaited the birth of his first child on that Monday, April 9, 1951, he immersed himself in the newspaper accounts of American troops under the command of General Douglas MacArthur, on the offensive against the Chinese Communists in the Korean War. Just hours later, he would be stunned upon hearing that President Harry Truman had relieved MacArthur of his duties for insubordination, abruptly ending the general's dynamic military career and reminding Nathan, a former soldier himself, that no leader, no matter how decorated, is ever bigger than the war itself.

The Dorrance family's genealogical history features a proud legacy of military service. Anson's great-great-great-great-grandfather Samuel Dorrance fought for the Continental Army in the Revolutionary War. Samuel's older brother Lieutenant Colonel George Dorrance also fought for the colonies, leading troops into the Battle of Wyoming, where he was wounded and captured by Indians near Pennsylvania's Forty Fort. Lieutenant Colonel Dorrance stubbornly refused to surrender his sword to his captors, so the Indians wrestled his weapon away from him and cut off his head with it. He died on Independence Day, July 4, 1778. Samuel's son, Captain George Dorrance, fought for his country in the War of 1812. George's grandson, George, fought for the Union Army at the second Battle of Winchester in the Civil War and later witnessed the assassination of President Abraham Lincoln at Ford's Theatre in Washington, D.C.

Anson's paternal grandfather, Albert Anson II, was a pilot in World War I. After the war, he moved to Shanghai, China, where he lived until World War II. There he was recruited as a supply pilot with General Claire Chennault's legendary Flying Tigers, a guerilla air force that supported the Chinese in their military struggle against Japan. Anson II flew arms from India into China over the Hump, a perilous labyrinth of 14,000-foot mountain peaks in northern Burma, until he was shot down, captured, and charged as a spy. He was eventually imprisoned in the hold of a Japanese ship, where he and his fellow POWs survived by drinking each other's urine. After two years in captivity, he was freed in a prisoner exchange.

At the same time that Anson II flew missions around Southeast Asia, his son Nathan, known to his family as Pete, also served in the Pacific theater as a Navy submarine navigator. Pete would name his first-born son after his late brother, Second Lieutenant Albert Anson Dorrance III, who perished on D-Day when the C-47 he piloted was shot down behind enemy lines in Normandy.

Both Pete Dorrance and Peggy Peoples were born and raised in China. Peggy's family came from North Carolina and worked in China as representatives of American Tobacco, while Pete's side worked there through Standard Oil of New Jersey, until both families were forced to leave the country at the beginning of World War II. The families had occasionally socialized with each other in China, but their children never met until a reunion in Washington, D.C., in December of 1949. Pete took Peggy out on a date the next night; they were engaged within a month and married in Bombay in May of 1950.

Pete followed in his father's footsteps as a Standard Oil executive. Since he was transferred regularly, the Dorrance family moved every three years or so, bivouacking from Bombay to Calcutta to Nairobi, Kenya, to Addis Ababa, Ethiopia, to Singapore, Malaysia, and then to Brussels, Belgium, when Anson was fourteen years old. During those years, Anson was attended by a fleet of servants, from nannies and maids to cooks and chauffeurs. That life of privilege was interrupted every few years when the Dorrance family returned to the United States on "home leave," spending several months at Anson's grandparents' farm in Louisburg, North Carolina. There young Anson primed tobacco and slopped hogs alongside the tenant laborers. The farm was owned by Anson's mother's father, who divorced his wife and later married Anson's father's mother.

As Anson bounced around the globe, he used sports as his road to acceptance. He taught himself how to play the most popular sports wherever he lived, like rugby, field hockey, softball, and soccer. But he never took to soccer much, bothered by his lack of instinct for the game as compared to his classmates who had spent their youth playing it daily.

Growing up in various British colonial outposts, Anson gained his first enduring memories of sport with his experiences at his British grade school in Nairobi. "Sport wasn't a choice; it was a part of our lives," Anson says. "There were four team colors in the school, and I was on Mead, and there was this sense of mission that we had every afternoon when we were competing for Mead. I loved playing this ridiculous game where everybody tries to run across the field and pick up a guy and scream out, 'British Bulldog!' and then throw him to the ground and he's dead. Mead came to represent something greater than ourselves, and that became a part of my personality."

After Anson, the Dorrances would add four other children: daughter Maggie, sons Pete and Lewjack, and finally another daughter, Chantal. To simplify life around the house, Anson's father was called Big Pete. Anson's primary sports role models were the women in his family, particularly Peggy, who was the family's most natural athlete. Peggy had grown up playing basketball, cricket, tennis, and golf. At American University in Washington, D.C., she was captain of the tennis team and set swimming records for the number of events won in a single meet. Anson's mother was the best adult athlete he knew, dominating everybody she met on the tennis court and incessantly teasing Big Pete about beating the stuffing out of him on the golf course. Anson's sister Maggie, one year his junior, was clearly a better athlete than Anson, as well as being so ferociously competitive that she was chosen before him in most backyard pickup games. One day seven-year-old Anson proudly arrived home with news that he had won a school boxing tournament. Maggie promptly slipped on his boxing gloves and knocked one of his teeth out.

If Anson had an athletic cross to bear, it was his stature. Throughout his childhood he was always among the smallest kids in his class, a deficiency that he blamed on his Hindu nanny in India, who, for religious reasons, had regularly removed the meat from his curry. Still, Anson always refused to use his size as a crutch. "My initial spark of competitiveness came from what they call in psychology 'the Napoleon Complex,'" Anson says. "I was always tiny for my age, and I always felt like I had to prove myself."

"As a young kid Anson would teach the other kids how to play the games, but he was too small to win," Peggy says. "He became extremely competitive, and I think that's because it was never easy for him as an athlete. He had to make a significant effort to be a good player, and he wanted to win so desperately that he struggled to keep himself under control."

Any activity became a competition for Anson. Once in Ethiopia, when he was riding a tandem swing with his brother Pete, Anson began to propel the swing so feverishly that Pete couldn't keep up. Pete's foot slipped off the pedal, and his leg snapped in two. Another time while visiting their grandfather in Hong Kong, Anson and Pete bought what are called "fighting kites," which have strings that contain ground glass. When Anson and Pete flew their new kites out the window of their grandfather's apartment building, Anson relentlessly sawed his kite's string across Pete's until his little brother's string broke and the kite soared off into the sky.

Anson also believed that a score should be kept in any game, and whenever he sensed that the environment wasn't competitive enough, he would intentionally say something to irritate his rivals, challenging them not to give up. *This could be a shutout! Do you want me to play with one hand?* In his mind, he would rather have someone beat him than let him win, so he did his damnedest to motivate his competition. "As Anson got older he was still smaller than anyone on the field, but you didn't feel that way after a contest," Pete says. "Every game he played, he kept score, and then he happened to be the guy who won."

In Singapore, Anson was the youngest and smallest kid on his fast-pitch softball team, but he was still chosen to be the team's pitcher. The best youth team in the city at that time, Boystown, was a squad of Catholic orphans who had produced a long winning streak until Anson pitched a 1–0 no-hitter against them, bunting home the winning run himself in the final inning. After the game, the vanquished Boystown team gave Anson a handkerchief with a note scribbled on it that read: *The day the little guy did the impossible!* "That's like a microcosm of his whole life," Pete says. "They probably looked at the little squirt on the mound and thought, 'No problem.' Then all of a sudden there are these bullets flying right past them and they're thinking, 'How does he do that?'"

Throughout his childhood Anson was constantly reminded that he was in the minority. Sometimes he *was* the minority. In Addis Ababa he was the only white kid in a student body of five hundred at St. Joseph's School. Anson compounded his racial minority status with his attitude. He wasn't afraid to tell any of his classmates that he was the proud son of an American imperialist whose family traveled around the world exploiting the natives in their own countries. He blindly supported the United States of America like a hometown team even though he had rarely set foot on American soil. So patriotic was he that he began to shun sports like rugby, cricket, and soccer, preferring to play only sports that were popular in the United States. "Being an American kid raised abroad you develop a tremendous patriotism because there is constant persecution," Anson says. "You become a radical American chauvinist because you're constantly defending your country and its actions."

Anson fought regularly on the school playground at St. Joseph's. Many scuffles began with a game that involved cards made from scraps of old cigarette cartons stacked in the center of a dirt circle. Players stood around the circle and won the cards by knocking them down with a rock, but the game sometimes devolved into throwing rocks at the white kid. Anson's schoolmates also clamored to play him in marbles because he was the rich foreigner with the shiniest marbles. Anson was good at marbles, which often meant that the only way to win his marbles was to beat him up for them. On more than a few occasions, Anson left school bruised and bloodied. "Most of the fights I got into were not because I was an asshole, but because I was an American," Anson says. "I've never been afraid of fighting. I didn't win that many because I was never very big, but I'd rather fight and lose than not fight at all. I learned that after someone pounds you there's nothing else they can do to you, and you gain a huge amount of power by not backing down. It's bizarre, but by the end of my time there I had earned respect from the African kids."

Meanwhile, during his occasional sojourns to Louisburg, Anson ran into trouble with race relations there as well. As a result of his time in Africa, Anson had become very comfortable befriending blacks. All of the tenant workers on the Louisburg farm were black, and Anson would play baseball with their children, mowing the diamond and clearing the basepaths in the pasture himself. Still mired in the twilight of segregation in the South, some of Anson's white classmates didn't appreciate his tolerance for blacks. "I developed this wonderful understanding of how it works on both sides of the divide," Anson says. "I'm beat up by blacks for being white in Addis Ababa and then I'm beat up by the whites in Louisburg for hanging out with the blacks. At the time I didn't see the obvious irony because I didn't know what irony was, but I had a suspicion that there was something very wrong about it."

As a fifth grader in Louisburg, almost every day as Anson walked to the school bus for the ride home, a collection of rednecks and sons of Ku Klux Klansmen shoved and harassed him. Anson never told any administrators at school or anyone in his family. He considered it a problem that he could handle himself. One day he left a classroom to go to the bathroom and discovered his most intimidating tormentor out in the hallway, the first time Anson had ever encountered the boy one-on-one. "There was a broom in the corner, and I grabbed it by the straw end and started beating the hell out of him with the stick," Anson says. "You could hear the blows, *Whack! Whack! Whack!* The kid started wailing and the classrooms emptied out into the hall and everybody was horrified. I went to the principal's office, and the principal asked me, 'Anson, what happened? Did you snap?'"

Anson refused to apologize for his outburst, acknowledging only that he shouldn't have tried to kill the guy. From that day forward, Anson required a personal escort each afternoon from the school to the bus, though it wasn't at all clear who was being protected.

A few weeks later, when Anson was assigned to deliver a speech in a history class, he pointedly selected the Gettysburg Address. Anson proudly recited the entire two-minute speech from memory, putting particular emphasis on the words *all men are created equal* as he stood before his white peers in the heart of Dixie.

A soldier was all Anson ever wanted to be. It was in his genes. He was fascinated by war. When he was a boy in Ethiopia he would line up two rival battalions of tiny metal infantrymen and conduct combat on his bedroom floor that would last for days. He came home one afternoon to find that the maid had swept the battlefield clean, and he was so devastated that servants were forbidden from ever entering his room again.

"Anson was always playing military board games, and even from an early age he was kicking everybody's butt," Pete says. "He was so competitive that I didn't really enjoy playing those games with him, because I didn't have the same cut-throat attitude and my brain wasn't wired the way his was. It was so easy for him to crush me whenever he wanted to and take over the whole world. It was like Genghis Khan sitting across the board from you."

Often when Big Pete came home from work, he would be greeted at the door by his eldest son, who was itching to go to war. Anson had already spent hours studying the game board for battle, plotting every strategy to destroy his father in a reenactment of D-Day or the Battle of the Bulge. He had calculated every conceivable counterattack that his dad might launch until he felt he'd created an overwhelming offensive game plan. Father and son would battle for two, three, four hours, sometimes deep into the night. "It was my dad's investment in me," Anson says. "Even though he knew I'd prepared for the game, like a good sport he always encouraged me and tried to beat me. If I won I knew it was still an achievement. He liked these kinds of confrontations, and I appreciated the way he competed so hard but was very gracious when I won."

Anson regularly organized the local boys and Maggie for war in the neighborhood. "Anson was always this kid with a dangerous edge to him," Maggie says. "He was always playing war games, and it was stunning how this little boy would just take command and tell us all where to go and what to do. He was the Clint Eastwood of all the kids."

Says Pete: "When we would play war in the yard, Anson was always the general, plotting where we were going to set up an ambush. Instead of us harmlessly trudging around with fake guns, he'd arm us with BB guns or rocks and slingshots and we'd actually inflict pain upon each other."

The points of reference were all too real during Anson's childhood. He spent the early years of the Vietnam War living in Singapore and studying the Domino Theory, which warned that Communist forces would begin by overtaking Vietnam and continue knocking down the countries of Southeast Asia like a series of dominoes. Malaysia was one of the dominoes, a daunting notion for a sixth grader whose headquarters for war games was an actual military bunker. Anson read about Che Guevara and digested every guerrilla warfare book he could find. He followed the Vietnam body counts and believed the American government's spin on the war as winnable, passionately defending American foreign policy against classmates who viewed the United States as a guileless bully.

While in Ethiopia, Anson had only to look out the window to study the strategy of war. When he was eight years old, rebellious members of the Royal Bodyguard attempted to overthrow the government of Ethiopian emperor Haile Selassie. The guerrilla attack passed down the street in front of the Dorrance family's compound, the rebels chasing after fleeing soldiers loyal to Selassie. One loyalist soldier surrendered and started praying for his life. A rebel pulled out his gun and fired a bullet into the base of the soldier's skull. Anson watched the young man die.

During the rebellion, Big Pete explained to Anson that their family was relatively safe, because regardless of which side triumphed, that faction would continue to value the American presence. Big Pete continued to go to work every day, and whenever shots rang out, the Dorrances would roll down the iron shutters that protected their windows. One evening Big Pete was reading in his favorite armchair when he stood up to get a beer. A few moments later, he heard a gunshot. The bullet penetrated through the metal shutters and pierced the back of Big Pete's vacated chair before ricocheting around the living room.

Anson wasn't frightened by the rebellion. He found it compelling, as if it were all just another war game. At one stage, the battle heated up to a point where Big Pete called home and told Peggy to drive the children to the protection of the American Embassy. Peggy piled her children into the car and floored the gas pedal, repeatedly screaming at her curious kids to duck their heads. The car careened right down the battle line through a crossfire produced by soldiers who had no idea they were shooting at Americans. When the Dorrances finally reached the embassy they found themselves in danger from scattershot mortars that were landing all around the grounds. Peggy quickly decided the family would be safer at their house and drove back through the gunfire. "It was very frightening driving down that road through this *bang bang bang* that sounded like Chinese New Year," Peggy says. "Up to that point I think Anson was too young to understand what war actually was. When he heard the panic in my voice, that finally made it real to him."

One snowy night in the dead of winter, Harry Dodson was stripped to his underwear and tied to a tree. It was 1968, and with the Dorrance family having moved to Brussels, Anson was in his third year at the Villa Saint-Jean, a Catholic boys' boarding school in Fribourg, Switzerland. Anson was still playing war games, and Dodson was his prisoner in Capture the Flag. While Anson eventually released Dodson that night after fifteen chilling minutes, the harsh consequences of failure were precisely what attracted Anson to the game. "Those nighttime raids taught us planning, risk-taking, teamwork, and, when we were caught, accountability," Dodson says. "Anson was a good leader because he usually had a great strategy, and his enthusiasm and humor convinced others that they should follow him."

Standing just four feet eleven as a ninth grader, Anson had the persona of a much larger boy. "Despite the fact that he was prepubescent, Anson had a very competitive, chip-on-the-shoulder attitude that translated into this fun kind of cockiness," Villa classmate John Akers says. "He was not an asshole, but he stepped on toes sometimes, and just as some bigger guy was about to pound him, Anson would crack a joke or deftly change the subject. He had a very good sense of how far to push someone before they reacted."

Says another Villa classmate, Alan Hirsh, "Anson was infectiously enthusiastic, never upset or apathetic or negative, and he liked to laugh at other students who took themselves too seriously. He spoke it as he saw it, and if you didn't like it, he didn't much care. He never minded being one against ten because he knew that rebels weren't chastised at the Villa. You were still a part of the community."

Daily activities at the Villa consisted primarily of classes, study hall, or sports. Anson felt compelled to participate in almost every sport offered because there were only two dozen boys in each grade, of which only ten were interested in athletics and only five were remotely coordinated. Anson played for the Villa teams in softball, tennis, track, and ice hockey, and he was one of the best basketball players on campus, practicing alone for hours by dribbling around the pillars that lined the Villa's makeshift court. He was the quarterback in touch football games; he earned a green belt in judo; and he treated mountain climbing field trips as competitions, delighting not in the scenic alpine vistas but in rushing to be the first to summit. On Villa ski outings he liked to careen down the slopes out of control, enduring catastrophic crashes and once flying off the side of a mountain, surviving only because he was caught in a net suspended over the gorge. As a senior his recklessness won him the school's giant slalom competition, even though he was not a member of the ski team.

The only Villa team from which Anson was ever cut was the soccer team as a freshman, though he did make the team as a midfielder in his final three years. He distinguished himself not with talent but with his boundless stamina, his thirst for practice, his distinctive tip-toed stride, and his acid commentary. Often, when a teammate misplayed the ball, Anson was heard to say, "You might want to try passing to someone in our colors!"

"Anson was not a particularly skilled or experienced soccer player, but he was a real hustler, and because of his size he often ended up flat on the ground," Dodson says. "In our team meetings Anson would be fighting a battle with himself to avoid monopolizing the conversation. The exuberant Anson versus Anson the team player. He seemed to have more energy and opinion than he knew what to do with."

During high school Anson began to broaden his interests beyond war and sport. He wore a Beatles haircut as the drummer in a campus rock band called the Leaves of Mercy, a not-so-subtle reference to marijuana. He participated in the choir and in debate and speech clubs, and acted in school plays, where his size and the lack of female students often compelled him to play women, like the role of Grandma in Edward Albee's *The American Dream*. He was the head of the Material Support Committee, which organized intramural sports on campus, and in his senior year he was elected vice president of the student council. In 1969, when students at the Villa organized a Vietnam War protest and refused to take final exams, Anson rebelled against the rebellion, conscientiously objecting to the revolt while reporting the movement's progress as the editor of *Vision*, the school's newspaper.

Such independent thinking was encouraged among the Marianist brothers on the Villa teaching staff, whose discipline was based on allowing students to experiment and learn from their mistakes. While some of Anson's classmates regularly got stoned, Anson's partying consisted mostly of Friday night outings after soccer matches, when the team would sneak off downtown to a bar for french fries and draft beer in massive steins that required two hands to lift. Despite the Villa's regular mixers with girls from nearby schools, Akers cannot recall that, over four years, Anson so much as talked to a woman who wasn't a nun.

Fribourg, considered the intellectual capital of Catholicism, attracted top students from around the world. The twenty-three students in Anson's 1969 graduating class came from twelve different countries. Anson, one of a half-dozen Americans in his class, was the only one who chose to list his home country as the United States in the Villa yearbook. He was poured into this scholastic melting pot with the progeny of a Turkish diplomat, a Spanish surrealist painter, a Philippine president, and a Cuban dictator. The school's most celebrated alumnus was the French writer, philosopher, and aviator Antoine de Saint-Exupéry, class of '35, author of *The Little Prince*. Saint-Exupéry's work was required reading, and Anson's favorite prank was to write a poem in the author's famously sparse prose, sign Saint-Exupéry's name to it, and plant it in the room of a naive Villa newcomer. The victim would then stumble upon it one day and think he'd discovered a priceless literary treasure, never stopping to ask himself why a Frenchman would have written his poetry in English. "Anson struck me then as a confident guy, and with good reason, because he seemed to accomplish things effortlessly," Villa classmate Thomas Brew says. "In high school one is always measuring oneself against one's peers. Who's the smartest? Who's the best athlete? While that kind of thing may not get articulated aloud, in my mental pecking order, Anson was one of the most gifted guys in the class of '69."

Anson studied under some of the most accomplished seminarians that the Catholic Church had to offer. His professors preached the power of dialogue, discussion, and debate. Anson embraced philosophical theology because that's what many of his mentors cherished. As a senior, he won the school's religion award for compiling the best four-year average in his theology courses. He was recruited for the priesthood by his theology teacher, Brother John Rechtien, and seriously considered that path before deciding that he was more of a philosopher than a theologian and that he didn't truly possess the judgmental spirit he felt was inherent in his Catholic faith.

His most taxing course was an English class during his sophomore year in which he was told to write a paper every day in class and another every night for homework. He wrote more than three hundred essays in one school year on a variety of subjects from "Why is Catholicism restrictive?" to "Why does the cafeteria food suck?" to "Why does the housemaid look ugly when you get here every fall and great by the time you leave in the spring?" The rules of Study Hall stated that each student had to sit up straight at his desk with a book open in front of him. No sleeping or reading of comic books was permitted, so Anson and many of his schoolmates became voracious readers because they had no other choice. Anson particularly enjoyed reading military history, and he was chastised on more than one occasion for reading contraband in class during lectures.

During Anson's junior year at the Villa, Anson's father satisfied his son's craving for war history when he drove the family from Brussels to the American Cemetery in Normandy. Big Pete led his wife and children through the grounds until they came upon his older brother's grave. He humanized the simple white cross by telling Anson that his uncle was a talented jazz musician who had once collaborated on a song called "Straighten Up And Fly Right" that Nat King Cole turned into his first hit. Anson whispered to his father that he was proud to be named after a war hero. When the rest of the family walked away from the grave, the teenaged boy lingered for a moment, both spooked and thrilled by the name on the headstone, *Albert A. Dorrance.*

Maybe it was that day in Normandy, or maybe it was his blood lust for fighting off the Commies, or simply the desire to live out his childhood fantasies. Anson isn't sure himself exactly why he decided to go to college at West Point. The notion had blossomed in the back of his mind since the moment when he'd read, as a young boy, that one of his military heroes, Gen. Robert E. Lee, had been trained there. Anson's father supported the idea. His mother did not. "I had a fit and told him, 'No way,'" Peggy says. "I think Anson would've made a good officer, but I don't believe in teaching a man how to kill another man. I thought war was a typical male thing and it was stupid."

"The way my mother said no made it clear to me that it wasn't going to happen," Anson says. "She was horrified. It was a visceral reaction. She had no illusions. She knew that war was no glorious mission."

So, as a senior at the Villa Saint-Jean, Anson applied instead to Connecticut's Trinity College and to Bowdoin in Maine, and was rejected by both institutions, he surmises, because he had flunked French at a school that taught the language for two hours every day and was located in the francophone region of Switzerland. His failure wasn't entirely unintentional. As part of his jingoism, Anson resisted speaking the language of a country he did not respect.

With no college acceptances at hand, one of Anson's teachers at the Villa suggested he attend another Marianist school, St. Mary's University in San Antonio, Texas, as a way of continuing his education under that order. "I imagine that for Anson it was a huge adjustment getting oriented to life in America," Brew says. "Attending a Catholic, all-male high school in a small town in Switzerland hardly prepared him for the tail end of the sixties in the United States. He might as well have dropped in from Mars."

Anson quickly discovered that even in central Texas, the Vietnam War was never very far away. One evening in the fall of 1969, Anson and a group of fellow students gathered around a television in a dorm lounge to learn their draft numbers. Everyone chipped in for a case of beer to be awarded to the guy with the lowest number. The "winner," who had received number 1, sat directly to Anson's right. Everybody else in the room found the guy's predicament amusing and drank his beer.

At St. Mary's, Anson earned a spot on what was arguably the best college soccer team in Texas. The Rattlers were a team made up largely of talented South American imports. Though Anson possessed the least skill on the St. Mary's roster, he was one of only two Americans to start, surviving on his energy and competitiveness. The Rattlers carpooled across Texas, playing all the top colleges, and lost just one game that season. They weren't even a varsity squad, just a club team.

Anson had chosen St. Mary's expecting it to be a Camelot like the Villa, having no idea that the school was located in a hardscrabble section of a city then known as the Murder Capital of the United States. There were almost constant undertones of violence. One night after a rugby match, Anson and his teammates went drinking at a pool hall near campus. It was the third bar they'd visited that night, and they'd been tossed out of the first two. As Anson and his buddies left the bar, a young woman was walking in, and one of Anson's teammates playfully slapped her on the butt. Moments later, a pack of strapping young men in cowboy hats stormed out the door, and a melee ensued. Anson fought his opponent to a draw, but many of his teammates were beaten up, including one who had his front teeth knocked out with a pool cue.

On another night during his first semester at St. Mary's, Anson was walking down the side of the road to an all-night diner when a beer can tossed from a passing car struck him on the back of the head. Anson instinctively picked up a rock and hurled it at the car, cracking the rear window. The driver hit the brakes and reversed back to Anson, and six people got out—three local teenaged boys and their girlfriends. "I tried to get myself out of trouble with my mouth," Anson says. "I suggested, 'Couldn't we just settle this one-on-one . . . with your smallest guy?' I was beat to crap. Two black eyes. When it was over I just kept walking and ate steak and eggs. Telling the story afterward made it worthwhile."

St. Mary's required ROTC for all freshmen. Anson felt comfortable with a gun because during his visits to Louisburg, he and Pete had ventured out on regular hunting trips to shoot turtles, frogs, and snakes, eventually graduating from BB guns to .22 rifles. At the St. Mary's rifle range, Anson earned an Expert shooting medal, easily piercing pop-up targets with an M16. He trained to act as a forward observer in the infantry, taking a class in coordinates and vectors to learn how to get an artillery shell to land on target. He relished the fact that when his ROTC instructors returned tests, they were not graded with the customary A, B, C, D, or F, but instead either "Alive" or "Dead." Anson always graded out "Alive," and he enjoyed mocking the cadets who had perished.

During one war games drill, Anson and the other underclassmen in his unit were scripted to be killed by the juniors and seniors, but Anson refused and ran off into the hills, much to the chagrin of his superior officers. "I wasn't a very cooperative soldier," Anson says. "I told them, 'There's no fucking way I'm going to die. I'm an expert in guerilla warfare. There's no way any of those guys is frying my ass. I'm immortal.'"

Cadet Dorrance was court-martialed for not dying.

3 | *A Right Nice Place*

Life is change. Growth is optional.

—Karen Kaiser Clark

One day Granny Rafaela sat her young grandson Anson on her knee beside a huge black cauldron and told the boy a story about the farm she proudly called home. She told him it was one of seven plantations owned by the sons of Jeremiah Perry prior to the Civil War, and that when each of the Perry brothers built their own plantation homes in North Carolina, the other six would send whatever slaves could be spared to help with the construction. After first laying the foundation stones, the slaves would place a black cauldron inside the square they formed and light a fire beneath it to cook a house-raising feast. All through that night, slaves would dance around the cauldron singing songs of the joys and hardships of life. When morning broke, the cauldron was dragged from the white ashes and set beside the house while they raised the walls and roof. The slaves contended that from that day on, whenever the wind was right, their songs would rise again from the cauldron. When Granny Rafaela finished the story, she stared at Anson with her steely blue eyes and explained that people can only truly appreciate the significance of a home to the extent that they have lived without one.

Rafaela had enjoyed an itinerant life, for years accompanying her first husband on journeys through China and Mongolia in his search for untapped oil. But when she'd finally settled down at the old plantation called Nutbush in Louisburg, she had come to realize the value of having a place to call her own. It was Rafaela who insisted that her son, Big Pete, and his wife, Peggy, bring their children to Nutbush on their home leaves every few years. Whenever Anson came to visit, Rafaela told him that it was her dream that he would someday put down his roots in North Carolina. No matter where in the world Anson wandered during his own nomadic youth, when anyone asked him where he was from, he promptly responded, "Louisburg, North Carolina."

It was toward the end of Anson's first semester at St. Mary's that he grew disenchanted with the school, partly because he wasn't being sufficiently challenged academically and partly because he felt his life was in mortal danger. When Dorrance considered transferring, he thought back to the previous summer's visit to Louisburg, when he'd become friends with George Blackburn and his cousin Charles Blackburn. Both had extolled the virtues of the freshman years they'd just experienced at the University of North Carolina in Chapel Hill. George's father, George Sr., the Dorrance family lawyer, lauded the school as "a right *niiiiice* place."

Returning to the Tar Heel state appealed to the young man who had always considered himself a North Carolinian. The elder George Blackburn pulled some strings to help Anson gain admission to UNC for the spring semester, and Anson called the Tar Heels' soccer coach and sold him on a tryout. Although he had never visited the campus, the kid who had already made no fewer than a dozen major moves in his first eighteen years decided to relocate to Chapel Hill in January of 1970. At the time he could not have imagined that he would heed his grandmother's wishes and never move again.

Less than a week after Dorrance first entered Teague dormitory at the University of North Carolina, the dorm's intramural sports manager, Danny Newcomb, knocked on his door. Newcomb handed Dorrance a list of all the intramural sports contested at UNC in the spring. "Which sports do you want to play?" Newcomb asked. Without even looking at the list, Dorrance simply responded, "All of them. If you want to win, put me on every team."

Newcomb thought Dorrance was kidding. He wasn't. Newcomb penciled in Dorrance for every sport.

Although Dorrance stood just five feet ten and weighed a mere 135 pounds as a freshman, his natural quickness and athleticism made him a force in everything from flag football to bowling, handball, and track. He often competed in four different intramural events during a single day. He used the badminton experience he'd gained while living in Asia to win an intramural tournament in that sport, and the martial arts he had learned there helped him triumph in a wrestling event. He even won a horseshoes competition in spite of never having touched a horseshoe before in his life. "It was pretty disheartening to the other teams when Anson strolled in and I asked, 'Do you know how to do this?' and he'd say, 'Nah, I'll pick it up on the fly,' and then he proceeded to beat the hell out of them," says Jack Simmons, who replaced Newcomb as Teague's IM manager in 1971. "Anson didn't just believe he could win. He *knew* it. Some people thought he was cocky, but I just thought he was very confident, and if there was ever any self-doubt in him, I never saw it."

Another dormmate, Freddie Kiger, remembers walking up to Dorrance before a decisive intramural ping-pong match and asking him if he could win it. "No question," Dorrance rejoined, "because I'm a competitor."

"He said it in the most casual way," Kiger recalls. "For Anson, it was not just a contest between two athletes playing table tennis, it was also about mental toughness. If he had an edge over everyone, it was the six inches between the ears. Anson won that match for Teague as if he'd just sheer mentally willed it."

"Anson sought out competition during the era of flower children, when everyone else was caught up in peace, love, and harmony," says Bill Griffin, one of Anson's roommates in Teague. "What was unusual about him as a competitor was there wasn't an ounce of malice in him. He competed with a joy about him."

After his intramural events, Dorrance delighted in a favorite post-competition ritual when he returned to his dorm room.

"How'd it go?" Griffin asked.

"The guy I played was really good," Dorrance responded.

"How good?"

"He was one of the best I've ever seen."

"So he beat you?"

"Well, he was absolutely the most amazing opponent I've ever faced."

"So what the hell happened?"

"*I kicked his ass!*"

Says Dorrance: "I absolutely loved sports, and on the athletic field I knew I was going to dominate. There was no way anyone was as competitive as me, and I also knew that part of my ability to beat people at everything is that they would always underestimate me. You'd look at me and say, 'There's not a muscle in his body. How can he do anything?'"

The other ingredient in Dorrance's competitive advantage was a keen sense of gamesmanship. As Teague's softball pitcher, he not only threw extra hard while warming up but also pretended to be myopic. He would tell his catcher to stand where the other team could hear him, and then Dorrance would say, "I can only see blurs. What color have you got on? . . . OK, red. I'll throw toward the red blob." The catcher played along and said, "I'll be the one crouched down. The guy standing is the batter. Try to throw it at me." It scared the hell out of undergrads with their whole lives ahead of them.

So confident was Dorrance in his abilities that one evening he decided he would challenge the entire campus. He designed a twenty-sport competition in which he would pick any ten sports and his opponent would choose the other ten. Dorrance believed he could win at least eleven events against anyone else at UNC. He wrote up a formal challenge with the intent of submitting it to the campus newspaper, the *Daily Tar Heel*. However, the more Dorrance thought about the logistics of such a plan, the more he realized that he simply didn't have enough spare time in his day to contest twenty different sports against all comers. So he reluctantly scrapped the idea.

Dorrance was not permitted to play on the Teague soccer team because he was a varsity athlete in that sport, so he became the team's coach. He trained a team that included only three players who had ever kicked a soccer ball before and coached them to a championship. "I'll never forget standing on the sidelines with Jack Simmons during a break in a soccer match, and Anson ran his eyes up and down me and Jack and then said to Jack, 'Freddie's in better shape than you are,'" Kiger says. "Jack was pissed, and I felt like I'd been blessed. Even though Anson was one of our own, he had the kind of respect that we *cared* about what he thought. That's the day Anson first became a coach in my eyes."

Whether as a coach or a teammate, Anson became notorious among his dormmates for his sarcastic criticism. "You'd go home a lot of days saying, 'I'm ticked off at that guy,'" Newcomb says. "But Anson knew how to step on your shoes without totally messing up your shine. I don't ever recall him turning on any of us in a malicious or butt-kicking way. It was always 'we,' always team first."

With the arrival of Dorrance in the spring of 1970, Teague rallied to finish third overall in the residence hall intramural standings, Teague's highest finish ever. Dorrance is convinced his dorm would have won the title had he been at UNC the entire year. In 1970–71, as a sophomore still ineligible to play with the soccer varsity because of transfer rules, Dorrance participated in eleven intramural individual and team sports and was voted the school's outstanding IM athlete as he led Teague to the dorm championship.

The men of Teague became more and more obsessed each year, spending entire evenings choreographing new flag football plays to add to the playbook or making up new team nicknames like the inimitable *Blood, Sweat, and Teague.* When Teague won the dorm title again in 1972, enemy dorms began accusing Teague of recruiting, which they clearly did. Teague residents would scour the incoming classes from their hometown high schools and suggest that the best athletes request to join them at Teague. Eventually 180 of the dorm's 200 inhabitants were participating in intramurals. When the IM officials tried to create a more competitive balance by dividing the dorm into two teams, Teague A on the upper floors and Teague B on the lower, all the best athletes moved downstairs, and the success continued unabated. "It was organized chaos that became a consuming, thriving mission that required a lot of work and an unbelievable commitment from everybody involved," Simmons says. "Yet we laughed and we had a blast while we were in pursuit of excellence."

Dorrance and his Teague descendants eventually captured a remarkable seventeen straight residence hall championships before the UNC administration, tired of the Teague boys' raucous campus-wide victory tours, abruptly cut off the streak by turning the dorm coed. "To understand who Anson is as a coach, to understand his drive for perfection, you need to understand what went on in Teague dorm," Kiger says. "It was a parallel universe to what was to happen later. We were all on Anson's team, despite the fact that he was playing with us. When Anson left Teague, he was very conscious of what we had begun to build in a historical sense. Anson was the first one in the dorm to use the word *dynasty*."

There was no master plan. The University of North Carolina men's soccer program began one morning in 1946 when Dr. Marvin Allen opened a closet door. The Second World War had just been won, and a Navy training facility that had been located in Chapel Hill was quickly abandoned. When Allen went poking around in a closet he'd never explored before, he stumbled upon some unused soccer uniforms that the Navy had left behind. At that same time, Allen was teaching a physical education course on soccer. So he sifted out the best soccer players from his P.E. class, dressed them up in the uniforms, and thus founded a soccer program. Soon after, he phoned a colleague down the road at Duke, some other nut like him who actually liked and understood this bizarre game played with feet, and the two schools arranged a scrimmage. The following year, North

Carolina men's soccer was granted varsity status, and Allen was given a part-time position as its coach. During the team's first two seasons, UNC competed in its hand-me-down uniforms. Nobody seemed to mind that the colors were navy blue and gold.

Most colleges in the South wouldn't follow Allen's lead and embrace soccer until at least a decade later. So it wasn't until 1958 that UNC could even cobble together a ten-game schedule, but Allen didn't mind the wait. Dr. Marvin Allen was the kind of guy you look for in a pioneer. He was simple, reserved, sturdy, dignified, straightforward, honest, a formidable rock upon which UNC soccer could be built. He was a native North Carolinian from Wilmington, and he absolutely loved the sport in a place where hardly anybody else did. Above all, he was humble. Even four decades later, whenever anybody mentioned that Allen had scored the first-ever goal for UNC's club soccer team back in 1938, he was quick to point out that the ball probably would have rolled in anyway. He just touched it last.

Allen was a phys ed teacher in every stereotypical sense of the term. He was balding and stocky, with a whistle perpetually dangling around his neck. At soccer practice he wore a ballcap, dark-rimmed spectacles, white socks pulled up high on his calves, and black sneakers. He dressed up in a sport coat and tie for every game. In a soccer era that is considered old-school, Allen was even older-school. He believed in a code of what he thought it meant to be a Southern gentleman, and that code wasn't all that far removed from the manners of the Old South.

A good Episcopalian, Allen lived his religion in his daily life. One of his players, Charlie Covell, can still remember one Sunday afternoon in the fall of 1955, during a team scrimmage on UNC's Fetzer Field, when he shanked a ball high over the crossbar with the goal wide open and loudly cursed his own error. On the sideline, Allen turned to one of Covell's teammates and said, "Didn't I see that boy carrying the cross in church this morning?"

Allen didn't have a lot of rules. His only pet peeve was what he called "extraneous" hair, a common style for his players, particularly in the late 1960s and 1970s. Allen asserted that short hair improved heading efficiency, but everybody knew that his disapproval was really more grandparental in nature. His rule on hair was simple: cut or be cut. "The first day I got to Chapel Hill I met Dr. Allen in his office, and he said, 'I want you to go uptown and get a haircut,'" says Kip Ward, who played under Allen from 1967 to 1971. "When I returned later that day, he said, 'I asked you to get a haircut, not *a hair* cut.' I wound up making three trips to the barbershop that day until I conformed to what Dr. Allen thought a Southern gentleman should look like."

Allen's soccer tactics matched his personality: conservative. He had discovered the sport as an undergrad in a phys ed class and had no formal soccer training, but he was a voracious student of the game, gleaning most of what he knew from the forty soccer manuals and textbooks that lined the bookshelf inside his office in Woollen Gymnasium. He believed in fundamental soccer and in the principles of creating space within his basic 3-3-4 formation. His vision of how the game should be played was very strict: stay in your position, stick to your role, maintain an attacking posture as much as possible, and shoot on goal every chance you get. He regularly shared with his strikers something one of his books told him: that "it takes an average of seven attempts to score one goal." Allen was not a tactical genius. What he appreciated most was the simplest quality for him to identify: effort.

Allen believed in the direct game, the European system, over the flashier Latin American possessional game. He rarely subbed, except on principle. Ward recalls the day he tried to score on a flamboyant bicycle kick and knocked the shot over the crossbar. The purist Allen yanked Ward off the field before the restart. But Allen was not totally without poetry. Often when he would roll the balls out for goalshooting practice, he would say, "You've got to see the goal in the theater of your mind." He believed in visualization before the term ever started being applied to sports.

Because Allen's players viewed him more as a gentleman who guided them than as a coach who drove them, very few ever called him "Coach." Most instead addressed the man, who'd earned a Ph.D. in physical education at UNC, as "Dr. Allen." Allen is described in an old UNC soccer program as "a great teacher and coach, speaking in a voice easily understood in times difficult to understand." He was erudite, though not particularly articulate. He was frugal with his words, but when he talked, his players listened, even though none of them can remember a conversation with Allen ever lasting more than thirty seconds. Allen rarely spoke on the sidelines during a game, and his brief pregame and halftime talks usually centered on reminding his players to try to do what they were supposed to do, only better. No matter how frustrated he became with his team's lackadaisical play or with an official's decision, he never lost his temper. Allen rarely raised his voice to anybody, and he never, ever, cursed. The closest he ever came was at a practice the day after one miserable loss to N.C. State when, still bitterly disappointed, he took the rare step of asking his team to gather around him as he reviewed all the transgressions committed the previous afternoon. Then he paused for emphasis. "Do you know what this team lacks?" Allen said, looking around at his players from face to face as they shook their heads tentatively. "This team lacks *balls!*"

Allen stood there expecting a reaction, but not the one he got, which was something between incredulous and dumbfounded. Some players even stared curiously at the practice bag full of balls beside the coach.

"No," Allen said. "You know what I mean. The *hangin' kind.*"

In case any of them had still failed to get the message, Allen ordered his players into his favorite practice drill, called "Suicide," in which he lined up half his team on each side of the center circle, with himself in between. He then rolled a ball between two players who charged headlong at one another without slowing down as Allen pointedly questioned the masculinity of those who did not tackle hard through the ball. On this particular day, Allen's all-conference center back tore up his knee in one of these dogfights and was done for the season.

Alas, whenever Allen lost a player to injury, there was rarely a credible replacement. His roster was always threadbare because he didn't believe in recruiting. For much of Allen's career, UNC offered him three full scholarships to distribute, but he refused to use them, believing in the purity of amateur athletics. He didn't want to be perceived as buying his players. While conference rivals like Maryland and Clemson were both importing foreign ringers by offering them scholarships, Allen relied instead on attracting players through word of mouth from his former Tar Heels. So his roster was stocked mostly with prep school players from New England and the Philadelphia area, and a few walk-ons chosen from campus tryouts. Nobody who wound up playing for Allen at UNC was ever wined or dined. It just kind of happened.

The only recruiting inducement Allen ever accepted was a set of four appeals each year that would let him admit talented players who wouldn't qualify for UNC on their academic standing alone. In the spring of 1970 Allen used one of those appeals on a skinny, mop-topped transfer named Anson Dorrance, from some nowhere school in Texas, whom he'd never even seen play. As soon as Allen first laid eyes on him, he knew something would have to be done about that hair.

That new guy with the pretentious name, well, he loved the ball. Adored it. Everybody could see that. There were times when he loved it too much. Whenever there was any break in soccer practice, Anson Dorrance would fool around with the ball at his feet, juggling it, trapping it in the air, trying a move somebody had told him was a Brazilian *somethingorother*. Allen would try to ignore it until he couldn't bear it anymore, and then he'd tell Dorrance to cut it out already. It wasn't meant as any lack of respect on Dorrance's part. It was just his natural hyperactivity. Finally, Allen told Dorrance that when he came to a huddle he had to hold the ball in his hands. So Dorrance taught himself to spin the ball on his finger. Allen could tolerate that because secretly he knew that all of this tinkering with the ball was really a good thing. Coaches lived for players who loved the ball so much.

When Dorrance first arrived at UNC in 1970, transfer rules stated that he had to be redshirted for one season. So during his first fall season he was utilized as a practice dummy. The eligible players executed their drills around him and nailed free kicks at him as a permanent member of the wall. When he wasn't doing that, he was a ball-shagger, standing behind a goal chasing striker Mack McKinnon's wayward shots. Between these humbling duties, Dorrance spent hours practicing on his own to improve his game. "I put a lot of time into being as good as I could be," Dorrance says. "When I joined the team I was a good header and tackler and I was aggressive, but that was about it. I had the touch of a barnyard animal and the creativity of a table."

"We saw what qualities Anson possessed very quickly," Kip Ward says. "He was a combination of pride and arrogance and determination and very little talent."

In his first season of eligibility, in the fall of 1971, Dorrance started on the forward line as a withdrawn striker and scored two goals in his debut match against Appalachian State. Dorrance was not a natural goal-scorer, but he did possess a solid strike that his teammates dubbed "The Thumper." Dorrance scored five goals that season, usually by pressuring a defender, stealing the ball, and thumping it into the net. His most notable goal occurred on October 23, 1971, against heavily favored Clemson on a rainy afternoon in Chapel Hill, when he battled for a loose ball in the box and blasted a shot into the lower left corner of the Tigers' net to forge a 2–2 tie. Dorrance never saw the goal, because as the ball crossed the line, he was face down in a mud puddle.

Before Dorrance's junior season in 1972, Allen switched him from forward to center halfback so he could have more effect on the run of play. Dorrance modeled his game after the European player he had grown up admiring most, the indefatigable Dutch midfielder Johan Cruyff, who was granted free rein to run from sideline to sideline and endline to endline. Because Dorrance was so extraordinarily tireless, he was the only player on the field allowed to roam freely in Allen's otherwise rigid system. "I tried to paint the field," Dorrance says. "Wherever the ball was, I was near the ball. I could run forever. I couldn't carve up six players and then drive one into the upper corner from forty yards, but I was a good ball-winner and a distributor, and I had a great work rate."

Dorrance's legend was enhanced one afternoon when he was running the mile at Fetzer Field in an intramural track competition, circling his astonished soccer teammates as they began warming up for practice. As soon as he crossed the finish line he ran right into a soccer drill without even stopping to catch his breath.

Dorrance's teammates dubbed him "H & H," which stood for Hack & Hustle, because when he wasn't running somewhere he was running into someone. Allen once described Dorrance as "the toughest 135-pound man I've ever seen." Dorrance treated every game like ninety minutes of Allen's "Suicide" drill. When it was over, if he left the field and both of his knees weren't bleeding, he wasn't satisfied with his effort. Says Dorrance: "I lived for the moment that me and my opponent were running towards a 50-50 ball and we didn't slow down and my forehead hit his forehead, our noses met, our teeth met, our chests met, our kneecaps met, and both of us were spitting out teeth, because I knew my pain threshold was greater than his, and eventually he'd surrender and say, 'This isn't worth that much to me.'"

"Anson was a ruthless tackler, but not dirty," teammate Geoff Griffin says. "You were not going to get the ball past him too often, but if you did you were going to leave part of your shin behind."

Whenever Dorrance got the worst end of a 50-50 encounter he still tried to leave his mark. "When I was tackled down, I tried to fall as hard as I could on the guy," Dorrance remembers. "I absolutely loved crashing into people. I think that's why I was made so small. If I was any bigger, I might have killed somebody."

A *Daily Tar Heel* reporter named Elliott Warnock wrote a preview of a UNC game against conference rival Maryland and included a typical quote from

Dorrance: "I would personally like to tear them apart. The only way I can accept losing is if I walk off the field and the opposing team doesn't."

"I remember he said it with a straight face," Warnock recalls. "He was kind of kidding, but at the same time, he really wasn't. Anson was the kind of guy who thought that if you can't win the game, win the fight in the parking lot afterward."

UNC committed nineteen fouls in that game, thirteen by Dorrance, including one on a Tar Heel corner kick when Dorrance was barreling through the penalty box and met both Maryland's All-America goalkeeper George Taratsides and the ball at the goalpost. Taratsides crashed against the post, collapsed in a heap, and was briefly unconscious.

Whenever Dorrance committed a soccer sin he would follow it up with a well-crafted angelic reaction. "What happens is the referee watches you cut someone in half and you get a card for the expression on your face right after you commit the crime. I always had this look that said, 'Oh my, what a shame, I've broken the poor boy's leg.'"

As a result of his convincing acting, Dorrance never once received a yellow card during his career, although he led the Atlantic Coast Conference in fouls in all three of his seasons. It's a testament to Dorrance's grit that he earned first-team All-ACC honors in 1972 without collecting a single goal or assist. It was discovered later that he'd played that entire season with a broken right foot, which had been misdiagnosed by doctors as a sprained ankle and was so excruciatingly painful that it prohibited him from shooting with that foot. "Anson pushed the envelope to the point of recklessness," says teammate Mark Marcoplos. "He never played any second of any game at 80 percent, and he had a confident, almost regal air about him. I remember even the cocky way he walked would tick people off."

Says another teammate Mark Berson: "I thought for a skinny little twerp Anson was the most arrogant guy that I'd ever met in my life."

When Dorrance was elected captain in his senior year, he expected everyone on his team to compete with the same passion that he did . . . or else. "If one of my teammates made a mistake that I felt was unforgivable, he heard from me instantaneously and it wasn't always the most positive leadership tone," Dorrance says. "I was not a gentle captain, but I had enough understanding of leadership that I only yelled at those who could take it and I didn't talk to the others. I wasn't afraid to whip them like dogs, and when I felt someone wasn't working on defense, I'd say, 'Don't worry, Kenny, I'll mark these two.'"

During the first half of a game against Virginia in Charlottesville, Dorrance took his leadership responsibilities too far. He dug a ball out of the midfield and passed it along the left sideline to Griffin, who misplayed the ball out of bounds. Dorrance got up off the turf and barked at Griffin, "*If you don't get your shit together, then get your ass off the field!*"

At halftime, Allen pulled Dorrance aside and gave him a stern lecture. "Anson, you're not the only reason this team wins," Allen told his captain. "You're not going to verbally castigate your teammates like that no matter how hard you're working." Dorrance was humbled because he knew that Allen was right. He spent the rest of the game literally biting his tongue to keep quiet.

"Anson didn't understand why all of his teammates didn't care as much as he did or didn't play as hard as he did, and he'd get after you," Griffin says. "Anson wasn't a polite person. You had to respect him for what he represented, but a lot of times you didn't appreciate his presentation. As a leader, he knew how to get you to raise your level, and that's why you wanted to play with him."

Dorrance's only loyalty was to Allen, whom he respected as a coach and a man. He realized that Allen's tactics were not on the cutting edge, but unlike his team-mates, who grumbled and blamed Allen's Paleozoic strategy for the Tar Heels' losses, Dorrance viewed his position as a contract. He believed that he and Allen were connected by a mutual respect for personal accountability. During Dorrance's first season at UNC, when the Tar Heels held a secret players-only meeting to trash Allen, Dorrance walked out. "Anson was the one guy who would run his ass off even if we were getting pounded," Berson says. "Anson never stopped trying, and Dr. Allen really respected that in him. Dr. Allen really took a liking to Anson. He saw himself in Anson."

Dorrance's most cherished memory as a player occurred after a 2–0 loss to Clemson in 1973 at Fetzer Field. "It was the greatest game I ever played," Dorrance remembers. "I don't remember missing a tackle all day. When the game ended I was so tired that I just stood still because my legs couldn't move. Dr. Allen ran out onto the field, shook my hand, and congratulated me for never giving up. That was the most exhilarating and satisfying moment of my career."

One afternoon before that season began, Allen had summoned Dorrance into his office for a private meeting. "Anson, you've worked so hard," Allen said. "I think you deserve to be rewarded." Allen then told him he was giving him a tu-ition waiver. In his long tenure as coach at the University of North Carolina, it was the first scholarship money that Allen had ever granted.

Dorrance never wore his soccer letter jacket. It remained in his closet, one of the few articles of clothing on a hanger. Soccer was not his life. It was just one of the things he did. He never wanted to glorify himself as a varsity athlete, and he despised the way other UNC athletes strutted around campus as if they were something special, including some of his own teammates. He particularly disliked the bravado of the Tar Heel football players. He resented the way the football team's most menacing player, 220-pound All-Conference linebacker Mike Mansfield, would brazenly cut in line at the athletes' training table. Finally, one day, Dorrance confronted Mansfield. "Who the hell are you?" Dorrance said. "Go to the back of the line."

"Who the hell are *you*?" Mansfield said, lumbering in Dorrance's direction. "What sport do you play?"

"I'm Anson Dorrance, and it doesn't matter what fucking sport I play. Get behind me!"

Mansfield charged him, diving across a dining table in an attempt to tackle Dorrance. But Mansfield's intended victim deftly stepped aside, and the huge linebacker pancaked an innocent Tar Heel swimmer right through a screen wall.

Dorrance didn't view his varsity soccer as any more glorious than his intramural horseshoes. On those rare occasions when Dorrance was interviewed after a UNC soccer game, he delighted in shocking reporters with his elite vocabulary and then reading the articles the following morning that described him as "surprisingly articulate."

"Anson had traveled all over the world with his family, and he was more worldly than most of us," Jack Simmons says. "The rest of us just wanted to make good enough grades to stay in school, play sports, drink beer, and pick up women, but Anson's goals were greater. He was not just another guy in the dorm. He was very busy doing Anson things."

One of Dorrance's trademarks was the singing of Steppenwolf's "Born To Be Wild" most mornings in the shower. It was a fitting anthem for his daily itinerary. *Get your motor running, head out on the highway, looking for adventure, or whatever comes my way.*

Dorrance spent two years as Teague's elected representative to the UNC student legislature. He would sometimes join George Blackburn at meetings of UNC's Dialectic and Philanthropic Society to debate such topics as The Erosion of the Southern Culture. In his senior year he moved into the coed fraternity, St. Anthony Hall, a roundtable of intellectuals whose most notable alum was the journalist Charles Kuralt. St. Anthony was a literary frat where every Wednesday night the members performed their "LDs" or literary duties. Inspired by a class on the Romantic poets, Dorrance loved to recite verses by Coleridge, reveling in the power of the cadence and lyrics, even if he didn't exactly understand what it all meant. Soon after his arrival at St. Anthony he discovered that there were only eight active members remaining in the chapter, which was $20,000 in debt and in serious danger of extinction. Dorrance appointed himself and Berson as rush co-chairmen, and the two set out on a recruitment drive. By the end of that year there were forty-five members and the frat was $40,000 in the black, an accomplishment for which Dorrance earned the St. Anthony secret society's loftiest title of "Most Noble"—the grandest identity he could imagine.

Each fall Dorrance began his school year flush with cash from summer jobs, but he never managed his budget well, burning through money on decadent meals at the Carolina Inn, the Carolina Grill, and the Carolina Coffee Shop. By late spring he would sometimes subsist for days on nothing but chewing gum, because he wanted to honor a deal he'd made with his father that he would pay for his own sustenance. Otherwise, Dorrance looked a lot like every other wanna-be rebel on campus in the early 1970s, which is to say that he didn't much care how he looked. He wore a faded green army jacket almost every day, along with horn-rimmed Coke-bottle glasses and, much to Marvin Allen's chagrin, horrifically unkempt hair.

At that time, the University of North Carolina was in a period of transition from genteel Southern university to more liberal bastion. So while many of his fellow students were protesting the Vietnam War, either because they hoped it might get them out of final exams or because they actually disapproved of the conflict, Dorrance refused to participate in the rallies. He still believed in the potential peril warned of by the Domino Theory, which had so troubled him as a boy in Singapore, and he was sticking to the conservative ideology that his father had so fervently drilled into him. Dorrance supported the war, and while he never considered dropping out of college to fight in Vietnam because of his mother's determined stance against the idea, he wouldn't have been against going had his draft number come up. "I remember when protestors closed UNC down during the Kent State shootings, but I wasn't anti-establishment," Dorrance says. "Sure, I was upset about Kent State, but I was appalled because our National Guardsmen took more than sixty shots and they only hit thirteen people. I was a radical, reactionary right-winger, a hawk in every conceivable way, and I saw the liberals as a passive, whiny culture who just happened to turn out to be right about the Vietnam War."

"Anson didn't suffer fools very easily, so he liked to stretch people or institutions by always asking, 'Why?' and then if the answer was bullcrap he'd call them on it," Freddie Kiger says. "He was always clever enough to be able to veer off-center politically, go through the median, run through a ditch, and then somehow be able to steer back onto the road unscathed."

It was a time on the UNC campus when drugs were readily available, but Dorrance did drugs only when challenged. "I didn't want anyone to assume I was afraid to try drugs," Dorrance says. "There was no way they were going to lord that over me. *Give it to me, I'll try it.* But ultimately I thought doing drugs was a waste of time."

Beer, however, was another matter. "I would go out on Friday night before a soccer game and get smashed, and the next morning I was so hung over I couldn't see straight," Dorrance says. "I couldn't wait for the game because like in medieval times, I would sweat out the demons. I remember I'd feel better and better as the first half moved along. By the second half, I was *invincible.*"

Dorrance's favorite bar was a dilapidated wooden lean-to called the Shack, where the motto was "Come down before it falls down!" Though the passage of Title IX in 1972 added a few female athletes to the UNC campus and would affect Dorrance's life considerably in the future, UNC's student body at the time was 90 percent male, so there were few girls at the Shack. Dorrance would socialize with all of his various communities, from his soccer teammates to his St. Anthony brothers to his intramural friends from Teague, and most often with the Blackburns.

George Templeton Blackburn III and Albert Anson Dorrance IV were drinking buddies at the Shack. The pair sat on rickety barstools, discussing everything from the war to Kierkegaard to how they could protest the rise in the price of Schlitz from forty cents to a half-dollar. Dorrance also was a fanatical foosball and pinball player, often with George or his cousin Charles as wingman. "I had led sort of a sheltered country life, and Anson made me real nervous because he was so brash that I was afraid he was going to get me into a fistfight," Charles says. "He would tell everybody how he was going to beat them in all these barroom games, but then he proved to be as good as his word."

Fortunately nobody in Dorrance's circle owned a car, so the boys walked back to Teague after a night on the town. Sometimes after a long stint at the Shack, Anson and Charles would return home to the dorm and spot Charles's collection of antique sabers that hung on the wall of his dorm room. They would nod acknowledgment to each other and commence a duel that would proceed through the halls of Teague and out into the woods behind the dorm, where they would strip to the waist and slash at each other. They never felt a thing, but the next morning each would wake up with crisscross welts that ran the length of their torsos.

Other times they would stop at Kessing Pool, just down the hill from the dorm. One of the two would wobble uneasily to the end of the diving board and begin to deliver oratory to the imaginary gallery in the pool. *Friends, Romans, Countrymen . . .* If the speech was botched, which it inevitably was, the orator would be punished with a push into the pool, fully clothed. On winter nights the speaker would sometimes find himself crashing through a sheet of ice, forcing the other to save his life with a daring water rescue. Charles once jumped in before he noticed that the pool contained only a foot of brackish water, a fall that might have killed him if he hadn't been so drunk.

Occasionally the two didn't make it all the way home. Charles can still remember one night carrying Dorrance out of The Shack over his shoulder and finally tiring just a hundred yards short of Teague. He laid Dorrance down gently in the boxwood shrubs that surround the campus bell tower. The next morning Charles found him there, still dozing peacefully.

Berson can still recall one morning he woke up at St. Anthony and noticed a trail of blood across the floor of the room he shared with Dorrance, who was sprawled across his bed with a crude bandage around his hand. Dorrance had spent the previous evening punching out windows in the Deke house in a competition to see how many he could break before splitting his hand open.

Dorrance's favorite drunken prank involved climbing to the top of the water tower behind St. Anthony. One night he carried a can of paint for the purpose of inscribing on the tower's bulb the word *smegma,* which is defined as the cheesy liquid under the foreskin of a penis. Dorrance's ascent began with a stairway, but to reach the top of the tower, he had to shimmy up the bulb on his belly without handholds, a stunt made more perilous because it occurred during a raging lightning storm. "Why did I do it?" Dorrance asks rhetorically. "Well, one of my favorite expressions is that the last thing a redneck says before he dies is 'Hey y'all, watchisss!' That's what I said right before I started climbing."

In a brilliant stroke of civic planning the Chapel Hill Police Department was located next door to the Shack. One night after last call, Dorrance, Charles

Blackburn, and another friend, John Berry, stumbled out of the Shack and spotted several cops standing on the steps of the police station. Naturally, they decided to serenade the law with some off-color rugby songs. Dorrance and Berry were collared and tossed in jail for being drunk and disorderly. Charles somehow evaded capture. The two convicts couldn't have been more pleased, for they got to meet fellow criminals and ask all kinds of classic jailhouse questions like "What are you in for?" Dorrance and Berry were unceremoniously released at seven the next morning. Unshowered and in the same clothes he'd worn in jail the night before, Dorrance decided to attend classes so he could share his tale of incarceration. He railed against the tyranny of the cops in his political science class. Then he wrote a short story about life behind bars for his creative writing class, concluding that his real punishment was not the time spent in jail, but his release just in time to go to his first morning class.

Dorrance was not a model student. His professors at the Villa Saint-Jean had taught him that learning was more important than grinding for grades, and he didn't really understand how to study. He was miserably disorganized, an inveterate procrastinator, and he rarely took notes during lectures. He treated his courses as reading lists, and his mission was to finish the list before the course was over. He faithfully attended only the classes of teachers whose lectures interested him, so eventually he stopped picking subjects as much as professors, believing that great minds could have an impact on him, regardless of the subject, and hopefully influence the way he conducted his life.

His favorite classes were his writing courses. Dorrance never needed to dream up an adventure; he just wrote about his own life and changed a few names. He particularly enjoyed the way one of his writing professors, Max Steele, taught by not overteaching. Steele sat back and let his students debate their stories among themselves and eventually bond over the experience. In the ensuing years, whenever Dorrance saw Steele on campus he was impressed when the professor remembered an obscure detail from one of his stories, and he came to realize just how much those moments built a connection between them.

Dorrance describes his college career as "three years of debauchery, one year of redemption." Determined to prove that he wasn't a total idiot, Dorrance cut back on drinking and intramurals in the spring of his senior year and took seven courses, including two that met at the same time. He finished that semester with 3 As and 4 Bs, and pulled his GPA up to a 2.7. "I grew up in my senior year when it suddenly struck me, 'Oh my gosh, next year I'm going to be supporting myself,'" Dorrance says. "I finally got bored with all of my sophomoric behavior and became disgusted with myself."

Dorrance intended to graduate with a B.A. in philosophy, but during his exit interview his guidance counselor informed him that he'd earned a degree in English as well. Without his knowledge, he'd compiled enough English credits to qualify simply because he adored nothing more than reading books. In a final visit with Steele, the professor told him, "You may never be rich, but you'll lead a rich life."

So Dorrance graduated in UNC's class of 1974 with a double major in philosophy and English. The running joke was that the only place that would hire someone with those degrees was the Carolina Coffee Shop. Dorrance applied there and got turned down. He had no job prospects whatsoever, but he was content. The kid from Louisburg looked around him and decided that he had finally found a real home. "After college I expected a life of impoverishment," Dorrance says. "I didn't know what I wanted to do, but I knew where I wanted to starve. I wanted to starve in Chapel Hill."

4 | *Big Pete*

Choose a job you love, and you will never have to work a day in your life.

—Confucius

In a fit of incredulity in 1967, Big Pete Dorrance stared down his sixteen-year-old son and uttered what from that day on would become the boy's favorite description of himself: "Anson, you are the most confident person without any talent that I've ever met."

Confirming the conclusion, Anson replied, "Dad, I'm taking that as a compliment."

Big Pete privately reveled in the dexterity of that retort because he knew in his heart that nobody was more responsible for his son's attitude than Big Pete himself.

When Pete Dorrance was just a teenager, he was already a lieutenant, third in command as the navigator on a World War II submarine that sank some Japanese Navy shipping in the Pacific. One evening he left the naval base for a few beers, and when he returned late that night the sentry ordered him to halt and identify himself. Pete stubbornly walked right past him, so the sentry shot him in the ass.

Truth is, Big Pete wasn't so big. He stood just five feet ten and weighed 170 pounds, but he radiated the presence of a much larger man. He had flinty blue eyes under thick dark eyebrows, and jet-black hair. And then there was that nickname. Big Pete. That fit. It made the guy sound like a mobster, and he had the personality to match. "When my father walked into a room people noticed," Anson says, "and it wasn't because of how he looked, it was because of who the fuck he was."

"Dad didn't just say things, he pronounced them," Anson's brother Pete says. "He made proclamations. He had the ability to crush you with just a glance or five words. He had the ability to absolutely snuff you, melt you in your boots, annihilate you with a stare."

Big Pete's aura came to be known around the Dorrance clan as "The Force," a term of mysterious power borrowed from the film *Star Wars*. "If my dad wanted to inject his presence he would hit a button and use 'The Force,'" Anson says. "There would be a visible metamorphosis whenever he wanted to dominate a conversation. It was tangible. You could *feel* it. It was not a quiet Tibetan monk kind of confidence, but an aggressive confidence that he was in the right whether he really was or not."

Big Pete was a fierce competitor, whether he was negotiating an oil contract or just socializing at a cocktail party where he would try to engage in any debate he could spark. He could discuss any subject from politics to finance to history to lawn care, and he would argue his point very passionately, but the dispute was nothing more than a game to him, an intellectual exercise. No matter how intense an argument might become, Big Pete didn't take it personally. That ability to distance himself emotionally enhanced his debating skills. He was the kind of debater who could argue either side of any issue, and when he knew he was on the wrong side, he would treat the encounter as a challenge to enhance the skills of his opponent. Then all of a sudden, when Big Pete determined that his foe had articulated the correct position sufficiently, he would stun the man by wholeheartedly agreeing with him, abruptly punctuating the dialogue by saying, "Good point!" Then he'd walk off to grab another beer and leave the guy reeling, wondering what the heck had just happened.

Anson loved to watch his father work a room, and as soon as he felt he was intellectually able, he stepped up to be his father's counterpoint. He adopted everything he could of his father's verbal arsenal and added an element of gamesmanship from the athletic arena. "To demonstrate to my father that he couldn't intimidate me, I recall one time when I continued to read the *New York Times* while I was debating him," Anson recalls. "Of course, I wasn't really reading the paper, I was furiously summoning every intellectual resource to combat this very intelligent and aggressive man, and my mother couldn't believe that I was doing it this way. She thought I was disrespecting my father, and she kept telling me to put the paper down and look him in the eye."

Pete believes that his father was harder on Anson than any of his other children, testing him intellectually to try to drill his own sense of invincibility into his eldest son. "I think Anson earned an odd kind of respect from my dad, who early on came to appreciate how mentally tough Anson was," Pete says. "Dad didn't take any prisoners when he got his dander up, but he couldn't really get away with that with Anson because Anson could verbally joust with him. When they were arguing Anson would always be giggling on the inside because he could think a move ahead of my dad. Anson honed his verbal skills in that crucible."

Once Anson felt comfortable with his own voice and confident in his own opinions, he became fearless. Rather than try to steer clear of conflict he, like his father, would seek it out. "In college there were many, many times when Anson took a stance that he didn't believe in just to spark a debate," St. Anthony roommate Mark Berson says. "He enjoyed the battle, the verbal dueling, and the mental gymnastics. It was part of his personality. He could look at both sides of an issue and argue either side passionately. I'm not sure how he did it, but sometimes he would defend both sides at the same time. I think in his own mind Anson never lost an argument."

There were many instances at home in Greenwich, Connecticut, where the Dorrances moved from Brussels in 1968, when Big Pete and his wife would disagree on an issue and Anson would support his mother's side just to provoke his father, with occasionally volatile results. Big Pete's one weakness was alcohol, which severely diminished both his wit and his patience. Too many beers brought out his temper, and he could erupt with rage in an instant. Once, when Big Pete was drinking, an argument with Anson became so heated from Big Pete's perspective that Peggy stepped in between them. "I told them, 'You're not hitting each other unless you hit me first,'" Peggy remembers. "Nobody hit me."

Anson's adaptation of The Force is more subtle and strategic than that of his father. "There's a softness in Anson that he got from our mom," Pete says. "He's always going to be under control. There's a calmness under pressure, an ability to rein in his natural blood lust when he has to."

Anson was also sensitive to his father's humility. Once when the Dorrance family went out to dinner, Big Pete was grumpily dismissive of a waitress when she asked for his choice of salad dressing. When the waitress returned to the table, she brought every flavor of salad dressing available and placed them all on the center of the table. "Here are your salad dressings, sir," she said to Big Pete, "just out of the reach of your wrath." Big Pete broke up laughing. He admired her spunk. "What everyone loved about my father is his wonderful quality of self-deprecation," Anson says. "Everything was funny to him, especially if the joke was on him. He could be intimidating, but he was not an asshole. When someone put him in his place, he loved it."

An engaging storyteller, Big Pete had a favorite war story about his duties as a censor, who had to read all the outgoing mail from the submarine to make sure that none of the letters gave away the sub's position. Everybody on the ship knew that Lt. Dorrance was the censor, so many of the letters began with the line, "The third in command is a real jackass." Big Pete laughed heartily at his own plight whenever he shared that story.

Big Pete loved nothing more than a good prank. Family legend says that he was expelled from UCLA for sneaking an enormous phallus into the football stadium and erecting it during a game. Another time, when his son Lewjack was fifteen years old and preparing for a date, Big Pete spotted the boy sneaking into the backyard with two beers and hiding them behind a bush. Big Pete replaced the two beers with a six-pack in a cooler. The next night at dinner Lewjack stared sheepishly around the table at his family and finally said, "Thanks for the beer, whoever that was."

All the Dorrance kids endured life lessons brought by their father's sarcastic sense of humor. Big Pete abhorred vanity, and Anson can still remember once in the late 1960s when his father, who skewed conservative in everything from his politics to his attire, blunted any temptation Anson might have to dress in the hippie trappings of the era by saying to him, "Why not dress conventionally and just act like an idiot? Then when you want to return to normal, you're not under pressure to live up to your clothes."

Big Pete was also a pathological teaser, a sadistic quality he bred into all the male members of the Dorrance family. "Thanks to my husband all the Dorrance boys can tease an unsuspecting victim to tears," Peggy says. "It's like scratching an itch until it bleeds, and they don't realize the damage they're doing until you kick them under the table."

"My dad was pretty sarcastic and he liked to have fun, often at other people's expense," Pete says. "Some people who didn't know him that well might not understand his humor, or they could get lost in his intimidating presence, but all he really wanted to do was provoke you for his own amusement."

The gauntlet Big Pete laid down for rest of the world could be summed up in the bumper sticker that he had plastered on the back of his Chevy Malibu for years. It read: *Nuke the Whales*.

Anson Dorrance first met M'Liss Gary when he was eight years old and she was seven. Like Anson, M'Liss was a globetrotter. Born in Lisbon, Portugal, she also lived in Delaware and Georgia before trailing her father, a colonel in the United States Air Force, to Addis Ababa, where he'd been appointed the American air attaché to the Ethiopian government in 1958.

The two American expatriate families, who lived just two miles apart in Addis Ababa, regularly mixed for parties and vacations, and their children grew close. M'Liss's older brother, Mark, became Anson's best friend. "I had a crush on Anson when I was little," M'Liss says. "I always wanted to be involved in any game he was organizing, and I'd try to get on his team because I thought he was cute."

M'Liss didn't think her feelings were reciprocated, but she was encouraged whenever Anson teased her. She understood that one of the ways a Dorrance shows affection is through mocking, and she was kidded mercilessly by Anson about her "ugly ballerina feet."

One weekend the two families shared a camping trip to Lake Awasa, an hour south of Addis Ababa. During one evening while the parents were playing bridge, the kids organized a game of spotlight tag. At one point when Anson was "it," M'Liss hid on the slope of a hill near the game's home base, where she thought she was secluded in the darkness. When Anson finished counting and left the base, he quietly sneaked over and sat next to M'Liss. "How'd you find me?" asked a startled M'Liss.

Anson replied, "Your hair was shining in the moonlight."

"I thought that was the most romantic thing anyone had ever said to me," M'Liss says. "I carried that with me for a decade."

For his part, Anson was merely answering the question.

Eventually the Garys were transferred stateside to Langley Air Force Base outside of Washington, D.C. They arranged reunions with the Dorrances whenever possible during the Dorrances' home leaves to the farm in Louisburg, but the two families sometimes went for years without any contact.

During his teenage years, Anson's extraordinary shyness around women basically precluded any contact with them. Finally, after one meeting of UNC's student legislature during Anson's freshman year, he mustered the courage to ask comely Marjorie Spruill out on a date. Spruill promptly turned him down, saying that she was dating a rugby player. When Spruill identified her boyfriend, Anson, who also played on the rugby team, felt like arguing that the guy was a poseur who barely ever played and wasn't half the athlete that he was, but he was not nearly as comfortable engaging in a debate with someone of the opposite sex. So he nodded and sheepishly walked away, vowing that he would never again ask another woman for a date. "When I got home from college that Thanksgiving my father was concerned about my lack of interest in girls, so he invited me out on the porch for a very serious father/son chat," Anson says. "He told me that the most wonderful part of his life was his relationship with my mother, and I could tell he was really worried about me. So, to take the pressure off, I vowed to marry the next woman who walked through the door."

During that same Thanksgiving weekend, Big Pete telephoned M'Liss, who was working as a ballet dancer in New York City, and invited her to Greenwich to meet a young man he knew who was working as a page on *The Tonight Show*. Big Pete figured that since they were both in show business the two might hit it off. "There had been a bit of distance between Anson and me as we'd grown up, but there was definitely still an interest there from me," M'Liss says. "Before that visit I told my roommate, 'They have this son who I've always thought was really special.' So I knew who I was interested in."

On a walk after Thanksgiving dinner, Anson and M'Liss kissed for the very first time. After that night the two began dating, though M'Liss was troubled by Anson's general disdain for women. "When we first started going together he didn't like women at all," M'Liss says. "He'd always say, 'You women are strange creatures.' He was always talking about how women were devious, untruthful, disloyal, and didn't have any good character qualities. He didn't trust women, and he didn't know how to communicate with them. He thought we got too emotional. He called us all 'psychos.'"

Over the next year, Anson would try to join M'Liss for her ballet performances whenever possible, but those experiences proved to be a struggle for him. "I was sort of one-dimensional," Anson admits. "It was tough for me to watch this woman that I'm in love with on stage in the arms of another man pretending that she's in love with him."

It didn't help that Anson was often accompanied by his brother Pete, who would constantly needle Anson about what they were watching on stage and what might be happening off of it. Anson became so jealous that M'Liss felt compelled to quit performing for a few months.

During Anson's Christmas break from UNC in 1972, M'Liss was performing in a ballet on the Harvard campus in Cambridge. On a snowy night, Anson jumped in his father's Malibu and barreled up Interstate 95 from Greenwich toward Boston. Anson was an inexperienced driver who had only recently obtained his license and had never driven in snow before, so he twice skidded off the road onto the shoulder. At one exit he failed to slow down sufficiently on the frozen off-ramp, and the car fishtailed into a snowbank. Anson eventually dug the car out of the snow and reached Cambridge late that night.

Because M'Liss had been set up to stay at the home of a local family she did not know well, and Anson couldn't afford a motel room, Anson decided he was going to spend that night in his car. The temperature was well below freezing, so

Anson would sleep for an hour until the intense cold would startle him awake, and he'd run the car heater for a few minutes and then fall back to sleep. "At one point I woke up and I swear I thought I'd died because I had no sensation in my limbs, and all the windows were fogged up," Anson says. "I thought 'Is this heaven?'"

The following evening M'Liss's dance company performed its rendition of *The Cherry Tree Carol.* M'Liss was playing the role of the Virgin Mary. Anson squirmed in his seat as Mary and Joseph cavorted around the cherry tree.

As soon as the performance concluded, Anson found M'Liss backstage, led her to the front steps of the theater, and asked her to marry him. He didn't even have a ring. He had proposed in a fit of passion, because he was jealous of Joseph.

Big Pete's professional dream was to start his own regional oil company. According to his blueprint, Carolina Refining & Distributing Company would produce thirty thousand barrels a day with refineries in Morehead City, North Carolina, Georgetown, South Carolina, Savannah, Georgia, and Jacksonville, Florida. Big Pete was a firm believer in nepotism, noting that labor laws prevented him from cussing the hired help with the same gusto that he could use on his relatives when they screwed up, so it was assumed that Big Pete's sons, Anson, Pete, and Lewjack, would join the company. Big Pete told Anson that he wanted him to be his corporate lawyer, joking that as the legal counsel for the family business, Anson wouldn't be tempted to steal from his estate. "I was on a railroad track as far as my career ambitions were concerned," Anson says. "The legal profession fit my personality. Combative. Competitive. Verbally argumentative. My father felt like this was a profession that he'd been training me for my whole life."

Anson and M'Liss were married in the summer of 1974, following his graduation from UNC, and at that point Anson began searching for any law school that might accept him with his mediocre grades. In the meantime, he needed a job. His work experience at the time consisted mostly of summer jobs as a door-to-door cookware salesman, a rent-a-cop, and a city park maintenance man painting lines on soccer fields. Shortly after his wedding, Dorrance took a job pounding the pavement of Chapel Hill, trying to drum up business for Kip Ward's fledgling printing company. Because Ward had virtually no money either, Dorrance agreed to be paid in land.

During the evenings and on weekends, Dorrance played and coached soccer in the Rainbow Soccer League, which Ward had created in 1972. Dorrance coached teams at four different age levels from six to sixty-six, running at least two soccer practices a day. Whenever Dorrance stumped for the printing business he also asked if the storeowner would be interested in sponsoring a recreation league soccer team, and he had far better luck gathering funds for the latter.

Ward envisioned Rainbow Soccer as a communal experience. There were no tryouts. Some teams did yoga as a warmup. Games were supposed to be more for fun than competition, so scores were only loosely monitored. No team won-loss records were kept. Dorrance ignored Ward's vision and trained his team to win.

He kept the game score in his head. He tracked his own won-loss record. One day Dorrance drove to a predominantly African-American neighborhood in town, recruited the best four black athletes he could find in the local park, and paid their league fees. He placed his new players up the middle as his center back, center half, and two inside forwards, and the team jelled. "Some of the other Rainbow coaches and parents told me I was taking the game too seriously," Dorrance says. "I told them, 'If winning doesn't matter to you, that's fine. But we've discovered our morale's a lot better when we win.' They didn't like that we buried everyone."

M'Liss couldn't help but notice her newlywed husband's passion for coaching soccer. One day she said to him, 'Anson, you spend all of your free time coaching, why don't you become a coach?'"

"Nah, that's not a real job," Anson told his wife. "It's not an intellectual pursuit."

During the summer of 1976, Dorrance was finally accepted to law school, at North Carolina Central University in Durham. One day during that summer he returned home and told M'Liss that he'd heard Marvin Allen was going to retire as UNC's men's soccer coach. M'Liss asked her husband if he wanted to apply for the job. "No," he said with a hint of resignation. "I've got to go to law school."

Dorrance had plenty of excuses for why he could never be a coach, but he understood which was the most prohibitive factor. Loyalty. This was one debate with his father that Anson feared he might not be able to win.

When Marvin Allen informed UNC athletic director Bill Cobey in the summer of 1976 that he planned to retire after the upcoming season, Cobey responded by asking Allen who he thought should replace him. The job was never advertised. There were no applicants. It was still a part-time position that paid $2,500 for the season, so there wasn't exactly a line forming outside Cobey's office. Cobey's primary criterion for his new soccer coach was simple. He had to live nearby. The university simply could not afford to fly its next coach to Chapel Hill or pay any moving expenses.

Allen provided Cobey with three names. Shortly thereafter, Cobey phoned Dorrance one evening at home and asked if he could stop by his office sometime to discuss the state of the UNC soccer program. A few days later, Dorrance showed up at Cobey's office in Carmichael Auditorium with a list of five top college coaching prospects that he felt might be interested in the UNC job. He never got to share it. After he and Cobey had talked about the UNC program for a few minutes, Cobey said, "I've been thinking about this and I had a chat with Marvin Allen, and I was wondering if you'd be interested in becoming our next soccer coach?"

Dorrance replied, "*Are you kidding me?*"

Dorrance had never even considered that a school like UNC would offer its head coaching job to a twenty-five-year-old who had never coached a soccer game above the club level. Allen had never once talked to Dorrance about becoming a soccer coach, and he wondered how he had earned his recommendation. Had Allen somehow heard about the way Dorrance often stood up for him when many of his fellow UNC teammates were ready to mutiny? Or did Allen know how badly Dorrance needed a job that paid in cash? Or had Allen wandered around the corner from his office one afternoon and seen Coach Dorrance sneaking his Rainbow team of nine-year-olds onto the dusty intramural fields across the drive-way and putting them through their drills? Dorrance would never ask Allen why he rubber-stamped him. Says Dorrance: "All I know is that Dr. Allen saw some-thing in me that I never saw."

Allen told Cobey that Dorrance understood soccer as well as anybody he'd ever coached, and that he could teach it. "I had seen how competitive Anson was as a player, and I've always thought that people coached the way they played," Cobey says. "Besides, I hated to fire coaches, and among my candidates I felt that Anson had the best chance to survive. Who knew if he would succeed? But he was the least likely to fail miserably."

"When Anson was offered the UNC job, I think a lot of people were sur-prised," Kip Ward says. "Anson was as shocked as anybody. I don't think any-body in the UNC soccer community had even considered it a possibility. We all thought they would want a college coach from the outside with a track record and not this little no-name guy with guile. There was a real question in everybody's mind whether Anson could be successful."

The day after his meeting with Cobey, Dorrance accepted the job. His hiring was never formally announced by the university, partly because he wouldn't offi-cially take over as coach until after an apprenticeship season under Allen and partially because hardly anybody in the general public would care. Dorrance never even bothered to tell Cobey that he also planned to begin law school at North Carolina Central that fall. In his own mind Dorrance still didn't view coaching as a serious profession, but more as a hobby, a part-time job to earn a little money in the afternoons to help pay for law school. He still had every intention of someday becoming Big Pete's corporate lawyer.

In retrospect, Bill Cobey acknowledges that he, too, was surprised Allen would recommend such a young candidate as his successor. However, to dismiss Dorrance on those grounds would have been hypocritical. Cobey himself had been named UNC's athletic director in 1976 at the relatively tender age of thirty-six, and he understood the value of youthful exuberance. "I have never thought that maturity or knowledge is necessarily chronological," Cobey says. "I was the right person to hire a twenty-five-year-old with no coaching experience. It was a gut feeling."

What Cobey didn't know at the time was that he hadn't exactly hired the man he thought he was hiring. After Allen had endorsed Dorrance, Cobey still main-tained some reservations about a recently graduated soccer player who might lack the necessary discipline for the job, so he asked his associate athletic direc-tor, Moyer Smith, to vouch for Dorrance's character. Smith thought about the young man whom he had met several times, dutifully performing administrative chores around the soccer office. Smith told Cobey, "I've found Anson to be a humble, organized, responsible, clean-cut guy, who seems to get along well with everybody." Trouble is, the man Smith was describing, the man he thought was Anson Dorrance, was actually Dorrance's teammate Geoff Griffin.

A few weeks later, when Smith was introduced to Dorrance and discovered his error, he was petrified that he'd committed a blunder that would cripple the UNC men's soccer program. Smith didn't tell Dorrance about his misidentification for nearly a decade. Once he did, whenever Dorrance ventured out on a university-related speaking engagement with Moyer Smith, he began his remarks by peeking over at Smith with a devilish grin and then saying, "Ladies and gentlemen, I want to share with you a little story about how we hire coaches at the University of North Carolina . . ."

5 | *Beginnings*

You see things; and you say, "Why?" But I dream things that never were, and I say, "Why not?"

—George Bernard Shaw

Laura Brockington was not a feminist. She was an opportunist. All she really wanted to do was play soccer. Brockington grew up in Chapel Hill, the only child of an anthropology professor at the university. She began playing soccer with the Rainbow Soccer program, competing in coed games with and against teams coached by Anson Dorrance. A striker at heart, Brockington always found herself banished to fullback with the other girls, where none of the boys ever passed to her.

For the first three years that Brockington attended Chapel Hill High School, no girls' soccer program existed. The few girls who played soccer were relegated to reserve roles on the boys' team. Brockington stood just five feet tall, and though her skills were honed by two hours of individual soccer workouts every day, the boys were still too fast and strong for her. She didn't want to play five or ten minutes a game. She wanted to play the *whole* game.

Early in the spring of 1977, Brockington broke her leg in a coed soccer game. The twelfth-grader was still wearing a full-leg cast when she appeared before the school board to lobby for a girls' soccer program at Chapel Hill High. While her leg was actually fully healed, and the cast was overdue to be removed, she wanted graphic evidence of what happens when girls play soccer with boys. Brockington captained the inaugural Chapel Hill High girls' soccer team later that spring.

When Brockington matriculated at UNC in the fall of 1977, she discovered that there was no women's soccer there either. Brockington met with UNC women's athletic director Frances Hogan about starting a UNC women's soccer club. Hogan patiently heard Brockington out. Then she told her to try field hockey. Brockington had never played field hockey, didn't want to play field hockey, so she scoured the UNC campus searching for as many women as she could find who were interested in playing soccer. She got three dozen or so to sign a petition. She lobbied the school's Sports Council into funding gas for the team's transportation. Then she arranged for a local sporting goods store to provide a discount on uniforms. The UNC women's soccer club was born, a team that would become known as the Pioneers. "Soccer was my passion, and I saw no reason to give it up just because the sport didn't exist for women at UNC," Brockington says. "I didn't do it for womankind. I did it for one woman. I did it for me."

"Laura looked so innocent I always expected to see a butterfly land on her nose," says club teammate Katherine Bliss. "But underneath she was a born leader who was tough enough to fight for what she wanted."

The club team began competing in the spring of 1978. There were no tryouts. Whoever showed up played. The team was a melting pot of undergraduates, grad students, and a few university staffers. Some were good. Some were not. Competing on the grass-deprived intramural fields because they were not allowed on Fetzer Field, the UNC club played equally primitive club teams from other North Carolina colleges and traveled to a tournament in Athens, Georgia, in the summer of 1978. They were dominant in most games. The only competition of any kind came in a scrimmage against Brockington's former team, the women's varsity at Chapel Hill High.

On the UNC club Brockington got to play forward, and she got to play for ninety minutes. An admitted ball hog, she considered any game in which she scored fewer than three goals to be a disappointment. She loved the scoring. She loved the winning. Sometimes she even looked around and noticed that her teammates were having fun, too.

Almost as soon as she started the club, Brockington set her sights on varsity status. It wasn't about her playing time anymore. It was about creating more female role models. Her idol growing up in the sport had been German national teamer Gerd Muller, a guy she identified with only because he too had to overcome stumpy little legs. "I remember in high school little boys asking me for my autograph, and I thought that was pretty cool," Brockington says. "But it struck me that they were little boys and not little girls, and I didn't like that. I didn't want little girls to grow up in the game like me, wondering, 'What happens when I get to college? Don't I get to play anymore?'"

Brockington knew she needed to prove that there was enough interest in the sport at UNC to merit a varsity squad. She spent as much time in the Sports Council office as she did in class, seeking out potential opponents by making phone calls or writing letters to 150 other colleges to identify which of them fielded women's soccer programs and which were intending to start them in the near future. When she was ready, she went over Hogan's head this time, directly to Bill Cobey. She entered her meeting with Cobey armed with a roster and a tentative schedule and anticipating a tough sell. She had no idea that Cobey was unaware that a UNC women's soccer club even existed.

Brockington told Cobey about the interest in the club and about how he could fund a women's varsity team for less than the cost of one football recruiting visit. Then she wielded her secret weapon. She just happened to let it slip that she'd been contacted by an attorney looking for a test case on Title IX, a law enacted in 1972 that encouraged proportional participation for female athletes at federally funded universities.

Brockington could not have been more stunned at the reaction of the man across the big desk. Before Cobey was promoted to athletic director, he had been the athletic department's Title IX officer. He'd had Title IX folders piled high on his desk, and he was the one who attended all the meetings. He thought he might know as much about Title IX as any other school administrator in the country. As a result, Cobey had constantly lobbied for more women's sports at UNC, a school which had no women's varsity teams until 1971, and he recognized the value of fielding as many varsity sports for women as for men. Adding a women's soccer varsity would bring UNC to twelve sports for each gender, the first time the university had ever fielded as many women's sports as men's. "I felt like that would protect us from charges of discrimination from some of the demagogues out there," Cobey says. "It was a problem prevention step, a way of protecting us from unjust criticism and potential lawsuits."

Beyond the practical reasons for considering women's soccer, Cobey also had a vision. Four years earlier, in the fall of 1974, Cobey was driving home past the campus Astroturf field, where the Chapel Hill High soccer team was playing a match. He recalled reading a local newspaper article about his friend Bill Basnight's daughter, Lorrie, who was playing on the boys' team because no girls' team existed. He decided to pull over and watch the rest of the game, and he was surprised at what he saw. He watched Lorrie, a speedy wing fullback, repeatedly streaking up the sideline with the ball at her feet past her slack-jawed male opponents. It was the first time Cobey had ever seen a girl play soccer, and he was impressed. "You have to get over these mental hurdles," Cobey says. "That night I realized that soccer is a game that women can play, too."

Memories of Lorrie Basnight flashed through Cobey's mind when Laura Brockington showed up in his office that day. He saw an opportunity for UNC to set the pace for an entire sport. Cobey had observed through his twenty-one years working in athletics that once a school established an athletic juggernaut, like Notre Dame in football or UCLA in basketball, it was extremely tough to compete against it. "What clicked in my mind was that maybe this is a time when we can get out ahead of everybody else and we can establish a tradition," Cobey says. "I knew there were only a handful of women's soccer programs in the nation, and that we had a whole lot of potential to build something special here."

Cobey eyed Brockington that winter day and delivered a cautionary message. "I don't know how good your club is, but if we get into varsity soccer we're going to be the best, and that means that maybe nobody on the club will even make the team," Cobey told her. "Do you still like the idea?"

Brockington didn't blink. "Sure," she said.

So Cobey took the soccer idea to Hogan, who floated it to the coaches of UNC's established women's sports. Most of them hated it. They were already running their programs on shoestring budgets, and they worried that another women's program would sap their resources even further. Hogan relayed their concerns back to Cobey and recommended that the plan be scrapped. "I told Frances that I was sorry, but we were going to do it anyway," Cobey recalls, laughing at his own bravado. "I didn't consult the chancellor. I didn't consult the Athletic Council. I just created a team."

The day Bill Cobey hired Anson Dorrance as his men's soccer coach, he gave him the same ominous pep talk he shared with all of his rookie coaches. *This is the University of North Carolina, and there are enough schools out there that would like to play us who I know we can beat. If you can't schedule a winning season, then something is wrong.*

With all due respect to Marvin Allen, Dorrance knew he was not inheriting a program rich in championship tradition. During Allen's tenure his Tar Heels churned out what many of his players jokingly referred to as "Southern gentleman seasons," solid but not spectacular, a reflection of the coach himself. Allen finished his coaching career with a respectable record of 174-81-23, but in his twenty-eight seasons Allen's teams earned just one Atlantic Coast Conference regular-season championship and one appearance in the NCAA Tournament.

During Dorrance's apprenticeship season as the Tar Heels' head coach designate in 1976, he studied how Allen coached the team and tried to educate himself as best he could. He read everything about soccer coaching he could find, and he attended every coaching course he could manage on his limited time and budget. In his first attempt, he became one of the youngest coaches ever to earn an "A" coaching license from the United States Soccer Federation.

When Dorrance took over the Tar Heels on his own in 1977, he began his coaching career with two victories, followed by a pair of defeats at the hands of UNC–Wilmington and Rollins. The day after the loss to Rollins, Big Pete wrote a letter to his son:

Dear Anson,

I'm compelled as an interfering parent to offer you some advice concerning your coaching.

1. You're the youngest major university soccer head coach in the U.S. That fact must have been a source of concern to other coaches in the A.C.C., as youth today seems to be riding the crest of the wave of success. Playing UNC this year, those coaches must have been surprised to be playing a suddenly inexperienced Dr. Allen rather than an experienced Anson Dorrance. Moral—Be yourself.

2. You have one thing going for you that none of your competing coaches has—recent game experience and demonstratively peak skills. These things should be the basis of what and how you should teach. Other coaches can teach only from memory and "the book."

3. Sports are a pleasure for the player because of the comradeship developed. You should encourage a close, almost exclusive, feeling within the team by making the team a distinctive unit within the student body. How? The uniform is an obvious unifying symbol on the field. What can you develop that would carry out that important family feeling off the field?

4. Sports need leadership. A leader is not a lonely, distant figure sitting isolated on a bench. You should participate in the game—patting butts, murmuring to players, encouraging the disappointed, vocalizing praise. You

*won't lose face or encourage familiarity. You'll develop friends and be a
part of the team. They'll be playing for your effusive praise.*

*5. Lastly—think out your game plan. Prepare mentally for the unex-
pected. What will you do if you're down 3 at the half? Change radically or
continue as you were doing? Prepare your team to cope with the unexpected
by not allowing anything unexpected to happen. If they have considered
the possibility of playing without their best goalie or center half, they won't
be surprised if it happens.*

With love and respect,
Dad

Dorrance's men finished that first season at 14-3-1 and swept their last eight
matches, outscoring opponents 28–3. Although the Tar Heels were disappointed
not to receive an NCAA Tournament bid, it was arguably the best season in UNC
history, and Dorrance was named Atlantic Coast Conference Coach of the Year.
He followed that up in 1978 with a 12-3-4 season against an upgraded schedule. In
his second season, Dorrance felt the team had turned a corner, and he pointed to
ties against Appalachian State and Clemson, the two ranked teams on the UNC
schedule, as evidence that the Tar Heels were now capable of competing with
any team in the country. "I don't think Dr. Allen would have handed over the
program if he didn't feel that Anson would take it and run with it," says Geoff
Griffin, Dorrance's assistant coach from 1977 to 1987. "Anson immediately
brought more energy and emotion. He had an opinion on everything. With Anson
in charge, the program wasn't going to stand still."

When he assumed sole responsibility for the program, Dorrance had grate-
fully accepted the three scholarships that Dr. Allen had always steadfastly refused. That allowed Dorrance to do some recruiting, something that Allen had
largely shunned, and in 1977, for the first time in the history of the program, the
roster included five players on athletic scholarship. Dorrance imposed only one
rule on himself in his initial recruiting classes. Even though Clemson was dominating the ACC at the time by handpicking its recruits from the Nigerian national team, Dorrance stuck to his nationalistic roots. He would recruit players
only from the United States, staying loyal to the belief that he could build UNC
into a national power with a roster made in America. In 1978 he signed two players off the U.S. junior national team, Ricky Marvin and Adam Abronski, estab-
lishing UNC as a legitimate soccer contender.

Dorrance treated every practice and every game as an experiment. He tink-
ered with all sorts of different systems, from aggressive four-fronts to bunkering.
He sampled every dribbling and heading drill he had ever witnessed, from Dr.
Allen's elementary stuff to what he'd picked up from watching European coaching videos. In the spring, Dorrance instituted off-season training and scrimmag-
ing three nights a week, developing the players year-round for the first time in the
program's history. He also initiated weight training, much to the dismay of most
of his players, and constantly whipped his team with the power of his personality.

Says Dorrance: "I kept challenging their manhood, which is a great way to get them to do something they don't like. *What? You don't think I'm man enough to drive a car off this cliff? Stand back!* Motivating men is such a simple process."

Then, in March of 1979, Dorrance received a phone call from Cobey asking if he could spare some time to help evaluate the UNC women's soccer club. Dorrance told Cobey that he didn't know anything about women's soccer or have any interest in it, and he'd had nothing to do with organizing the club, but he agreed to help out as best he could. As Cobey and Dorrance walked over to the Astroturf field one chilly afternoon to watch the women's club scrimmage, it was the first time Dorrance had ever seen the club play. He had absolutely no inkling about Cobey's meeting two days earlier with Laura Brockington or about what was running through Cobey's mind at the time. After the pair watched the scrimmage, Cobey asked, "Well, do you think they can compete as a varsity?"

"Yeah, this is a good club," Dorrance replied. "They're well organized. They play a relatively attractive game."

A week later, Dorrance received another call from Cobey, who got right to the point this time. "Anson, we'd like to make you full-time, and we want you to coach both teams," Cobey said, "the men and the women."

On September 12, 1979, Anson Dorrance's two families were born at the same time. An hour before Dorrance was scheduled to leave with his team for UNC's first-ever women's varsity soccer match, a road game against the UNC–Wilmington club, M'Liss sat up in bed that morning and asked if maybe he could send Geoff Griffin instead. "Why?" Anson asked. M'Liss told him she was going into labor. The Dorrances' first child, daughter Michelle, was born the same afternoon that UNC defeated UNC–Wilmington 7–1. So let the record state that Dorrance did not actually coach the first match in UNC women's soccer history.

Dorrance learned that he'd earned his first victory as a women's soccer coach on a phone call from Griffin while sitting in a hospital room beside his wife and his newborn baby. He told M'Liss that the women's team had won and then the UNC men's team had tied its game 1–1 in the nightcap of the doubleheader in Wilmington that day. "It must be prophetic that we just had a daughter," M'Liss told her husband. "Maybe it's your women who are destined for greatness."

As fate would have it, Laura Brockington wasn't with the Tar Heels in Wilmington that day either. That summer she had taken a job as an au pair in Caracas, Venezuela. During her stint there she dutifully followed Dorrance's training program, running sprints through the smoggy streets. Dorrance phoned her a couple of times in Venezuela just to remind her, "I need you!" He had no idea that Brockington was also receiving calls from a new boyfriend, and that she was more excited by those conversations. Brockington had fallen in love, and in order to be with her boyfriend, she made the agonizing decision to drop out of UNC and move to California that August.

That same summer, as Dorrance was unsuccessfully wooing Brockington to be the cornerstone of his new program, he attended a coaching clinic in New Jersey where he introduced himself to a Dallas club coach named Ray Thomas. Dorrance asked Thomas his pat question: "I hear that Dallas is a good area for girls' soccer; do you know anyone?" Thomas mentioned a scrappy girl he coached who he claimed had produced 180 goals in 140 club games. A kid named Janet Rayfield.

Janet had only begun playing soccer in the summer after the fourth grade because the Rayfields had moved to a new house in Dallas; to help Janet meet new friends, her mother enrolled her in the local YMCA sports program. The only sport with space remaining was soccer, so Janet played that. Eventually Janet and her soccer buddies formed a neighborhood club team. Because there was no women's high school soccer, she played exclusively for clubs.

The same day that Thomas told Dorrance about Rayfield, the UNC coach began recruiting her, sight unseen. He phoned the Rayfield home and learned that Janet was away at summer camp, so, unbeknownst to her, Dorrance and Janet's parents made arrangements for her to make a recruiting visit to Chapel Hill as soon as she returned home from camp. On a Friday that July she flew to North Carolina, and when she got off the plane she stood in the gate area for twenty minutes, waiting for Dorrance. Finally, Rayfield spotted a guy walking briskly toward her, with thick glasses and hair all over the place. She was wearing a khaki skirt with pantyhose and sandals. "When I saw him I was thinking, 'This *can't* be him!'" Rayfield says. "And I'm sure he was thinking, 'This *can't* be her!'"

Rayfield's recruiting visit lasted only three hours, including the admissions interview and a quickie campus tour. She was certain she was not qualified to be admitted to UNC and only agreed to the trip to appease her parents. She had already been accepted to go to Regis College in Colorado, where she planned to try to walk on to the volleyball team because Regis had no soccer team. She thought her soccer career was over.

Toward the end of Rayfield's campus tour, Dorrance noticed that they were running late for the trip back to the airport. He hurdled a short stone wall, but when Rayfield tried to follow him her sandal clipped the wall, and she fell on her face. She put a run in her pantyhose, and her shin began bleeding from a scrape, but she pulled her dress down over it, hoping Dorrance wouldn't think he was recruiting a total klutz. "There was a certain symbolism in that," Dorrance says, "because my first recruit was recklessly leaping over obstacles behind me and suffering the consequences every step of the way."

In his final recruiting pitch, Dorrance told Rayfield, "I want to build the best women's soccer program in the country. Our administration is supporting us; we feel like soccer is about to explode, and we want to be ahead of the curve."

After the flight home, Rayfield and her family took a twelve-hour drive into the Rocky Mountains for a vacation at a dude ranch. "I kept thinking, 'I won't get a second chance,' Rayfield says. "I loved soccer, and the thought of never playing again bothered me. I thought if I didn't go to UNC I might regret it for the rest of my life."

The dude ranch had no phones in the cabins. The only phone was located in the country store. Dorrance called Rayfield at that phone fourteen times over the next few days to try to seal the deal. She never got his messages. Finally, after several days of deliberating on her own, Rayfield walked into the store and phoned Dorrance to tell him she wanted to come to UNC. Dorrance was elated.

Rayfield was one of three "recruits" on the 1979 team, along with midfielder Kelly Haines and wing forward Emily Scruggs. Haines was steered to Dorrance by one of his male players, who had helped coach her at Greensboro's Grimsley High. Scruggs aspired to run track at UNC, but when she mentioned some soccer experience on her application, she received a phone call from Dorrance. The UNC coach filled out the rest of his roster by holding campus tryouts which attracted twenty-five players, many from the club team, all but one of whom earned a spot on the inaugural roster, because somebody had to.

In its promotional literature, the UNC athletic department referred to that first season as "an experiment in ladies' soccer." Brockington's stubbornness and Cobey's calculated vision had combined to create just the nineteenth varsity women's soccer team in the nation, and the only one east of Colorado and south of Connecticut. During a 12–0 win over Duke's club team in UNC's second-ever game, one Tar Heel heard a Blue Devil player ask her own teammate, "What's your name again?"

"You definitely knew you were at the beginning of something," says Rayfield, who led UNC with thirty goals in just twelve games that first season. "We were doing instep passing drills in every practice. We had a lot of girls who had never played competitively. It was odd for all of us to be training every day. But even though we were extremely raw, there was always a feeling that we were expected to succeed."

Due primarily to superior fitness and organization, and the presence of Rayfield, UNC would beat Duke's club team three times that season, along with wins over the club teams from Georgia and James Madison. In early November, UNC traveled to Fayetteville to play in a tournament involving the best soccer teams in North Carolina. The Tar Heels defeated a club called the Fort Bragg Chargers 11–1, and later that same day downed the UNC–Wilmington club 4–0. The next day in the finals, UNC was matched against its own club team, the squad from which the varsity had been born a few months earlier, and the second-best team in the state. UNC's varsity won 4–1 behind a hat trick from Rayfield. With nothing else available to play for, the UNC players dubbed themselves winners of the 1979 state title. The Tar Heels were champions in their very first season, in their own minds anyway.

The UNC Law School library is located on the third floor of the school, which stands just a hundred yards behind the soccer goal at the east end of Fetzer Field. In 1979, when Dorrance agreed to accept the UNC women's coaching job, part of the deal included a transfer to UNC Law School. In the late afternoons, when his men's and women's soccer practices were over, Dorrance would walk over to the law library and study at a table in front of the huge floor-to-ceiling window that overlooked the soccer field. He merely had to peek over the edge of his tort tome to see the white lines, the green grass, the two opposing goals. Some days he would notice somebody jog onto the field to kick around a soccer ball. Often somebody else would join in, and Dorrance would get the itch. By the time Dorrance noticed a third player showing up to play, he realized that he could form a 2 v. 2. He was out the door.

In order to have enough time to coach the men's team during his first three years of law school at North Carolina Central, Dorrance had taken one course shy each semester, four courses instead of the usual five. Most of the students he had started with there had already earned their law degrees by the fall of 1979. Dorrance needed to complete just six more courses.

During those three years in law school, Dorrance had never truly embraced the task before him, comparing the vast memorization of tedious facts to his days as a Catholic youth memorizing the catechism. The only moments of law school he enjoyed were the mock trials. He relished the debate, the strategy, how the pitched battle taught him to think on his feet and even to creatively bullshit at times. In fact, the competitive nature of those classes reminded him of what he liked so much about his other career. But he knew that his dad's dream was for him to become a corporate lawyer, not a trial lawyer, which would be primarily a paper job and wouldn't involve much time in the courtroom. He grew increasingly miserable as a law student, realizing more and more that his becoming a lawyer was Big Pete's dream rather than his own.

Dorrance had accepted the job of coaching the UNC women's team with a resolution that he wasn't going to do anything less in training them than he was doing for his men. He'd train each team for two hours a day then write recruiting letters in the law school library into the wee hours of the morning while he prepared briefs for cases. On many nights he'd literally fall asleep on his typewriter, but he was still making Cs in his classes—he was spending so much time coaching that he was falling desperately behind in his schoolwork. For the first time during their marriage, Anson was going to bed later than M'Liss each night and getting up earlier the next morning, averaging four hours of sleep per night. It got so bad that Cobey called Dorrance into his office and told him that he was one of only two coaches in the UNC athletic department who was still married to his original spouse, and to please spend more time at home to try to keep it that way.

After juggling the responsibilities of law student and coach of two soccer teams for about six weeks into the fall semester of 1979, Dorrance drove home one night and told his wife the news that she'd been expecting for several weeks. *Honey, this is just too much. Something's got to go.*

Dorrance never pretended that this was a decision he could make for himself, because it affected his family's future. He was making only $11,000 coaching both soccer teams, so the Dorrances were supported primarily by M'Liss's salary as a ballet instructor. Now he was weighing a lucrative law career against a subsistence-level coaching job, so he tried not to influence his wife's opinion in any way.

"Anson, you know what's got to go, don't you?" M'Liss replied. "I think you really love this coaching thing. Why don't you drop out of law school?"

"It wasn't until then when I really thought about coaching soccer for the first time, and it was obvious that I loved it," Anson says. "It was automatic. It was like breathing. M'Liss understood that, and she shoved me in the right direction. She was the one who knew that my passion for coaching was overwhelming, and she must have thought that I could make something of it. All I knew is that it would be fun, but at what cost?"

"I wasn't worried about the money," M'Liss says. "Coaching had always been part of Anson's personality, from his days as a kid telling the other kids what to do in backyard games. I had a chance to follow my childhood dream to become a dancer, and I always thought that coaching was Anson's true calling. I thought, 'How can you not do something that you love?'"

Anson knew that making the decision to drop out of law school was the easy part. Telling Big Pete was the hard part. The phone call to his father amounted to an apology. "I was shocked when Anson dropped out, and I know dad was totally shocked and a little pissed," Anson's brother Pete says. "Dad couldn't believe Anson would do something so stupid."

Big Pete unleashed the full power of The Force to try to change Anson's mind. For months after that, he would phone Anson regularly at work to tell him about other jobs that were available. Real jobs. Peggy believed the soccer thing was just a phase her son was going through that surely wouldn't last. Every time UNC Chancellor Ferebee Taylor ran into Dorrance, he encouraged the young coach to please complete his final six law school classes, just in case.

Dorrance wouldn't listen to any of it. He was preparing to scale another water tower in a rainstorm. *Hey y'all, watchisss!*

6 | *Pioneers*

In the land of the blind, the one-eyed man is king.

— Michael Apostolius

Billy Palladino was supposed to be Mickey Mantle. The kid could hit. The kid could track a ball down in center field. The kid dreamed of nothing but making the bigs.

Not long after the Palladino family moved to Chapel Hill from Washington, D.C., when Billy was three years old, he became a fixture on the local athletic scene. His family grew close to the family of UNC basketball coach Frank McGuire, and eventually Billy met Dean Smith through McGuire when Smith arrived at UNC as an assistant coach in 1958. When Smith took over as the Tar Heels' head coach in 1961, he signed up Billy for UNC basketball camp each summer, and whenever Smith spotted Billy at camp, he would call him by name and offer a personal tip on his jump shot.

Billy was a sports junkie. He sneaked past security into Woollen Gym for pickup hoops games, rode his bike around UNC's Finley Golf Course raking sand traps in exchange for a free round, and taught little kids how to swim for a dollar an hour at the campus pool on summer mornings. Because youth soccer did not exist in North Carolina when he was growing up, and there was no soccer team at Chapel Hill High, Billy never kicked a soccer ball until the summer before the tenth grade. A couple of his close friends had gone off to prep school up north and returned with an interest in the sport, and they talked him into joining them in a summer soccer league, composed of UNC varsity soccer players, football players trying to stay in shape, international students, and a few random high school kids. Billy had no idea what he was doing, so he chased the ball all over the field.

While Billy played varsity football and basketball in high school, his true love was baseball. He grew up assuming he would attend college at UNC, but the Tar Heel baseball program showed no interest in him, so he decided to attend East Carolina University in Greenville, where the Pirates coach had promised him a chance to pursue his goal of playing pro ball. At East Carolina, Palladino struggled mightily through fall baseball, distinguishing himself more as a 50-yard freestyler on the swim team. Realizing his baseball aspirations were slipping away, Palladino decided to transfer home to UNC after one year.

During that summer of 1970, Palladino showed up for daily soccer pickup games at Fetzer Field that included several players from the UNC varsity team. These players recruited Palladino to try out for the Tar Heels that fall. He agreed at least in part because he was fond of Marvin Allen, who had been ten-year-old Billy's first Little League baseball coach.

It was at those UNC tryouts that Bill Palladino first met a spindly fellow transfer student named Anson Dorrance, who was also forced to sit out the 1970 season. The pair spent that fall relaying Mack McKinnon's wayward practice shots back to the field and shuttling between the varsity and the J.V., welcomed by neither except as ball-shaggers.

Palladino was an athlete, not a soccer player, with good size, speed, and strength but limited ball skills. He was a marginal player who started a few games for UNC as a defender in 1971. In the summer before his senior season he broke his right big toe in a pickup soccer game and played sporadically in his final season of eligibility.

He majored in psychology at UNC with a minor in chemistry. After graduating in 1973, he commuted to N.C. State in Raleigh for three years, where he earned his master's degree in biology. Then he returned once again to Chapel Hill and accepted a job doing research in a lab at the department of surgery in the UNC School of Medicine, most days working alongside another young chemist named Jerry Greenfield. The two men often lamented the sterile environment of the lab, and Jerry used to speak often about quitting his job to pursue his dream of selling ice cream with his buddy, Ben Cohen. Palladino laughed incredulously about the plans of Ben & Jerry and skeptically teased his friend, asking, "You two are going to open an ice cream store . . . *in Vermont?!*"

One day in the fall of 1978 when Palladino was walking to lunch on Franklin Street in downtown Chapel Hill, he bumped into Dorrance. The two had lost touch, not having spoken since before Dorrance had accepted the UNC men's coaching job two years earlier. They struck up a conversation, and Dorrance asked his old teammate, "Why don't you come out and help me?" For a guy working full-time in a lab, a chance to escape each afternoon and soak up some sunshine sounded appealing. That fall Palladino helped Geoff Griffin coach UNC's junior varsity team. The following year, when Dorrance took on the women's coaching position as well, Griffin focused more on the men's varsity, and Palladino ran the men's junior varsity as a part-time coach, paid $50 for the season. When Dorrance needed a women's assistant coach in 1980, he first offered the position to Griffin, but he preferred coaching men. So Dorrance offered it to Palladino, with a raise to $300 for the season.

Palladino was apprehensive about the offer because he hadn't coached a female since he'd taught swimming lessons as a teenager. He wondered how he might be received as a man coaching women. Dorrance told him he needn't worry about that because judging by his own recently completed inaugural season as the women's coach, he obviously hadn't the slightest idea how to deal with them either.

At the same time as Palladino was pondering a stab at women's soccer, Bill Prentice was driving up Interstate 75 in southern Michigan. He was a few weeks away from finishing up his Ph.D. in sports medicine at the University of Virginia. Prentice was twenty-seven years old, married, and flat broke. Looking for a job. *Any* job.

He was on his way to a physical education conference in Detroit because one of Prentice's college advisors, Bob Rotella, had told him that it was a good place to look for work. Prentice left Charlottesville, Virginia, one night at 10 p.m. and started driving north. Sometime around 5 a.m. he dozed off and veered toward the median, where he believes his life may have been spared when he slammed into the guardrail and skidded safely to a stop.

When Prentice finally arrived in Detroit that day he couldn't afford a room, so Rotella offered him the opportunity to sleep on the floor of his hotel room. It was so small that Prentice had to sleep in the closet for three nights. Rotella's roommate on that trip was John Billing, who had just been hired as the new exercise and sports science department chairman at the University of North Carolina, and one night when Billing and Prentice went out for a drink, Prentice told him he would love to work at UNC someday. A month later, Billing phoned Prentice for an interview, and Prentice accepted a job as an assistant professor.

Prentice's primary duty was as a teacher, but he hoped to also work with some of the school's renowned athletic teams. UNC's coordinator of athletic training, Dan Hooker, asked Prentice to work with wrestling, track & field, and swimming. Then Hooker told Prentice about a new program that had just begun competing the previous fall ... women's soccer. Says Prentice: "I'll never forget my very first thought was 'You've got to be kidding me. I've just spent all these years getting a Ph.D., and now I have to work with the frigging women's soccer program? Working with some coach named *Anson Dorrance*? What kind of a name is that? Where's this guy from, Tasmania or someplace?' I really did not want to do it. I can't emphasize enough how much I did not want to do it."

Prentice didn't like soccer. He considered it a Third World sport. He had no idea about the rules. And *women*? He didn't even know they played soccer. But he had only been on the UNC staff for a few weeks. He could see no way out.

So, on a late August afternoon in 1980, Bill Prentice reluctantly showed up for his first women's soccer practice. He stuck out his right hand and introduced himself to assistant coach Bill Palladino. The two men stood together on the sideline at Fetzer Field and watched Dorrance lead the players through a scrimmage. After a few minutes, Prentice turned to Palladino with a stunned gaze and said, "Wow, these girls are awesome!"

Susan Ellis had never played an organized soccer game in her life, never tried the game at all outside of a phys ed class, as she entered her senior year at Chapel Hill High in 1979. The following spring, many of her friends, who had never played the game either, suddenly started getting excited about trying out for the school's women's soccer team, which was coached by UNC assistant Geoff Griffin. Ellis had no idea where the newfound interest in soccer was coming from. Then one afternoon, Ellis' best friend, Liz Phillips, approached her and said, "Why don't you come play soccer? Coach Griffin is *soooo* cute!" That's all it took. Ellis became a soccer player because the coach was cute.

Growing up, Ellis had played some basketball and tennis, and she swam all the time in the summers, but her only athletic claim to fame was that she was the fastest kid, boy or girl, in the sixth grade at Glenwood Elementary School. Ellis adapted surprisingly quickly to soccer, and during that 1980 summer she and some of her high school teammates joined a group of UNC players to form a team coached by Dorrance that won the North Carolina state championship. Though Ellis was still extremely raw as a player, Dorrance offered her the opportunity to come to UNC and try out for the Tar Heels.

Ellis had already been accepted into the college where she really wanted to go, Springfield College in Massachusetts, a school that specialized in physical education. She hoped her degree there would springboard her toward her lifelong dream of becoming a P.E. teacher and basketball coach. When the offer came from UNC, Ellis couldn't help but think back to the many times when her father, Bill, a devout Tar Heel fan, sat Susan and her four siblings down around the dining room table and told them only half-jokingly that they could go to any college in the country, but that he would only pay for one: the University of North Carolina. As Susan weighed her two college options, Bill maintained that she was free to make her own decision. "I remember coming down to breakfast one morning and my dad asked me if I'd made my choice," Ellis says. "I said, 'Yeah, I think I'm going to Springfield.' My dad lowered his newspaper and said, 'Not going to let you do that, Susan.' It was the best decision of my life, and I didn't even make it."

In the first two years of the UNC women's soccer program, most of the players weren't so much recruited as invited to a party at the new guy's house that nobody was sure would be all that fun. From Chapel Hill High, Dorrance also lured Liz Phillips. Nancy Clary transferred in from Mary Washington College, where she had played on the basketball team. Rosemary Carbery earned a promotion to the Tar Heel varsity from the women's soccer club after a stint with UNC's junior varsity basketball team, and Elley Jordan followed the same path after distinguishing herself in the Ultimate Frisbee club. Katherine Bliss had never played soccer until she tried it in a phys ed class as a UNC sophomore, after which Jordan talked her into joining the club team. Carbery, Jordan, and Bliss were among seven refugees from the club team to make the varsity, including Liz Crowley. Crowley had recently set the UNC record in the javelin when she met Laura Brockington, who convinced her to play for the soccer club in 1978. Then, in the fall of 1979, Crowley was in the midst of a self-imposed semester sabbatical from UNC when she attended a Tar Heel volleyball game and ran into Dorrance, who remembered Crowley as an aggressive defender for the club. He wanted her to try out for the varsity the next fall. "What are you doing now?" Dorrance asked Crowley.

"I joined the Army," she said.

"*What?*" Dorrance said. "Did you sign anything?"

Crowley's induction had been deferred, so Dorrance contacted a law school buddy who suggested that he issue Crowley a letter of intent to help her get released from her military commitment. Crowley returned to school that spring and began playing soccer in the fall. "When I left college it was because I felt a little bit lost," Crowley says. "When I started playing soccer it was like I finally found my niche. To be on a varsity soccer team in college was my dream. It was about being part of something. That something wasn't necessarily defined, but it was grand enough just to be on a team, to win a letter and wear a shirt with *Carolina* on it. I thought the idea of playing soccer for Carolina was the greatest thing in the world."

The UNC roster was extremely fluid, and nobody was quite sure who would turn up when each season began. "I remember showing up for my freshman year in 1980, and some of the girls thought I was just there hanging out with my friend Liz Phillips," Ellis says. "About a week into practice someone asked me, 'Are you actually on this team?'"

This was the ragtag bunch that Dorrance carried into the 1980 season. The team's talent had improved significantly over his first season, and some of the players had also benefited from a year's experience. The young coach ordered the most basic dribbling drill performed over and over until his players vowed to shoot themselves if he ran it again. So, of course, he did. Then he demonstrated the more advanced fundamentals himself, putting forth a level of skill to which each player could aspire in the theater of her mind. Says Crowley: "Anson took a team with lots of players who had never played organized soccer, who had been coached mostly by P.E. teachers who just said, 'Shoot!' and 'Kick it out of there!,' and he organized us, and he already knew ten sessions down the road what he wanted us to achieve. He led us step by step until he took us to the top of the ladder, and then we concentrated on climbing the mountain."

While the 1980 Tar Heels did suffer three losses to an elite high school all-star team, they dominated the rest of their regular season schedule, winning all twenty games by a combined score of 96–3. During the season, Dorrance asked each of his players to write a letter to John Swofford, who had replaced Bill Cobey as UNC's athletic director, asking for extra funding to attend the season-ending Association of Intercollegiate Athletics for Women invitational tournament in Colorado. Dorrance then set up a meeting with Swofford to discuss the proposal. Swofford had always liked Dorrance since the days in the early 1970s when Swofford played football and Dorrance played soccer on opposite sides of Stadium Drive, two undersized athletes with oversized hearts, largely overshadowed by the burgeoning success of Dean Smith's basketball teams. Dorrance told Swofford that the trip would cost $9,000, double his operating budget for the entire 1980 season. Dorrance didn't think he had a prayer, but he sold the argument that going to this tournament could put UNC women's soccer on the map, even though he had no idea what the map looked like. Swofford asked one question. "Anson, do you think we can win it?"

"No," Dorrance told Swofford, "but it will be a great launching pad for our recruiting. If you send my team out there we can tell every recruit that this is the place to come, because we're making a commitment to women's soccer. I'm a good recruiter. You give me this weapon and I'm going to bring in the best kids in the country and . . ."

Swofford interrupted Dorrance mid-pitch and said what he knew he was going to say all along: "Let's go."

In early November, the Tar Heels flew to Colorado Springs on the first airplane flight for the program. "It felt like a huge step," Janet Rayfield says. "It was the first time we really felt legitimate."

Amidst the flurry of excitement for the journey, nobody had planned for the cold of Colorado in the late fall. Fortunately, the used men's jerseys Dorrance had borrowed for the trip had long sleeves. The team drove to Kmart, and all the players bought long underwear that stuck out from beneath their shorts. They wore plastic bags over their socks to combat the snow on the field, which was deep enough that it obscured the sidelines.

The Tar Heels showed their inexperience and nerves. After defeating Texas A&M in the opener 1–0, UNC lost to UCLA 3–2 in the semifinal, in a game decided by an own goal. Then in a 5–3 loss to Harvard in the consolation round, UNC endured three more own goals and finished the tournament in fourth place overall. The championship was won by Cortland State, a school that none of the Tar Heels had ever heard of before the tournament.

Dorrance was not disappointed by his team's results. The tournament had given his young program, which had never traveled beyond Washington, D.C., or played any team from outside the Southeast, a much-needed frame of reference. "Colorado benefited everyone," Dorrance said upon his return to Chapel Hill. "It showed we are competitive at the national level. We didn't know how strong we were and to see that we were that close is exciting. Our goal is within our reach."

"We're going to win the national championship this year," Dorrance announced at a UNC faculty/athletic department banquet in the spring of 1981. When the audience stopped buzzing, Dorrance spread it on even thicker, facetiously suggesting that if his team didn't live up to his prediction, the coach should be fired.

As Dorrance walked off the dais, he felt his arm grabbed by UNC wrestling coach Bill Lam, who said, "Anson, that was very foolish."

"What do you mean?"

"That was very foolish to predict that you are going to win a championship."

"Bill, I *am* going to win."

"Well, regardless of whether or not you're going to win, it was dumb, because what if you don't?"

"Bill, *we're going to win.*"

Lam thought Dorrance had unnecessarily drawn a target on his chest, but Dorrance had his reasons. He correctly assumed a comment like that would leak out beyond the walls of UNC, and he wanted to draw some attention to his fledgling program and leave other soccer coaches wondering why he would say such a damn fool thing. Dorrance also knew what nobody else in that room, nobody else around the country, could possibly know. He knew about a conversation he'd had just days earlier with Moyer Smith, the new head of UNC's Educational Foundation, the fund-raising arm of the athletic department:

"Congratulations on helping our women's team get off to such a great start," Smith had said during that talk. "We'd like to help you. How many scholarships are you currently working with?"

"Less than one," Dorrance said.

"What's the maximum number of scholarships the NCAA will allow you to have?"

"Eleven."

"You got 'em."

Dorrance's eyes grew wide for one of the few times in his life. "OK, then," he said, "we're on our way."

Suddenly Dorrance had all the recruiting ammunition he could want. He could sell the commitment of the university, which had ignored his paltry budget and flown his team to Colorado, *and* he had scholarship money to offer before most schools even had a team. "The university handed me a recruiting bazooka and I wielded it," Dorrance says. "We told our recruits that we weren't interested in assembling an ordinary team. We wanted to assemble the best team in women's collegiate soccer. I told them we're going to build something extraordinary here, something that no one's ever seen. Then I asked them, 'Do you want to be the best?'"

Dorrance began with one basic tenet. Recruit players who are good enough to beat you. Laurie Gregg was taking a one-year academic sabbatical from Lehigh to Harvard when she helped the Crimson defeat the Tar Heels in the consolation game of the 1980 AIAW tournament. A few months later, faced with returning to Lehigh, where she played on the men's junior varsity team because there was no women's varsity, she phoned Dorrance, and he talked her into transferring to UNC. Dorrance scouted other potential recruits by scheduling games against every elite high school club team he could find. After losing twice to a talented club from northern Virginia, Dorrance eventually signed Ginger Hurst, Suzy Cobb, and Kathy Kelly from the opponent's roster. After his club team was destroyed 8–1 in a summer game by the nation's top club, the Dallas Sting, Dorrance raided the Sting for Wendy Greenburg, Marianne Johnson, Meg Mills, and Amy Machin. Toward the end of that blowout against the Sting, Machin already had two goals when she scored again on a spectacular side volley from the top of the penalty box that rocketed into the goal's upper corner. Dorrance approached Machin afterward and said, "I've never seen a girl do that before."

"Well," Machin replied, "I'm not a typical girl."

Indeed, Dorrance was beginning to recruit an entirely different breed of athlete. Emily Pickering was the first girl ever to play Little League baseball in

Massapequa, New York. She defined "tomboy," so much so that her third-grade teacher once anxiously asked Emily's mother if her daughter had any female friends, because she was always playing with the boys. Pickering was introduced to soccer when the coach of the New York Cosmos, Gordon Bradley, moved in two doors down; he had two sons Emily's age who played in the street with her. "On her recruiting visit, we took Emily to a bar and she was smoking cigarettes," Susan Ellis remembers. "Well, the 1980 team was a bunch of sissies. No one drank, no one smoked or did anything bad. We went back to Anson and told him Emily smoked cigarettes, and he thought it was great because she didn't genuflect to anyone; she was her own person."

About that time Dorrance had driven to northern Virginia to recruit striker Stephanie Zeh, to whom he was considering offering a small scholarship. As he walked among a group of spectators while scouting Zeh, several parents told him that he might not want her because she was too selfish. One of them described her as "a bitch." Dorrance loved the idea of this seventeen-year-old maverick, and after hearing how much everybody detested Zeh, he offered her a larger scholarship.

For the 1981 season, Dorrance brought in a total of eleven freshmen, all of whom were among the top twenty recruits in the country, and he did it while spending only three and a half scholarships. Planning for long-term success, he knew he didn't have to offer full scholarships, because nobody else was offering them. Dorrance's theory in recruiting at the time was the one he'd been taught at the outset of Rainbow Soccer: *Gather as much milk as you can, and the cream will rise naturally.* "What Anson did was assemble some of the best female athletes in the country, and then he taught us how to play soccer," Machin says. "We had all played mostly basketball, tennis, volleyball. We weren't girly-girls. We were tough girls. We had the arrogance of youth. We had seven or eight snot-rubbers."

"I knew we were going to win because no one did the work I did that year in recruiting," Dorrance says. "I saw a lot of girls' soccer players, and I got the best. I knew that Wendy Greenburg could run, I knew that Amy Machin could trap and pass, I knew that Stephanie Zeh could score goals, I knew that Emily Pickering could run my midfield, I knew that Suzy Cobb was a fierce defender, and I knew that Marianne Johnson was the best goalkeeper that I'd ever seen."

These new girls were different, all right. "Going to the library" for them was code for going downtown to get wasted. These girls didn't drink out of bottles; they drank out of bongs. During one night out, the girls bet a teammate five dollars each that she couldn't drink an entire pitcher of beer with a straw. The only restrictions were that she couldn't leave the table and she couldn't throw up. Only a few gulps away from collecting $100, she vomited her guts out while her teammates grabbed their money, hopped over the back of the booth, and made a run for it.

On another evening out drinking the players engaged in a game called "Magnet," borrowed from UNC soccer practice, in which one girl is declared the magnet, and everyone else attacks her and piles on until she screams for mercy. Unfortunately, on this night the magnet happened to be sitting on the toilet at the time, and when a dozen girls piled on her, the toilet tore away from the wall and sent water spraying everywhere.

One of the new girls grew marijuana plants in her closet, and some smoked pot before practice. The competition on the field sometimes extended to who could bring the most guys home, at least until the word got out that a UNC player had knocked out her boyfriend with one punch and been kicked out of her dorm. During one early pit stop on a road trip, Dorrance climbed out of his van and announced, "There'll be no drinking, smoking, or swearing on this trip." A few of the new girls responded in unison, *"Fuck that!"*

At one point, when the NCAA mandated that athletes stop cursing during games or risk red-card disqualification, Dorrance reluctantly arranged for a graduate assistant coach, Caroline McLaughlin, to check a player's name every time she cursed. Each transgression would be punished with a mile run after practice. Pickering reacted by spewing a stream of curses in McLaughlin's face and then brazenly asking, "How many miles is that?" After a few days, Dorrance told McLaughlin not to bother.

On the field, some were known to belch or blow "snot rockets." Some with tiny bladders subtly relieved themselves during the game rather than sub themselves out. "I was very naive and sheltered, and this wasn't like any of my past experiences with women," Dorrance says. "These girls were soccer renegades, and in some respects they horrified me, but they knew down deep that I admired their spunk and combativeness. I identified with the reckless quality they brought to soccer, and I didn't really want to know about anything else. If they had gone out the night before and drank half of Chapel Hill dry, and came in the next morning hung over, they didn't whine about running fitness, they just frigging did it, sweating alcohol out of their pores. These were *hard chicks* who partied hard, trained hard, played hard, and I loved coaching them."

Says Pickering: "I think Anson was only horrified because we were women. Men did the same things we did, but that was OK in the good ol' boy network. We did what *he* did in college, but he didn't expect that from women. We acted like college students."

With the influx of these cocky and talented new recruits, the UNC roster turned upside down. A team that had enjoyed blissful chemistry during its first two seasons was thrown into turmoil. "The trauma was that I benched all these sweet, hardworking, wonderful kids who founded the program in favor of these talented, abrasive street toughs," Dorrance says. "The new kids were like, 'Hey, thanks for coming, but you're in my spot so you're outta here. Bring the water at halftime, I might be a little thirsty.'"

During a team meeting before the 1981 season, the freshmen told the veterans that it was their team now. They called the older players *Dinosaurs*. "We were cocky and immature, and we didn't care what came before us," Machin says. "We thought we were the chosen ones brought there to win national championships."

Ellis remembers going to dinner with Pickering during her recruiting visit when Pickering said, "You tell Nancy Clary that she's not going to be playing center midfielder next year. I'm taking her position."

Two weeks before the 1981 season opener, Ellis clipped out a newspaper article in which Dorrance predicted there would be only two starters left over from the 1980 team. She knew he was talking about Rayfield and Clary, so she taped the article to her mirror and looked at it every day for motivation. By the time the season began, the UNC starting lineup consisted of eight new starters, seven freshmen and the transfer Laurie Gregg. The only three returning starters were Rayfield up front, Ellis in the back, and Clary at center midfielder. A disgruntled Pickering started at outside midfielder.

Ellis laughs at the memory of a game early that season, when Pickering grew frustrated with her and screamed to her teammates, "Would you quit passing the fucking ball to Susan, because every time you pass it to her, she knocks it out of bounds!"

"If you messed up on the field, Emily would drop a few F-bombs on you," Ellis says. "It was get it done or get your ass off the field. That was a hard transition because most of the freshmen were better than the rest of us, and they weren't humble about it. We were like this tight family, and they were assholes. Our chemistry off the field was awful. There were two distinct camps."

On road trips the two factions on the team rode in different vans, slept in different rooms, ate at different restaurants. Dorrance took a very hands-off approach to the schism, too busy juggling two teams to officiate the unrest, so as the team captain, Rayfield reluctantly assumed the role of mediator. The bookish computer science major became the team's gracious public face, which concealed the divisiveness from the outside world. While Rayfield shared Dorrance's troubled view of the young heathens, she followed her coach's instincts not to be too judgmental and risk losing them. The new kids rewarded Rayfield for her diplomacy by sarcastically dubbing her "Mom."

It was tough on Rayfield, who, despite her exceptional talent, had come to UNC with no scholarship offer, no sense of entitlement, just because it was the only school that offered her the opportunity to play varsity soccer. "That was my most painful and difficult year personally," Rayfield says. "There were a lot of growing pains. I was trying to meld our former club team players with a bunch of freshmen that had no appreciation for the fact that our varsity hadn't always been there. They were the first class that had played soccer in high school, and they saw college soccer as a right, while we still saw it as a privilege. We thought they were too wild, and they thought of us as goody-two-shoes."

Truth be told, some of the new freshmen didn't even get along that well with each other. Machin resented how Pickering would go out drinking and carousing on nights before games. Pickering gave Machin insufferable crap for being a virgin. "But when it came down to us against another team, nobody messed with us," Machin says. "Plenty of times during games Emily and I screamed at each other, *Fuck you! No, fuck you!* But when somebody whacked me, Emily whacked them. We had each other's backs."

The UNC players grew to respect each other, if only because they could help each other win. "Even though we didn't like one another personally we joined arms and made it happen," Machin says. "Anson picked some pretty extraordinary people. It was part luck, part wisdom, and part self-awareness. He identified certain players who refused to lose, and he egged us on. We were all winners. We didn't know any better."

As the 1981 season progressed, many of the Tar Heels had no idea that the first-ever sanctioned national championship tournament awaited them at the end. A year earlier, Dorrance had lobbied the AIAW to create such an event and then offered to host the twelve-team showdown at Fetzer Field and Kenan Stadium, where the football team played. "I can remember we had a reception before that 1981 tournament began," Rayfield says. "I remember seeing Anson speaking on the stage and thinking that something that he promised several years earlier was coming to fruition."

Entering the AIAW tournament, the Tar Heels had a spotless 20–0 record that included one dominant three-game stretch at a tournament in October, when UNC defeated Alabama 9–0, Georgia Tech 12–0, and Duke 5–0 while outshooting those three teams by a combined 161–0. The Tar Heels allowed only four goals to collegiate competition that season, while winning seven games by eleven goals or more, led by thirty-six goals from Zeh and thirty from Rayfield. The prolific UNC offense averaged more than eight goals per game and scored at least four in every contest except for a benchmark mid-season 2–0 victory over No. 1-ranked Connecticut in Storrs. Even after that victory, in the minds of the New England teams with longer legacies in the sport, the Tar Heels were still upstarts with no credibility.

In the AIAW tournament, playing on three consecutive days, UNC defeated Massachusetts 6–0 in the opener, and then, in a rematch of the earlier game, the Tar Heels defeated UConn 5–0 in the semifinal to set up a final with Central Florida, a team that had lost only two games all season, both to UNC. In a championship match played before 3,531 fans at Kenan, the Tar Heels dominated the game, outshooting UCF 30–8, but the only goal came with 19:36 left in the first half when UNC's Diane Beatty scored off a corner kick by Kathy Kelly. As Kelly's serve flew across the penalty box, Beatty's mind clicked on one of Dorrance's favorite lessons. *Always head the ball back toward the corner of the goal it is served from, so if you miss you still have the entire face of the goal to potentially score.* "Sure enough, I mishit that ball," Beatty says. "The goalie was caught leaning the wrong way, and my mishit found an open net just as Anson said it would. It was a great goal in my mind, not because of me, but because of Anson's repeated coaching on the technique. The only goal in the first national championship was a coach's goal."

Dorrance had won a championship largely of his own creation. The AIAW title was only UNC's third national championship in school history, and the first produced by a women's team. Ellis gave the first autographs of her life that day at the stadium where she had once roamed the stands selling hot dogs and sodas at football games, never dreaming of ever playing college soccer or winning a national title. The UNC players tried to take a victory lap around the stadium, but they only made it halfway because the trophy was too heavy.

After winning the title game to complete a 23-0 season, Dorrance proclaimed that UNC now stood for "Undefeated National Champions." The Tar Heels had fulfilled their coach's preseason prophecy. In the bleachers that day, Frances Hogan walked up to Bill Cobey with a grin, half proud and half sheepish, and said, "Bill, you were right and I was wrong."

Throughout the UNC program's infancy, Dorrance's eyeglasses were held together with a safety pin. They were still the same nerdy black horn-rimmed spectacles that he'd worn throughout his college days. Pickering took to calling him Clark Kent. Unfortunately, his glasses were the only thing that Dorrance wore in those days that was not white. Every day was the same. White T-shirt, white cotton shorts, white soccer socks pulled up high on his calves, and white sneakers, an outfit chosen by a man who didn't want to have to worry about matching his clothes. Betsy Johnson called him "The Man From Glad." Because Dorrance's demeanor was as regimented as his fashion, Ellis called him "Prissybritches." The hair remained the same. It was thick and wavy, styled in a sort of disheveled pompadour, and he refused to get it cut. The girls lamented that they never expected to have a coach with bigger hair than their own.

Alas, the players weren't much more stylish. For the first three seasons they wore their own clothes to practice. Most wore UNC T-shirts they'd bought for themselves, but others wore tank tops. UNC's uniforms also were not uniform at all. When the Tar Heels' 1981 championship team photograph appeared in the *Chapel Hill Newspaper* showing players wearing a wide variety of sweatsuits, and a letter to the editor promptly followed saying the team's appearance was embarrassing, a set of twenty-five baggy but matching UNC sweatsuits mysteriously turned up before the next season.

For practice each day in 1982 and 1983 the players wore university-issued gray gym shorts and T-shirts in wildly random sizes. The girls knew they might be wearing the same shorts that a wrestler had worn the day before. Each day they would turn them in and try again until eventually they got shorts that fit. Finally, in 1984, players were given two sized pairs of practice shirts and shorts to rotate. Everybody got new uniforms, but the seniors chose first. The underclassmen received the leftover irregulars that didn't fit anyone. Everybody was on her own for shoes. At the beginning of each season they were each issued a soccer ball that they had to bring to practice every day.

Fetzer Field was also used for lacrosse, track & field, football practice, and parking on football Saturdays, which explains how in the midst of a slide tackle during one of his college soccer practices, Dorrance got a chicken drumstick lodged in his knee. The field was so dry and dusty that the players alternately called it "Fetzer Desert" or "the lunar surface." Because of the neighboring broad-jump and pole-vault pits, the field was a narrow 62 yards wide, and it had such a big crown built into it for drainage that coaches had to sit on the top of the bench to see players along the opposite sideline. Because the stadium had no lights, practices toward the end of each season concluded when it got too dark to see the ball.

Women's soccer games were only sporadically covered by the school newspaper. The Tar Heels played home games in front of an average crowd of about twenty people, a count that included players' parents, a few really, really close friends, and the random joggers circling on the track that bordered the field. With so few varsity soccer programs in the area, scheduling was a headache, and matches were often arranged only days in advance. The Tar Heels played NAIA teams like Guilford and Erskine. They played Nassau Community College. They played club teams called the Braddock Road Cobras and the Fairfax Burgundy Belles. "At the beginning of the women's program it felt like we were traveling shoe salesmen," says Kip Ward, a part-time UNC assistant. "We went to every little hamlet in the Carolinas that could muster up a team."

Scheduling became even more problematic as North Carolina's reputation grew. In 1982 Virginia and UNC–Wilmington both dropped the Tar Heels from their schedules to avoid the humiliation, and a William & Mary invitational tournament was canceled after UNC was invited. The Tar Heels were so feared after the undefeated 1981 season that Dorrance could find only five schools that would agree to play UNC in a dual match. The team's other thirteen regular-season games were all part of exhausting tournaments, including one that required UNC to play five games in just three days.

In that era, UNC women's soccer couldn't afford to travel west of the Mississippi River, so the team shuttled up and down the East Coast from Massachusetts to Florida on rides as long as sixteen hours each way. They rode either in vans four to a row, with their luggage stuck beneath their feet, or on a rickety old school bus known as the Blue Goose, which had been in operation since the early days of Marvin Allen. The women's team almost always traveled with the men's team, so on the Blue Goose players often had to sleep in the overhead luggage racks. Each player had a $3 limit for meal money on the road, and the team ate at McDonald's so often it was renamed McDorrance's.

Whenever possible on road trips the team stayed in the homes of players' parents, sleeping on couches or the floor. When they did stay at motels, they slept four to a room. They would drive five hours to James Madison, play the game, and then drive five hours home that same day, just to save money on lodging. On the way to one game in Washington, D.C., the team changed into its uniforms at a gas station, and the cashier was so amused that he closed up shop and attended the match.

Dorrance's total women's soccer operating budget began at $4,665 in 1979 and grew only slightly with each passing season, a princely sum that had to cover everything except for the coach's salary and office supplies. In each season-ending

annual report, Dorrance implored the athletic department to come up with funding for more coaching help. He concluded his 1984 report with one simple
multiple-choice request: *Full-time assistant or divorce lawyer!*

Right there on the field at Kenan Stadium after the 1981 championship game,
the Tar Heel freshmen made a pact among themselves to finish every season the
same way. They parted that day by gathering in a huddle and chanting, "Go for
four!" They knew then that they had the talent and depth to win four championships in a row, and it turned out that a long-term goal would prove inspirational
as the players muddled through the many lopsided and monotonous games they
would endure throughout the next three years.

Entering the 1982 season, the Tar Heels' roster featured a whole new dynamic
of growing pains, which actually helped improve the team's chemistry. "That year
the freshmen from the previous year had matured a bit, and the former club players had all graduated," Rayfield says. "Now we were all in it for the same reason,
to win. Suddenly a lot of those freshman phenoms were fighting for their jobs
against new freshman recruits."

After winning their first ten games that season, the Tar Heels traveled to a
tournament in Orlando, Florida. Over that same weekend, the UNC men were
playing two games in Tampa, and Dorrance chose to coach them, leaving the
women's team to Palladino. The UNC women lost 2–1 to Missouri–St. Louis in
their tournament opener, breaking the team's thirty-three-game winning streak.
"I think our team felt a little bit slighted," Ellis says. "We were undefeated, and
the men weren't doing so well, but Anson chose to go with them. We didn't play
well, and there were lots of young players on our team who had never lost a college game and had no idea how to deal with defeat."

Many of the players drank in the hotel bar after the loss to console themselves, and then went out the next day hung over and lost to Cortland State 2–1.
After the team's second consecutive loss, Zeh couldn't contain her anger. She
told her teammates, "I've had enough of this shit. I'm going to walk back to Chapel
Hill." Emboldened and embittered by a few drinks, Zeh left the hotel and started
to walk north along the interstate. Bill Prentice chased her down and insisted
that she come back with him. When Zeh refused, Prentice flung her over his
shoulder and began to carry her, but she fought him off, landing a few solid punches
that made him leave her behind on the highway. The next morning Zeh showed
up for the bus ride home with the rest of the team.

After the Orlando debacle, Dorrance wondered if his team could still qualify
for the national championship tournament. The Tar Heels responded by winning their final six regular season games by a combined score of 43–0 to put
Dorrance at ease.

Playing in the first-ever National Collegiate Athletic Association Tournament,
the Tar Heels returned to Orlando and changed accommodations, refusing to
stay in the place they called the "Loser Hotel." In the semifinals they had a chance
to avenge the loss suffered there earlier in the season to Missouri–St. Louis, and,

sure enough, they reversed the score this time and won 2–1. The next day in a rematch of the 1981 AIAW title game, UNC defeated Central Florida 2–0 to win its first NCAA championship, a bittersweet victory because Zeh was taken to the hospital late in the first half after suffering what would be a career-ending knee injury. Zeh had drawn a penalty kick on the final play of her career, and it resulted in the game-winning goal.

In 1983, UNC lost its opener 3–1 at Connecticut. Dorrance reacted with a new strategy, holding a series of individual player conferences on the bus ride to Boston that night to help players define their roles on the team. The next day the Tar Heels defeated Boston College 5–2, beginning a string of nineteen wins in a row that concluded with a 4–0 shutout of George Mason in the national title game.

During the summer before the 1984 season, confident UNC parents began making hotel reservations for the Final Four in Chapel Hill. The Tar Heels were so deep that eighteen different players scored at least one goal, and most of UNC's reserves would have been stars at other programs. Even Machin, a two-time All-American who had led the country in scoring in 1982, came off the bench as a reserve in six games that year. In an attempt to spare UNC's future opponents some embarrassment, Dorrance privately instituted what would become known as the "9–0 Rule," forbidding his players from scoring double-figure goals in a game. Therefore it was no coincidence that the Tar Heels won three of their first seven games in 1984 by a score of 9–0.

During one practice on the eve of the 1984 national semifinal, several UNC players were warming up, and Machin was clearly preoccupied. Unbeknownst to her teammates, she was thinking about her mother, who was undergoing cancer surgery that day. At one point Pickering turned to Machin and barked, "Get your fucking head in the game."

Machin responded, predictably, "Fuck you!"

A couple of teammates had to tackle them to keep Machin and Pickering from beating the crap out of each other. The next day, with five minutes remaining before halftime and UNC trailing California 1–0, Machin was undercut by the Cal goalie and carried off the field on a backboard. When it was clear to her that she could still wiggle her toes, Machin sat up and figured she'd better get back in the game. Streaking toward the goal on a near-post run, a run Dorrance had nagged her to make all season, Machin scored the game-winner in overtime.

The NCAA final against Connecticut was somewhat overshadowed by a controversy that had begun a couple of weeks earlier, when some of the Tar Heels watched the movie *Apocalypse Now*. The UNC players identified with a famous line from the film: "I love the smell of napalm in the morning. It smells like victory." After UNC's 2–0 defeat of Connecticut completed a 24-0-1 season, Tar Heel fans paraded through the stands with a banner bearing the phrase *UNC Women Love the Smell of NAPALM in the afternoon: NCAA Champs,* while other fans chanted "Napalm! Napalm! Napalm!" In the ensuing days, Dorrance received criticism from the local press as well as a wrist-slap in *Sports Illustrated* for his team's insensitivity, in what would become a trend from reporters who were already searching for stories beyond UNC winning national titles—that was no longer considered news.

The Tar Heel seniors preferred to concentrate on the fact that with the 1984 national championship, UNC women's soccer had produced more titles than all of the other UNC sports combined, and more NCAA championships than any other ACC program, male or female.

In the 1984 championship team photo, Pickering, Machin, Beatty, Cobb, and Kelly are all holding up four fingers representing the four straight titles they'd vowed to win three Novembers earlier in Kenan Stadium. Palladino and Prentice are also in the photo, celebrating along with Susan Ellis, who after being redshirted for a season with a knee injury, had come back to win her third title in 1984. The least skilled player among UNC's starters, Dorrance played Ellis because nobody got past her unscathed; she was an indispensable grinder on a team otherwise filled with genius. Ellis reminded Dorrance of himself. She had that extraordinary intensity that he had yet to label with a specific name, but one that would be shared by all the finest Tar Heel players yet to come.

"When I stepped on the field I never, *ever*, expected to lose," Ellis says. "I don't know if that's because I was smart and I knew the quality of players on our team, or whether it was Anson making us feel like we were better than we were. He made me feel like I was awesome, even though I wasn't, and he created an aura around the whole team that we were supposed to win every national championship."

For his part, Dorrance was just beginning to recognize the big-picture reality of UNC's situation, even if his players didn't have to because their careers were finite. By 1984, he had already evolved from exultant to relieved whenever a national championship was secured. "There is always pressure to be the best in every game," Dorrance said after the 1984 title game. "We wanted to win four in a row. But it's gotten a lot harder each year. The teams are much better. There is more tension to stay at the top."

Motivated by a family tragedy on the eve of that season, Peggy sat down with her son shortly after the 1984 championship game and asked him, "Anson, how long are we going to keep winning?"

"Mom, I don't know."

"Will you keep winning until I depart the world?"

Peggy's son made no promises.

7 | *Man and Women*

A man walking along a California beach asked the Lord to grant him one wish. The Lord said, "Because you have tried to be faithful to me, I will grant you that wish."

The man said, "Build me a highway to Hawaii so I can drive over anytime I want."

The Lord said, "Think of the enormous challenges for that kind of project. The supports required to reach the bottom of the Pacific! The concrete and steel it would take! Take a little more time and think of another wish."

The man thought about it for a long time and finally he said, "Lord, I wish that I could understand women. I want to know how they feel inside, what they are thinking when they give me the silent treatment, why they cry, what they mean when they say 'Nothing,' and how I can make a woman truly happy."

The Lord replied, "You want two lanes or four?"

—from an e-mail sent to Dorrance by the father of a UNC player

On Sunday night, October 28, 1979, the Dorrances found a babysitter for their newborn daughter Michelle and went to the movies to help take Anson's mind off soccer for a while. The following afternoon at Fetzer Field, Dorrance's men would play perennial conference powerhouse Maryland, and he thought his Tar Heels had a fighting chance. Dorrance enjoys movies that involve anything military, so he dragged M'Liss to see *The Great Santini,* a film about a Marine pilot, Lieutenant Colonel Bull Meechum, a frustrated warrior in peacetime. Dorrance has always watched movies looking for analogies to his own life, and he couldn't help but notice shades of himself and his family in the *The Great Santini*. The domineering father who moves his brood from place to place, from culture to culture, smacked of Big Pete. Anson liked to think of himself as a warrior without a war. Midway through the film, Meechum turns to his wife in bed and explains the legacy he wants to leave his children. *I want my sons to have the gift of fury. I want them to gobble up the world. Eat life or it'll eat them.*

Until that moment, Anson Dorrance could never define exactly what burned inside him and fueled him through his athletic career—his whole life, really. He could never pin a name on what had compelled him to pick up that broom in Louisburg, or to take on those three toughs in San Antonio, or to bounce that Maryland goalkeeper's head off the goalpost. Sitting in the movie theater that night, he was thunderstruck by the phrase that for him would epitomize that quality from that moment on: *The Gift of Fury.*

The next afternoon, UNC took Maryland into overtime scoreless. Dorrance walked over to his exhausted men who were in need of some inspiration for the extra session. *Listen, I don't care what you do in this overtime technically and tactically. I want you to get the ball and whack it toward the Maryland goalmouth and go charging in there like a bunch of Neanderthals. Take the ball, the Maryland defense, and the goalkeeper, and stuff them all into the back of the net. I want you to reach down and find that gift of fury that all of you guys naturally possess, and I want you to unleash it upon them.*

The players rose as one, reinvigorated. They loved these instructions because their coach was telling them that they didn't have to think, just attack with all the passion they could muster. Eleven minutes into the overtime, the ball was launched into the Maryland box, and half of the Tar Heels furiously stormed the goal. Sure enough, the ball got stuffed into the back of the net. "My players are carrying me off on their shoulders after the game and I'm thinking to myself, 'Knute Rockne, move over, a new motivational genius has arrived,'" Dorrance says. "I couldn't wait to unleash *The Great Santini* on my women."

Six days later, Dorrance's women were getting outclassed after one half by the McLean (Virginia) Grasshoppers, the Under-19 national club champions. The Tar Heels trailed 2–0 at the intermission, but Dorrance wasn't the least bit concerned because he had his magic bullet. "I started talking to the girls about the Gift of Fury, gobbling up the world, eating life before life eats them." Dorrance says. "They're looking back at me with all these vacuous stares and I'm thinking to myself, 'OK, they've obviously internalized this information, and as soon as the second half begins we'll start ripping the legs off these Grasshoppers.'"

UNC lost 4–0.

When Dorrance accepted the job of coaching the UNC women, he still viewed females as strange creatures. As a guy who'd attended an all-male high school and a college that might as well have been, Dorrance believed he understood how men think, but these girls were still a mystery. So Dorrance did what he always does when he needs to bone up on a subject. He read. He read all the books he could find on feminism. He read *Ms.* magazine and *Cosmopolitan* and *Glamour.* He read newspaper articles about the ongoing battle over passage of the Equal Rights Amendment, which stated that by law men and women must be treated equally. All the feminist literature of the 1970s was telling him that there were no inherent differences between men and women and that only environmental influences forked the two genders in different directions. "So I was going to try to correct decades of sociological influence," Dorrance says. "I would treat my men and women exactly the same."

Because Dorrance's athletic role model as a youth was his mother, and because he had grown up largely without access to television and therefore had never become attached to the usual male sports idols worshiped by other boys, he had never been tempted to buy into any social prejudice that women couldn't compete like men. He coached essentially the same training sessions for his men and women, with only a slightly lower expectation of what the women could handle physically, though he expected the same skill level from both. He addressed the players on each team by their last names. He systematically ran them through the same drills. He spoke to his players only on the field and only in an instructional sense, except when he occasionally grew frustrated and would ask the offending player, *"What kinda crap was that?"* When one of the girls would burst into tears, he was stunned. "Anson treated the women exactly like the guys," Bill Palladino says. "He was just as harsh with them when it came to delicate issues of playing time or starting. Anson at times could be really abrasive and matter-of-fact, and that caused some stress on the women's team."

Dorrance dislikes jewelry and had never worn a wedding band, but one day in his first season as the women's coach, he began wearing one to create a distance from his players that he felt he needed. Even after winning a national championship game, when everybody else was bear-hugging each other, Dorrance always extended his hand first to congratulate his female players, leaving it up to them to initiate a hug. "Anson wasn't really sure how to deal with his women's team," Janet Rayfield says. "His personality was very strict and military. He was very standoffish, very conscious of not sending the wrong signals as a young male coach of a women's team."

"At that time I don't think Anson was comfortable with coaching women at all," Diane Beatty says. "In fact, I think women just made him uncomfortable, period."

"He was so robotic," Betsy Johnson says, "that I don't know that we thought of Anson as a person."

Early in his career coaching the women, Dorrance would regularly make speeches to the UNC booster club or to whomever else would listen to him, preaching that men and women were not different. They needed to be trained exactly the same. People showed up and listened to him because he was winning championships, but something still nagged at him. His teams were successful, sure, but that was mostly by overwhelming opponents on raw talent alone. He sensed that there was a flaw in his approach that he would have to address at some point if he was going to keep on winning. But what?

April Dawn Heinrichs was a soccer prodigy who started playing the game at age six, using old copies of *Reader's Digest* as shin guards and sleeping in her cleats. She eventually led her teams to five Colorado club championships and two state high school titles at Heritage High in Littleton, where she was twice named a high school All-American. However, despite writing to every college she could think of as a senior in the spring of 1982, including UNC, Heinrichs was not offered a dime to play collegiate soccer anywhere—no coach would spend the time and money to scout her in what was considered a soccer backwater. So Heinrichs committed to attend Mesa College in Grand Junction on a basketball scholarship. That October she was spotted during a club soccer tournament at Brown University by another club coach who tipped off Dorrance.

Dorrance flew out to see Heinrichs in February of 1983, but in the middle of winter in Colorado there weren't many options for an audition, so he watched her practice with her former high school teammates on a slippery gymnasium floor. Dorrance saw something special that afternoon. He saw a competitor. He saw the Gift of Fury. He wanted April Heinrichs to be a Tar Heel in the worst way.

Dorrance was still in the very early stages of recruiting women when he was chasing Heinrichs. He felt much more comfortable recruiting men. "With guys it was an incredibly simple process," Dorrance says. "You call the young man and say, 'Hello, this is Anson Dorrance, I'm from the University of North Carolina. I saw you play last weekend. I think you can step in and start for us. We're going to give you a scholarship.' He grunts a couple of times and I say, 'Great, I'll see you in August.'"

So when Dorrance phoned Heinrichs, he told her she was going to start at right midfielder and she would get some scholarship money. Assuming she was sold, he began to hang up the phone when she suddenly said, "Wait, how does your team get along?" "I was thinking, 'Who cares?'" Dorrance recalls. "When I played at UNC I never cared that our right back was a hillbilly who didn't shower for weeks and had poor dental hygiene because I didn't have to associate with him off the field. I didn't care that our center forward was an asshole as long as the balls I served him ended up in the back of the net. Caring how a team got along didn't make sense to me. I told April something like, 'They get along great.' To be honest, I really didn't know and I didn't care. As long as I could get her to come to UNC."

Every time he phoned Heinrichs that spring, she would listen to his pitch about scholarship money and playing time, and then she kept asking him that same question. *How does your team get along?* It would become the single most important question ever asked of Dorrance in the history of the UNC women's soccer program, because it provided a spark. For Dorrance, the question began to hammer home a suspicion that he had begun contemplating about how men and women weren't really the same after all. The question would prove to be the beginning of his developing theories on specific areas where he felt men and women actually needed to be trained and coached differently.

Dorrance on the use of videotape:

Men: "Men need videotape. I have never met a male athlete who has ever felt that he made a mistake in any athletic competition in his life. Videotape is proof. If we had a miserable game defensively, I'd tell them, 'Defensively we were a nightmare.' Every guy in the room is nodding because he agrees with me, but what he thinks is that it's all the guys around him that were the problem. *Yeah, I was the only one working out there. The rest of you were useless.* Then we'd watch tape and I'd say, 'Look, you're number five and they're going through you like a knife through butter.' And number five would be incredulous. He can't believe that that was him. A guy needs to see his faults on videotape, and even then he'll probably come up with an excuse."

Women: "When you make a general criticism of a women's team, every woman in the room thinks you're talking about her, so you don't need videotape. I am constantly amazed at how little confidence even my most talented female players have, so if you tell them they did something wrong, they'll believe you. Video makes it worse, because they see how bad they actually were. A woman takes full responsibility for her problems emotionally, and you have to be careful not to destroy her psychologically. I stopped using videotape for the women except to show the positive aspects of their play to try to build their confidence."

On halftime talks:

Men: "The greatest halftime talk I've ever given to a men's team was when we were playing against Wake Forest back in the early years when we didn't think they should be able to compete with us. All of sudden I'm in there at halftime, and it's 0–0, and I'm ticked off. We had done nothing right in the first half, no energy, no technical understanding, no tactical confidence, no leadership. It was an absolute disaster. What's critical when you're upset with a team is that they can sense it. So I come in, and I'm pacing back and forth like this caged tiger. But the trouble with men is that they're not terribly sensitive, so it takes awhile for them to gather that I'm upset. Eventually it quiets down, and when I can hear a pin drop, that's when I turn to face them. I didn't know what to say, but out of the corner of my eye I saw a wastepaper basket, so I sprinted over there, and with my right instep I drove that sucker through a window and I stormed out. Let me tell you something about human evolution. That spoke volumes to the men in the room. In the second half everything changed. All of a sudden, we had great energy, tactics, shape, and the game totally turned around and we destroyed them."

Women: "If you kick a trash can in front of the women, they think you're a frigging idiot. And, if you think about it, you are. This is how a halftime talk has to work for women. If they've played poorly you still come storming in like a caged tiger, but because these are women they can sense immediately that you're upset. The critical thing is tone. You turn to face them and you calmly say, 'Well, what do you think?' Now you can hear a chorus of self-flagellation as every woman in the room is taking full responsibility for the disaster that is taking place. Even the bench players are saying that they haven't been cheering hard enough. I haven't criticized anybody, and I don't need to because they're their own worst critics. Then you start to impart some wisdom and you say, 'You know the girl who scored five goals in the first half? Hey, why don't we mark her?' Now they think you're a coaching genius. You haven't criticized them at all, you've just reconstructed them a bit, and now when the halftime talk ends they are willing to die for you because all you've done is support them."

On lineup changes:

Men: "When you bench a guy from the starting lineup of a men's team, the other guys say, 'Sounds good. Bobby'll be OK.'"

Women: "Women are easier to coach than men because they listen to criticism, but they're difficult to manage because most are sensitive to slights, and their bond is stronger than on a men's team. Therefore, when you bench a female player, her teammates feel empathy. They experience a debilitating catharsis towards that player and it affects them, whether the benched girl gives a damn or not."

On praise:

Men: "Men love public praise. When a young man dominated for us in a game, in the locker room afterward I'd say, 'Mark, today you carried our team on your back.' Every guy in the room says, 'Yeah, Mark!' It's great because Mark's heart is soaring like a hawk, and the whole team rallies behind him."

Women: "After a woman plays a remarkable game I'll say, 'Mary, today you were superb.' And there is total silence. Every woman in the room now hates Mary with a passion. Not only do they hate Mary with a passion, but they hate me with a passion for not praising them. And Mary hates me for humiliating her in front of her teammates. If you want to praise a female player, the most powerful form of praise is personal, one-on-one. As she's walking off the field, you're on her shoulder, and in a voice only she can hear, you say, 'You were awesome today!' Or after the game you write her a note about what you think of her. She just wants you to feel that she's something special, and you have to figure out a way to communicate that personally. No one else has to know it."

Dorrance justified his revised conclusions about the inherent differences between men and women through his reading about female developmental psychology in the early 1980s. He'd stumbled upon a new strain of feminism. In reaction to previous feminist assertions that the only differences between men and women were culturally determined, psychologists began exploring the possibility that the differences between the genders might not be cultural after all. Dorrance read *Toward A New Psychology of Women* by Jean Baker Miller and Carol Gilligan's *In a Different Voice,* and he saw how those authors concluded that by claiming differences, women could claim their true power. Those books asserted that society has traditionally devalued women's emphasis on feelings and relationships. From his reading, Dorrance also concluded that men and women speak different languages.

"Men speak English and women speak Hidden Agenda, and because it took me a while to realize this, I made so many mistakes with my women's team," Dorrance says. "I learned that in talking to a woman there is a whole different conversation going on that is above and beyond her intellectual interpretation of what is being said. Women are looking at body language and tone and deciphering exactly what you are thinking regardless of what you are actually saying. When a man is criticized on the soccer field he understands that a coach is taking his game apart, not his life apart. A woman does not separate the two."

This was never more obvious to Dorrance than one game day in 1983. The Tar Heels were playing a men's and women's doubleheader, and Dorrance preferred to schedule the men's game first because he considered them harder to coach. On this day he paced the sideline throughout the men's game, carping at his players. Then, as soon as the women's game began, his grumbling resumed. Finally, UNC's Betsy Johnson completely stopped playing as the game continued to swirl around her, turned to Dorrance with her hands on her hips, and yelled, "Anson, this is your women's team. *Sit down!*"

"To coach men, you've got to dominate them, drive them with the intensity of your personality and walking up and down the sidelines burying them always seems to get them going," Dorrance says. "I always wanted to rail at my women the same way, but while it made me feel good, I learned they weren't going to hear a thing. I could vent my spleen and have a heart attack, but it's not going to make them better players. You don't drive women, you lead them, and you don't lead them effectively with intimidation. You relate to them personally. You lead them by caring about them. Women have to understand that your relationship with them is never in jeopardy."

Dorrance altered his approach to training women gradually. Initially, whenever he began to inch toward some humanity with his women it was met with skepticism. During one practice early in her career, Rayfield was involved in a shooting drill and couldn't find the net. Dorrance walked up behind her, put his hand on her shoulder, and said, "Don't worry about it." Rayfield turned to him and snapped, "Don't patronize me."

"I didn't want him to be nice to me just because I was having a bad day," Rayfield recalls. "Compassion wasn't part of Anson's coaching personality yet. He was always learning and developing, figuring out how to manipulate the psychological makeup of the team. In those days he learned a lot about himself from trying to get the best out of us. He tried different personalities every year, trying to get a sense of who he really was as a coach. Eventually Anson became more relaxed. He became a part of us, instead of just our coach."

"It was like trial and error," Palladino says. "Sometimes it would be either a stroke of luck or a sheer accident that Anson would try a different tactic with the women and it just happened to work."

Dorrance started calling his female players by their first names while he was still addressing his men by their last names. He encouraged the women to address him as "Anson" instead of "Coach," and he scrapped his coach's whistle to instruct them only with his voice. He invited them all over to his house after practice sometimes for pizza or banana splits. His personality began to emerge through sarcasm. During fitness testing, when he measured Rayfield's vertical jump, Dorrance pulled out a credit card to see if he could slide it under her feet. When one of his players limped off the field and Bill Prentice diagnosed the problem as tendonitis, Dorrance responded, "The only place she has tendonitis is between her ears." He often punctuated disagreements with his female players by asking them the same philosophical question: "If a man speaks in the forest and there is no woman there to hear him, is he still wrong?" The players began to feel comfortable teasing Dorrance as well, initiating "Anson Day" at practice, when every player wore white from head to toe. Dorrance even started giving roses to his seniors before their final college games.

Occasionally, Dorrance learned his lesson the hard way about bonding with his players. In June of 1983 the Tar Heels took a trip to Denmark, partially funded by the players themselves. The team was lodging in a hostel, and one night Dorrance overheard a rowdy pillow fight developing in the room where his players were staying. Trying to quell the scuffle, Dorrance was instead ambushed by Betsy Johnson, Suzy Cobb, and several other players who began wrestling with him, until eventually Johnson pinned Dorrance's arms behind his back.

Betsy: What are you doing?

Suzy: I'm kicking him in the balls!

True to her word, Cobb kneed Dorrance square in the groin. Dorrance doubled over in pain and then crawled off and locked himself in the bathroom to recover in private. The next morning, Dorrance shuffled gingerly into the breakfast room and the players started giggling. He held his hands apart the width of a basketball and announced, "Ladies, if you could see the size of my right testicle . . ."

Unfortunately for Dorrance, the team's itinerary for that day called for a walking tour of Copenhagen, and he was in agony. The following morning he decided to go to the hospital. The doctor asked him how long he'd been suffering from this affliction. Having heard that socialized medicine would cover his treatment free of charge for up to twenty-four hours after the injury, Dorrance told him the incident had occurred twelve hours earlier. The doctor shook his head ominously and gave Dorrance some bad news. They'd have to amputate. Thinking fast, Dorrance asked if the length of time since the injury would affect the diagnosis. When the doctor nodded, Dorrance confessed that he'd actually been incapacitated for the last thirty-six hours, and he was treated with drugs instead.

Yet another sign that Dorrance was becoming less of a male had nearly left him less of a man.

He delivers it to insurance salesmen in hotel ballrooms; he delivers it to young coaches at soccer conventions; and he delivers it to high school kids in cafeterias with the cuss words edited out. Dorrance's twenty-minute stump speech about the differences between training men and women is his staple on the rubber-chicken circuit. He always opens the speech with the disclaimer that his experiment has been executed by only one scientist with virtually no background in the subject matter, but what he fails to mention is that his are far from ordinary lab rats. Then he delivers his conclusions as if the data were definitive and irrefutable. You would never know that when he was young and naive twenty years ago, Dorrance was delivering the polar opposite speech.

In the mid-1980s, when Dorrance first started preaching the differences between men and women, he was in the distinct minority. He was once invited to join a panel discussion on the subject at a coach's convention. Alongside him on the dais that day was Yale coach Felice Duffy, who was there to act as Dorrance's counterpoint, to argue the classical feminist viewpoint that to accept that men and women are different is to open up the possibility that the genders are unequal. As the only male on the panel, Dorrance wasn't expecting much support for his viewpoint, so he arrived armed with that week's issue of *Time* magazine, which coincidentally featured a cover story about how men's and women's brains differ biologically, prompting diverse behavior. Much to Dorrance's surprise, when the questions were posed to another panelist, sports psychologist Colleen Hacker, she generally came to his defense. "The panel was lined up to be everybody against Anson, and he was taking quite a few hits," Hacker recalls. "There was a group of people who were just dismissive of him. They didn't like what they were hearing, and they didn't like who was saying it. It's important to understand that it was a number of years ago, and this notion of what was complimentary to women and what was condescending, what was empowering and what was limiting, wasn't as clear. It was more contentious. With us or against us. Right thinking or wrong thinking. And I just felt that many points that Anson was making were accurate in terms of his own observations and experiences."

So sensitive were Dorrance's opinions on gender at the time that he would refuse to identify groups who had invited him to speak on the issue. He once tried to co-author an article with UNC sports psychology professor Charlie Hardy about the male/female dynamic for the magazine *Psychology Today*, but Hardy eventually abandoned the project, telling Dorrance that the research was too anecdotal and not scientific enough. Hardy later admitted to colleagues that he was scared off because Dorrance's theories were simply too radical and controversial.

To this day, there is still a segment among Dorrance's own UNC soccer alumni who suspect that he doesn't necessarily believe everything he preaches, that a lot of what he says and does to motivate his women, he does just because that's what has worked for him. In fact, nobody is quicker to criticize Dorrance's views prompted by his early contact with April Heinrichs than Heinrichs herself. "During my recruiting I did ask him how his team got along because even though I was a big fish, I understood the danger of cliques and the value of team unity," says Heinrichs, who coached the U.S. women's national team from 2000 to 2005. "But I don't believe that you treat women with kid gloves the way that Anson suggests. It's dangerous that some of his anecdotes become translated into fact because then all the male coaches in America go around saying, 'All I have to do is treat women with respect.' The underlying commentary there is that you can drive and scream and push and prod and holler at men, but you've got to fluff women up. There are very few men out there who would say they want a coach to yell at them and treat them like dirt."

By the time Marcia McDermott began playing for UNC in 1983, Dorrance had already arrived at many of his revised gender conclusions. McDermott, who would eventually coach the Women's United Soccer Association's Carolina Courage to the 2002 league championship, has been Dorrance's touchstone for most of his feminist arguments over the years and has recommended to him most of the literature he's read on the subject. "People ask me all the time if I think Anson has solved a great puzzle with his philosophy of coaching women versus men, and I confess that I don't know because I have never coached men," McDermott says. "There are a lot of people out there who cringe when Anson starts talking about the differences between coaching men and women, but I really believe in my heart that what Anson professes as the best way to coach women is simply the best way to coach. Men or women. Believe in your athletes as people as well as athletes, set a high standard, demand the best from them, and accept them regardless of the outcome on the field. Over the years I think Anson has just evolved to be a better coach."

Dorrance labels himself a feminist, but the one segment of the movement that rankles him is what he calls *victim* feminism. "I believe in making women strong, not in making laws to protect them which turn them into victims," Dorrance says. "I want to help build powerful, confident, aggressive women that don't genuflect to anything or anyone, including me. Part of that process is saying things that I know drive them crazy but which force them to stand up for themselves."

Whenever Dorrance was criticized for his views, or when it was suggested that for UNC to be successful he must be creating a negative environment, he pointed to his players. Amy Machin was so fascinated by the gender issue that she often showed up early to watch Dorrance's men practice while the rest of her team-mates watched *General Hospital*. "I think Anson is right, that there is a big difference between coaching men and women," Machin says. "When his male coaching style started failing and girls were in tears, he figured he'd better try something new, and then he changed more and more over his career because the modern players are more cultivated prima donnas who require a lot more pampering."

Like Machin, Heinrichs believes Dorrance's evolution derives from the ever-changing personalities of his players. "My generation of players provided the transition between the hard-exterior, callused women who came before us and the blonde-haired, blue-eyed, bushy-tailed America's sweethearts who came after us," Heinrichs says. "We laid the foundation for him on how to treat individuals because we forced him to take the time to have conversations with us. He learned as much from me and my generation of players as we learned from him. I think he uses certain women that he's coached over the years as guinea pigs. *Let's try this with April and if she'll buy into it, then we can get anybody to buy into it.* In the long run, I think that him bumping into me and some of my strong-willed peers helped him realize that coaching women is complicated, and it requires a lot of thought and sensitivity."

Over the last twenty years, Dorrance has evolved from generally being perceived as an inflammatory crackpot on the gender issue to a national expert who is quoted on book jackets. In 1994, The Citadel deposed him as an expert witness during the school's attempt to bar Shannon Faulkner from enrolling as the academy's first female cadet. Although the judge in that case declined to allow Dorrance to testify, stating that his decision would not be based on gender differences, Dorrance had argued in his deposition that allowing Faulkner into The

Citadel would destroy either her or the school because men and women can't be developed the same way. For Faulkner, who joined the corps of cadets in August of 1995 and dropped out five days later, citing exhaustion and maltreatment, Dorrance's opinion would prove to be prophetic.

No matter how controversial his views may be, whenever Dorrance has discussed the gender issue in recent years, he has defended his stance by insisting that nothing should be considered more wholesome than the truth. "People have accepted the genetic proof that men and women think differently, but out of a noble desire to see men and women treated equally our culture has bent political correctness into a misguided weapon. If I have learned one thing about men and women in the past two decades it's that they are wonderfully different. Different doesn't mean unequal. It just means different."

When UNC blew a three-goal lead to tie George Mason 3–3 in the 1985 season opener at Fetzer Field, it confirmed the suspicions of many around the program. Another championship was no gimme. The Tar Heels had lost nine of eleven starters from the 1984 team, which had won four consecutive national titles, and they did nothing to refute the notion of their vulnerability when they suffered a 2–0 defeat at Massachusetts in October. That loss broke a 57-game unbeaten streak and a string of 112 straight games in which UNC had scored at least one goal.

Still, as the season wound down, the Tar Heels looked like their old selves. Heinrichs, the defending National Player of the Year, led the Tar Heels in goals and points as they completed the regular season with a 16-1-1 record. Just days before the NCAA Tournament in a scrimmage against a team of male UNC students that usually proved to be a struggle for the Tar Heels, the UNC women destroyed the opposite sex 4–0. Confidence was so high that nobody seemed too worried when starting goalkeeper Kathleen O'Dell broke her wrist a week before the Final Four and had to play in a cast. There was still that familiar feeling of invincibility at tournament time.

On the eve of the NCAA championship game, a rematch of the season opener against George Mason on the Patriots' home field, Betsy Johnson's brothers, Bob and Bill, had gone out to drink a few beers. The Johnson brothers wound up at a Wal-Mart, where they bought a few gallons of Carolina blue paint. Then they sneaked past a security guard and crawled out to the center of the game field, where they painted a crude Tar Heel that stretched across the diameter of the center circle. The next day, when UNC arrived at the field, the Tar Heel had been painted over in green paint, but it was still visible enough to be instantly detected by Dorrance, who correctly identified the likely perpetrators. Dorrance approached Betsy Johnson before the game and asked, "What were your brothers thinking?" Meanwhile, in the Patriots' locker room, coach Hank Leung motivated his players by asking, "Can they come here and desecrate our house?!"

While the Tar Heel starters and reserves had flown to Washington, D.C., for the Final Four, Bettina Bernardi had driven there with the rest of UNC's walking wounded to support the team. Bernardi was recovering from a knee injury that had sidelined her for all but four games that season, and she had desperately wanted to play in the Final Four, but Dorrance had decided to hold her out to maintain the team's positive chemistry. Says Bernardi: "I remember watching our team play the first fifteen minutes of the final and turning to my teammate Lisa Duffy and saying, 'There's something wrong! That's not our team out there.' It's like they were playing not to lose."

UNC lost the game 2–0.

In the locker room afterward, Dorrance began his remarks to the team with the word he had used to sum up every setback since his college days; "Bummer." Then he assumed full responsibility for the loss. "It's my fault," he told his players. "I didn't prepare you well."

For the UNC players it was a total shock. They didn't know whether to be angry or embarrassed. They had known nothing but winning in the postseason, and they had all been wary about what to expect from their coach. "I had seen Anson be hard and push us, and the response I expected from him was to have him say, 'That's not good enough,'" McDermott says. "He showed tremendous class and compassion that day. For me it felt like a personal failure, and that was certainly motivation enough; there was no need to be berated beyond that. Obviously we all felt awful losing, yet we still found a way to celebrate the season."

Assuming a victory, one of the UNC players' parents had rented a party room in a local restaurant and hired a DJ. There was food and an open bar. Initially nobody wanted to be there, and everybody just stood around, some players crying and others consoling, as if it were a wake.

Then the alcohol kicked in. Several players chipped in ten dollars each to dare McDermott to dance with a newspaper reporter. At one point Dorrance was hoisted onto the shoulders of his players. He held up two fingers and everybody started chanting, *We're No. 2! We're No. 2!* "It was one of the all-time great therapeutic activities ever devised," Palladino says. "We went from being totally dejected to enjoying one of the best parties in the history of the program. The healing process took about an hour."

Toward the end of the night, Dorrance walked up to Bernardi and said, "You should have been on the field today. That's my fault. Here, you fly back. I'm going to drive back."

"He handed me his airline ticket and I was just bawling," Bernardi says. "That was a pretty memorable moment for me."

During the evening, talk turned to the future. For the first time, every player in the room had something greater to aspire to the next season. Bill Prentice was sitting at a table with freshman Wendy Gebauer when he casually said to her, "You know, this really sucks. From this point on, we never fucking lose again." Prentice liked the sound of what he'd said and he shared it with Dorrance, who appreciated the defiant sentiment. For the rest of the evening Prentice repeated it to whomever he stumbled upon. The players embraced the idea because it freed them somehow to party lustily once they'd each vowed allegiance to that solemn oath. By the end of the party, the phrase had filtered through the entire room, and there was a palpable commitment from everybody to regain the Tar Heels' rightful pedestal atop the women's soccer world. Their final act as a team that evening was to gather in the middle of the makeshift dance floor and chant their new mantra as one:

WE NEVER FUCKING LOSE AGAIN!
WE NEVER FUCKING LOSE AGAIN!
WE NEVER FUCKING LOSE AGAIN!

Adolescence

8 | *Competitive Cauldron*

Our deepest fear is not that we are inadequate. Our deepest fear is that we are powerful beyond measure. It is our light, not our darkness, that most frightens us. We ask ourselves, Who am I to be brilliant, gorgeous, talented, fabulous? Actually, who are you not to be? . . . Your playing small does not serve the world. There's nothing enlightened about shrinking so that other people won't feel insecure around you. . . . It's not just in some of us; it's in everyone. And as we let our own light shine, we unconsciously give other people permission to do the same.

— Marianne Williamson

The University of North Carolina Tar Heels would never fucking lose again in the 1980s. They would not lose again in their next 103 games. They would not lose again for 1,764 days. UNC would not lose the national championship again for an entire decade.

What started as a casual remark in a drunken haze, sprouted into a mindset, a credo, a pact. During the 1986 season, some Tar Heel players swear they could still hear Dr. Bill Prentice's voice ringing in their ears, *We never fucking lose again.* After UNC defeated George Mason 4–2 in September on the same field where the Tar Heels had lost the NCAA final in 1985, Anson Dorrance said, "We as coaches are involved, but this is the girls' program now. They carry on the tradition. The mission of the players is to go out there and say, 'This is the University of North Carolina and we own that championship. Some team is just renting it now, but it's ours.'"

After exacting further revenge against George Mason in the 1986 NCAA semifinals with a 3–2 victory in overtime, then defeating Colorado College 2–0 in the final, Dorrance reiterated how winning felt different this time. "I wanted this championship more than the others," Dorrance said after the game. "We've won championships in the past for different reasons. We won because we had superior talent or because of tradition. This championship is very special to me and to the players because you can appreciate it more when you haven't won it."

The championships once again started coming as surely as another winter. In 1987 the Tar Heels recorded twenty-two shutouts in twenty-four games, including all three games in the NCAA Tournament. UNC permitted only fifty-two shots all season, allowing only two goals. And one of those was an own goal, leaving George Mason's Sherry Bardell as the answer to the trivia question, "Who is the only opposing player to score a goal against UNC in 1987?" UNC's starting goalkeeper, Anne Sherow, surrendered only one goal that season, producing a microscopic .05 goals against average, the lowest in team history.

The Tar Heels were so stacked with talent that Sherow lost her job the next season. Merridee Proost took over in goal in 1988, and the Tar Heels "struggled" through the season, allowing nine goals and enduring three ties on the way to an 18-0-3 record and a third straight NCAA title.

In 1989 the Tar Heels added a freshman striker by the name of Mariel Margaret Hamm. She went by Mia. Hamm led the Tar Heels' offense with twenty-one goals and helped that year's senior class of Julie Guarnotta, Shannon Higgins, Ava Hyatt, and Carla Werden leave UNC without losing a single game in their four seasons. In UNC's 2–0 victory in the national championship game over Colorado College, Higgins scored the game-winning goal in the NCAA final for the third time in her brilliant career.

Finally, on September 22, 1990, UNC lost. The 3–2 overtime defeat at Connecticut ended the Tar Heels' 103-game unbeaten streak and caused UNC to forfeit the No. 1 national ranking for the first time in forever. As fate would have it, the two teams met again in the NCAA final in Chapel Hill. Before that game, Dorrance took out a piece of chalk, walked to the blackboard, and simply wrote down, 3–2. It was the shortest pregame talk in UNC history. The Tar Heels won the game 6–0.

UNC produced its tenth national championship in eleven years in 1991 with a 24-0 season, despite playing the entire year without Hamm and ten games without Dorrance; both were off with the United States national team at the World Championship in China.

In 1992 when the term "Dream Team" was coined at the Olympics in Barcelona, a lesser-known Dream Team thrived in Chapel Hill. Hamm returned to join Kristine Lilly and Tisha Venturini to make up what Dorrance considers to be the best team in the history of women's college soccer, and the one that best represents UNC's dominance during the era. Dorrance calls Hamm's record ninety-seven points the greatest season ever by a women's college soccer player. By herself, Hamm outshot UNC's entire opposition 117–113.

On the way to a 25-0 record in 1992, the Tar Heels won every game by at least two goals. Dorrance tried to challenge his team in October with four tough West Coast road games on four straight days, including three against Top 20 teams. UNC won them all by a combined score of 22–2. The Tar Heels outscored their opponents 132–11 overall that season, and trailed only twice all year, including a 1–0 deficit in the NCAA final against Duke. On a sloppy rainy day at Fetzer Field, Duke scored that first goal seventeen minutes into the first half, prompting Bill Palladino to turn to Dorrance on the UNC bench and say, "That's good for Duke. I'm glad they scored." UNC then responded with four goals in the next eleven minutes. Following Duke's goal, the Blue Devils managed one shot the rest of the game while UNC took twenty-seven. UNC's 9–1 victory set records for goals and margin of victory in an NCAA final. After the game, Duke coach Bill Hempen called it a "privilege" just to watch UNC play.

The Tar Heels followed that up with another perfect 23-0 season in 1993, closed by a rousing 6–0 pasting of George Mason in the NCAA final that punctuated a mind-boggling stretch of seven seasons during which UNC had trailed in their games for fewer than seventy-four minutes *combined.*

In 1994 the Tar Heels broke their own NCAA record by extending their winning streak to ninety-two games before it was stopped in October against Notre Dame by a scoreless tie. Then, seventeen days later, UNC lost to Duke 3–2, the program's first loss ever to a college team on Fetzer Field. There was so much stage whispering about how this was going to be the season when UNC finally lost in the NCAA Tournament that Venturini, who was selected as UNC's seventh straight National Player of the Year in 1994, called the 5–0 rout of Notre Dame in the '94 NCAA final the most satisfying game of her soccer career.

The program's unimaginably consistent success prompted UNC's shoe sponsor to publish a full-page ad that featured the Tar Heels' team picture after a championship game, with index fingers raised in the air and the caption: *It's not a championship, it's an anniversary.*

By that point, people in the soccer world had long since stopped asking "How many?" They were more interested in simply asking "How?"

Dorrance's coaching adolescence began one morning in 1982 when he was reading a newspaper article about UNC basketball coach Dean Smith's practice schedule. It explained how Smith's practices were blocked out to the minute. *5:00 Dribbling Warmup, 5:03 Stretching, 5:07 Layup Drill. . . .*

"I'm thinking to myself, 'How is this possible?'" Dorrance says. "Not only was Dean organized down to the minute, but he posted his schedule before he ran practice, and I thought that was insane because then he had to stick to it."

At that time, Dorrance's practice organization consisted of an approximate starting time and three possible tempos—hard, medium or light—depending on the length of time until the next game. When Dorrance read about Smith's technique, he just had to see it for himself.

Dorrance didn't know it at the time, but he was seeking out a mentor. There weren't too many tutors available in the soccer world then, so Dorrance would go to the most obvious candidate on his own campus. Dorrance believed that all coaches, no matter the sport, were simply leaders of athletes, and one of the most accomplished leaders in collegiate sports worked right down the hall.

Unfortunately, attending one of Smith's practices involved more than just wandering into the gym when basketball practice started. Everybody knew Smith's practices were closed. Tarps hung over each portal inside Carmichael Auditorium to shield Smith's workouts from the outside world. Practices were invitation-only. Dorrance was reluctant to phone Smith, so he went through a basketball assistant, Bill Guthridge, who brokered the deal. Dorrance's visit would be coordinated and chaperoned by one of the team's female student managers, who explained the protocol to him ahead of time. No food, no drinks, no talking. The young woman never had any idea who Dorrance was. Dorrance even dressed up for the occasion. "It's almost like you've been brought in to watch the Pope give Mass and you're invited to sit in the front pew," Dorrance says. "Obviously I had a very high expectation about what I was going to see, and it was even better than I thought. I didn't really think you could structure a practice so meticulously, a practice that could waste so little time."

Everything seemed to happen in explosions. Nothing was done casually. Shooting drill. *Boom.* Wind sprints. *Boom.* Half-court trap. *Boom.* Even the water breaks were structured. No waiting in lines. Everybody had his own water bottle. It felt like there was some sort of vacuum sucking the players to wherever they had to be. Dorrance occasionally peeked down at the practice plan in his hand and shook his head in disbelief. All the times were right on the minute.

What struck Dorrance most about Smith's practice was how everything was recorded. Smith posted student managers all over the floor, and whenever a player made a shot or missed one, it was noted. Free throws, rebounds, steals, turn-overs—every statistic was recorded as if it was an actual game. Every time a player competed in a 3 v. 3 drill, he got a win or a loss. Smith created intensity by keeping score, and Dorrance saw that because their performance was constantly being measured, the players kept pushing themselves through even the most mundane drills. At the end of practice, the managers sprinted to the scorer's table to compile that day's practice stats. Then, when Smith finished addressing the troops, he'd turn around, and the head manager handed him a ranking of that day's practice performance. Based on that ranking, players left practice immediately to shower or else had to run sprints. Dorrance thought that keeping stats provided a meaningful incentive to compete and concentrate in practice, and it was an ingenious way to convince the players that everything makes a difference. Everything counts.

One other aspect of that practice also impressed Dorrance. "From all my reports of Dean Smith I thought it was going to be this passionless clinic," Dorrance says. "Here's how you shoot. Here's how you rebound. All these machines moving around. But it was filled with passion. Dean was driving the soldiers. If someone wasn't working hard enough, this man that I assumed would gently prod a guy to go for a rebound is all of a sudden yelling at him to perform. Within the structure, he retained the passion. Usually you don't think those two can coexist. I told myself, 'I can do this. I can soccerize the whole thing.' It was exciting because I coach with passion, and I saw that could still have a place within a structured practice."

After practice, Dorrance was too intimidated to talk to Smith. He wrote and rewrote a thank-you note and dropped it off on the desk of Smith's secretary. When Smith read it, he was surprised. He'd had no idea that Dorrance was even there.

April Heinrichs really did care about how the team got along. She understood that chemistry was important. She wanted to like her teammates, and, more importantly, she wanted them to like her. But when Heinrichs stepped onto the soccer field all that getting-along stuff seemed to vanish. The Gift of Fury consumed her. Chemistry be damned. When Heinrichs first showed up at UNC soccer practice she had the talent and competitive fire to humiliate any of her teammates, and when that started happening, predictably, everyone did not get along. It is one of Dorrance's favorite stories.

When I watched April's first preseason practice in 1983, I was in shock. From the first minute this woman was an absolute shark. She chewed everyone up. First, she carved up all the freshmen and let them know, 'This is my class.' Then she carved up all the sophomores to let them know, 'Listen, I know we're close in age, but you're no competition for me.' And before she was done, she'd carved up the juniors and seniors. She had no hesitation at any minute of any practice against any player. She was going to win. It didn't matter what it took. She was going to bury everyone. I was ecstatic. All of a sudden one player after another came to my office during that preseason and asked, 'What are you going to do about April?' I was thinking to myself, 'Clone her?!' I asked them, 'What do you want me to do? Convince her to transfer to Duke? You want to play against her?'

'Oh, no, we don't want to play against her.'

'No, you don't want to play against her. You want to play with her. In fact, I want all you guys to play just like her.'

April was a player who ultimately didn't care what anyone thought about her. She knew that the object of the game was to stuff the ball in the back of the net as many times as you could in as short a time as possible. She was the best player I've ever seen at that. She was an extraordinary competitor. And even though April wanted to be accepted, wanted to be liked, she still refused to sacrifice her own amazing standards of excellence to be like most people, wonderfully mediocre. We have built our program's culture at North Carolina on her phenomenal example.

Heinrichs completed her UNC career in 1986 with eighty-seven goals and fifty-seven assists, leading the Tar Heels in scoring all four years. She was a three-time first team All-American, a two-time National Player of the Year, and according to Dorrance the most dominant player of any era in the history of women's collegiate soccer. "I think Anson and I were meant to collide," Heinrichs says. "Anson was a competitive guy looking to create an environment where competitiveness could get him the things he wanted. He helped me by creating a protective climate where I could excel, and for that reason I'll be eternally thankful, because had I been criticized, had I been thwarted, had I been ostracized, it would have been a much less pleasurable experience."

Dorrance came to realize that Heinrichs's story could be used as a model to protect each of the viscerally competitive players he recruited. "As a young girl I was always pretty good at sports, but I was never allowed to feel as good about it as the boys did," says Mia Hamm, the National Player of the Year in 1992 and 1993. "Lots of people thought I was too competitive until I came to UNC, where Anson told me right away that if I didn't go all-out in practice I'd be cheating myself and my teammates. It felt great not to have to apologize anymore whenever I got mad at myself for screwing up."

"I remember growing up playing sports I was always trying to win every game I played," says Cindy Parlow, the National Player of the Year in 1998. "People would always ask me, 'Why are you playing so hard? Why are you trying so hard?' It was frustrating. Anson said it was OK to try to carve people up. It was such a relief. For the first time in my life, I felt it was OK to win."

Not everybody who comes to UNC is like Heinrichs, Hamm, and Parlow. In fact, hardly anybody is. Which is the other reason Dorrance needs to tell the Heinrichs story. He believes he is fighting against a sociology that discourages most women from being competitive. "So much of what girls have been taught growing up is about cooperation and acquiescence," Dorrance says. "Women have the superior understanding that friendships are more important than winning the game, and there's really nothing in their culture that encourages them to be competitive. Girls who compete are considered bitches. Girls would rather be accepted and liked than be competitive and respected. We want the girls in our system to understand that we don't want you to be popular, we want you to be respected. My job is to change their natural course."

Sitting in Carmichael Auditorium that afternoon, watching Smith run a basketball practice, Dorrance discovered how he could push his women to be more competitive. He started to choose the ingredients for what years later he would call the "competitive cauldron." Following the example of Smith's practice, Dorrance decided that every single time a player touched a soccer ball, she could be graded in some way, and from those evaluations he could build a report card for the season. He could regularly post the rankings on a bulletin board for everyone to see, and players would be more likely to hold themselves accountable. "Players tend to be more forgiving of their faults if it's in a nebulous fog of subjective criticism," Dorrance says. "We wanted to make it very clear with numbers. Charting was a way for me to coach women without the intensity of my personality. Instead of me whipping them verbally, the numbers would be whipping them. It would not be personal. We wanted to create a competitive fury in practice so that once they got into a game it would be like Brer Rabbit in the briar patch. We wanted our kids to feel at home in intense competition."

It all sounded great. But who had time to do all that work?

Tom Sander hated soccer. Growing up in Lancaster, Pennsylvania, he watched his two younger brothers excel at the game in youth leagues, but he thought it was a decidedly boring game, just a couple dozen idiots clumsily kicking a spotted ball around, and he couldn't stop wishing that all of them would just pick up the damn thing.

On the afternoon of November 18, 1990, Sander, a sophomore at UNC, was walking down a footpath beside Teague dorm on his way back from the library when he heard some cheering on a nearby athletic field. He peeked through the chain-link fence and saw two teams of women playing soccer. Sander looked up at the scoreboard and it read *UNC 5, UConn 0*, with 10 minutes left in the game. Sander sat down and watched the last few minutes of the match through the fence. He was surprised at how skilled the women were and thrilled by the excitement of the Tar Heel players winning a national championship. When he arrived back at his dorm he figured out that the game would be shown tape-delayed on television, so he phoned his mother and asked her to record it for him. Sander watched the videotape of the game a half-dozen times over his Christmas break. The following fall he started attending women's soccer games at Fetzer Field. "I basically became a soccer freak," Sander says. "I still didn't really understand the game. I just liked watching them play because they were successful."

Watching the videotape of that 1990 championship match, Sander was particularly struck by the pregame and postgame interviews with Dorrance. He was captivated by the UNC coach's speaking presence. Sander gushed about Tar Heel soccer all the time to his best friend, Greg Randall, a wrestler at UNC. One day when Randall spotted Dorrance in the UNC weight room, he asked the coach if there might be a position available for Sander to help out the team with statistics. In the spring of 1992, Dorrance invited Sander to stop by his office and talk.

Dorrance showed Sander the team's bulletin board that included six sheets of notebook paper with some barely legible statistics scribbled on them. To Sander they read like hieroglyphs. These numbers were computed with pencil and calculator and required hours of work for Dorrance. The coach asked Sander if he thought he could organize the stats for him and track how they developed over the course of a season. "Sure, I love numbers," Sander told him. "This is right up my alley."

Once Sander started working with the team and listening to Dorrance explain the intricacies of the sport, he was hooked. "Soccer became so logical," he says. "It's like chess. All of sudden I realized that players do everything for a reason, it's not just people running around chasing a ball. It became fascinating to me."

Trouble was, after working with the team during the 1992 season, Sander graduated in the spring of 1993. While biding his time to obtain residency in North Carolina so he could go to veterinary school at North Carolina State, he continued to volunteer with the UNC soccer team. He took on odd jobs so he could afford to feed himself and have the schedule he required in the fall to attend Tar Heel practices and games, and to travel on road trips. Sander loved the soccer staff lifestyle, but he was having trouble not starving to death. First, he worked as a cook and dishwasher at the UNC cafeteria. Then he delivered UPS packages during the day and pizzas at night. Sometimes he'd disappear for three or four days to participate in drug studies where he'd receive $500 to swallow a pill and see if it made him nauseous or caused any other debilitating side effects. He even submitted to one study where he was quarantined and injected with a cold virus to see if he got infected. Sander was a human lab rat, but it allowed him to keep working with the soccer team.

Each year, as Sander grew thinner, the stat package grew fatter. Sander and Dorrance kept tinkering with their competitive matrix. Dorrance busted the budget for a laptop computer so that Sander could sit in the press box during games and chart every shot, every pass, every trap, every tackle, until nobody could run more data, crunch more numbers, than UNC soccer. Sander eventually settled on a total of twenty-four different categories, from power heading to clearing to Dorrance's personal favorite, the 1 v. 1 duels. Eventually Dorrance reached a level of science that Dean Smith could never have imagined. "Once Tom started doing the stats players could really see the areas of the game they needed to work on," Susan Ellis says. "UNC had come a long way from my era when we just had Emily Pickering saying, 'Hey, you lost every drill, what the fuck is wrong with you?'"

"I didn't look at the stats every day, but sometimes you wanted to see 'How am I doing?'" says Siri Mullinix, a UNC goalkeeper from 1995 to 1998. "I would sneak a peek at the bulletin board when there was no one else around so that nobody saw me reading it. If I was having trouble finding motivation, I felt like I could always compete against that piece of paper."

Dorrance sometimes ratchets up practice intensity even further by declaring that a particular drill carries a penalty of twenty sit-ups for the losers. To encourage competition and discourage collusion, any players who tie are sentenced to twenty-five sit-ups. If the coach is still dismayed by the lack of passion in training, he will huddle his players around him and tell them about the time Michael Jordan stormed out of a Chicago Bulls practice because of a disagreement over the score of a scrimmage. "I want every kid I train to compete in every drill like it's for a world championship," Dorrance says. "Is winning that drill important? No. But does it matter? *Yes!* The environment we create here is cold-blooded. You either win or you lose. Recording stats forces everyone to know that it matters to try to win at all times."

The UNC statistical matrix has never determined playing time, but it does evaluate effort, and while it is not fully compiled until the end of each season, it winds up being an accurate predictor for who performs best during the season. "Whenever I bring Anson the stat sheet he sits there reading it like it's the Holy Scripture," says Sander, who finally joined UNC's paid staff with the title of director of operations in 1998. "He pores over everything, saying 'Wow! . . . Wow! . . . Wow!' He'll talk about this girl moving up the rankings, this girl moving down. He's looking for an angle to present to the girls. It's either ammunition against them or it's something on paper to show them that their work's paying off."

Dorrance believes one of the primary advantages of the stats comes in their shock value. Invariably they expose an established player who isn't performing up to her capability or a talented freshman who isn't psychologically prepared for the competitive cauldron. "The best players in the world come here and suddenly they're ranked eighteenth in something and that horrifies them," Dorrance says. "They're going from being trained all their lives to be sweet into an environment where they're given permission and endorsement to beat the shit out of everyone or risk not playing. We unite them by pitting them against each other because if you create an environment where the girls are encouraged to win and then post the results, there's no 'bitch' factor. The girls at the bottom of the rankings don't look at the girls at the top as bitches, they look at them as winners. They all want to be winners."

She wasn't just your typical new meat. No, freshman Anne Remy arrived at UNC in August of 1998 as the perfect mark. She wore heavy mascara and she polished her fingernails fire engine red. Tar Heels just don't do that. Dorrance wasted no time picking a nickname for the new girl: "Princess." During her first fitness test, Remy was struggling. On one of her final sprints, she crawled on her hands and knees across the finish line in wicked pain and whimpering, "Help me! Please! Help me!" Senior Tiffany Roberts, slumped over in exhaustion beside her, grabbed Remy by the ponytail and said, "Help you? Help yourself, bitch!"

Freshmen at UNC are traditionally the ultimate peons. Depending on the level of sadism of the upperclassmen, Tar Heel rookies in years past weren't even spoken to until October. Dorrance blithely jokes that some of his incoming freshmen may need the suicide hotline. Laurie Schwoy calls the preseason of her freshman year "the toughest two weeks of my life." Schwoy and her roommate Lorrie Fair tacked up a calendar in their dorm room and marked off each day of their freshman season with an "X" the way convicts do. Kalli Kamholz sums it up thusly; "As a freshman, you feel like a piece of crap."

"You come to UNC as a new recruit and the players on the team ignore you, won't acknowledge that you're alive, basically do everything in their power to make you miserable," Libby Guess says. "I'd call home and say, 'Get me the hell out of here!' Then I'd talk to friends who were freshmen at other schools and they'd have to hang up on me because their seniors were picking them up to go out, and I'd say, 'You mean they *talk* to you?'"

Even preexisting soccer stature is not a mitigating factor. Says Mia Hamm: "When I came to UNC I was already on the U.S. national team, and my new teammates were like, 'Who cares? You haven't done anything here yet.' Basically they were asking, 'Why should we invest in you?'"

Says Catherine Reddick: "As a freshman I showed up as the best player in Alabama, and suddenly I'm practicing against the best player from California, the best player from Texas, the best player from Michigan, and none of them give a darn about what I've done in the past. Welcome to UNC. I wasn't prepared for that, and it was a blow to my pride."

Shannon Higgins vividly remembers after the first couple of days of preseason when she and fellow freshman Lori Henry walked to town to buy sandwiches and stopped on the way back, sitting together on the base of a statue. The two girls began crying and then through their tears both simultaneously blurted out, "I want to go home!"

"Every day I came back to my freshman dorm during the preseason I wanted to quit," Lindsay Stoecker says. "I'd ask myself, 'Why am I playing soccer?' I'd call my father and ask him if he would pay for my tuition if I quit, and he'd tell me to give it a little more time."

By far the least favorite day for every freshman is her first official team scrimmage, when Tar Heel starters play against a team of reserves and incoming freshmen. The seniors consider it their opportunity to initiate the freshmen on the field. Dorrance stokes the fire. "I go to my starters and tell them, 'All right, I'm going to walk over to the reserves, point to you guys, and tell them if they want your position to go get it.' Then after I do that the starters are all huddled together saying, 'No frigging way some freshman is taking my spot. We've been reading about her, well, I think that's a crock.' They're over there frothing at the mouth. Meanwhile all these freshmen are thinking, 'Oh my god, I should have gone to Duke.'"

In the opening scrimmage, rules are ignored. No fouls. No whistles. No holds barred. During Fair's first scrimmage as a freshman on a rainy day she was rudely upended by junior Aubrey Falk and wound up face down in a mud puddle. By the time Fair was a junior, she took it out on Remy, bloodying her nose with an elbow in Remy's first scrimmage. That same afternoon, junior Rebekah McDowell issued a warning to freshman Jena Kluegel. *If you ever steal the ball away from Cindy Parlow, either give it right back to her or run as fast as you can in the other direction.* "The first time it happened Cindy steamrolled me," Kluegel says, "and while I was lying on the ground seeing stars, Rebekah stood over me and said, 'You should've listened to me.'"

Later in the scrimmage, freshman Danielle Borgman made the same mistake with Parlow. "Cindy picked me up and threw me across the field," Borgman says. "There was a message. 'This is our program and this is how we play. How are you going to deal with it?'"

"I basically just threw Jena and Danielle down on the ground on purpose," Parlow recalls with a laugh. "It was a test. A rite of passage. 'Are these girls going to fall down and whine about it? Or are they going to try to get me back?' They came right back after me, and that's when I knew they were going to be good."

Surely the worst first day in UNC history occurred on August 14, 2001, when freshman Annie Felts, the 2000 Missouri Player of the Year, took the field for her first scrimmage. Though Felts suffered from alopecia, a skin disorder that had caused her to lose all of her hair, there was no sympathy from the UNC veterans. Only a few bad bald jokes. Felts's opening scrimmage remained tied late into the game, when she attempted to slide-tackle Remy just outside the penalty box. In the violent collision, Remy's knee struck the back of Felts's head. Felts fell down on her back and couldn't get up. She remained prone there for twenty minutes with a concussion. "I could hear the ambulance coming, and all I could think was, 'Oh, great, now all my teammates are going to hate me for being the little freshman who interrupted the game," Felts says. "Then I thought, 'Is this how it's going to be for four years? Maybe this is a bad omen.'"

Meanwhile, the Tar Heel veterans sat around the center circle massaging each other's calves and discussing summer-school GPAs. They laughed about how Remy might have broken one of her precious red fingernails in the crash. Nobody seemed at all concerned about their fallen teammate, except perhaps for the one Tar Heel player who said, "What's wrong? Is she dead or something?"

Meanwhile, Dorrance chatted with his wife on his cell phone. Though he would visit Felts in the hospital later that evening, this scene was nothing new for Dorrance, who had experienced similar incidents a dozen times before in his career. Eventually Felts's head was immobilized, and she was loaded onto a backboard and driven away from her very first Tar Heel practice to the emergency room. None of her new teammates made a move to see her off.

Instead, moments later, Dorrance called an end to the scrimmage, and the Tar Heels gathered around a birthday cake. They each grabbed a hunk in their bare hands and giddily stuffed their faces, the vanilla frosting sticking to their cheeks along with various blades of grass and sweat. In the frenzy, the salutation swirled in Carolina blue icing was quickly smudged before any of the Tar Heels even got a chance to notice it. It read, *Happy Birthday Annie.*

During the first game Carla Werden ever played as a freshman at UNC in 1986, April Heinrichs ran by the Tar Heels bench and screamed, "Anson, get Carla off the field. She's killing us!" Like many other rookies who had come through Dorrance's boot camp, Werden admits that at that moment she wanted to go home to her mommy.

Werden was an admitted homebody who was initially afraid to go away to college and wanted to stay close to her family in Dallas. UNC was the only school that was recruiting her, and she had never even considered playing soccer at an elite college level. The first time Dorrance phoned her, Werden responded, 'You want *me* to come play at *your* school?' The next few times that Dorrance phoned the Werden house, Carla ducked the call, whispering to her mother, "Tell him I'm not here."

Dorrance eventually sold Werden on coming to UNC. When she arrived in Chapel Hill, Werden discovered that the entire Tar Heel defense had graduated the year before. As a freshman she was going to have to step in and start right away at sweeper without the usual cushion of a year or two to grow accustomed to playing in college. "I was this shy, skinny, weak freshman coming in from one thousand miles away, and I didn't have any idea what I was in for," Werden says. "I was just so lame. I didn't want to have to play right away. Most competitive people would want that, but there were plenty of times as a freshman when I didn't want to be on the field."

In the seventh game of that season, against George Mason, the tense rematch of the 1985 title game, the Patriots' talented striker Lisa Gmitter was regularly causing havoc in the UNC box. At one point, Werden attempted a clear and kicked the ball right to Gmitter, who didn't even have to break stride as she then dribbled around Werden and rifled a shot at the Tar Heel net. As the shot flew over the crossbar, Werden broke down, bawling uncontrollably on the field. She unsuccessfully begged Dorrance to pull her from the game.

Werden discovered that the hardest part of playing for the Tar Heels was at practice, where she was asked to compete with her teammates as if they were her mortal enemies. She didn't like to hammer them or be hammered by them. During the 1 v. 1 drills contested against each of her teammates over the course of her entire freshman season, Werden didn't win a single game. Dorrance even tried matching Werden against Jo Boobas, who had recently torn her ACL. Werden still lost. "Coming in as a freshman you're supposed to know your place, so competing with teammates, kicking each other, it was all a bit of a shock," Werden says. "These are your friends, and you don't want to hurt them or hurt their feelings if you beat them. That made me nervous and afraid, and I didn't want to be there."

Werden thought about quitting all the time, but she was haunted to some extent by three players who had grown up playing alongside her with the Dallas Sting. Wendy Greenberg, Mary Smith, and Toni Catchings had each left UNC after just one season at least partly because of homesickness. Werden never told her coaches or teammates that she wanted to go home, but she cried every time she called her parents, and she flew back to Dallas every chance she got. During each trip home, when it was time to return to UNC, she would be begging her parents, "Please don't make me go back." Werden's parents always talked her into giving it another month.

Every day before practice Werden dreaded having to face the cauldron's lists. She tried to avoid them, but there they were prominently placed on the bulletin board beside the door. You couldn't miss them. Werden was embarrassed to see her name at the bottom of the 1 v. 1 column and many of the other columns as well. She fantasized about how she could somehow dispose of the lists.

Eventually, however, she realized that the stats set her free to compete. "I was not a naturally competitive person, but I learned a lot of my competitiveness in those drills," Werden says. "I was humiliated and knew that I had to get harder and tougher. As a player you want to have your teammates believe that you belong there. You want them to respect you."

"Somewhere between her freshman year and her senior year, Carla made a decision that it was OK to compete, it was OK to be the best," Dorrance says. "Her skills didn't get that much better between her freshman and senior years. What changed was her decision to win."

Werden gradually worked her way up the lists with each passing season. They became validation for her, but she no longer needed to study them. She absolutely craved the battling in practice and constantly encouraged her teammates to fight harder. "One day I realized that I was having a ball," Werden says. "By the end of my sophomore year, junior and senior years, I loved the competition. It was all just about being comfortable with it."

The same girl who had never won a 1 v. 1 duel as a freshman, didn't lose a single 1 v. 1 duel as a senior. She was named captain in her senior year, completed her four seasons with four national championships, and later, as Carla Overbeck, went on to captain the U.S. national team. During her time in Chapel Hill, Werden willed herself into one of the fiercest competitors in the history of the program, undergoing the most definitive metamorphosis in the annals of UNC's competitive cauldron.

During one game in her senior season, Werden turned to the bench and yelled to Dorrance, "Anson, you've got to sub out Rita. She's killing us!"

9 | *Mentality*

Come to the edge, He said. They said, We are afraid. Come to the edge, He said. They came. He pushed them . . . and they flew.

—Guillaume Apollinaire

They couldn't have been more different. They couldn't have been more the same. Anson Dorrance was an overprivileged white boy born into an oil family who traveled the world. Staci Wilson was an underprivileged black sister born into Jersey City who pretty much stayed there. But look beyond that. Check out what's inside. Dorrance and Wilson both grew up small for their gender and compensated with grit, both mouthing their way into playground fights as kids to prove their mettle. Both grew up knowing what it's like to be a minority on the athletic field and the prejudice that entails, yet both remained thoroughly imperturbable in that arena. Both arrived fashionably late to soccer and made up for their lack of experience by doing something anybody could do, tackling with a vengeance, each unleashing their gift of fury. Wilson is the player closest in mindset to Dorrance of all the women he has ever coached. "Staci embodied one of my favorite qualities in a player, a capacity to take physical risks," Dorrance says. "Here's this kid barely five feet tall charging in on 50-50 balls like David against all these Goliaths, and she just felled the giants with her incredible courage. She'd cut them in half. It was not a personal thing. It's *who she is.* When you played against Staci you thought that she's psychotic, and there's this lingering feeling that you just might die that day, and she'd do nothing to cause you to think any differently."

"Anson asked me to run people over and unleash my will, and I thought, 'Sweet, this is awesome!'" Wilson says. "He always encouraged me to train on the edge, to kick everybody's ass and not give a shit about the consequences."

Wilson competed with such a fervor that her own teammates hated playing against her in practice, and even Dorrance dreaded the spring scrimmages when a lack of healthy bodies compelled him to join the game. Wilson, a defender, seemed to take extra sadistic pleasure in marking her coach, leaving welts and scars that are still visible on Dorrance's shins today.

Dorrance called her *Buzzsaw*. He loves these noms de guerre. He called diminutive Tracey Bates the *Tiny Terminator*. Mia Hamm was *Hammer*. Heather O'Reilly was alternately known as *Wild Thing* or *The Angry Chicken*. He started recruiting Alyssa Ramsey the moment he heard her nickname, *Yellow Card*. Even Anne Remy, the girl with the prissy makeup who was initially dubbed *Princess*, learned to play so hard that whenever Remy bowled over a teammate during practice, Dorrance would proudly chirp "Nails!" which was definitely not a reference to her manicure.

Dorrance likes to say that he is breeding "Natural Born Killers," and he often refers to his players as "savages" or "blunt instruments." His pet peeve is what he's dubbed "chickenshitism," a grievous offense committed by players he calls "hummingbirds," girls who hover near the fray but shy away from any physical contact. All of which explains why he encouraged his early teams to engage in the bruising drill called Magnet.

Neither rain, nor sleet, nor snow prevents Dorrance from running his Tar Heels through their practices. "I remember one day we ran a fitness session through blinding rain in the middle of a hurricane," Sarah Dacey says. "Anson was telling us that this is what makes us champions. I remember that day just feeling very accomplished and proud . . . and wet."

It's all about creating a mentality. Creating alpha females. Creating snot-rubbers. Creating more Staci Wilsons. At the Tar Heels' annual season-ending banquet each spring, the last and most coveted honor Dorrance bestows on a player is not the team's Most Valuable Player Award, it is the Gift of Fury Award. The UNC coach feels the easiest way to toughen up his players is to crash them into each other, 1 v. 1, his version of Marvin Allen's infamous Suicide drill. Dorrance's interpretation is known as Top Gun, the soccer version of basketball's one-on-one. Two players. One goal. Robin Confer recalls competing in Top Gun against Cindy Parlow when the competition became so heated that the two began throwing punches, the one and only brawl of Confer's life. "Anson made me a believer in 1 v. 1," Confer says. "It encompasses so much more than just being able to beat somebody. It's a huge mental battle, a huge physical battle, an ego battle. It teaches you so much about yourself. Are you going to crumble, or are you going to find a way to win? You're so exposed. It tells you how tough you really are."

Dorrance ultimately wants UNC practices to be fiercer than games, so he concludes nearly every training drill by shouting, "Good enough," a calculated mix of praise and caveat, suggesting that the quality can always be improved. In team scrimmages he regularly scripts his starters behind by one goal with just ten minutes left to play. He wants his players to grow accustomed to adversity, even to losing, so they won't fear it. Even those Tar Heels who never lost a match in their careers didn't view themselves as undefeated. Once, when Danielle Egan played for a U.S. youth national team and her team lost, Egan's coach teased her afterward by asking, "You've never lost a game at UNC; what does it feel like to finally lose?"

Egan replied, "Coach, at UNC I lose in practice every day."

"You can't go through four years of UNC women's soccer drills and not be tough," Lindsay Stoecker says. "When it comes to game time we're bonded, because we're all so relieved not to be killing each other for a change."

Dorrance views practice as a natural transition to mentality in games. The last thing the Tar Heels see as they exit their locker room for the pregame talk is a poem taped beside the doorway. The poem is titled "Push":

The challenge isn't someone else
The challenge is within
It's the aching in your lungs
And the burning in your legs
And the voice that yells can't
But you don't listen
You just push harder
Then you hear a voice whisper can
And you realize the person you thought you were
Is no match for the one you really are

Dorrance emboldens his players in his pregame talks, constantly reminding them that UNC's mission is not just to defeat its opponents, but to relentlessly sap their will until they can seize on an opportunity to break them. Concluding his remarks before a game against Villanova during the 2003 season, he said, "My thrill during our games is the understanding that every team that leaves the field against us knows they were beaten by a greater force. No, not a better team. They ran into a *force.* They found the center of our chest and it was hard and they couldn't knock us down. So when you're tackling out there today, I want you to throw your body at the girl with such a clattering of bones and gristle that she'll be worried about having a scar from her kneecap to her ankle. I want her wondering, 'If I finish this game, will I ever be able to wear a skirt again?'"

During one halftime speech against Duke in the early 1990s, Dorrance's notorious rallying cry was, "They're coming after you. Well, tough, *fuck that shit!* Let's go after *them.*" For every game since then the Tar Heels' final chant before taking the field is, "Tough! F!T!S!"

Says Susan Ellis, "I once heard someone describe UNC by saying, 'They're not women, they're animals.' I'd say on the field the Tar Heels are like a pack of hungry dogs. Sometimes when opponents talk about us, I can hear they are scared. The only thing on our minds has always been to win and play at the highest level, but if that means decking somebody, that's fine with us."

"When you watch UNC play, you can see the aggressive edge they have," Santa Clara coach Jerry Smith says. "It's actually beyond aggressiveness, it's a meanness. They don't care how many fouls they have or how they're perceived. Their attitude is, 'I will do anything to win this game, even if I have to hurt you, and when I have your jugular exposed, I want to see it spit blood all over the field.' The rest of us struggle to match their ferocity."

Says Catherine Reddick: "I think a lot of college soccer people are bitter toward our program. We are segregated from everybody else as players who appear to be saying *Die! Die! Die!* whenever we're on the soccer field. That take-no-prisoners mentality comes from Anson, and it bothers people outside the program who like to say, 'Why not just play the game and have fun?' Playing hard is what's fun for us. What's wrong with that?"

Whenever Dorrance designs a drill, he considers not only the tactical, technical, and physical ingredients, but also a psychological component. The Tar Heels don't employ a sports psychologist, like many other college programs, because that element is already integrated into their training. "In our game there is a line drawn as to how much contact is allowed within the rules," Dorrance says. "We want our players to come right to the edge of that line, because a lot of your success has to do with your ability to intimidate your opponent."

"Playing for Anson wasn't easy, and I think that's very valuable that it was so hard," Marcia McDermott says. "I loved playing Carolina soccer, but everything was earned. Playing time was earned. Winning was earned."

Says Amy Machin: "Anson created an environment where there wasn't any sympathy for 'I don't feel good' or 'I've got my period.' Girls who couldn't hack it just disappeared."

If Dorrance has a signature coaching pose, it is standing amidst the frenzy of a Tar Heels practice, arms folded across his chest, eyes darting from player to player, the man watching his women, evaluating their every move for clues about how hard they really are. Dorrance admits that one of his favorite aspects of coaching is thinning the herd, seeing which players can stand up to the challenge of his program. He will actually encourage anybody who isn't sufficiently dedicated to quit the team, and several freshmen have done so even before the end of their first preseason. "The kids who play at UNC are going to be severely tested in every area, because we're always essentially asking, *Whatcha got?*" Dorrance says. "They're all going to fail at some point, and then we get to see whether that forges their character or shatters it. We have a sink-or-swim philosophy. There aren't any hand-holding pop psychology sessions of singing 'Kumbaya' together. If you're going to roll over and die, this culture is not for you. Join a sorority."

po-ten-tial *n.* not worth shit yet.

It is the most-often-quoted definition in the Dorrance dictionary. If there was ever any doubt that his players got his drift, Dorrance posted a sign at the practice field that reads, *You Can't Build a Reputation on What You Are Going to Do.*

Dorrance's ultimate objective for his players is simple: excellence. And Dorrance doesn't believe it is that difficult to achieve. He subscribes to a theory he once read in an article entitled "The Mundanity of Excellence," which states: *Excellence is not out of reach. It is accomplished through deliberate actions, ordinary in themselves, performed consistently and carefully, made into habits, compounded together, and added up over time.*

It's all part of Dorrance's continuing effort to demystify the sport for his players. One of his favorite phrases is, *Isn't this a simple game?* "I remember I was horrible one day in practice and Anson walked up to me, leveled my shoulders, and said, 'You're just off balance,'" Mia Hamm says. "Sometimes as athletes, when things aren't going right, you think you're doing everything wrong. He gave me that one easy thing to work on, and I thought, 'Really? That's it? I thought I just completely sucked.' In that moment he'd relieved all of my doubts, and I immediately started playing well again."

At the outset of nearly every UNC practice, Dorrance bellows loud enough for the whole team to hear, "Let's get better!" His favorite phrase to encourage an individual is "There's another level in you." No player knows exactly how many levels there are, only that there always seems to be another one to be reached. "Winning is not what we talk to our players about," Dorrance says. "We judge our performance against the ideal game. We want perfect passing, perfect finishing, perfect organization overall. So we're not really playing against our opponents, we're playing against the game. It's impossible to beat the game, but we want to keep trying."

Carla Werden recalls one practice when Dorrance asked her to pass a 40-yard ball along the ground to Marcia McDermott's left foot. Says Werden: "I tried the pass eight or ten times before finally I kicked one to her right foot, and Anson says, 'Carla, do you know the difference between left and right?' I could never put it exactly on her left foot, and I felt like an idiot, but Anson's a perfectionist and he wanted me to know that precision is important."

Tar Heel players keep fighting this indomitable foe because they know their playing time depends on it. Dorrance doesn't hesitate to demote one of his starters to the reserve squad at any moment during any practice. "Many coaches have a fear about declaring a starting lineup, but why?" Dorrance says. "I'll say, 'All right, Catherine switch with Julia.' And everyone knows that means Catherine's had a great practice and Julia hasn't, and now Catherine's the starter."

Says Jena Kluegel, "I remember once when Anson stopped a scrimmage and said, 'Jena, put on a pinnie.' Suddenly I was on the reserves. Some players would just stand there and cry, but I got pissed off and tried to prove to him that I wasn't that bad. That fired me up. *I'll show him!*"

Dorrance believes the three key ingredients to every player's success are self-discipline, competitive fire, and self-belief, and he tries to identify and fortify each player's fragile areas. He also believes a player's development is largely based on her ambition, and while he may extol past Tar Heel legends as carrots, he doesn't try to pigeonhole every new recruit into becoming the next April Heinrichs or Mia Hamm. "I never think of players in terms of other players, because I believe every player is incredibly unique," he says. "My job is to find out a way to let her know she's unique, accelerate her unique qualities, and hide her weaknesses."

"Anson finds a player's spark, her personal nuance, and refines and cultivates it so he doesn't just crank out UNC robots," says Colleen Hacker, a former U.S. women's national team psychologist and college coach. "He's saying, 'This is what makes you special. How can we maximize that?' I saw Kristine Lilly being more of Kristine Lilly and Mia being more of Mia, but I never saw Kristine trying to be Mia. This gave them each a confidence and a belief and a power because they were not asked to subjugate core aspects of who they are."

Naturally there's a different ceiling for every UNC player, but Dorrance wants each one to be as excellent as she can be. "There isn't a single player that he doesn't deem important, from the All-Americans to the walk-ons," Marcia McDermott says. "It's a tribute to Anson that a freshman benchwarmer often becomes a senior starter and a highly touted recruit often manages to become a star on the national team."

Dorrance considers his player development one of his primary strengths as a coach. He believes there is a greatness in all of his players, and it's his job to coach it out of them. For each player, Dorrance asks himself the same series of questions: *How can I make this player the best she can be technically and tactically? What can I say to her to make her more confident? What can I say to make her more hardworking and disciplined? What can I do to create a more competitive soccer warrior?* He proclaims that he can make poor players fair, fair players good, and good players extraordinary. For example, he transformed Keath Castelloe from a plodding, meek freshman walk-on who apologized in practice when she bumped a teammate into a two-year starting defender. He also turned a barely recruited "project" named Louellen Poore into an All-American and a confidence-challenged Carla Werden into one of the best players in the world. Also, Dorrance can point to how he often does not sign the nation's top-ranked recruit but then does produce the Player of the Year four seasons later.

Like every other coach, Dorrance truly lives for the wondrous few, the players who he says "change the temperature of a game." April Heinrichs. Mia Hamm. Kristine Lilly. Cindy Parlow. Staci Wilson. Lindsay Tarpley. Heather O'Reilly. Dorrance pushes his best players the most, imploring them to dominate games with their individual talent, to be what he calls "the margin of victory." Dorrance believes the word "selfish" should have a positive connotation for his most gifted players, and he often reminds them of what Michael Jordan once said: "There is no *I* in *team*, but there is in *win*."

"Anson has always believed in stars," Bill Palladino says. "His coaching methodology is to affirm greatness, and he asks the truly extraordinary ones to never be afraid to say, 'Gimme the friggin' ball!'"

When a star player falls into a scoring drought, Dorrance tells her another Michael Jordan story about when Jordan returned to Chapel Hill from an upset loss to Indiana in the 1984 NCAA Tournament. The next day, Jordan was out on the court at Carmichael Auditorium, practicing the exact shots that he missed in the game until they became routine. Dorrance will tell his elite strikers to do the same, and he believes the truly extraordinary players are the ones he must tell when to stop.

"I like to ask all of my players, 'What separates you?'" Dorrance says. "There's something that truly separates a great one from the rest. I'm going to push her to her psychological edge because I'm convinced that sort of agitation is what creates the pearl inside the oyster. She has to embrace the phrase, *To whom much has been given, much will be expected.* She has to want to be a champion, to do things that ordinary people would not do, because talent at our level is very common, but what you invest on your own to develop that talent is the critical final measure of athletic greatness."

Early one morning during the spring of 1994, Dorrance was driving to work past a local park when he spotted a lone figure running sprints in the gloaming.

Dorrance slowed down and recognized the runner, so he pulled over his car to get a closer look. Unnoticed, he watched her finish each sprint, her chest heaving, hot breath streaming from her lungs, her body straining so hard it was quivering. A chill ran up Dorrance's spine. "It was right then when I knew that Mia Hamm had crossed over to extraordinary," he says. "She was on her way to ascending into the stratosphere and becoming the greatest player in the world."

Dorrance drove to his office, sat down at his desk, and proudly wrote Hamm a brief note: *The vision of a champion is someone who is bent over, drenched in sweat, at the point of exhaustion when no one else is watching.*

In the summer of 1970 George Blackburn visited the Dorrance family in Connecticut, and one night he and Anson rode the train into New York City. The pair made the rounds of bars in Chinatown and Greenwich Village and eventually missed the last train home. They wound up spending the night on a traffic island where a group of hippies was encamped. When Blackburn woke up the next morning, Dorrance was gone. One of the hippies told Blackburn that a street gang had stolen Dorrance's watch, and he had run off after them. A few minutes later, Dorrance returned with his watch in hand. When Blackburn asked his friend how he had recovered the watch, Dorrance said, "George, it was great! They were so amazed that I was idiot enough to chase after them by myself that the guy dropped it on the sidewalk and took off."

Dorrance directs his players to treat the soccer ball the way he once treated his wristwatch. Behave like it belongs to you, chase after it with reckless abandon, and don't ever think about the risk. It is why he can ask his teams to play in an unusual formation known as the 3-4-3, the soccer equivalent of football's all-out blitz or basketball's full-court press. Three backs. Four midfielders. Three forwards. It is the riskiest formation played in all of college soccer, and Dorrance has used it in every women's match he's ever coached. Ask him why and he simply says, "To make shit happen."

The 3-4-3 system places a tremendous burden on each of the Tar Heel players. Yes, even Dorrance's formation is designed to forge his team's mentality. Dorrance is the antithesis of the classic conservative soccer coach who overloads the backline, clogs the midfield, and hopes to score on a counterattack, a blueprint designed to limit the possibility that a team will be humiliated at the expense of a chance at overwhelming success. Dorrance's 3-4-3 comes from his youth, when he admired the arrogant Dutch master Johan Cruyff and the hell-bent attacking style of Holland's national team in the 1970s, as well as from his early years as UNC's men's coach, when the Tar Heels played inferior competition, and their coach would implore them to never stop sprinting, calling for pressure, pressure, pressure.

Playing three forwards is Dorrance's idea of soccer suffocation. For an opposing back there is rarely a comfortable pass or an easy clear. There are more UNC players flooding the penalty box on offense, so each player is responsible for covering less ground, and a three-front allows UNC to frame the goal, running a player at each post and another at the goalkeeper as often as possible. But the primary reason UNC plays three up front is that women's collegiate soccer has yet to evolve to a point where this kind of elementary pressure doesn't work. Dorrance realizes that his female players aren't as skilled as men, so he is increasing their odds to score. Says Dorrance: "Lots of times a girl will dribble to the endline, and she'll try to serve the ball back post, and she'll shank it near post, but because of our system we'll have a near-post runner who tries to finish it, but she mistimes her header and flicks it off her ear back to the slot, where because we have numbers in the box we have another girl, and she tries to hit it and it goes off her kneecap towards the back post, but since we've framed the goal, it deflects off another girl's stomach and into the net."

For years the Tar Heels even ran a finishing drill in practice called "Controlled Chaos," but while UNC scores its share of goals through pure frenzy, there is also a well-rehearsed choreography to the team's attack. During the 1997 NCAA final Raven McDonald executed a blind headball flick to Cindy Parlow, who was cutting behind her to the near post, and then Parlow tipped it over the head of the Connecticut goalkeeper for UNC's first goal. After the game a reporter asked McDonald if she knew Parlow was in position to receive her pass, and when McDonald admitted that she did not, Parlow interrupted by saying, "She knew I was supposed to be there, let's put it that way."

In Dorrance's blueprint, each of the Tar Heels must move as a unit or the system collapses. There is no place on the field to hide or relax as there are in less aggressive formations. Prima donna forwards must play defense, defenders attack, and the goalkeeper is asked to act as a sweeper and charge any balls played through the back line. Every player is implored to dominate her zone of the field with what Dorrance calls "an animalistic territorial imperative." Dorrance substitutes whenever he senses a player is tiring, hoping to play the entire game at a furious sprint that will eventually demoralize opponents. Effective pressure limits the extra risk of fielding only three defenders. While the 3-4-3 would seem to be designed to supplement the offense, the key to UNC's success is that all eleven players, from the strikers to the goalkeeper, exhaust themselves in pressure defense. "A player's attacking personality is ephemeral; it could be absolutely brilliant one day and totally gone the next," Dorrance says. "So if you want to have consistent value, you must play defense. Defense is not a talent. It's a decision, and if any of my kids decides they're not going to work on defense, they are sitting next to me on the bench."

"When you play North Carolina, right from the starting whistle you have to brace yourself for what's about to happen," Georgia coach Patrick Baker says. "It's like a storm, and you're trying to hold on through the wind and rain. They keep running at you with so much team speed that as a player what you think you're seeing on the field can change in a heartbeat. It feels like you're playing short-handed the entire game."

Says UCLA coach Jill Ellis: "I'm not sure Anson feeds them the week prior to a game. They come out extremely hungry, like they are rabid, and the question is,

'Can we handle the pressure?' You tend to struggle when you can't think quickly enough to deal with it."

Coaches who have never played North Carolina before have a hard time preparing for an intensity they have never experienced. Some have tried to scrimmage against an opponent with as many as fourteen players, but even that doesn't accurately simulate the situation because UNC substitutes so much that fresh bodies come off the Tar Heel bench in waves. April Heinrichs put it best when she coached at Virginia against UNC and said, "There are some teams that can play with Carolina for seventy minutes. Trouble is, the game is ninety minutes."

The foundation of Dorrance's system has remained remarkably consistent over the years, so much so that when he recently stumbled upon some notes he had taken at a coaching school in the 1970s, he discovered one tenet after another that he still follows today. Tar Heels who played in the 1980s swear they can accurately predict what Dorrance will do on any given day in practice. The only significant system change occurred in 1996, when Dorrance suddenly decided his team could not win the NCAA title that season using its longstanding combination of man-marking and zone defense. So at halftime of a game against Vanderbilt he switched to a straight zone defense. The Tar Heels improved in the second half in their new set, and Dorrance never went back to the marking defense.

Beyond challenging his players with his system, the man who played on all three lines during his college soccer career isn't afraid to shift players around within it. Part of Dorrance is still that little boy staring at the gameboard and trying to figure a way through the Khyber Pass, shifting his pieces around until they can engulf and dominate an opponent. Two games into Heinrichs's freshman season, Dorrance informed her he was moving her from the midfield, where she'd grown up playing, to the forward line, where she would become the Tar Heels' third-leading career goalscorer. During the 1996 championship season he switched Laurie Schwoy from striker to midfielder and Cindy Parlow from midfielder to striker, the positions where they would both become dominant forces and play for the national team. All three of the Tar Heels' starting defenders in the 2001 season had arrived at UNC as forwards.

Dorrance has also perennially tried to construct the most challenging schedule of any program in the country, facing as many ranked teams as possible, almost always away from Fetzer Field. Seeking team development, recruiting exposure, and the financial guarantees that the Tar Heels earn for playing away from home, UNC typically plays at least twice as many games on the road as in Chapel Hill, including one stretch during the 2002 season when the Tar Heels endured forty-one days between home games. It isn't so much a schedule as a gauntlet, but it pays off when UNC reaches the NCAA final and the Tar Heels have already played their opponent earlier that season in a more hostile environment. Ever since his team began cranking out national titles, Dorrance has even tried to arrange what he calls "scheduled losses," a script that the Tar Heels tend not to follow. "Early in every season we try to gain some humility by getting our ass kicked," Dorrance says. "We throw our kids into the fire by traveling to the farthest team away from

Chapel Hill that can beat us, maybe take a loss, and then reconstruct ourselves the rest of the year, chomping at the bit to play them again and beat them. That was our plan from the beginning. It isn't very sophisticated."

UNC doesn't scout its opponents with the detail that most schools do because Dorrance doesn't want to overwhelm his players with information, and because he isn't going to make any adjustments in his system anyway. Says Palladino: "Part of our pregame message is that if we play our game and play it well, regardless of what they do, chances are we're going to win."

Since most of the time UNC doesn't face teams with comparable talent, the scouting report often enhances opponents' strengths to make them more dynamic, more of a threat than they actually are. Palladino is usually in charge of scouting, so during the week he phones a few coaches who have played UNC's upcoming opponent. Sometimes he reaches them. Sometimes he doesn't. If his scouting report doesn't include any specific names of opposing players, the Tar Heel players know that Palladino is fudging it.

Even the way Dorrance asks questions in the pregame meeting is designed to harden his players. Because he was an apathetic law student, Dorrance learned the value of the Socratic method. He doesn't tell his players what they should do, he *asks* them what they should do. He recalls the fear of sitting in a law class when a professor posed a question and then looked down at the roll for a random name to call on, and he realized that during that pause everyone in the room responded to the question in their heads because they all dreaded the potential public humiliation. So Dorrance won't say, "Leslie, if the ball is on your left foot here, where does the pass go?" Instead, he'll say, "If the ball is on your left foot here, where does the pass go . . . Leslie?"

"I always stayed focused in pregame because you never knew when Anson was calling on you for a little practice test," Wendy Gebauer says. "If you let yourself daydream and he noticed it, then he would try to fry your rear end in there."

Dorrance even takes a hard-line view toward injuries. One of his pet theories is that pain is manageable, which has credibility coming from someone who once played an entire soccer season on a broken foot. Dorrance has no tolerance for the time-honored soccer tradition of writhing on the ground after a foul. One day during a UNC men's practice, striker Billy Propster was clipped by a vicious tackle. As Propster was rolling in the grass in apparent agony, Dorrance stood over him and said, "Billy, I know it hurts, but if you were to die now, is this the way you'd like us to remember you?"

Everyone on the field broke up laughing. Even Propster.

Dorrance is a man who has never taken a sick day in his career and sincerely tells his players that he considers being ill a sign of weakness. At the outset of each practice he doesn't ask Dr. Prentice for an injury report but instead a "Hypochondria Report," and when he is particularly incredulous about the number of walking wounded who are sitting out, he will inevitably shout, "The few, the proud, the Tar Heels!" In order for a player to legitimately miss practice, Dorrance wants to see a bone sticking out.

Fortified by her coach, Amy Steadman played her freshman season with a torn ACL. During one game when goalkeeper Jenni Branam got spiked in the forehead, a wound that initially needed twenty-two stitches and eventually required plastic surgery, Branam looked up at Prentice as soon as she reached the UNC bench and asked, "When can I go back in?" The only time Staci Wilson ever admitted to being hurt was during the 1994 national title game when she butted heads with an opponent and suffered a severely broken nose. "Anson came out and saw that my nose was pointing toward my ear, but he didn't say, 'Are you OK?' Wilson remembers. "He said, 'Can you still play? We really need you out there.' So Prentice taped it pointing forward again, and I checked back in the game."

Dorrance flunked one college class. It was an Intellectual History course taught by Dr. John Headley. On the first day of class in the fall of 1971, Dr. Headley announced that grades would be docked incrementally by absences. No excuses would be accepted, not even the athletic absences that were approved by almost every other UNC professor. In the midst of the Tar Heel soccer season, Dorrance understood instantly that he would miss too many classes during road trips to pass the course under Headley's strict standards. But Dorrance continued to attend the class anyway, as often as he could, because he enjoyed the lectures, never bothering to explain to Headley why he'd missed so many sessions. Despite Dorrance's solid performance on the exams and other assignments, Headley gave him an F.

When Dorrance saw that F on his transcript, he wasn't disappointed. He was inspired. More important than anything else he had learned in the class, Headley's decision would become a huge piece of Dorrance's intellectual history. Dorrance learned a lesson about setting a standard that he would respect for the rest of his life.

"Someone has to draw a line that is incontrovertible, unimpeachable, and then once you earn the right to stand on that platform, you can see the greater possibilities," Dorrance says. "Evil is anything that imperceptibly lowers our standards just a hair."

It's why UNC women's soccer seasons have always begun with the Cooper test. Players are required to run seven and a quarter laps around the Fetzer Field track in twelve minutes. As introductions go, it is not a particularly friendly one. "On my first day I remember thinking Anson would welcome us or at least talk to us about what to expect," Julie Carter says. "Instead we warmed up, walked to the starting line, and then Anson said, 'Ladies, this is a test of your mentality. Go!' We took off running, and then it is all psychological, all about overcoming the overwhelming desire to stop."

Johanna Costa lost control of her bowels during the Cooper one year and kept running anyway for two more laps. Louellen Poore ran stride-for-stride with freshman Lori Walker for nearly seven laps, barking at her like a drill sergeant to keep running as Walker cussed back. Aubrey Falk once ran ten yards of the Cooper, sprained her ankle on the track's inside rail, and missed three weeks of preseason. There are still some conspiracy theorists who suspect that Falk maimed herself intentionally. Moments after winning the 1983 national championship, Susan Ellis was asked what she was thinking about and she said, "Running the Cooper next August." It got so bad that Carter composed a song about the run called "The Cooper Blues":

> I made it to a mile, boy I'm on my way
> Now I'm over pace, oh these mind games Anson plays
> On Lap 6, Sanchez passed me by (again)
> I feel so bad, I just wanna lay down and die
> Number 7 has come and I hear the countdown
> 5, 4, 3, 2, 1, and I just can't be found
> (I'm in the bushes throwing up)
> Well, I got the Cooper Blues
> Relieve my pain and throw me a bottle of booze

Putting her own spin on *The Cooper Blues*, Donna Rigley prepared for the Cooper one year by drinking a 32-ounce beer. When Dorrance asked her why, she said, "Because when I get drunk and I run home at night, I feel like I'm flying." Rigley ran eight laps, one of the best Cooper performances in UNC history.

In the early days of the program, those who didn't pass the Cooper were sentenced to run five miles a day for a week as well as jogging the mile-long hill between campus and the UNC practice fields during two-a-day preseason practices. When it was discovered that some players asked their roommates to meet them with mopeds at secluded locations near the bottom of the hill, Dorrance knew he needed to devise a new plan. When only two players passed the Cooper and then UNC lost its 1983 season opener against Connecticut, Dorrance told the unfit players they had to lose two pounds a week or run extra fitness after practice. The players jokingly dubbed themselves the "Chub Club," started visiting the sauna before weekly weigh-ins, and became so dehydrated they could barely stand up during practice. Finally, Dorrance instituted the "Breakfast Club," a gaggle of the sleep-deprived who meet at seven o'clock each weekday morning to re-run the Cooper until they can conquer it. Lori Walker failed to pass the Cooper a record twenty-nine times one season before she was finally pardoned. Whenever Palladino chaperones the club, he likes to punctuate a workout with a box of Krispy Kreme donuts, or what he likes to call the "Breakfast of Champions." Alas, the ultimate punishment of the Breakfast Club is for those who have 8 a.m. classes, because they don't have time to shower before class and must attend in a full sweat.

During the preseason, Dorrance also demands that his women pass ten timed 120-yard sprints and a brutal shuttle run, which is exactly the same fitness standard he once asked of his men, and has come as a physical shock to many of his incoming freshmen. "I thought I was fit, but my first day of preseason I realized that I didn't even know what fitness was," Siri Mullinix says. "I ran one 120 and I panicked. I started hyperventilating, breathing into a brown paper bag, trying to get some color back into my face."

Wendy Gebauer and Tracey Bates lost ten pounds each during their first pre-season, and Gebauer took to calling Bates "Honeybun," because she would regularly empty the dorm vending machine of those treats to try to maintain her weight.

The fitness standard for UNC women's soccer is based on the advice NBA Hall of Famer John Havlicek once received from a doctor. Havlicek, an asthmatic, was told not to worry about overtraining because "you'll pass out before you die." Dorrance is only half-joking when he tells his players they must reach his fitness standards or pass out trying. The team runs fitness once a week during the season, a day affectionately known as "Terrible Tuesday," such a despised day that when Vanessa Rubio blew out her knee during her senior season her first reaction was, "At least I never have to do fitness again." Palladino often greets the players on Tuesdays by saying, "OK, what is fitness?" The players mockingly reply, "Fitness is our friend." Then the grind begins. It became almost routine for Bettina Bernardi to finish a Tuesday sprint and wander off for a moment to vomit, and then return just in time to run again. "I was scared of doing fitness until my junior year," Mia Hamm says. "Even for the fittest player, it sucks at times. One of the main reasons you do it is for the psychological uncertainty you must fight through. Sometimes playing in team sports you can become dependent on others, but fitness is just about your own mentality. It's a personal test, and everyone learns how to conquer it in their own way."

Says Helen Lawler: "Anson always told us that we'd pass out before we die, but in the middle of that eighth 120, I wasn't sure if I believed him. I dreaded every Tuesday for four years. I couldn't sleep the night before, or eat that day, and I felt like I was entering the Gates of Hell as we lined up on the starting line, but the accomplishment in pushing my body to its physical limit and succeeding was indescribable."

The team's mantra on fitness days is *No Fucking Babies*. "Fitness helps us physically, but I think Anson liked to really mess with us mentally to pick out who were the weaklings," Tiffany Roberts says. "We're on this line together as a team. The power in the individual comes in the belief that if we all need to do something then I'm not going to be the one who lets us down. It was the perfect credo for our program. It was like saying, 'I'll pick you up, but you better prove that you can pick yourself up first.'"

After famously admonishing rookie Anne Remy to "Help yourself, bitch!," Roberts eventually helped pull Remy across the finish line that day. Dorrance sometimes pairs his fittest with his least fit, and the strongest players routinely grab the weakest links by the jerseys and literally drag them through fitness, until it becomes less about doing it for themselves and more about doing it for each other. "Let's face it, in most youth cultures it's cool to be lazy, cool to rebel, but we have created a culture at North Carolina where it's not cool to be unfit," Dorrance says. "Our seniors are convinced that if the underclassmen don't get fit that they're going to lose a championship because the frigging lazy slackers didn't buy into the program. So there is no honor in cutting corners at UNC."

Dorrance expects his players to train harder in the off-season than any other team because of the impending Cooper as soon as they arrive back on campus each summer. On the final night of a team trip to England in August of 2003, UNC players scattered for various forms of revelry. Many didn't sleep at all, but at 6:30 the next morning the entire team still gathered for a voluntary fitness session. The Tar Heels ran 120s on a cement-hard field pocked with potholes in preparation for the fitness testing two days later in Chapel Hill. "We all ran them, cursing on the sprint down and cursing more on the jog back," Jordan Walker says. "Then we collapsed on the field together, puking, crying, and dehydrated. But no one quit."

Dorrance believes that anyone who thinks talent is the only factor in winning is missing a critical element to his success. "No matter how talented a player is, with every 120 or every 50-50 ball in a game there's a raging debate going on inside her," Dorrance says. "There's a devil on one shoulder saying, 'This hurts! Quit! *Quit!*' The angel on the other shoulder is saying, 'Keep going. Don't bail!' You need players who only listen to the angel. Find a core of people who just refuse to quit, and then surround them with these talented dancers and magicians, and then you've got a team that can win championships."

10 | *Pushing Buttons*

Wit is a sword; it is meant to make people feel the point as well as see it.

—G.K. Chesterton

Watching us practice the last few days is like watching soccer underwater. Most of you guys are just standing there with your frigging thumbs up your nostrils, and I swear if you played any slower you'd be moving backwards in time. That's got to change tonight or we're in trouble, because Wake Forest can play. Right now what I'm seeing from us are isolated pockets of effort and a lot of you bailing out. If someone is cringing on a 50-50 ball, call her out on it. And when someone does something absolutely courageous, they should hear from everyone then as well. Does this make sense? At the core of every successful team that plays a contact sport is fight. Not one player fighting. All eleven that fight. You understand what I'm saying? What has set our team apart since 1979 when we started playing this game is that we outfight everybody for ninety minutes. We have built a tradition out of beating these teams that don't make the same physical investment that we do. Now guess what? I'm watching us lately and we're exactly like every-frigging-body else. Nothing separates us. We are incredibly soft. It's like, 'I'm not going to take a physical risk now, I've got the cotillion this weekend. I don't want to mess up my pretty face.' I gave a speech to all the UNC freshman athletes the other night, and this debate broke out about what's a game and what's a sport. I told them that I think sports are environments where you take physical risks, where you can get hurt, where someone can come after you. My first semester of college at St. Mary's in San Antonio, Texas, I thought about playing on the tennis team until it dawned on me why I could never play tennis. Some country club fairy across the net could beat me because I couldn't bring to bear what I think is critical about sports, which is going after it physically. I hated that I couldn't run around the net and cut the jackass in half. And what I admire about you guys when you play your best is that those are the sorts of risks you take. You get to demonstrate your courage tonight. Can you show everyone that you care so much about this team that you will take a risk to make shit happen? I can handle a loss, but what I can't handle are people who don't try, people who play without passion, who play without caring, who play without risk. That tells me something about their character that I don't like. What I'm talking about is not something that you're born with, it's not a talent that you're given by God. It's a choice you get to make about who the fuck you are. That's how the great ones are remembered until the end of recorded time. It's a statement about their

humanity that is unique. Do you know what I'm trying to say? . . . Are you guys
ready? . . . All right, let's demonstrate to them who the fuck we are. Are you with
me? . . .

It was Winston Churchill, of course. Who else would Anson Dorrance pick?
Who else would a devout anglophile bred in the colonial British school system in
the aftermath of World War II select as his motivational mentor? Dorrance read
every biography he could find about Britain's legendary Prime Minister, and as a
teenager he even listened to Churchill's speeches over and over on crackling au-
diotapes, held rapt by the raw power of the words. The more Dorrance listened,
the more he noticed the rhythm, the cadence, the tone, and he realized that it
was from these things that so much of the strength emanated. The *force.* Dorrance
would memorize Churchill speeches and recite them in an affected British accent to his friends and family, often against their will.

Dorrance's favorite speech is one that Churchill delivered on June 18, 1940,
before the Battle of Britain. He appreciates it because of the remarkably dire
circumstances under which it was given, with the Allies losing on all fronts and a
German invasion of England imminent. With little left but hope, Churchill
searched for the right words to buoy his troops and his people. *Let us therefore*
brace ourselves to our duty, and so bear ourselves, that if the British Empire and
its Commonwealth last for a thousand years, men will still say, "This was their
finest hour."

When Dorrance repeats those words years later, he admits that they give him
the same goose bumps he experienced when he first heard them on tape. Dorrance
adores that quote because it was not only powerful and eloquent, but wonderfully prophetic. "I think Churchill is the greatest leader of all time," Dorrance
says. "Nothing except the strength of his own personality could save Western
Civilization. Churchill was talking about freedom, about good and evil, and there
was no reason for hope except the will and the inspirational voice of one man.
When you're searching for people to be inspired by, who do you choose? You
choose someone who represents everything that's meaningful for you."

Listening to Churchill, Dorrance realized that while sometimes it was the
gradual crescendo of his speeches that packed the power, other times it just required one phrase, a simple captivating moment. He realized that it doesn't necessarily require a lot of time to say something of value.

Some of Dorrance's most efficient speeches have been among his most effective. At halftime of the 2000 national championship game against UCLA, the Tar
Heels trailed 1–0 after a botched play in their defensive box cost them a goal.
Dorrance walked into the locker room, sipped a cup of water, and said, "I know
we're going to win this game, because that's the worst we've played all year long and
we're only down one goal." That was all he said. The Tar Heels rallied to win 2–1.

Preparing his team for overtime in a 1999 game against Notre Dame, Dorrance
addressed his team's tentative play. "Look guys, there's no reason to play scared,"
he said. "If you don't play well and we lose, it's not like your parents are going to

be taken out in the woods and shot after the game." The Tar Heels laughed and relaxed and won the game.

In times of high tension as a UNC player, Dorrance had always been impressed by the coaching demeanor of Marvin Allen. He respected the way Allen could make his point without ever browbeating his players. Dorrance reminds himself of that whenever he is tempted to morph back into the alpha male who once delivered the infamous Great Santini speech that infused his women with nothing but the Gift of Worry. He has learned over the years to coach with calm, because that communicates confidence and eliminates any anxiety in his players about potentially being berated. "I'm not aware of any time when he's yelled at his players," Tracy Noonan says. "Not a single moment. Never in anyone's face. Even when we played like absolute crap and deserved to get yelled at, we'd never see him stressed, and I always wondered, 'How does he do it?'"

The only time Dorrance will ever express displeasure with his team during a game is when the Tar Heels are leading but still underachieving in his eyes. He will tell them that they are too casual, too sloppy, too unplugged, but as he castigates them it is never designed to obliterate, only to construct. Whenever the Tar Heels are behind at the half, Dorrance greets them with an upbeat attitude. "He'd just sit quietly and tell us, 'We're fine,'" Mia Hamm says. "It is crap. It's not the truth. But as a player, when you're expecting a coach to come in mad and he does the opposite, that makes you feel better. You think, 'Maybe we are all right.'"

After a miserable opening half in a game at Duke in 1999, UNC trailed 2–0 when Dorrance led his team out to the center circle and issued a matter-of-fact statement: "Forty-five minutes is plenty of time. We're going to go out and keep working, and we're going to score three goals, and we're going to beat them."

"Just when I thought it was hopeless, it was like Anson had seen the future, like he was telling us how a book ends," Tom Sander says. "He said it so calmly and so confidently that I remember thinking, 'We *are* going to win this thing.' It was the biggest mental 180 I've ever done. Sure enough, we scored two goals in the first few minutes, and then later we scored on a free kick to win the game. It was eerie. Afterward I thought, 'Gosh, did we win that game because of the way Anson said we would or would that have happened anyway?' To this day I don't know if he believed it, but he made us believe it."

Dorrance emphasizes his points not through raising his voice, but with a strategically employed curse. "Anson's swearing let us know how passionate he was," Shannon Higgins says. "It adds drama and power and urgency to a speech, and he knows it can be inspiring. That's one way he humanizes himself with his players. It let us know that he's right there with us."

Dorrance says he employs an occasional curse as an exclamation point for his thoughts. During a game against Wake Forest in 2000, Dorrance stood before his team and implored them to play more recklessly in the air. *Stick your head in there so they're leaving their fucking teeth in the back of your skull, and then look at the girl and say, "How does that feel, bitch?"* Perhaps taking the speech a bit too literally, UNC's Maggie Tomecka subsequently jumped for a header and actually felt two of Demon Deacon midfielder Katherine Winstead's teeth lodge in her scalp.

One of Dorrance's motivational masterpieces occurred at halftime of a game on September 20, 2002, against Marquette. Less than four minutes into the match, UNC lost its best defender, center back Catherine Reddick, when she tackled a Marquette striker from behind in the penalty box and got whistled for a red card, all while UNC right back Leslie Gaston was bent over tying her shoelace. The ensuing penalty kick put UNC behind 1–0, and for the rest of the opening half, the Tar Heels played on the verge of panic.

As the UNC players moved to one end of the field and sat down in a circle for the halftime talk, there was a sense of dead women walking. Dorrance began his halftime discussion with his favorite questions. *What do you guys think? Are we still in this? Who's the better team?* There were nods and a few meek voices supplying the appropriate responses. Dorrance then began discussing tactics, formation adjustments to show how UNC might best attack Marquette despite being a player down. Dorrance then threw the talk to Palladino for his strategic input as the head coach composed what would be the true message of the intermission. When Palladino finished his remarks, Dorrance asked his girls to stand up and gather around him in a tight circle so that nobody off the field could hear what he was about to say. *In all my years here, we've never been in this spot before, down a goal and down a player, and to tell you the truth I am intrigued. I'm curious. This is your chance to write history. I'm excited to see what's going to happen. We can win this because we are the fucking University of North Carolina. Let's stick one early and stun them, and then let's break them. You know what I mean? This is a great opportunity. All of you have a chance to write history. Are you with me?*

The Tar Heels came out rejuvenated and scored four goals in a devastating twenty-six-minute span for the final margin of 4–1. UNC had followed up its worst half of the season with its best. After the game Dorrance gathered his team around him again. *I am an old man and I've been coaching a long time and that was one of the greatest comeback victories I've ever seen. You did exactly what we talked about at halftime. You bent them and then you broke them. You'll remember this for the rest of your fucking lives.*

Anson Dorrance is a reb. It's the Louisburg in him, the Southern blood. Somewhere in the theater of his mind, he is a Confederate soldier, and he will tell you that he is still fighting the Civil War. His Confederateness is not about those ideals, which he knows are indefensible. It's about the pride, the guts of the severely outnumbered rebel troops, that he so admires. He believes there have never been more noble military victories than those won by the underdog Confederate soldiers in the War Between the States.

Dorrance loves nothing more than competing from the perspective of the underdog. He understands the power of that position because it is what he felt growing up, and he'll try his damnedest to maneuver his UNC teams there. From a motivational standpoint, his favorite Tar Heel national championship occurred in 2000, because that year's team lost three regular-season games and received its lowest NCAA Tournament seeding ever. Throughout the NCAAs he got to use his beloved rallying cry: *They think we suck!*

"Those speeches were so simple," Dorrance says. "*They think we suck!* Is there a better motivation than that? It's fabulous. It's simple. It's visceral. In soccer, it's worth a goal or two a game. As the UNC coach I know that they don't really think we suck, but whether or not they think we really suck, it's guaranteed to stir our players into a froth."

Dorrance wonders why opposing coaches haven't been using this strategy against him for years. Instead they're usually providing Dorrance with ammunition. What other coaches say to the press to inspire their own team winds up motivating the Tar Heels. The man who adores quotes so much has rarely coached a game when the opposition has not provided him with some fodder. UNC doesn't actually need a bulletin board because Dorrance *is* the bulletin board. After digging up a quote from a Santa Clara player about UNC's vulnerability, Dorrance walked into the team meeting room before a game against the Broncos and drew upon his days as an actor at the Villa Saint-Jean. In a performance inspired by Robert De Niro's character in *Taxi Driver*, Dorrance turned to his players with fire in his eyes, read the offending quote, and then said, "*Are you coming after me? Are you fucking coming after me? Well, fuck that. I'm coming after you!*"

Most of the time he sticks to a more tranquil yet still goading recitation of a demeaning quote. Before the 2002 ACC Tournament he read a quote from then Florida State coach Patrick Baker, who said, "We don't fear anybody in the ACC. We all used to be fearful of Carolina, but now I don't think anybody is going to say, 'Oh my God, we have to play the Tar Heels,' because for the most part everyone has played them very well this year. I think this will be the most competitive and exciting ACC Tournament that we have ever had." The Tar Heel players bristled at the words and subsequently outscored their three conference opponents 13–0.

Over the years some opposing coaches have become smarter about inflammatory quotes, which has forced Dorrance to become more creative. "Sometimes he'll hold up a newspaper and say, 'You should see what it says in here about you guys,'" Sander says. "Then he'll spew out some quote, but if you look closely, you'll find that there's nothing in that paper about UNC soccer." If Dorrance doesn't create quotes altogether he will often sensationalize the propaganda for a more insulting effect.

Meanwhile, through studying Dean Smith's rhetoric, Dorrance has learned how to sandbag his opponents masterfully, trumpeting all of their strengths to the media while lamenting his own team's multiple failings. Dorrance relishes the opportunity to play these mind games; it's just that he doesn't enjoy that much press. Dorrance is careful that neither he nor his team inspires an opponent through senseless bravado, and he has occasionally needed to censor one of his players when he didn't approve of her word choice.

Dorrance dismisses all postmodern motivational gimmicks. He mocked UCLA for wearing blue T-shirts with the word *Believe* etched on them before the 2003 NCAA semifinal against the Tar Heels. And it did not go unnoticed by the UNC coaching staff when Santa Clara coach Jerry Smith showed up at consecutive Final Fours in 2001 and 2002 sporting bleached-blond hair and a mohawk, respectively, coiffures that he had offered up as a potential reward for his players to reach that stage.

Dorrance would rather inspire passion through language. He will often close his pregame remarks with some poignant words from a leader like Alabama football coach Bear Bryant or Antarctic explorer Ernest Shackleton. Whenever possible he will read a letter, note, or poem written by somebody connected to the program that unites the players behind a cause. Before the 1989 ACC Tournament final against rival N.C. State, Dorrance read a poem written the previous evening by UNC's student manager Kevin Markle:

> There are times in our lives that the world lets us show
> The things of ourselves that now only we know.
> Of course people say, "They're so fast!," "They're so strong!,"
> But in thinking that's us, they're totally wrong.
> Sure, the skill and the strength are keys to our fate,
> But they're not the main things that make this team great.
> No, those on the outside can't see why we win
> Because they cannot see what we all have within.

According to Dorrance, there is no surefire formula for motivation. He will try anything if he thinks it can be connective. "Being inspirational is never a given," Dorrance says. "Just because the game is big doesn't deliver it, and just because the game isn't big doesn't mean it can't be delivered. Motivation is not a skill; it's an art form. It's about pushing buttons. It's an interplay between the coach and players, and its power is related to a personal connection. It can lift a team, but not as significantly as your year-round fitness preparation or commitment to mentality. It's a tiny percentage, but sometimes the margin of victory can be unbelievably narrow, so any impact might be the difference."

Dorrance is convinced that his players must ultimately be motivated by playing for each other so that they are passionate for every game. He knows he can't whip them into a frenzy for two dozen games each season because there is only so much juice to tap. He tries to build gradually toward an operatic inspirational climax at the Final Four when he dismisses his seniors from the locker room and reads the letters he has written to them. UNC senior associate athletic director Beth Miller recalls her astonishment the first time she attended an NCAA final and noticed the Tar Heel players emerging from their dressing room in tears before the game. "I thought, 'My God, what in the world did Anson say to them to get them so upset?'" Miller says. "I'd seen players cry after a loss, but never walking out onto the field for warmups."

Says Jena Kluegel: "Whenever he started reading the senior letters, I started bawling. I'm not a very emotional person, and I'm crying my eyes out and thinking, 'What is going on here?' But I was always really moved by the things he said."

The senior letters have become so popular that many of UNC's alums have asked to join the team in the locker room to listen to the readings. In 1994 Roz Santana was the first of many UNC seniors who left a tape recorder behind in the room so that she might later hear her letter read. "Those letters are one of Anson's greatest gifts to us," Cindy Parlow says. "I love going back and listening to him read them. There are times when you think he doesn't notice the little things, and when you hear those speeches you realize, 'Holy crap, he *saw* that!' That rallies the team together. It's during those moments that he makes you feel that everything is possible."

Mia Hamm was nervous. She was sweating profusely in Dorrance's office, sitting across the desk from her coach. It was Hamm's first goal-setting meeting of her sophomore year, and she felt woefully unprepared. She'd been through these things before, and she knew what the critical question would be, but she had yet to figure out the right answer. Stalling for time, she spoke first, and her coach nodded a few times and waited patiently for Hamm to take a breath. Then he leaned over the desk, stared her down with his piercing blue eyes, and asked what he always asks, "Mia, what do you want?"

Hamm had a million things swirling through her mind, but she didn't want to give him a dumb answer. "Ummmmm, to be a good soccer player?"

"Can you be a little more specific than that?"

Hamm cautiously threw out some numbers about the goals and assists she'd like to accumulate that season and then immediately began questioning herself, "Are those too high? . . . Too low?"

"But what do you really want?"

Hamm was dumbstruck. She couldn't think of anything to say. Suddenly, instinct took over and she blurted out, "To be the best." It sounded as much like a question as a statement, but Hamm still couldn't believe what she had just said. The words sounded crazy to her, but the more she thought about them, the more she realized that they were sincere. She sat in her chair, silently waiting for her coach to tell her to be serious.

"Do you know what the best is?"

Once again Hamm sat there clueless, perspiring and praying that the question was rhetorical.

Finally, Dorrance stood up and walked around the desk behind Hamm. He flipped the light switch off. The two sat in darkness for a moment. Then Dorrance flipped the lights back on. "It's just a decision, a light-switch decision," the coach said. "That's all it takes, but you have to make that decision every single day. You can't make it today and then say, 'Whew, glad that's over.' You have to make it tomorrow and the next day and the day after that for the rest of your career."

"I guess deep down I wanted to be great, but I had no idea what that really meant when I first said it in the meeting," Hamm says now. "On that day being the best became something tangible, no longer abstract. It would require a huge commitment made up of a series of smaller efforts. The most important thing was that when I walked out of his office I didn't feel like Anson had set my goals for me. I did it."

Dorrance wrote the goal down that day in Hamm's file. *Be the best.* He records all the goals. He believes that a critical element of his environment is for his players to determine specific goals. He conducts three player conferences each year: during the first month of the soccer season, shortly after the season, and at the end of the spring semester. He breaks each player down into her pros and cons, and then he pulls out her file, and they compare how she's done both athletically and academically to what she said she wanted to do the last time they met. Then they consider what she hopes to do in the immediate future and how Dorrance can help her reach those goals. Beginning with the very first player conference he also insists on determining a career goal, even though most of his players have no clue at the time. He won't ask, "What do you want to be?" Instead he asks, "What are your dreams?"

These goal-setting meetings are Dorrance's best opportunity to motivate his players on an individual basis. He is blunt. Realistic. He won't allow them to fake it. Any player who says she aspires to play soccer professionally must also choose a backup career just in case. "A player conference is about sitting a player down and challenging her to be extraordinary and then giving her hope to achieve it," Dorrance says. "My job is to explain to a kid what she's capable of, and then all I can do is ask, 'Do you want to go there?' If you play at UNC, you can't tell me that you have no ambition. You knew coming in that you were going to have to try hard. A part of every player wants to affiliate with that."

Still, each player must be handled differently. Early in her career, Dorrance saw defender Carmen Watley as the type of athlete who'd invent injuries as excuses not to train. He teased her incessantly about bent hair follicles, sarcoid problems, sleep deprivation issues, but the ribbing seemed to have no impact. Watley insisted she had a lung ailment that would prevent her from ever playing more than fifteen minutes at a time. Dorrance told Watley that her doctors underestimated the human spirit. "Carmen, let's go to the future," Dorrance said in one player conference. "You have just finished college. You have said you want to be a pharmaceutical salesperson. It's 5:30 in the morning and you're alone in some hotel room and you're getting up to drive to Wilmington to sell your drugs. Catherine Reddick is sleeping in some fancy hotel somewhere, and her alarm is set for 10:30 a.m. She's going to get up and have a leisurely breakfast in preparation for a national team game. At breakfast she decides whether to go to the mall that day or have her nails done, and by this time you have already been thrown out of your fifth doctor's office because he doesn't want any drugs from you. All of this because she ran her 120s and she didn't beg out of practice."

Dorrance believes that it was about that time when Watley made her own light-switch decision to step out of her comfort zone and be extraordinary. In her senior year Watley earned All-America honors, played ninety minutes in all but two games, and looked insulted whenever Dorrance subbed her out.

As a rule, Dorrance doesn't believe in comparing players to predecessors, but sometimes in his player conferences he will use the past to motivate and measure progress. During his very first player conference with Lori Chalupny in 2002, he pulled a UNC media guide off his shelf and turned to the page that details the feats of Tisha Venturini.

"Shall we dream a little?" Dorrance said.

"OK," Chalupny said.

"This is Tisha Venturini, the greatest scoring midfielder in our history; let's look at her numbers and let's beat her numbers in your four years. What do you think?"

"OK."

So Dorrance grabbed a pencil and divided Venturini's career goals and assists totals by four. He then scribbled the numbers down on a piece of paper and said, "Here's what you need to do each year."

"OK."

"You're pretty low-maintenance, huh?"

"Yup."

Four seasons later, in Dorrance's estimation, Chalupny joined Venturini among the five best players in the history of the UNC program.

Over the years, Dorrance has also learned that not every player is poised to switch on the light. When Nel Fettig arrived at UNC as a freshman, Dorrance quickly realized that she was twice the player he thought he had recruited. He couldn't wait to have his first player conference with her because he wanted to tell her how he believed she could play on the national team someday. On his legal pad, Dorrance began mapping out a future national team lineup with Fettig in it, when he began to sense her discomfort. He assumed Fettig was just intimidated by him, as so many freshmen are. In the next player conference, he told Fettig what a great debut season she'd had, and again she began fidgeting, looking around with her arms folded over her chest. Then all of a sudden in the spring conference, Fettig interrupted Dorrance and said, "Anson, did you know I was a nationally ranked tennis player as a kid, and do you know why I don't play tennis anymore?"

Bells started to go off for Dorrance. He knew exactly what Fettig was going to say.

"I don't play tennis anymore because my mother and my father and my coach were always telling me how great I could be if only I did this or that. You know why I play soccer?"

Dorrance knew, but he shook his head.

"I play soccer for fun."

Dorrance scribbled down Fettig's new goal as *Enjoy life!*, and for the remainder of that player conference and every other one for the rest of her UNC career, Fettig and Dorrance would spend a half hour chatting about what was on sale at the mall or her family's summer vacation plans, anything but soccer, and Fettig became a three-time All-American.

Outside of his goal-setting meetings, Dorrance has a cornucopia of tactics to push individual players. One day in practice Bettina Bernardi and two other reserves were playing a 3 v. 3 game against three starters, April Heinrichs, Shannon Higgins, and Lori Henry. "Anson's laying odds on how badly we're going to get beat," Bernardi says. "We're like, 'Oh yeah. Screw you!' He lit a fire under us and we ended up winning just to spite him. That happened a lot."

"I remember one practice when Anson called us all in and said, 'Some of you aren't giving 100 percent,'" Emily Pickering says. "He purposely didn't point out specific players, so at first I looked around at all the usual slackers, but then I thought, 'Maybe I could be giving more? Maybe I've got another 10 percent?' He knew exactly how to get more effort out of each of us."

During the 2001 NCAA semifinal game against Portland, Dorrance was looking to sub in a reserve. Says Dorrance, "I started talking to Dino about putting Anne Felts in, and then I see Elizabeth Ball listening to me, and I see her head drop a bit and I think what's going through her mind is, 'Oh my god, I played so badly in the first half that he's not going to play me in the second half.' Now I've got her. I walked over to her and I said, 'E.B. I think you can play better. I'm going to put you in. You're one of the best players on our roster.'" Ball scored what proved to be the game-winning goal just eighteen seconds after she entered the game.

For each player, it is about finding the right button to push. Dorrance thought Jena Kluegel played with too much tension, proved it to her with photographs of her agonized facial expressions during games, and challenged her to relax on the field. He tweaked Lorrie Fair simply by referring to her by her detested middle name, Ming. He identified Heather O'Reilly as a dreamer and motivated her with vision, concluding an April 2002 letter right after she signed to come to UNC with the words, *Now go about the business of becoming the best you can be and remember the sky is the limit for you . . . yes, all of us think you can be one of the best we have ever seen.* He saw Stephanie Zeh as a fighter and motivated her with fiction, preceding the 1981 AIAW tournament semifinal by walking up to the tempestuous Zeh and telling her that he'd heard that Connecticut had concocted a scheme to try to rattle her into a red card. Jacked up by the information, Zeh scored three goals in the game, yapping at the Huskies after each one about how they would never get under her skin. The Connecticut players had absolutely no idea what Zeh was ranting about and thought she was a lunatic. It turned out Dorrance had made the whole thing up.

"Anson could sit you down and tell you that you were going to walk on water, and you firmly believed you could walk on water," Venturini says. "I remember one night the team went to a barbecue at Anson's house, and my boyfriend joined me. We were having dessert; and Anson stood up and said a few words about teamwork and his love of the game. My boyfriend leaned over to me and whispered, 'Oh my god, I feel like playing right now. I'm fired up.' Anson can inspire anyone."

During cocktail parties at the Dorrance compound in Addis Ababa, Big Pete indulged in a regular ceremony when introducing his eldest son to his guests. He ushered Anson into the room and cleared his throat for a formal announcement. *I'd like to congratulate my son publicly for winning an academic award at St. Joseph's School. He won the English Award and we're very proud. He accepted the award at the royal palace from Emperor Haile Selassie . . . oh, did I fail to mention, he's the only English-speaking person in the school?*

The room typically erupted with laughter. Big Pete cracked his devilish grin. Anson bowed dramatically. He was never embarrassed. Anson knew that Big Pete was not disparaging the English award so much as subtly pushing his son to win the Math Award.

You can hear Big Pete's sarcasm every day on the soccer field at the University of North Carolina, such as when Anson walks up to a confused reserve goalkeeper during a training drill and asks, "What the hell are you doing?"

"I don't know."

"Aren't you at all curious as to what everybody else is doing?"

A misplayed ball will elicit a comment from Dorrance like "Touch of a billygoat!" or "Replace your divot!" A weak shot will bring "She hit it with her purse!" A spectacular fall will prompt "Yard Sale!" When a player is too stationary he'll refer to her as a "cone," comparing her to the orange pylons placed on the field as directional markers. When a drill is being performed too languidly for his taste he'll start chanting, "Monday, Tuesday, Wednesday," suggesting the turning of calendar pages. When his players aren't training hard enough he accuses them of playing "Grabass."

When one of the Tar Heels makes a clumsy play in a game, Dorrance bellows, "Hey, don't forget, it's left, right, left, right," or "Ask Susie if she wants to put on one of their uniforms?" or "Hey, we're wearing the blue jerseys!" or his personal favorite, "It's lucky they don't let me carry a loaded weapon on the sideline, because I would have shot you by now."

Says Jena Kluegel, "In my first game as a freshman Anson called me over to the bench and said, 'Jena, tell Borgman to head the ball in the direction that she's facing.' I said, 'OK,' and then I ran back on the field and thought, 'I'm not going to tell her *that!*'" Kluegel then turned back toward the UNC bench and saw the entire UNC coaching staff in hysterics.

During Shannon Higgins's first game she recalls Dorrance making sarcastic remarks every time she cut the ball inside from her flank midfield position. Eventually Higgins, who is partially deaf, began pretending that she couldn't hear Dorrance. So he started teasing her in sign language.

During practices and games, Dorrance often doesn't so much speak as communicate through a series of proclamations. "Anson's not a yeller because he's so smart he knows that he doesn't have to yell to make you feel an inch tall," Jordan Walker says. "I remember my first game as a freshman I was petrified, standing like a statue in one spot on the field, and balls were bouncing off my shins. Finally, Anson told me, 'Jordan, we're going to need you to be involved either offensively or defensively. Preferably both, but at least one.'"

Says Dorrance: "Some people use sarcasm as a weapon. I use it as editorial. I use it to have my players self-reflect."

Dorrance tends to dig at the players he feels are the most resilient. It is designed to deconstruct, not to demoralize. "Anson busts on them to fire them up to go to the next level," Palladino says. "I like to describe the humor as felt-tipped darts. It hits you and bounces off. The remarks are not really searing, but they get the point across."

During a 2002 game against Stanford, a frustrated Dorrance barked at Alyssa Ramsey, "Pass it to the other team, maybe you'll hit one of us." The next time Ramsey touched the ball she scored the winning goal in UNC's 1–0 upset of the No. 1–ranked Cardinal. A minute after subbing Brynn Hardman into a game against Florida International in 2002, Dorrance bellowed from the bench, "Brynn, are you on drugs?" The entire crowd hushed. Hardman looked mortified. A few seconds later, she scored the first goal of her career.

While this notion will provide little comfort to them, what the players on the field can hear isn't nearly as bad as what they cannot. The UNC sideline during a game is much like a celebrity roast, with Dorrance and Palladino maintaining their own expletive-laden color commentary. While the coaching staff is venting, most of the bench players congregate as far away from them as possible. Says Dorrance: "One year a reserve came up to me and said, 'Anson, I've been listening to what you say about the starters out there. I'm a reserve. What happens when I go out there?' I told her, 'Well, of course, it's worse. You're a frigging reserve. You're not as good as they are.' It was horrifying for her."

Dorrance also finds time for some positive reinforcement. He often asks his players to applaud themselves after a crisply performed training drill. As Dean Smith once did, Dorrance will use media interviews to compliment specific players who displayed the qualities that reporters tend to overlook, and he will individually tell a player what she does that is extraordinary as a means of constructing her. Says Kristine Lilly: "Anson constantly reminded me of what I did best, which was great for my confidence."

Bernardi recalls one game in which the Tar Heels were struggling against George Mason until she came off the bench and produced a goal and an assist. Late in the game, UNC earned a free kick, and Dorrance called April Heinrichs off the ball and told Bernardi to take it. "The next day in study hall Anson came up to me and said, 'I wanted you to take that kick because you were playing great and I was proud of you,'" Bernardi recalls. "Anson does that to players. He always makes sure to tell them when he thinks they've played well."

Then there are those times when it's hard to distinguish between Dorrance's sarcasm and praise. Stacey Blazo says the most curiously gratifying moment of her career occurred during her first start, when she dribbled up the sideline in front of the Tar Heel bench and heard Dorrance say, "That fucking cone can play!" During a practice in 2003, Dorrance sat down on the field with his strikers in a circle around him and told them an instructive story about former Tar Heel forward Carrie Serwetnyk. *I coached Carrie in the '80s, and if there were four runs to make, I swear Carrie would always pick the dumbest one. I couldn't wait for her to graduate, but then two months into the next season, I realized that Carrie did one thing well. She ran! If you're running, the defense doesn't know that you're an idiot who has no idea where you're going, so they're likely to chase you. That's what makes us so dangerous, and without Carrie our offense lost all its personality. So if there's a time when you don't know what to do, think of Carrie Serwetnyk and just keep running like your hair's on fire.* As in so many of his stories, Dorrance somehow snatched dignity from the jaws of defamation.

Dorrance used to zing reserve goalkeeper Kristin DePlatchett mercilessly for what he called her "chicken dance" whenever she was indecisive about charging a ball. DePlatchett found Dorrance's sarcasm so amusing that during the 2000 soccer season she compiled a thirteen-page pamphlet of his most creative commentary and titled it *The Journal.* DePlatchett has shared the document with players from other generations like Rayfield and Hamm, who relished it because much of what Dorrance says hasn't changed in twenty years. "One of the most important things I will take from my experience as a Tar Heel soccer player is that you should never take yourself too seriously," DePlatchett says. "At first I used to hate being picked on, but eventually we all had a great time laughing at ourselves when we made mistakes, and we were our greatest source of entertainment. The coaches helped us realize this."

The name that appears most often in *The Journal* is Danielle Borgman. Borgman once made the mistake of telling Dorrance that her grandmother offered her fifty dollars for every goal she scored during a high school tournament. So when Borgman missed a shot in a UNC practice, Dorrance liked to say, "Somebody call Grandma Borgman. Borgs needs some incentive." Whenever Borgman made a mistake in a game as a freshman, Dorrance exclaimed, "Dammit Borgman!," until it became a running joke that she'd changed her first name from Danielle to *Dammit.* "Anson liked to pick on me, but he didn't do it because he hated me, he did it because he cared enough about me to be honest," Borgman says. "It sounds funny, but I'll always carry those *Dammits* with me."

"There were times during my first two years when Anson was so brutally honest with me that I thought he was the Devil," Tracy Noonan says. "Anson didn't sugarcoat his opinions, and in retrospect that was good for me. When he's proud of you, he will tell you, and when he thinks you stink, he will tell you that too. The way he handles it fuels your fire. If you hate him for it, he's fine with that. He might even laugh about it on the sideline with Dino."

There's a general feeling that the worst thing Dorrance can say to a Tar Heel player is nothing at all. "Anson can be insulting at times, but I know that if he hadn't criticized me then I would have been scared that maybe he didn't have any hope that I could get better," Anne Remy says. "He has a way of humorously breaking you down and then building you back up."

Dorrance describes his tough-love approach by adapting a favorite line from the movie *Legends of the Fall:* "He is the rock they broke themselves against." In Dorrance's interpretation, his Tar Heels are generally steeled by what they hear from him. "Sometimes it might sound like he's ripping you apart, but he's actually teaching you," Blazo says. "I never had another coach who says what he has the guts to say. He's not afraid to hurt your feelings, and I think women sometimes need that. It's time for us to grow up. Quit babying us. When you get to this level you respect that from him, not to be treated like a little girl."

Says Higgins: "I'll never forget the practice when he told both Wendy Gebauer and I that we didn't have a move to save our lives, and he was absolutely right. It's a love-hate thing. You're young, you're dumb, you're impressionable, and your ultimate goal is to prove to him that you're good through all of this crap that goes on. Your first year you play to spite him, and as your career moves on you play less to spite him and more to please him."

Aubrey Falk recalls a scrimmage as a freshman in the spring of 1995 when she slid for a tackle and bruised her knee. Because the team was short on players, she limped through much of the rest of the game, before she eventually collapsed on the ground in tears. "Then in front of everyone, including my mom, I heard Anson say, 'Get up! This is a contact sport, not fucking badminton!'" Falk says. "So I got up and I played the rest of the game thinking, 'What an asshole, how dare he embarrass me like that.' I was so mad at him, but I was not about to give him the satisfaction of me coming out of the game. I built some character that day. Of all the things Anson has ever said to me, it's funny how I remember him saying that most of all."

Marcia McDermott says that every Tar Heel has a pet story to tell about a time when Dorrance eviscerated her publicly, while somehow conveying his faith in her potential as well. McDermott recalls Dorrance comparing her to a three-toed sloth, a water buffalo, and a tugboat turning in a small harbor . . . and those were the polite remarks. "At the time it was torture hearing those things, but it made me better," McDermott says. "I'd go home and tell my friends outside of soccer about some of the names Anson called me, and they would say, 'Gosh, you should quit!' It was liberating for me that they saw it that way, but it was still a preposterous notion. As I've often said, 'Mental health does not lead to greatness.'"

For all of Dorrance's editorializing over the years, it was one former Tar Heel, Elley Jordan, who enjoyed the ultimate comeback. Jordan, a nurse at UNC hospital, just happened to be on duty as the United States national team prepared to depart for the 1991 World Championship in China. The coaches and players required some inoculations for the trip, and Jordan was chosen as one of the nurses to administer the shots. When she opened the door to one examining room and discovered her former soccer coach she was initially taken aback, but then she composed herself, told Dorrance to bend over, and calmly needled the needler. "It was great to finally turn the tables on him and have Anson be the vulnerable one," Jordan says. "There was definitely some revenge in me for all of his sarcastic comments. But I was also thinking about how confident I was in that pretty intense situation, and how I owed some of that to the guy with his pants down."

11 | *Democracy*

An army of deer led by a lion is more to be feared than an army of lions led by a deer.

—Philip II of Macedon

It was a locker room with no lockers and hardly any room. A half-century-old building so nondescript that it was not even included on campus maps, it was constructed of stucco with a roof of terra-cotta shingles, many of which were missing. It featured fake wood wall paneling, a boarded-up fireplace, one sporadically functioning toilet, and tiny windows, which meant that most of the light came from fluorescents industrially buzzing from a ceiling of patchwork asbestos tiles. Most of the furniture looked like hand-me-downs from a frat house, including a wicker couch and a warped foosball table donated by Susan Ellis's boyfriend. In the center of the room were six benches rife with splinters and rusty nails, where the women sat for pregame talks, squinting at diagrams on their coach's legal pad because for years there was no blackboard. It was dingy and insect-infested and had absolutely no privacy, akin to a cabin at summer camp. One October somebody brought in a pumpkin to liven up the place, and there it remained, overlooked and decomposing in a corner until it had run its entire ecological course and turned to dust. Anson Dorrance's tiny "office" in the back was originally designed as a storage closet. The whole place was a firetrap whose only door was secured with a padlock.

For thirteen seasons, from 1984 to 1996, "the Hut" was the humble clubhouse of UNC women's soccer. "The place was so cramped that getting dressed for a match was like a game of Twister," Lorrie Fair recalls. "But you still walked inside there in awe, knowing that most of the history of women's college soccer evolved in that messy little space."

Says Kristine Lilly: "I thought it was great that here's this soccer powerhouse, No. 1 in the country every year, and everyone thinks we had so much money and so much prestige and the best facilities, and they come and see this mildewing shack. It was a dump, but it was *our* dump. It was my home away from home, my favorite place in Chapel Hill."

Moyer Smith recalls one bitter cold day when he made a rare visit to Dorrance in the Hut and found the coach bundled up in a huge parka and gloves with a space heater pointed at his desk. Dorrance had been working there through several winters, never telling anyone that the building had no heat. It didn't matter to him. The Hut personified Dorrance in the early days, stark and unadorned, held together with safety pins, functional and totally without vanity. "There's a climate in athletics where every coach wants a bigger budget, better facilities, more glitz, but we built this program in a ramshackle hut and I loved it," Dorrance says. "That's the slum from which we ascended, like a gang of street urchins rising to the throne of England."

In 1983, thirty-two-year-old coach Anson Dorrance was invited to a Fédération Internationale de Football Association Academy in Atlanta for a seminar led by celebrated German coach Heinz Marotzke. Marotzke spent the seminar's entire opening day introducing a concept he called the "personality coach." The UNC coach didn't get it. Says Dorrance, "I thought to myself, 'My gosh, when is this guy going to start talking about attacking or defensive shape? When is he going to talk about box organization? When is he going to talk about something that is going to have some meaning for me?' I was too young, too naive, to be in that course and to understand what was critical for me to develop into an elite coach."

At that time, Dorrance was still an avid drill collector. At the annual National Soccer Coaches Association of America conventions he would shuttle from clinic to clinic, searching for the ultimate finishing exercise, the ultimate possessional game, the ultimate clearing drill. He thought great coaches were nothing more than great clinicians. But after listening to Marotzke it gradually dawned on him that the guy was right, that after a while developing as a coach ceases to be about newer ways to organize practice. Dorrance began to study how the top coaches drive players to perform at higher echelons. "Twenty-five years ago, when I was starting out, I was such an idiot it's a wonder they gave me a license to coach," Dorrance says. "I thought that if a clinic had a good flow and the kids were enjoying themselves that it was successful, but a clinician is like an animal trainer at the circus, running his animals through these routines in front of an audience. It's a performance. He's acting like he's a great leader, but he's just a frigging actor, and the sort of person you want as a leader is not a clinician, but a powerful personality. A coach needs to try to create a connection, do something to stimulate the community, or he isn't worth a damn."

Dorrance decided that his animals would learn by falling on their faces. He wouldn't just coach the basic stuff, he'd coach everything and push his players beyond their comfort zone no matter how uneasy that made them or him. "I realized that a leader's challenge is to somehow assert yourself into the session you're running and be a powerful life force," Dorrance says. "I saw that my strength in coaching is having the courage to constantly deal with the athletes that unconsciously try to take things a bit easier, and the way I'd lose the respect of my team is by not being demanding enough, not making a passionate, stressful investment. My challenge would be to never surrender my standards to be more popular with my team, but to push my players to transcend ordinary effort in every training session and every match."

In order to pull that off, Dorrance realized he would need to surrender some of his own power. He would have to spread the leadership responsibilities around to everybody on his staff and on his team. The day Dorrance started to figure it out is the day he started concluding nearly every team meeting by scanning the room and asking one simple question: *Are you with me?*

Right about the time a practice was scheduled to begin during the 1995 season, Bill Palladino was nowhere to be found. When one of the Tar Heels asked Dorrance where Palladino was, he guessed the two most likely places, the refrigerator or the golf course. This was hardly the first time Palladino had gone AWOL. Dorrance joked with his players that the way Palladino often left them all looking to the horizon for his arrival reminded him of the Beckett play *Waiting for Godot*. Since then, whenever Dorrance is anticipating Palladino's late arrival, he describes his vigil as "Waiting for Go-dino."

There is time. And then there is DinoTime. Palladino famously sets his watch and his clocks fifteen minutes ahead and then still arrives a half hour late for everything.

Due at least in part to his pathological inefficiency, Palladino no longer participates in UNC recruiting. Outside of his coaching responsibilities, he is asked to handle only UNC's annual scheduling of opponents. For that purpose, Palladino has a spacious office which he visits so rarely that Dorrance likes to joke that it is the least used workspace on campus. Once, when Palladino went a couple months without an office visit, the rest of the staff hatched a practical joke to convince him that for lack of use his office had been deeded over to the UNC rowing coach. There are invariably two dozen pink phone message slips piled up outside of his door, and opposing coaches looking to schedule a game against UNC call Palladino ten times. When he doesn't return the tenth call, then they phone Dorrance. The UNC head coach only half-jokingly describes Palladino as "a dependent."

"My fantasy is that Dino live for one month in the world that he creates for other people," Dorrance says. "During that month nobody returns his phone calls. I'd like to have him experience what it's like to have the lights go off all around him."

Tom Sander says that Palladino's life can be summed up largely in three of his favorite sayings:

I'm on my way.

Check's in the mail.

Where are the chicken wings?

Yet without Bill Palladino, a consensus of UNC players insists, the program would never have become so successful.

Bill Palladino didn't begin coaching the UNC women's team until its second season. Naturally, he was a little late.

As he stood there beside Dr. Bill Prentice on the sidelines at his first practice in 1980, Palladino's skepticism about coaching women was erased before the end of the workout. "This is the way coaching should be," Palladino told Prentice that day. "It's so different from coaching guys. These girls are actually listening and learning. You show them how to do something and they actually try it. This is fun."

Palladino had never really considered himself coaching material, despite his background in swimming lessons and coaching Little League baseball or Rainbow Soccer for Kip Ward. He'd always rejected the notion of coaching as a career. Yet every afternoon that he sneaked out of the dank and sterile research lab for the fresh air of the soccer field, his resolve weakened. He felt burned out on science and began to equate coaching with freedom. Finally, one day in 1988, he quit his research job even though he wasn't sure how he'd support himself.

They made a fascinating duo, Dorrance and Palladino. One man who had grown up all around the globe paired with another man whose home address since he was old enough to remember had always been Chapel Hill, North Carolina. Their differences were a lucky accident that would wind up creating the necessary balance for the program. "It's hard to really think about Anson without thinking of Dino," Pete Dorrance says. "It's a yin-yang thing going on. I think it's helped flesh out the personality of the program. It's a collaboration, like Rodgers and Hammerstein or Lennon and McCartney, or maybe Abbott and Costello. They are so intertwined. If Dino hadn't come along I don't know how all of this would have worked."

In many ways Palladino, whose title is assistant *head* coach, has filled the coaching profile that Bill Guthridge embodied for so many years as the basketball assistant to Dean Smith. The nurturer. The ultimate foil, but never the buffoon. Palladino thinks like the players, and he is another set of educated eyes for Dorrance. Like so many assistant coaches he is usually cast in the role of the good cop. "Dino allows Anson to be the cold, hard, insensitive decision-maker," Sander says. "Dino's the warm-hearted, fuzzy guy that comforts them after Anson chews them out."

While nobody enjoys torturing the UNC women during Terrible Tuesday fitness more than Palladino, he is also known to time the sprints with, quite fittingly, "an elastic watch." His count for a thirty-second sprint is noticeably malleable: . . . *25* . . . *26* . . . *27* . . . . . *28* . . . . *29* . . . . *30.*

Palladino is the program's comic relief. The crackup. When the players stand on the line for 120s and Dorrance is reminding them that their playing time depends on passing, Palladino is invariably doubled over chuckling after spotting someone picking their nose. "He's our yeast," Sander says. "You can have all the other ingredients, but you need that in order to make the bread. Without Dino, we're just a pile of dough."

Tactically, Dorrance runs the offense, Palladino the defense. The two can engineer an entire practice without consulting one another, Dorrance flogging the forwards with shooting drills on one end of the field while Palladino patiently explains the same concepts of defensive shape and positioning that he once learned as a Tar Heel player from his assistant coach, Frank Nelson, the first All-American to play at UNC. Rarely does Dorrance address a talking point after practice without asking Palladino to elaborate. Midway through every pregame and halftime talk, a certain amount of time is always reserved for Palladino to speak his mind, a critical respite that Dorrance uses to organize his final thoughts. "The relationship between Anson and Dino is worth studying," April Heinrichs says. "Dino balances Anson's inhuman moments and inhuman qualities. He is the person that dredges the good qualities out of people. He is the person who gives Anson insight into all the things Anson doesn't know about. He is the person who picks up the pieces when Anson has blown into a room and shattered all the china. He is the one who made you laugh when you really needed a laugh. He is the person who gives Anson balance on the bench. Anson has some Type A personality qualities, but he's been around Dino for twenty-five years, who is a Type Z."

Palladino is also Dorrance's devil's advocate, and he often has a polar opposite opinion on issues within the program. When Dorrance brought in a personal growth coach for the team, Palladino refused to listen to him. When Dorrance brought in a consultant to create a PowerPoint presentation of the UNC teaching technique, Palladino skipped the meeting. Palladino believes that Dorrance sometimes emphasizes his beloved statistical matrix over the performance of the players on the field, and Palladino loves nothing more than calling out Dorrance when he feels he is bullshitting.

"In my relationship with Anson, I think of myself as a reality check," Palladino says. "When Anson starts blue-skying about stuff, I'm there to shoot him down. Nobody else is going to say 'no' to Anson. If I don't think he's doing something right I don't have any qualms about telling him that it's idiotic. To Anson's credit, whenever I question him he'll say, 'OK, why?' We see no difference in stature between the two of us. It's like parenting."

Palladino says his relationship with Dorrance reminds him of something that T.J. Williams, his UNC graduate assistant soccer coach, once wrote to him in a card: *If you have two heads that think alike, then you only need one.*

"If you look at people who hang around Anson a lot, they tend to try to impersonate him, try to act like him, talk like him, look like him," Heinrichs says. "But over the years from what I've seen, Anson has become more like Dino rather than Dino more like Anson and that's really a credit to Dino and his self-confidence."

Says Dorrance, "Dino and I are a good counterbalance because I trust absolutely everybody and Dino trusts absolutely nobody and the truth is usually somewhere in between."

Palladino constantly brings fresh ideas into the program. He is the one who introduced Dorrance to the zone defense. He is also the one who initially pushed Dorrance to consider the differences between coaching men and women. After losing his father at age nine and being raised by his mother and an older sister, Palladino had more of a comfort level around women off the field. He understands that in part the road to these girls' hearts is through their stomachs, and he wins them over with team barbecues and homemade banana pudding and his regular pit stops for snacks on the road.

As a result Palladino is more plugged into the players than Dorrance is. "Dino knows what's going on with the team much more than Anson does," Pam Kalinoski says. "He was a critical buffer because there are times when you don't like Anson, but during those times, you can always like Dino. For the first two years whenever I went to see Anson for a meeting, I was so intimidated that I would just stare at the wall, and then I'd walk out of his office and see Dino and say, 'Dinooooo, want to go grab lunch?'"

Says Bill Prentice: "In the early years Anson was so egotistical and so wrapped up in whatever it was he was doing and not being in tune with everybody's personal life that he would have failed miserably had it not been for Bill Palladino. I once told Anson, 'If Dino wasn't here, you would have got everybody so pissed off that they all would have left, and you'd be back in law school.'"

In 1991, when Dorrance traveled to China to coach in the first Women's World Championship, he left Palladino to coach UNC in the NCAA Tournament. Other than a few faxes to wish the team good luck, Dorrance handed over the team completely to his assistant. He never consulted with him about any game lineups or strategy. He was just a fan. UNC won the national title, prompting Palladino to be named the Southern Regional Coach of the Year despite having coached only ten games. "A leadership quality in Anson that's outstanding is that he has shared the space with Dino so well," Marcia McDermott says. "You won't hear any of the players talk about Anson without Dino. Dino's impact is huge. When I was a player I would have said that Anson was very tough and Dino was very kind, but when I look at them now I see Dino as the one holding the line. Dino's not a big ego, but you have to have enough ego to be the other half of Anson. He is very aware of how and why the program succeeds, and what Dino's very good at is being what's needed."

Bill Prentice is 6-0 as the head coach of the University of North Carolina women's soccer team. Not bad for a trainer. Those six games all occurred back in the early 1980s when Dorrance was off on a road trip with the men's team and Palladino was stuck in the lab. Prentice admits that he had absolutely no clue what he was doing on the sideline. He told the team what he remembered hearing Dorrance tell them. *Kick it far post!* or *Get stuck in!* Prentice didn't know what any of that meant, but he won anyway.

Two decades later, Prentice is like another assistant coach. He'll yell at the referee over a bad call. He'll even suggest personnel changes. When the Tar Heels were trailing Santa Clara 1–0 in the second half of the 2001 NCAA final, Prentice sidled over to Dorrance and Palladino and said, "Nobody's doing anything offensively. How about throwing Catherine Reddick up front? At least she'll shoot." The two coaches looked at each other, nodded, and made the change.

As a doctor, Prentice is among the most accomplished in his profession. He has treated UNC players on the field for everything from a compound fractured leg to a fly lodged in a player's throat. He taped Bettina Bernardi back together so many times that she started saving the used tape, and at the end of her career she presented her trainer with the giant tape ball. Prentice has also proven particularly helpful with a more subtle female health issue. In 1983 when many of the Tar Heels were destined to endure their periods on the day of the NCAA final, Prentice anticipated the problem with estrogen treatments, thus delaying the affliction until after the game. Prentice also can rid a player of menstrual cramps in about three minutes by massaging an acupuncture point on her back, relief that can last as long as eight hours.

Prentice says that the majority of his doctoring is psychological. "I think 80 percent of what I do is manipulating their heads," Prentice says. "You really can't separate mind and body. I figured out that Mia Hamm needed to have a reason not to play well in order to play well. She needed something to fall back on, like her ankle's a little sore or her hamstring's a little tight. So if she came in and said her hamstring was sore, I didn't doubt her, I put a hot pack on it. I've done that with a lot of girls."

Because the soccer team is not Prentice's primary job, and he has no bearing on anybody's playing time, the players view him as a safe haven and never hesitate to confide in him about a flunked biology test or a flunked boyfriend. One Tar Heel player consulted with him about a pregnancy before she had even told her parents. "While Anson can be gruff, I have a more nurturing, caring, let's-put-things-back-together personality," Prentice says. "I've always seen the most important part of my job as mothering the players. They all have their problems, and you've got to take them under your wing, pat them and dry up their tears, and tell them everything's going to be all right."

Says Heinrichs: "On the medical side, Prentice has patched together quite a few players, including myself, and he's great at judging when to get an injured player back on the field or take her off. But it's just as important that when a player has a bad day with Anson, Prentice isn't afraid to say, 'Aaaah, he's a lunkhead. Forget him.' He's never disloyal, but he's the voice who really keeps everything in perspective. Sometimes you need a doctor to remind you that soccer is not life and death."

Like all of Big Pete's stories, the one about being the outgoing mail censor on the submarine had a larger message. After the laugh, he would clear his throat and tell his children about how the lack of writing skills among his fellow seamen embarrassed him. He told them it was that experience that convinced him that if he survived the war and someday had kids, he would take their education seriously. He would encourage them all to read and read and read as he did.

Naturally, Anson fought the reading bug at first, until the eighth grade, when his mother gave him a copy of Nicholas Monsarrat's *The Cruel Sea*. That book combined the subject matter Anson loved to read about, war, with a lyricism that he had never experienced before in the more strategy-oriented military books he'd studied to that point. Dorrance hasn't stopped reading since.

These days Dorrance reads for at least an hour every night, his version of continuing education. He requests nothing but books as gifts, maintaining a literary wish list that he distributes to his wife, M'Liss, and his three children, daughters Michelle and Natalie, and son Donovan, before each Christmas and Father's Day. Dorrance owns a collection of more than a thousand books in his home, including a vast library that he inherited from Anson Dorrance II. In order to discipline himself to read from different literary genres, he divides his reading material into eight categories, and he will read one book from each category before he can restart the cycle. He has always loved biographies of great leaders the most, from President Lyndon Johnson to John D. Rockefeller to Charles Lindbergh, and he underlines every word or phrase that interests him, especially inspirational quotes. "Everything I read impacts on the way I think," Dorrance says. "Great quotes put into words what I genuinely believe in."

Like Big Pete, Anson has tried to pass along his love of reading to anyone who will listen. When Natalie asked for a car one Christmas, her father told her he would buy her one the next Christmas if she would read for at least an hour for each of the next 365 days. Whenever Donovan is grounded, the only way he can reduce his sentence is by reading an entire book. When it comes to Dorrance's players, a UNC campus library tour is part of every recruiting visit. Dorrance revels in pointing out how he had four high school valedictorians on his 2001 team. He is also proud that women's soccer players have always maintained a higher GPA than the average female student at UNC, and that all but two of his four-year players have graduated.

Dorrance is a fan of language, of the power of words to construct, destruct, reconstruct, and especially to empower. Inspired by an article Dorrance read in the *New York Times* about the lost art of committing poetry to memory, he asked his 2003 seniors to memorize motivational poems and then foist them upon the underclassmen during the season. He also likes to challenge his players with an occasional pricey vocabulary word. *We need someone with some perspicacity to know when to knock a long ball out of the back.* "There were tons of times when he'd use a word in practice that most of us had never heard of," Meredith Florance says. "We'd look to a player who had straight A's and ask, 'What does *that* mean?'"

Dorrance has never forgotten a particular day in an English class at UNC, when his professor read a stream-of-consciousness passage from James Joyce's *Ulysses*, then segued right into a letter from his mother, and then back to *Ulysses* without the class realizing the gimmick. Says Dorrance: "All of sudden I thought, 'Literature is life. Why can't I read like that? I'm just reading a book, but this professor is consuming life. He was teaching me how to read, and now that's what I try to do. I want to teach my players how to read and how to tie what they read into their lives."

Because NCAA rules prohibit Dorrance from giving books to his players, he has written each of his rising seniors' parents during each of the last ten Decembers and asked them to buy their daughters a Christmas gift on his behalf, a book called *Man's Search For Meaning*. The book was written by a Holocaust survivor, Jewish psychiatrist Viktor Frankl, about his experiences inside the Auschwitz concentration camp during World War II. When Kalli Kamholz began reading *Man's Search For Meaning*, she thought she'd surely been given the wrong book. She is not alone. "Frankl is pretty deep for senior leadership," Jena Kluegel says. "Initially you're comparing Auschwitz to Carolina women's soccer and thinking, 'Hmmmm, that's a stretch,' but it started a lot of good discussions."

Hoping to transform his readers into leaders, Dorrance conducts a thirty-minute meeting with his rising senior class once a week during spring semester, and they discuss Frankl's book and how it applies to the UNC program's core values of attitude, character, performance, discipline, community, and ambition. "Some of our players are wonderful leaders with our core values already embedded, but others act like these values are hieroglyphics from an alien civilization," Dorrance says. "All we are trying to do is to let them know how we expect them to behave, but it is shocking to see how few understand the value of something as simple as nobility."

With Dorrance acting as a philosophy professor in these leadership meetings, eventually the players begin to see the connection between Frankl and their lives. Dorrance regularly reads what he feels is the seminal quote from the book:

> If there is a meaning in life at all, then there must be a meaning in suffering. Suffering is an ineradicable part of life, even as fate and death. Without suffering and death, human life cannot be complete. The way in which a man accepts his fate and all the suffering it entails, the way in which he takes up his cross, gives him ample opportunity—even under the most difficult circumstances—to add a deeper meaning to his life.

For Dorrance the quote is a scathing indictment of whining, which he sees as one of the most destructive aspects of athletics. He believes that whining not only degrades the person indulging in it, but also anybody who listens to it and tolerates it. "Frankl writes about the nobility of suffering, and his basic message is that you can't always control the events in your life, but you can control your attitude toward them," Dorrance says. "Most of our players play less than they would like, but adversity doesn't necessarily have to be defeatist. What we try to teach our leaders is a kind of decorum and presentation when they're sacrificing themselves for a greater mission. Athletics doesn't develop character, but it clearly exposes it and when that happens then I feel it has value."

Dorrance's reading has convinced him that in civilian life coaching is the profession closest to the military, and that a person who succeeds as a leader in one field would likely thrive in the other. In fact, Dorrance rarely uses the word *coaching*, but prefers *training*, which suggests guidance beyond the soccer field. He often refers to practices as "sessions," as if they were visits to a psychologist's office, which they often are, and when he spots a mistake he likes to call the team together by saying, "Bring it in. Let's review this." Dorrance essentially takes the college athletic experience and makes it a think tank in which his players can reflect and hopefully develop a spirit and strategy they will use to face all the succeeding challenges of their lives. This is how he's ultimately justified his career decision, how he's turned coaching into an intellectual pursuit, an honorable profession.

Thus Dorrance doesn't measure the true success of his program by the attitude of his stars, but instead by that of the easily overlooked half of his team who rarely or never plays. His appreciation for their plight dates back to 1975, when he watched his brother Pete, a UNC soccer walk-on, ride the bench throughout that soccer season without complaint. For many years, borrowing another idea from Dean Smith, Dorrance started all of his seniors, including his walk-ons, in every NCAA Tournament game as a tribute to their contribution to the program, choosing to honor people over honoring talent, at the risk of sacrificing a national championship. In recent seasons he expresses his appreciation for his walk-ons at the end of every season, when the NCAA limits his traveling squad to eighteen players at the Final Four, by paying out of his own pocket for every player on his roster to go. "Because our heads are always turned by the decisions we have to make to win, we risk failing in our ultimate mission," Dorrance says. "The worst criticism for a successful program is that it's just a factory, that it's a program without soul. The walk-ons are the ones experiencing the soul of the team, and they must get a sense of our emotional commitment to them as well."

Dorrance's favorite embodiment of this idea is Elizabeth Marslender. Nobody on the 1996 Tar Heels worked harder than Marslender. Nobody had a more positive attitude. Nobody played less. Yet it was Marslender who scored what Dorrance calls "the most celebrated goal in UNC history." With UNC leading William & Mary 4–0 in the final minutes of the 1996 NCAA tourney opener, Dorrance inserted Marslender into the game, and with just twelve seconds remaining, she scored the only goal of her career on her only shot of the season. As soon as the game ended, all of Marslender's teammates dogpiled her, including Vanessa Rubio, who had recently torn her ACL yet still crutched out to the scrum, mangling her knee further when she hurled herself into the joyous heap. What seemed like a meaningless goal was loaded with significance for Dorrance. "Elizabeth's teammates were celebrating the goal, but really they were celebrating the fact that this girl who never played was the one who passed fitness every week with a smile on her face, and the first girl to greet anyone who came off the field and tell them how great they did," he says. "They were celebrating effort, courage, competitiveness, all the qualities that are truly admirable in athletics. They were celebrating Elizabeth's nobility in suffering."

From Dorrance's opening senior leadership meeting for the class of 2004 on December 9, 2003:

You guys are now the caretakers of the program. You guys will make a lot of collective decisions about what we do from here. Basically you are being placed in positions of leadership. Does that necessarily give you any leadership power? No. You're going to have to earn your right to lead anyone, and the first person you've got to lead is yourself. Most of you in this room don't lead yourselves very well, and the best way to establish credibility is to work. Your teammates are not going to listen to a damn thing coming out of your mouths if you don't work with them. They'll be thinking, "You're telling me to do this when I've been carrying your fucking ass all year?!" You've got to demonstrate through your leadership that you're not just taking care of yourself, you're taking care of everybody. Let's face it, our soccer team is a laboratory of the human spirit. Some people are going to respond to you, and some are going to be a royal pain in the ass. Great leaders never quit on anyone. They're not judgmental, and this loyalty toward everyone on the team is critical. You've got to make uncomfortable decisions that aren't going to be popular. You've got to say uncomfortable things to people who are not going to like you because you called them out. Your job is not to be anyone's friend. Your job is to take the people who are following you to their full potential, and some people are going to fight you every step of the way. Your challenge is to take them there anyway. Are you with me?

Dorrance says he has adapted his leadership style from a book called *The Female Advantage* by Sally Helgesen, which asserts that a good leader of women should be positioned in the center of an organizational spider's web, connected personally with everyone in the group. Unlike male leadership, which is more hierarchical and tends to function through intimidation and memorandum, Dorrance's leadership style is designed to be more respectful and receptive.

Dorrance likes to call UNC women's soccer a democracy. He allows his players their say on virtually everything except who plays and for how long. He's been known to ask his senior leadership to decide whether or not they think the team should practice on a particular day. He prepares for every game by having the players rehearse their formations for set pieces during pregame and decide their own alignments. He encourages his senior leaders to stop by the office to discuss the chemistry of the team, a tradition that dates all the way back to Janet Rayfield, because he knows that in most matters his seniors are more tuned in than he is. Says Danielle Borgman: "Your freshman year you hardly ever talk to Anson, sophomore year you talk to him a little bit more, junior year you're comfortable talking to him, and by senior year you're like, 'OK, listen up Anson, this is how it is."

Dorrance is grooming his players to be leaders on the field, like he once was. He understands from his playing days that you must be in the action to truly feel the pulse of a game. He subscribes to a theory he once heard proposed by German national team player Paul Breitner, who said, "Coaches run the game until the whistle blows, and then it becomes the players' game."

Unlike most any other sport, there are no timeouts in soccer, no breaks in the action when the coach can consult with his team and draw up a new plan in the dirt. Other than his occasional sarcastic remarks, Dorrance hates to give any direction from the bench because in his mind it connotes panic. He'd rather his players solve it on the field. "If you're constantly screaming at your players from the sideline it's because you haven't prepared them properly," Dorrance says. "Coaching isn't knowing the game; it's figuring out a way to have the players do what we want. Coaching is about having an effect."

Trailing Santa Clara 2–0 at the half in 1993, Dorrance simply told his team, *Well, girls, no Carolina team has ever been down 2–0 at the half. You guys wanted to make history, well congratulations, you did it!* "We're sitting there thinking, 'What? That's it? We need help out here!,'" Mia Hamm recalls. "What ended up happening is that players started standing up and saying, 'We're not going to lose this game.' I remember Tish Venturini said, 'I don't know what you guys need to do in the next five minutes to get your heads on straight, but you better do it.'" UNC won 3–2.

In the final minutes of a game at Texas in 2001, Tar Heel goalkeeper Jenni Branam grew frustrated with midfielder Sara Randolph's tracking back on defense from her flank midfield spot, so Branam ordered Randolph to switch positions with Anne Felts and move to forward. Dorrance didn't realize what had happened until after the game, but he supported Branam's leadership voice. Dorrance encourages all of his players to talk to their teammates with enough urgency that it is accepted, but not so much that it offends. "One of the huge challenges in women's sports is to find a vocal leader, and when you get one it's like gold," Dorrance says. "She must have unbelievable personal strength because everything in her culture is telling her that if she opens her mouth on the field everyone is going to think she's a bossy bitch."

Dorrance says he has never coached a better natural leader than Jordan Walker, a high school valedictorian and a regular at UNC summer camps who is one of the least athletic players ever to be recruited to UNC. The Tar Heel coach once told Walker's father, Randy, that if Jordan came to UNC he couldn't guarantee that she'd ever play a minute, but he saw the ingredients of a leader who would be his captain someday. Walker is one of the few players in UNC history who constantly exhorted and excoriated her teammates throughout a game. "It was very hard for me to tell other people what they should be doing, but the tone you use to convey your message means much more than what you actually say," Walker says. "It's a fine line between being encouraging and still holding people to a high standard. If someone trips over themselves or kicks the ball into our own goal, you don't say, 'Nice try!' You had to know who you were talking to, because we had some girls on our team who I could rip and they responded exactly how I wanted, and there were others who started crying on the field."

During Walker's freshman year of 2000, the Tar Heels lost three conference games during the regular season. Then Dorrance inserted Walker into the starting lineup at attacking midfielder, and the Tar Heels didn't lose again that season. After Walker scored the game-winning goal in the NCAA semifinal against top-ranked Notre Dame, Dorrance sent Randy a newspaper photo of his daughter that included his own caption, *And a child shall lead them.*

Dorrance also credits the 2003 NCAA title to his decision mid-season to put an injury-riddled Walker back into the lineup during a tough game at Navy. Walker won that game 1–0 with the fifth game-winner of her nine-goal career, and the Tar Heels were never threatened again in an undefeated season. During the NCAA semifinal that season, Walker displayed her nobility by asking not to play in the second half against UCLA because she assessed that she couldn't keep up with the speed of the game. "Jordan's a wonderful lesson in leadership," Dorrance says. "Even though she lost almost every duel, even though sometimes teams went through her like she didn't exist, even though there was no frigging way she should ever have been on the field at this level, when she was out there our team always got better. It's because she could handle crisis. When you tell Jordan that the house is burning down, she says, 'Oh really, which room?'"

A few players, including Shannon Higgins, Carla Werden, and Walker have achieved a status where they are referred to by Dorrance as *Coach*. With UNC ahead 2–1 during a brief break in the 2001 NCAA semifinal, Dorrance was warning his team that they needed to keep playing aggressively when he was suddenly interrupted by Walker, who said, "Hey, y'all, we're going to keep running until we pass out and we're going to win this frigging game!"

Says Dorrance: "At that moment I was thinking, 'This is the ultimate evolution. I'm just an appendage here.' But that's what you love. It was a defining moment. That's why I should never be running the team. My hand is on the tiller, but it's a soft hand. Every once in a while they'll make a mistake and you're there to help them correct it, but they are running the ship."

During a tight game against Texas in 2003, Dorrance told Maggie Tomecka he was subbing her out of the game for the second overtime. Walker studied Tomecka's reaction, sidled over to Dorrance, and said, "Leave Maggie in. I think she's still got something left."

Dorrance reluctantly agreed, and four minutes into that second overtime, Tomecka dribbled through the Longhorns defense and blasted a shot into the back of the net. Dorrance quickly found Walker, gave her a hug, and told her, "Coach, I owe that victory to you."

It's called the "Ring Toss Theory," an idea Dorrance once absorbed from a college psychology textbook. The premise is based on the carnival game during which a contestant chooses to toss a ring at one of three pegs set at various distances. The closest peg is easy, the next challenging, and the farthest one virtually impossible. Dorrance equates the decision to the one that arises on a soccer field whenever a striker dribbles toward goal with one defender to beat. His most tentative players shirk their responsibilities completely by passing back to a teammate, the equivalent of shooting at the closest peg. Others avoid their obligation by blasting a low-percentage twenty-five-yard shot rather than take on the defender, and then when they miss they can claim that the shot was next to impossible anyway. Dorrance wants all of his players to take on the defender 1 v. 1, to embrace personal responsibility for whether they succeed or not, to go for the middle peg.

The UNC coach laments that most young players are not being bred to strive for that middle peg. "What we've created are pampered protected babies because too many kids are told how great they are when they're not," Dorrance says. "We're thinking by praising them and loving them and excusing them that we're constructing them. We're *not*. It's better for players to know the truth. When UNC plays poorly and wins, I'll tell my players that we dodged a bullet. I won't let them make excuses."

Dorrance tries to create personal accountability through peer pressure. At the end of each season he asks his players to participate in a confidential evaluation of every Tar Heel's attitude, performance, character, and discipline as a way for them to motivate teammates and, hopefully, themselves. Then each spring he conducts a player draft and posts the pecking order so that every Tar Heel can see where she stands in the eyes of her teammates. If Dorrance believes one of his players isn't trying hard enough, he isn't afraid to tell her that he's recruiting on top of her and even name the player he believes is going to eventually put her on the bench. "Some players have to be constructed and some have to be deconstructed, and I do that in a public forum," Dorrance says. "I see through every corner they cut. I see through all of their bullshit. They are glass houses."

Personal accountability begins with the competitive cauldron, but some players need an even bigger push. Meredith Florance, an unfit and lazy underachiever during her first three seasons at UNC, grew so tired of hearing Dorrance's derisive use of the word "potential" when describing her that she dedicated herself to getting fit as a senior and won the 2000 National Player of the Year award. Emily Rice remembers arriving late to practice on her third day as a freshman and expecting to run sprints. Instead, Dorrance told her to step aside while her teammates ran instead, some cussing at her the whole time, and Rice never arrived late for a practice again. Pam Kalinoski, whose moody demeanor earned her the nickname *Brat*, once asked Dorrance a question in practice, received an answer she didn't like, and walked away from him with her shoulders typically slumped. Dorrance fell into line behind her, imitating her hangdog gait for twenty yards as the rest of team cackled. "I had a real love/hate relationship with Anson in college," Kalinoski says. "I was like this weeble wobbling but never falling down. He would do or say something to humiliate or embarrass me, and I would think, 'Are you for real right now?' I remember one game when my parents had driven seven hours to watch me play, and Anson knew that. I played twenty minutes in the first half, and he didn't think I played well, so I never went back in. At that point I hated him so much I could have punched him, but in our next practice I killed myself, and I won back my spot in the lineup. That night I realized, 'Damn, he won the game again.'"

Even after the Frankl and the leadership meetings and the lectures on accountability, some players still don't catch on. Nobody in UNC soccer history felt less personal responsibility than Dawn Crow. An extremely talented sweeper who could serve the ball on a dime, Crow never earned the playing time she deserved because she wouldn't get fit, insisting that her position didn't require the same fitness as the other field players. Crow was one of the girls who just happened to mysteriously pull her hamstring before nearly every Terrible Tuesday. Dorrance went so far as to institute an extra 120-yard sprint that the rest of the team had to run to make up for Crow's lack of fitness in hopes of goading her into better shape, but like every other attack on Crow's malingering nature, the plot failed miserably. Finally, Dorrance stumbled upon a George Bernard Shaw quote, asked Crow to memorize it, and then, whenever she was ducking fitness or whining, he would stop practice immediately to ask her to recite it to the rest of the team. *Be a force of fortune instead of a feverish, selfish little clod of ailments and grievances complaining that the world will not devote itself to making you happy.* Alas, even that didn't work. Crow never took to heart what she was reciting, but everybody else did. The quote became the foundation of UNC's core values and finds its way onto the blackboard at some point every season, because there are new Dawn Crows every year.

"It boils down to the reality of what's really important in life," Dorrance says. "Count your frigging blessings, and if anyone's feeling sorry for themselves, tell them to 'Shut up!' We've had some frigging assholes who come in as freshmen, and I wonder, 'Why did I ever recruit this selfish jackass?' Some of them evolve into something more powerful. Some don't. Then you've got some people like Leslie."

The personification of Dorrance's theories on accountability is Leslie Gaston. By the time Gaston's UNC career ended in 2002, she'd endured eleven surgeries on knees so scarred they both looked like tic-tac-toe boards. She also stashed an inhaler in her shorts that she used to combat her asthma. Gaston was considered such a medical marvel that during her junior year her story of perseverance was featured on the Discovery Channel. Even though Gaston knew that her soccer career could end with any collision, she was the most relentless tackler of her era. The Tar Heels lost eight games during her career, and Gaston thought every one of them was her fault, but she was particularly distraught after the loss in the 2001 NCAA championship game, after which she wrote a message to Dorrance that she read to him in his office three days after that game:

"My tears can't express what my words can say, but my words get lost because my tears often get in the way," Gaston read to Dorrance. "Passion is the only word I can find to describe what I feel so often. Through all of my unfortunate surgeries, I have been given a gift, an extra-sensitive heart. It has made me care so deeply for all those around me and expect only the highest standards for myself in certain areas of my life, including soccer. I told myself before our last game that I was not going to let our seniors leave without another ring. If I had sprinted only seven yards to block a shot, or headed a ball a foot more to the right, the outcome may have been different. I know that everyone makes mistakes, and I also know that I can do nothing about that game now, but I do know that I can learn from my mistakes and only improve on them. In the meantime, however, I may be hard on myself only because I expect more out of myself. If I did not care so much I would not enjoy my time here as much as I do . . ."

At that point, Gaston stopped reading, broke down, and wept.

On a chilly, sunny January morning in 1997, a backhoe leveled the Hut to its foundation in just twenty-two minutes. Palladino scoured through the wreckage that day for a few roof shingles to use as flagstones in his yard. Prentice saved one brick from the fireplace. Sander grabbed some curtains that still hang in his house. Dorrance bore less sentimental witness to the demolition that day, standing beside one of his players, Sarah Dacey.

Seven weeks earlier, just two hours before UNC's final pregame meeting in the Hut, Dacey, who had fought through an up-and-down career to earn a starting midfield spot as a senior, had restlessly sat down in her dorm room and written about her reaction to suffering. She dropped off the note with Dorrance when she arrived at the Hut before the game. When Dorrance read the note he saw it as more than a farewell letter, but also as a plea that the spirit of the Hut, the spirit of that Tar Heel era, not be lost in the new building. Dorrance knew it would be the last note he ever read to his team in the Hut, and the first he ever read to his team in its replacement soon to be raised on the same ground.

"This being our last meeting in the Hut," said Dorrance, opening his pregame remarks that day, "I'm going to talk to you guys a bit about what you guys are a part of. You guys are a part of soccer history. You guys are a part of the longest collection of great American soccer players, dating back to names you guys probably don't even know. Janet Rayfield was my first recruit; Emily Pickering one of the meanest women I've ever coached in my life, but a great player; Marcia McDermott, April Heinrichs, the Hamms, the Venturinis, the Lillys, to the people who have Olympic gold medals who are sitting here in the room. All of them are a part of the tradition in this building. They all met in this building. What I want you to do is when you walk out of here for the last time, I just want you to turn around and remember that the thing I like about this building is it is very symbolic of where we started and where the game started in America. It's a very humble building. Even though we've had the greatest soccer players in the history of the American game come through this hut, every one of them had a humility about the game they compete in and about their own level, and this building is reflective of that. It may be a dilapidated hut, but it is held together by a spirit that transforms the architecture. I don't ever want you to forget that."

Dorrance then dismissed Dacey and the other seniors from the room and pulled out Dacey's note. He told those who remained that Dacey's mother had died just six months before Sarah arrived at UNC as a freshman, which many of them did not know. Then he read her letter:

Anson,

Well, I'm finally returning your Frankl book that I borrowed in preseason. I'm sorry it's taken me so long to bring it back to you. I was flipping through the pages and read all the things that you had underlined and realized that Frankl says a lot of things that I can relate to in my life and I'm sure many people can relate to. The quote I especially liked was, 'Life is suffering. Survival is finding meaning in the suffering.' It's funny, because for my 21st birthday I received many cards from friends and family and I found that in many ways all my family's cards were the same. They wrote, 'We're proud of the young woman you have become.' That obviously made me feel good, but it also got me to thinking. I'm not trying to toot my own horn, but I just don't think I would be who I am now if it weren't for my environment and the friends that surround me. Sure, my family has had a huge impact in helping me along the way, but they weren't actually here all the time. My friends, my teammates, always showed me how much they cared. Their friendship helped to guide me in the right direction. I also want to thank you Ans, you have taught me so much over the years. One of the things that you've ingrained in my head is that I can choose either to feel sorry for myself and everything that's happened or choose to fight back and rise above it. Of course, my life hasn't changed overnight and there are times when I am not proud of my behavior and attitude and I know that I have many more years ahead of me when I will come across conflict and strange happenings and I will have to go through the process all over again. But I guess I just wanted to thank you for supporting the fighter in me and helping to bring it back to the surface. I'm sure there have been times when you have been disappointed in me and my actions and for that I am sorry. But you were always there for me, encouraging me, pulling for me, putting an arm around me when I was hurting and needed it most and you have helped me to grow and learn and I just wanted to say thank you. Coming to this school and playing on this team was the best thing that could ever have happened to me. I will always cherish the people who have touched my life and will also cherish everything this team has taught me: determination, hard work, desire, responsibility, heart, and especially love. Thank you for the experience and everything along the way.

Sarah

12 | *U.S. vs. Them*

We must walk consciously only part way toward our goal, and then leap in the dark to our success.

—Henry David Thoreau

Anson Dorrance isn't qualified. So said the United States Soccer Federation in 1985 after Dorrance applied to coach the first U.S. women's national team. Sure, Dorrance had already coached his North Carolina Tar Heels to four straight national collegiate championships, but he was just a college coach. He wasn't ready to coach America. Dorrance was told that the criteria for the national team job included experience coaching in a USSF-sanctioned event, a prerequisite he could not meet at the time, and it just so happened that the woman who informed the young coach that he wasn't qualified had a daughter who had recently been cut at a regional tryout camp by Coach Dorrance.

Dorrance suspected that this Machiavellian mom might not be his only enemy in the cutthroat world of the USSF. He hadn't exactly endeared himself to many of the Federation's grand poobahs ever since the days in the early 1980s when he formed the North Carolina Soccer Association and represented the state at the USSF annual convention, thus becoming a reluctant politician as well as a regional coach. While many of Dorrance's fellow coaches were intimidated by the USSF administrators who held the coaches' fates in their hands, Dorrance spoke his mind. He preached the value of regular coaching turnover and hoped to court support by vowing to resign after three years as a regional coach. He scoffed at the idea that at national camps the Federation wanted to mix up the regional teams to make the players adjust to new teammates, and chose not to keep score in the matches. Dorrance argued that his coaching colleagues were afraid to put their reputations on the line and play to win. He also made it no secret that he hated the way the USSF administrators, many of whom were doctors or lawyers with little soccer background, made critical decisions about player development instead of the coaches, and the way that then, when a coach lost a few games, he was fired, while the administrator escaped unscathed. At one USSF meeting, Dorrance proposed a resolution that every administrator who appoints a coach should be fired when that coach is fired. Nobody seconded the motion. Before long, Dorrance wasn't being invited to the meetings anymore.

"Anson was an abrasive combination of politically incorrect and noisy," says Chuck Blazer, then the USSF executive vice president. "The administration at that time generally wasn't sophisticated enough to see the potential in that."

Dorrance didn't care about politics. He just wanted to win. He flouted USSF rules by training his regional team before its camp was officially scheduled to begin, subjecting his players to fitness testing, and hiring an assistant coach. After his South region team clobbered all the other teams at national camp, even though the South was considered a weak region, Dorrance received antagonistic memos from the Federation about how his preparation was unfair. He wrote back, *What is our objective? Aren't we trying to build the United States into a world power? Why do you want to restrict me from training and developing my players at my own expense when my only goal is to kick everyone's ass at every level from now until the end of recorded time?*

"Getting those paper tigers to understand anything about developing players was maddening for me, so I never did anything according to any of their rules," Dorrance says. "I always did whatever the hell I wanted, and it drove those assholes absolutely nuts."

After the USSF said he needed experience at a Federation-sanctioned event, Dorrance entered a team in the USSF's amateur championships in the summer of 1985. Dorrance aimed to prove that the top collegiate players could be competitive on a national level, so he fielded a team stocked with Tar Heels called the Chapel Hill Kixx. Dorrance couldn't technically coach the Kixx, which included Susan Ellis, April Heinrichs, and Emily Pickering, because of NCAA restrictions on summer coaching, so he watched from the stands as Ellis's boyfriend patrolled the sideline. The University of North Carolina, disguised as the Chapel Hill Kixx, won that amateur championship, ripping through teams that included national team players. Dorrance made his point.

Meanwhile, the USSF had chosen Mike Ryan as its first women's national team coach. Ryan, an Irish expatriate, was a Seattle club coach whose teams had recently dominated the Federation's amateur championships. Ryan understood the game. Unfortunately his Irish brogue was so thick that many of his players couldn't understand him. That hardly mattered to the USSF, because at the time nobody could envision Ryan's national team actually scheduling a game.

Then, a few weeks later, an invitation suddenly arrived for the U.S. team to play in the Mundialito, a mini-World Championship staged in Italy that summer. Ryan quickly summoned the hypothetical roster he'd chosen at the 1985 National Sports Festival, including Michelle Akers and Lori Henry off Dorrance's South region team. Two Tar Heels, Henry and Stacey Enos, started in the very first U.S. national team game, a 1–0 loss to Italy on August 18, 1985. While the U.S. team surprised many just by being competitive with more experienced teams from Europe, the Americans finished the tournament with three losses and one tie, and Ryan was unceremoniously dismissed as coach.

The following spring, the USSF invited several dozen coaches to Dallas to audition for various national coaching positions. Dorrance was among them. At age thirty-five, he was the youngest coach invited, and while he still coveted the women's national team job, he had absolutely no expectations of landing it. Then things started to fall his way. With his evaluators sitting in the stands out of earshot, Dorrance watched a boys' team struggle through a nightmarish first half. At the break, he cracked a couple of jokes and then told them to go out in the second half and kick ass. Dorrance walked back to the bench, playfully flashed his evaluators the "OK" sign, watched his team score a goal immediately off the kickoff, and then gestured toward the stands that he rested his case.

Later when asked to analyze another men's game, he eschewed the banal soccerspeak favored by the other coaches. Instead, because he was currently recruiting a lot of the guys in the game to come to UNC, he loosened up his fellow coaches by promising to give out coveted information like home phone numbers for many of the players. The whole room cracked up. Dorrance was in command. Toward the end of the auditions, Dorrance buttonholed Blazer, one of the Federation's most powerful evaluators, and boldly lobbied for his own appointment. "Chuck, give me the job," Dorrance said, "because I am going to win."

Dorrance got it.

Dorrance's mission statement was modest: *Beat Canada!* When Dorrance accepted the women's national team coaching job in 1986, nobody at U.S. Soccer dared to dream that American girls could compete with the rest of the world in soccer. They just hoped to compete in the neighborhood. Maybe start with North America and work their way out. For a team that had scored just three times in four games at the Mundialito, the team's goals were, well, goals, *any* goals.

In Dorrance's first game as coach of the U.S. national team on July 7, 1986, against Canada in Blaine, Minnesota, he started five Tar Heels: Pickering, Heinrichs, Henry, Enos, and Joan Dunlap. The U.S. earned its first international victory, 2–0. Two days later, with six Tar Heels among the starting eleven, the U.S. beat Canada again, 3–0. Suddenly Dorrance realized that it was safe to expand his team's aspirations beyond beating the Canadians. Later that summer, the United States returned to the Mundialito and finished with a 3–1 record, including wins over China, Brazil, and Japan, along with a loss to Italy. With talk of an impending inaugural World Championship (FIFA, soccer's worldwide governing body, chauvinistically refused to acknowledge the women's tournament as a World *Cup*), Dorrance had to figure out a way to catch up to the more established European national teams like the Italians, who had started their women's team in 1968 and played almost one hundred games, and Norway, which had formed its team in 1978.

In the summer of 1987, Dorrance scouted the U.S. under-19 national camp in Marquette, Michigan. It was at that event where sixteen-year-olds Julie Foudy and Kristine Lilly and fifteen-year-old Mia Hamm crossed paths for first time. That U-19 team then traveled to Blaine for a tournament that also included Dorrance's full national team. The two teams never played each other, but the U-19s fared better overall than the full team. Dorrance watched every move of the young talent in training and in games, and he saw some unique ingredients: Hamm's acceleration, Foudy's presence, Lilly's energy. He considered a radical youth movement for the national team. It was a gamble. Bringing in players too young could destroy their confidence, but Dorrance couldn't resist the opportunity to expedite their development against the best competition. When his national team lost its final two games of that tournament to Sweden and Norway, Dorrance's mind was made up. He wanted to add the three teenagers to his roster for an upcoming two-game trip to China. At the time, Lilly wasn't even aware that the U.S. national team traveled internationally.

The three teenagers, who would become known as "the Babies," all traveled to China. Hamm and Lilly debuted as starters in the August 3 match against China in Tianjin, which the United States won 2–0. Ten days later, they started again in a 1–1 tie, with Lilly scoring the United States' goal. Foudy, who had yet to prove to Dorrance that she could play sufficient defense, wouldn't become a starter until the following year.

In deciding to trade experience for potential, Dorrance cut some of the national team's most established players, angering the USSF regional coaches who felt he had selected the wrong players because he didn't select *their* players. The burden to win grew exponentially with every decision to get younger and more Carolina blue. "When you pick a lot of your own players for the team, the only way you can justify that is by winning," Dorrance says. "We were always under great pressure, and there were charges of nepotism even though I felt it was unjustified. Obviously, you're going to select a lot of players from the dominant college program in the country."

After losing to New Zealand on December 15, 1987, with six Tar Heel starters, five days later the United States lost 2–1 to an unheralded Taiwan team in Taipei. Dorrance joked with Hamm and Lilly that he hoped he wasn't fired before the plane touched down back in the United States. "I had burned all the bridges around me, and I didn't have a political leg to stand on," he recalls. "I was only standing on my success, and I was convinced that loss was the end for me."

Though Dorrance survived those defeats, the national team's record stood at just 7-5-3 in the two years following his decision to go young. He was being skewered after every disappointing result like the one on June 21, 1989, when the United States managed only a scoreless tie against lowly Poland with seven Tar Heels in the lineup.

The following summer at the 1990 Olympic Sports Festival, instead of having the four regional teams compete, the USSF brought in the national team, the under-19 team, and two teams comprising the best remaining American players. They played round robin, and Dorrance felt considerable outside pressure about the roster he'd picked, which was typically filled with Tar Heels at the expense of some other excellent players. The national team won all of its games easily, but after a 2–0 win over the Under-19 team, some of those younger players left off the national team began to grouse that they were better than Dorrance's reserves. So, in a rematch against the Under-19 team, Dorrance made the bold decision to start seven of his reserves. Unbeknownst to Dorrance, Heinrichs gathered those players together before the game and told them, "Just so you guys know, everyone out there is criticizing Anson, and he is playing you because all the people

Nine-year-old Anson Dorrance (popcorn salesman, *center*) and eight-year-old M'Liss Gary (ballerina) at a costume party in Addis Ababa, Ethiopia, 1961. Anson and M'Liss were married in 1974, and both followed career paths foreshadowed by this photograph. (Courtesy of the Dorrance family)

The Dorrance brothers, Pete, Anson, and Lewjack *(left to right)*, in Singapore, 1962. Growing up, Anson dreamed of becoming a soldier and regularly organized war games in the neighborhood during which, his sister Maggie says, "it was stunning how this little boy would just take command." (Courtesy of the Dorrance family)

The Dorrance family *(clockwise from left):* Pete, Anson, Big Pete, Maggie, Lewjack, Chantal, and Peggy, in Brussels, 1967.
(Courtesy of the Dorrance family)

Anson *(center)* with sister Maggie and brother Pete at the gravesite of their uncle Anson Dorrance III, in the American Cemetery in Normandy, France, 1967. A voracious reader of military history, Anson was fascinated to read his name etched on the headstone.
(Courtesy of the Dorrance family)

Anson drumming with his band, the Leaves of Mercy, as a student at the Villa Saint-Jean in Fribourg, Switzerland, 1968. The Villa is where Anson began broadening his interests beyond war and sport.
(Courtesy of the Dorrance family)

Dr. Marvin Allen, who founded the UNC men's soccer program and coached the team from 1946 to 1976, on the sideline in his customary jacket and tie. His tradition of sartorial formality on game days was carried on by Dorrance, Allen's handpicked successor, who says, "Dr. Allen saw something in me that I never saw." (Courtesy of UNC Athletic Communications)

Dorrance, UNC's senior captain in 1973, admits he was not a naturally skilled soccer player. Admiring his grit, Dorrance's teammates nicknamed him "H&H" for hack and hustle, and his coach, Marvin Allen, once called him "the toughest 135-pound man I've ever seen." (Courtesy of UNC Athletic Communications)

Jack Simmons, Freddie Kiger, and Dorrance (left to right) pictured as UNC intramural badminton champions in 1971. Dorrance competed in eleven different intramural sports as a sophomore and helped launch Teague dormitory's "dynasty" of seventeen straight residence hall championships. (Courtesy of UNC Campus Recreation)

Dorrance with his first women's recruit and captain, Janet Rayfield, in 1981. Rayfield scored ninety-three goals in her Tar Heel career, second only to Mia Hamm, during a primordial era when many of her teammates were playing soccer competitively for the first time. Says Rayfield: "Even though we were extremely raw, there was always a feeling that we were expected to succeed." (Courtesy of UNC Athletic Communications)

The 1981 Tar Heels pose with the trophy after winning the sport's first-ever national championship tournament and fulfilling the bold prophecy of their coach, who had publicly boasted before the season that UNC would capture the title. After this photo appeared in a local newspaper and a letter to the editor promptly followed from a reader aghast at the team's mismatched clothing, an anonymous fan donated twenty-five new sweatsuits to the program for the following season. (Courtesy of UNC Athletic Communications)

Emily Pickering *(far left)* heads a ball during the Tar Heels' 1984 national title victory over Connecticut. The infamous banner hanging on the fence states, "UNC Women Love the Smell of NAPALM in the afternoon: NCAA Champs." The war reference created a backlash in the press, which threatened to overshadow the remarkable achievement of the Tar Heel seniors, who had delivered on a vow made as freshmen to win four straight national championships. (Courtesy of UNC Athletic Communications)

Dorrance walks off the field while comforting senior back Stacey Enos after the Tar Heels lost to George Mason in the 1985 national championship game, UNC's first-ever defeat in the NCAA tournament. The moment captures a crossroads for the program, illustrating that the Tar Heels were no longer invincible, just as Dorrance was realizing that he needed to be more emotionally supportive of his players. (Courtesy of UNC Athletic Communications)

April Heinrichs, Marcia McDermott, and Bettina Bernardi *(left to right)* celebrate the Tar Heels' 1986 national championship. Of regaining the title after losing it for the first time in 1985, Dorrance said, "This championship is very special to me and the players because you can appreciate it more when you haven't won it." (Courtesy of UNC Athletic Communications)

The Hut, UNC's locker room from 1984 to 1996, had no lockers, no blackboard, no heat, no privacy, and only one sporadically functioning toilet. Dorrance believed that the dilapidated building symbolized the program's rise to prominence during its era, calling it "the slum from which we ascended, like a gang of street urchins rising to the throne of England." (Photograph by Delaine Marbry)

Teague dormitory *(left)*, Fetzer Field *(center)*, and the McCaskill Soccer Center *(right)* are all bunched onto a tiny tract of real estate where many of the seminal moments of Dorrance's life have occurred. From his office window in McCaskill, which is built on the same ground where the Hut once stood, Dorrance can see the field where he played his college soccer and the dorm room where he lived during his first five semesters as a student at UNC. (Photograph by Jeffrey Camarati)

Linda Hamilton *(left)* and Kristine Lilly *(right)* help Mia Hamm off of Fetzer Field after UNC's dramatic 4–3 overtime victory against North Carolina State in the 1990 NCAA quarterfinals, a match later called "the greatest game in women's soccer history." This is one of Dorrance's favorite photographs because it evokes the physical and emotional investment required to win a postseason game against an archrival and it reminds him of the iconic American image of the Fife and Drum Corps. (Courtesy of UNC Athletic Communications)

The Tar Heels gather around yet another trophy in 1990 after winning their fifth consecutive national championship and the program's ninth in ten seasons. To underscore his assertion that the Tar Heels' success is primarily a result of players and not coaches, Dorrance has never appeared in a UNC championship photo. (Courtesy of UNC Athletic Communications)

Dorrance and his U.S. national team pose for a picture in Blaine, Minnesota, during the North America Cup in August of 1990. After the young and talented U.S. team, which included nine Tar Heels, shut out the Soviet Union, England, and Germany, Dorrance dubbed the tournament "our international coming-out party." (Photograph by Phil Stephens)

Dorrance watches his U.S. national team defeat Martinique 12–0 during the 1991 World Championship qualifying tournament in Haiti. Seated to Dorrance's right is Michelle Akers, a player who admits that she disliked Dorrance intensely until she began playing for him on the national team. To Dorrance's left is Carla Werden, a Tar Heel whom Dorrance would groom to be the national team's future captain. (Photograph by Phil Stephens)

Dorrance poses with the trophy on the night that the United States defeated Norway to win the 1991 World Championship in Guangzhou, China. Initially told he wasn't qualified to be the team's coach, Dorrance took over the position in 1986 with a mission to silence the many critics of America he had encountered in the various foreign countries where he'd grown up. Says Dorrance: "I was the ultimate patriot, and I turned that on my women for reasons that were visceral. I wanted to win more than breathe oxygen." (Photograph by Phil Stephens)

Tisha Venturini (13), Mia Hamm *(right with arms extended)*, and Kristine Lilly *(center)*, the three most prominent stars of the 1992 UNC team that Dorrance considers to be the finest ever in women's collegiate soccer, celebrate a goal on the way to dominating Duke 9–1 in the NCAA title game. After the game, the Blue Devils' coach said it was a "privilege" just to watch the Tar Heels play. (Courtesy of UNC Athletic Communications)

Debbie Keller *(center)* rejoices after her goal that won the 1996 NCAA Championship, surrounded by her UNC teammates *(left to right)* Aubrey Falk, Rakel Karvelsson, Nicole Roberts, and Sarah Dacey. That the Tar Heels needed two overtimes to finally defeat Notre Dame 1–0 confirmed Dorrance's suspicion that UNC had embarked on a new era during which championships would become far more difficult to win. (Photograph by Michael Stahlschmidt)

Assistant head coach Bill Palladino, UNC's second in command since 1980, is Dorrance's counterpoint and the program's comic relief. (Courtesy of UNC Athletic Communications)

UNC goalkeeper coach Chris Ducar is also the program's recruiting coordinator, the talent scout who lays the groundwork that allows Dorrance to close the deals. (Photograph by Jeffrey Camarati)

Dr. Bill Prentice, with Tar Heel alums Sarah Dacey (left) and Ange Kelly, has been UNC's trainer for twenty-six seasons, and is 6-0 as the team's head coach. (Courtesy of Bill Prentice)

After overcoming his initial hatred of soccer, UNC director of operations Tom Sander is the program's travel agent and equipment manager, as well as the chief statistician for Dorrance's competitive cauldron. Sander, who joined the program as a student manager in 1992 and never left, echoes the sentiments of his colleagues on the Tar Heel staff when he says, "I just kept thinking I'd do it until something better came along. That hasn't happened yet." (Photograph by Jeffrey Camarati)

Dorrance, at work amidst the rubble of his office, claims he is comfortable in chaos because he was born into it. There is a placard often buried on his desk that reads, "If a cluttered desk is a sign of a cluttered mind, of what then is an empty desk?" (Courtesy of UNC Women's Soccer)

The 2001 Tar Heels posed for this preseason team picture. Dorrance's belief that his players stick with his program as much for the camaraderie as the championships is epitomized in this photograph of the Tar Heels mugging for the camera while the 2000 NCAA Championship trophy sits obscured at the foot of the stairs. (Courtesy of UNC Athletic Communications)

Dorrance says that his philosophy of life is embodied in this comic strip, which he has taped to his office door. The Tar Heel coach, who all of his staff members insist is the most optimistic person they have ever met, tries to teach his players how to live an existence of "never-ending ascension." (CALVIN AND HOBBES © 1990 Watterson. Dist. By UNIVERSAL PRESS SYNDICATE. Reprinted with permission. All rights reserved.)

Dorrance's quote book, given to him by his daughter Michelle one
Father's Day to help her dad catalog the inspirational quotes he
likes to share with his team. According to Michelle, the cover photo
depicting a directional road sign peppered with bullet holes
symbolizes "what I've taken from what my dad taught me."

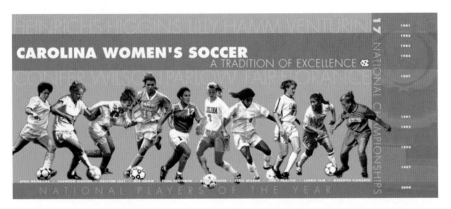

This poster printed in 2002 honors UNC's pantheon of National Players of the Year,
including *(from left to right)* April Heinrichs, Shannon Higgins, Kristine Lilly, Mia Hamm,
Tisha Venturini, Robin Confer, Staci Wilson, Cindy Parlow, Lorrie Fair, and Meredith
Florance. The Tar Heels' other Player of the Year at that time, Debbie Keller,
is not pictured. (Courtesy of UNC Sports Marketing)

The Dorrance family *(left to right)* Natalie, Donovan, Anson, M'Liss, and Michelle at their Chapel Hill home in 2006. Natalie is a teacher who helps her father at UNC's summer soccer camps; Donovan is a tenth grader at Chapel Hill High; M'Liss is a ballet teacher and choreographer; and Michelle is a professional rhythm tap dancer. Admitting he has sacrificed some priceless time with his family for soccer, Anson jokes, "I was never part of my daughters' lives when they were kids, which might explain why they're so successful." (Courtesy of the Dorrance family)

Dorrance's other "family," like his eldest daughter Michelle, was born on September 12, 1979. In this photograph, the Tar Heels punctuate one of Dorrance's more than 600 victories with the team's traditional Fetzer Field curtain call. When asked about his legacy, Dorrance says, "I'm especially proud that we've laid to rest the insult, 'You play like a girl.'" (Photograph by Jeffrey Camarati)

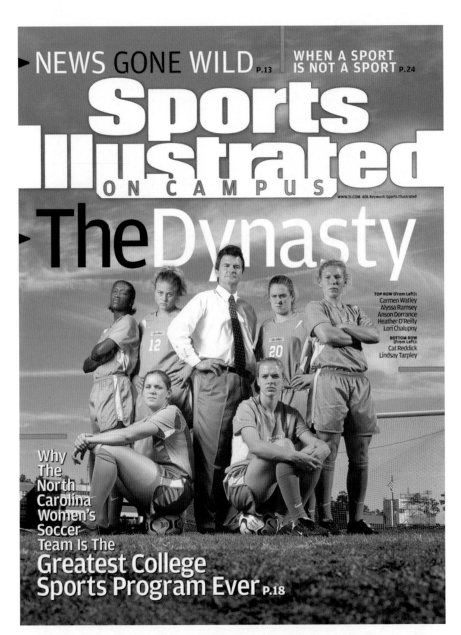

The November 11, 2003, cover of *Sports Illustrated On Campus* places the UNC women's soccer program's accomplishments in a historical context. Dorrance is flanked by *(clockwise from his left)* Heather O'Reilly, Lori Chalupny, Lindsay Tarpley, Catherine Reddick, Carmen Watley, and Alyssa Ramsey. A month after this issue was published, the Tar Heels enhanced the program's label as "the greatest college sports program ever" by completing another undefeated UNC season with a 6–0 victory over Connecticut in the NCAA final, holding the Huskies without a single shot on goal. (Greg Foster / *Sports Illustrated*)

you're playing against feel they deserve your positions. So let's make a statement about the team he's picked."

In a devastating performance, Dorrance's team led 9–0 early in the second half when he finally subbed Heinrichs into the game to play in possessional mode, as dictated by his longstanding 9–0 Rule. Meanwhile, former Tar Heel Julie Guarnotta, who was in the stands, began placing sucker bets with some of the male players at the Sports Festival that, as unlikely as it seemed, the national team would not score another goal. A few minutes later, Dorrance's team earned a corner kick, and when the ball found Heinrichs at the top of the penalty area, she blasted a side volley into the net to make it 10–0. Heinrichs stared over at her coach to make sure that they both knew she was making a statement to his critics. Guarnotta shook her head in impoverished disbelief.

When the game ended, Dorrance was extremely satisfied with his team, hoping that he had quieted his detractors. "That was one of the finest days of my career," he says. "I was proud of April and proud of the team. We couldn't have put on a better display of soccer. In my mind we'd silenced all the critics, but I didn't care about that as much as I wanted all these people to join my community. I wanted them to say, 'He is a winner. He picked the right players. He's got some great ideas. Let's back him.'"

Moments later, he was pulled into the team locker room by USSF Secretary General Keith Walker, expecting a warm hug and congratulations. Instead, Walker said, "What is this I hear that you've left some of the best American players off your team?"

"I'm looking around the room thinking, 'Are you fucking kidding me?'" Dorrance says. "All the players he was talking about were on the team that just got annihilated. I was incredulous, and finally I said, 'What game were you watching?'"

Walker then said, "Germany is coming over soon, and I refuse to be embarrassed when the Germans come in to beat us."

Four weeks later in Blaine, with Walker sitting amongst an awed German delegation, the United States easily defeated Germany 3–0. That summer the U.S. team also defeated England for the first time ever, defeated the Soviet Union by eight goals, beat powerful Norway twice, and began a streak of fourteen consecutive shutouts in international play.

Maybe this Dorrance guy was qualified after all.

In his very first letter to the U.S. national team pool of players in 1986, Dorrance had informed his prospects that he'd be placing an increased emphasis on fitness training because that was something they could all control. *If you don't come in fit, I will cut you!* Sure enough, Dorrance cut goalkeeper Barbara Wickstrand, the player who arrived in camp in the worst shape, sending her home on the very first day. His message was clear: the United States might not be the most skillful women's team in the world, but it would be the fittest. Dorrance believed that in a sport still so early in its germination, Darwin's theory of evolution might go a long way toward success.

Anyone in camp who had never played for Dorrance was initially shocked by the intensity of his competitive cauldron. Dorrance told them he wouldn't play anybody in a match until they proved they could tackle. He had already trained the perfect role model for how he wanted his new team to compete in Heinrichs, the very first player he selected for his national team. Says Dorrance: "In practice I would walk by her huddle when we were playing 5 v. 5 games, and April would be saying, 'You go here, you there, you do this, get me the ball and then stay out of my way.' Everyone was nodding. Then I'd go over to the other huddle, and all the best players in the country are talking about is 'How are we going to stop April?'"

The foundation Dorrance laid out for the national team was similar to the one he'd been developing at UNC. Prepare and train on your own. Play for each other. Compete with intensity, respect, and guts. Train and play on the edge. "Anson's mantra was always, 'We set the standard for women's soccer in the world and I don't care what people think about us, we're going to get out there and battle,'" Julie Foudy says. "The thing I love about Anson is that he was the first one to condone women being competitive, ripping opponents' heads off, chewing them up and spitting them out. Basically a 'fuck you' mentality. He allowed me to be the competitive sonofabitch that I knew I was. We were all competitive, but not everybody knew it until he brought it out in all of us."

Between the time when the Babies joined the national team in August of 1987 and the 1991 World Championship in China, the national team played forty-three games outside the United States and only seven home games. Many of the younger players, particularly Lilly, suffered acute homesickness. The team traveled to Italy on a cargo plane and then practiced on a field composed primarily of gravel. They rode seventeen hours through China on a coal train, arriving at their destination with soot covering their faces, and then stayed in a hotel so grimy that they slept with their clothes on. They often traveled to games on rickety old school buses, sometimes accompanied by the team they were about to play. There weren't many perks. They wore hideous pink-and-green sweatsuits and uniforms handed down from the men's national team, many of which were so threadbare that the shorts had split in the back. They were not paid, attendance was paltry, and media attention was virtually nonexistent. For obvious reasons, the players were skeptical whenever their coach waxed poetic about a Women's World Cup or participation in the Olympics, but Dorrance kept selling a dream.

For Dorrance, it was his American dream. At the beginning, the national team was so low-profile that some of the players didn't really understand that they were playing for their country. Often when Dorrance phoned a player to invite her to train with the national team, it was the first she'd ever heard of it. The U.S. women's *what*? When he first asked talented Cal–Santa Barbara striker Carin Jennings to join the national team in the summer of 1986, Jennings turned down the invitation, choosing to hang out at the beach instead. Jennings agreed to join the team the following summer only because it meant a free trip to Asia.

"When Anson first told me he wanted to take me for the national team in 1987, I had no concept of what that meant," Foudy says. "I'd been on the road for weeks, I didn't have any money, I was tired, and I just wanted to go home. I made up some lie about having to go back for summer school, and Anson said, 'Yo, do you understand what I'm asking you? This is your *national team.* You have a chance to play for the United States of America.' It finally hit me. What am I doing? He's right. I need to go. It was my first experience with his expertise at persuasion. He sold me on becoming an American pioneer."

"Patriotism was his prime theme, his ace-in-the-hole to get people motivated," says Brandi Chastain, who joined the national team in 1988. "Whether you're wearing red, white, and blue or Carolina blue and white, for Anson it's all about where you come from and who you represent."

Dorrance's nationalism had been ignited back on the playgrounds in Addis Ababa by the rocks bouncing off his head, by his British classmates in Nairobi who refused to admit that they'd actually lost the Revolutionary War, and by the students in Singapore who decried the American imperialism in Vietnam. For Dorrance, U.S. had come to stand for what it spelled, *Us.* Us against them. By the time he coached his first national team game on foreign soil against China in Jesolo, Italy, on July 20, 1986, the anthems and flags sent shivers down his spine, the most exciting feeling he'd ever experienced in athletics. Dorrance realized that in his mind this was so much more than one soccer team against another. It was one country against another. One culture against another. "Coaching the United States national team was my mission." Dorrance says. "It was a part of my core as a human being because of where I was raised. This was a sport the world invented and dominated. So this was a wonderful gift to me, a crucible, to take the United States, which had absolutely no respect from the rest of the world in this game, and gain a respect. *You think we suck at this, well, give me a couple of years and I'll beat you.* I was the ultimate patriot, and I turned that on my women for reasons that were visceral. They felt it every training session, every pregame, every halftime. I wanted to win more than breathe oxygen."

Dorrance had no idea when he arrived in Port-au-Prince, Haiti, for the first World Championship qualifying tournament in April of 1991 that he was about to experience what he calls "an epiphany."

The matches were played before beyond-capacity crowds of 35,000 fans pounding steel drums at Sylvio Cator Stadium, and they were televised live in Haiti. In the tournament opener on April 18, the United States trounced Mexico 12–0, ignoring Dorrance's 9–0 Rule because qualification could be determined by goal differential. The Americans then defeated Martinique 12–0, destroyed Trinidad & Tobago 10–0, and in the semifinals pounded home-standing Haiti 10–0. As the tournament progressed, people on the street began to ask April Heinrichs and Michelle Akers for autographs, the first time any American players had actually been recognized in public.

In the final, the United States easily shut out Canada 5–0 with an appreciative Haitian throng chanting *U.S.A! U.S.A!* In five games the United States scored forty-nine goals, including eleven by Akers, eight from Heinrichs, and seven by Chastain, while Carla Werden led a defense that didn't allow a single goal. The U.S. team was so dominant that during the win over Martinique, the Americans strung together more than one hundred consecutive passes without losing possession.

After the victory in the final, Dorrance sat in an interview room addressing a gathering of international soccer press. His team had just played the finest soccer he'd ever seen produced by women, and he was as proud as he could possibly be. He had exorcised his own lingering doubts that he was a coaching poseur riding on the coattails of talented players. He felt a part of this triumph, a man who had truly arrived as a coach, and he had this powerful feeling that his team could conquer the world. The reporters were clearly stunned to watch an American team produce such an awesome display of attacking soccer. They were even more surprised that it was a women's team. They were extremely skeptical, trying to sort out some sensible reason why the Americans played so well. One reporter asked Dorrance about his training methods, and when the coach shared his thoughts, he noticed that nobody wrote his answer down.

"Where were your players raised?" another reporter asked.

"They were raised in the United States," Dorrance responded.

"Were they coached by foreign coaches?"

"No, most of them were coached by American coaches. In fact, most of them are collegiate players."

"Did they play in foreign leagues?"

"No, they are American college players who came up through American youth leagues."

Nothing convinced the press. They couldn't be persuaded that elite soccer could be produced in America by Americans. Finally one of them stared down Dorrance and asked, "What is your background?"

"Well, I was born in Bombay, India, and at the age of three I moved to Calcutta. Then I moved to Kenya and from there to Ethiopia, and to Singapore, and from there my family was transferred to Belgium, and while we were there I was sent to a Swiss boarding school . . ."

As Dorrance described his childhood odyssey, the reporters began nodding and scribbling in their notebooks. Finally, they'd unearthed the answer they were looking for. They could accept that Dorrance's foreign lineage had produced such sophisticated soccer. As Dorrance watched them writing, he experienced a defiant moment of clarity. Up to that point in his career, as a young and insecure coach, he had always trumpeted his foreign pedigree, because he thought it gave some credibility to what he feared was a lackluster résumé. However, bolstered by his team's success, Dorrance finally mustered the guts to embrace his true background for the first time. Dorrance concluded his answer to the reporters by proudly stating, ". . . but I learned how to play soccer at the University of North Carolina in Chapel Hill, and I learned how to coach soccer at the United States Soccer Federation coaching schools and from the National Soccer Coaches Association of America convention clinics. I learned everything I know about soccer *in the United States of America.*"

Six days before the World Championship final in China and half a world away in Chapel Hill, the University of North Carolina faced Wisconsin for the 1991 NCAA championship. By request of the nine former and current Tar Heels on the national team, Dorrance phoned the press box every few minutes during the NCAA final. The Tar Heel nine sat in the hallway of the White Swan Hotel in Guangzhou, anxiously awaiting updates. Dorrance had no angst about leaving his UNC team behind because he is not a micromanager; he trusted Bill Palladino at the helm. When Dorrance phoned for the final time and learned that UNC had won the game 3–1 to capture its tenth national title despite missing its two best players, Hamm and Lilly, the coach signed off by saying, 'Great, tell the girls I said, 'Hi.'"

Dorrance was excited to be in China because of his family's historical connection to that country. His players did not share his enthusiasm. In the city where the team was residing, Guangzhou, there is a saying that they eat everything with four legs except the table. The players were served dog, ox, and cat, which meant they mostly ate Snickers, available in bulk because the candy's company was an event sponsor. The players did receive a $10 food per diem, but what were they going to buy? More dog?

In team meetings before the tournament began, Dorrance coaxed each of his players to win the championship in the theater of her mind, by asking, "How many people ever get the chance to be the best in the world at something?" Then he told them all that they could pursue their goal in one of two ways. They could try to sneak up on the world and win it, or they could decide to go in with a favorite's mentality and let everyone come after them, leaving no doubt he preferred the more aggressive approach. He hammered the point that to win the World Championship they all must win their individual duels by repeatedly telling them, "I respect talent, but I admire courage." He then assured them that whatever success they had would be their gift to the United States, but warned them not to succumb to the pressure of trying to win for America, because if they played for themselves they'd play with more freedom. Finally, he lowered outside expectations by telling the press that a U.S. win would be equivalent to a Russian baseball team winning the World Series, and he kept his team loose by sharing an old joke about sending an all-female army to fight a war. *If we win, that's great. If we lose, we just say, "Big deal, you just beat a bunch of women."*

Dorrance's personal incentive entering the World Championship came from reading the comments of Hubert Vogelsinger, a prominent German soccer clinician, who said that the American team was talented, but they lacked the necessary understanding of what the pressure is like to win a world title. Dorrance thought Vogelsinger was dead wrong. He thought his team was ready.

There were landmark victories along the way. After the United States shut out Brazil 5–0 in Panyu on November 19, Brazilian coach Fernando Pires gave his counterpart one of the greatest compliments Dorrance believes he's ever been paid by another coach, when Pires said, "I would like the American coach to know that of all the teams in this World Championship, including my own, his plays most like Brazilians."

Eight days later, the United States faced Germany in the semifinals. Dorrance was convinced that the Germans would be too proud to alter their style of working the ball mechanically out of the back, so he told his forwards to play furious high pressure and tackle for turnovers. Jennings scored three goals and Heinrichs added two as the United States played its best game of the tournament and destroyed Germany 5–2, after which the German coach, Gero Bisanz, launched into a tirade about how thuggishly the Americans had played. A few minutes later, German assistant coach Tina Theune-Meyer stopped Dorrance in the bowels of the stadium and apologized for the remarks of her boss. Theune-Meyer told him, "We all want you to know that you and your players had a tremendous game plan and they played a great game, and that's how we all really feel."

Newspapers around the world ran flashy stories throughout the World Championship and television crews beamed games back to more than one hundred countries, but not to the United States. When the tournament began, the American media contingent consisted of *Soccer New England, Soccer America, Soccer International, Shots On Goal,* and just one daily publication, *USA Today,* which sold out before dawn to fans in America's few soccer hotbeds. Many U.S. players sent home faxes to their friends and family to report the results. As the U.S. team advanced through the draw, the *New York Times* and the *Washington Post* dispatched stringers, and *Sports Illustrated* sent a correspondent from Beijing who had never covered a soccer match. Dorrance welcomed the lack of American media coverage because it afforded him an escape from second-guessing.

The starting lineup for the World Championship final included six Tar Heels: Hamm, Lilly, Heinrichs, Werden, Linda Hamilton, and Shannon Higgins. Yet another Tar Heel alum, Birthe Hegstad, started at midfielder for Norway.

Dorrance began the pregame by reading a poem that he told the players was written by one of their mothers:

> *Years ago when you were born*
> *Women's team sports was an oxymoron*
> *We held you close and searched your face*
> *For signs of your talent, your fate, your grace.*
> *I thought you'd be a teacher, nurse or aesthetician*
> *Didn't think of president, lawyer, obstetrician*
> *It wasn't that I doubted you*
> *It's just the way it was*
> *But then, I didn't know then you'd grow up*
> *With such a cause.*
> *Yes, you've arrived, the goal is in sight*
> *But the cup is not all, let's get this right . . .*
> *Along the way you grew up well*
> *You're beautiful people, we're proud as hell!*
> *No matter what happens, I know what you are*
> *I didn't really have to come this far*

> *To see it inside you, to see it so clear*
> *You're a woman, of course, and a CHAMPION, my dear.*
> *Mom*

When Dorrance finished reading the poem, there were a lot of tears in the room. Dorrance intentionally did not reveal whose mother had written it because he wanted every player to wonder if her mother had penned the words; that way it touched all of his players with the same power. Higgins didn't learn until after the game that her mother was the poet.

Dorrance then concluded his pregame remarks by dictating a laundry list of why the United States was going to win. *We are the best team. We are the fastest. We are the fittest. We are the smartest. We are the toughest. We are the best headers. We are the best tacklers. We are the best 1 v. 1. We are the best team . . . We are the best team.*

It was clear to Dorrance from the opening minute of the final that his team had emerged from the brutal semifinal victory over Germany exhausted and spent, and hadn't sufficiently recovered in time for Norway. Still, despite his team's tired legs, Dorrance ordered the same maximum high pressure that had withered the Germans. Akers scored for the United States in the twentieth minute on a header off a pass from Higgins, and Norway answered eight minutes later to tie the score 1–1 at halftime.

Dorrance recalls that intermission as being the most disjointed of his entire career. Higgins, his brain on the field, was trying to explain to him all the things that were going wrong, but the list was so extensive and left so little room for optimism that Dorrance was afraid that sharing it might shatter his team's fragile confidence. He addressed a few of Higgins' key points and then explained how the Americans could win the game in the second half.

During that final half, Dorrance was concerned about his weary players, but he made no substitutions because his team hadn't played enough international games to develop any experienced depth, and he sensed that substituting might suggest concern. Norway clearly controlled the run of play after halftime, pinning the fatigued American players back in their own end of the field. Still, the game remained tied 1–1 into the final minutes as the 59,000 Chinese fans, then the largest crowd ever to watch a women's soccer game, cheered decisively for the Americans.

With only three minutes left in regulation time, Norwegian defender Tina Svensson misplayed a ball back to goalkeeper Reidun Seth. Akers intercepted the back pass, dribbled around Seth toward the left goalpost, and paused for a moment before the open goal with the ball at her feet. Time stopped for Dorrance as Akers shifted her body to shoot with her dominant right foot instead of the left, just to make sure she wouldn't miss. When Akers tucked the ball into the back of the net, Dorrance's immediate thoughts were not of victory, but of all the games he'd seen lost with a lead in the final minutes. Heinrichs pulled the American team together and said what she'd heard her coach say so many times in that situation. *We've only got a few more minutes. Hang on! Ride this sucker out!* Dorrance stood up off the bench for the first time in the game and implored his team: *No fouls! No fouls!* The final minutes seemed interminable for him. Seconds turned into hours. Finally, the whistle blew.

At the end, everybody on the U.S. bench, from coaches to reserve players to trainers to equipment managers, rushed joyously out onto the field past Dorrance, who was walking in the other direction, back to the bench, where he sat slumped, looking more like the beaten coach. "When we won I was shocked by what I felt," Dorrance says. "I felt absolutely no joy, no excitement, no thrill of victory. I was just glad that it was over. It was more a sense of relief and duty served. I felt like a sentry who had completed the midnight-to-8 a.m. shift, and I was just glad nothing had been screwed up on my watch."

Dorrance didn't have a chance to speak to his team after the game. There were fireworks. Jennings, the World Championship MVP, led the U.S. team on a victory lap around Tianhe Stadium. Akers was joined on the field by her husband, Robbie, who was crying for the first time she could ever remember.

In the postgame press conference, Dorrance genuflected to Norway's coach Even Pellerud, conceding that Norway outplayed his team and that victory could easily have been theirs. Pellerud responded by saying, "Perhaps we did play well today, but in my mind and in the minds of everybody in this tournament, the best team in this world championship, from the first game to the last, was the United States."

As the Americans exited the stadium, Chinese fans clamored around the team bus for autographs. On the ride back to the hotel, the team savored its victory to the soundtrack of the movie *Working Girl,* the story of a woman succeeding in a male-dominated world. When the Americans arrived back at the White Swan, the Swedish players had spelled out *Congratulations United States World Champions* with their yellow socks in the hotel hallway.

The U.S. team then attended a FIFA championship banquet at the hotel, where Tracey Bates followed through on a promise she'd made to Jennings if the United States won, by drinking the first and only beer of her life. Then the players organized their own after-party across the hall from the banquet. Dorrance returned to his room before the latter celebration began. He was in bed reading himself to sleep when he received a phone call from one of his favorite players, Joy Biefeld, saying, "Anson, we'd like to have you come and be with us." It was an offer he couldn't refuse. Dorrance joined his team at the party, where he listened to a victory poem from team poet laureate Amy Allmann and watched some improvised team skits before his players eventually implored him to share his feelings and the room fell hush. "Tonight was one of those wonderful opportunities that only comes around once," Dorrance told his players. "What excited me about it so much is how incredibly unlikely it was. I've got years of dealing with the love-hate attitude toward America, and I had a lot tied up in this. This was more than a soccer game for me. This is a validation of our way of life. This is their game, and they respect the people who play this game well, and we won the damn thing.

What I wanted to do was something absolutely unprecedented in our game, an American team to win a world championship in soccer. This was their game and we beat them at their game. All of them." Then Dorrance paused for a moment and concluded, "I am damn proud to be an American."

When the world champions arrived back on American soil at John F. Kennedy Airport in New York the day after the tournament, there were three people there to greet them.

It wasn't until the following morning, when Dorrance sat up in his bed back in Chapel Hill and looked through some recent newspapers, that he recognized what he'd just done. He was stunned to see an article on the front page of the *Washington Post* tucked below the fold in the bottom left corner. The headline read, *A Dream Comes True in Soccer*. He stared at those words, realizing when he saw it in black and white that his dream hadn't really been a dream after all. He got up from the first long and peaceful sleep he'd enjoyed in a month and turned on the stereo, allowing himself to celebrate for the first time. Still dressed in his pajamas, he cranked up the music as loud as the dial would permit, and he jumped around his bedroom like a little kid. He was joyous, totally relaxed, and proud of what all of his hard work had produced. He didn't have a worry in the world for the first time he could remember since he'd taken the national team job five years earlier.

Wherever Dorrance traveled in the months that followed, he spouted the same themes. *I am proud to be an American, I am proud to be a product of our coaching system, and I am proud to be a world champion.* He was bemused by the leverage he had suddenly acquired in the soccer community. "By winning you actually gain an unrealistic credibility," Dorrance said four days after the final in China. "Because we are the world champions and because I am the world championship coach, I will have a ridiculous credibility now. So whatever I say, everyone will suddenly think it has some meaning. Isn't that absurd?"

Dorrance promised to take advantage of his increased visibility by stumping for his sport as much as possible. "Anson had a vision back then," Julie Foudy says. "His constant mantra at the World Championship was that this was a chance to impact the way people view soccer in the United States. You have to sell the sport to America. It sounded great. We bought into it. Of course that didn't happen right away. When we came back nobody knew where the hell we'd been."

Akers remembers a plane trip shortly after the 1991 World Championship, when she was seated beside an elderly woman. Akers mentioned that she had just returned from a trip to China.

"What were you doing in China?" the woman asked.

"Playing soccer," Akers said. "We just won the world championship."

"Oh, that's nice, dear."

In January the team was invited to Washington, D.C., for a celebration with President George Bush. At the White House the players were asked by the press to line up in alphabetical order so that they could be identified. At the ceremony

President Bush said, "They say that sport is the great equalizer of the genders; for the sake of the male ego, let's hope the men catch up . . . soon."

Dorrance wasn't scheduled to speak at the reception, but as soon as Bush completed his remarks and turned to shake Dorrance's hand, the coach stepped to the podium and delivered his stump speech about defeating the world at its own game, selling the sport, and winning more world championships in the future.

During a layover in the midst of their fifty-two-hour plane journey home from China, Dorrance and his assistant coach Tony DiCicco had huddled in the Admirals Club in Zurich. Scribbling on cocktail napkins, they forecast future U.S. national team lineups, plotting how the Americans were going to win the next one, constructing a dynasty.

Three years earlier, he'd quit the first time. Back in the days leading up to the 1991 World Championship, Dorrance had informed Art Walls, one of his few allies at the USSF, that he would resign immediately upon completion of the United States' last match in the tournament. Dorrance refused to give his many enemies in the Federation the satisfaction of firing him if he lost, and if he won, great, he would go out on top. Dorrance had effectively given his two weeks' notice. "I wanted to leave, because the way the Federation treated coaches was abominable, and I didn't ever want to let those assholes determine the quality of life for me and my family," Dorrance says. "It was a very, very lonely job, and I had to watch my back every single day. They were dying for me to fail. I had too much power and influence for them. I could walk into a room, and no matter who else was in the room, if they had an opinion and I had an opinion, my opinion would rule, and they hated that. The only reason I was still employed was because I could win."

After the United States won the World Championship, Walls implored Dorrance to remain as national team coach, convincing him that nobody was properly prepared to replace him. Dorrance felt an obligation to use the team's success to sell the game, and though he no longer wanted to be the coach, he couldn't bear to watch what he had struggled so hard to build promptly crumble in his wake. Walls assumed that he had coaxed Dorrance back for the long haul, but Dorrance refused repeated offers to quit his job at UNC and join the Federation full-time, a move he viewed as tantamount to professional suicide. Instead he used the next two years to surreptitiously groom his successor. Ever the strategist, Dorrance had devised a plan to allow him to determine the coach to take his place. He waited until the U.S. Cup tournament in the summer of 1994. Dorrance was convinced the national team would play well in that event, so on July 29, 1994, two days before the tournament began, he informed USSF officials that he would sit on the bench during the tournament as a figurehead, but that Tony DiCicco would do all of the actual coaching. Though Dorrance received credit for the final victories of his national team coaching career, DiCicco coached the United States to victories over its three staunchest rivals, Germany, China, and Norway, over the next ten days. The USSF had no choice but to confirm

DiCicco and appease Dorrance, who had promised to keep his resignation secret until after the event, when it would look like promoting DiCicco had been the Federation's idea all along.

Hours before Dorrance told the Federation of his decision to resign, the U.S. women's national team gathered for a meeting in a hotel conference room in Columbia, Maryland. The players expected a strategy talk, and none had any inkling of what was coming. Against his custom, Dorrance had written out his entire speech word for word and rehearsed it several times, so that just in case he choked up he would be able to continue his thoughts. During the five-minute address, he didn't talk about the past, only the future. He told the team they were young and would only get better under DiCicco's guidance. He assured them that anytime they'd go in hard on a tackle he'd still be right there with them. He found it cathartic to share his affection for them. Then he concluded with one of his favorite quotes, a line from Charles de Gaulle: *Graveyards are filled with irreplaceable men.*

"I was shocked and saddened because Anson was our fearless leader and he left so suddenly and so unexpectedly," Foudy says. "I remember that meeting like it was yesterday. I remember the room. I remember the tears. I remember thinking that this would be a huge loss for us."

Later that evening Tisha Venturini visited Dorrance in his room. During her four seasons at UNC, Venturini had always been quiet and unemotional, rarely saying more than three words at a time. "When Anson quit I was so distraught, and it hit me that I respected and loved the guy a lot, but I'd never told him that," Venturini says. "I wanted to thank him for everything he'd done for my career and my family, and I just started bawling."

Says Dorrance, "I'd never seen that side of Tish before, and I was touched. It melted me. I thought, 'My gosh, these girls really care about me.' It was kind of a shock."

Dorrance resigned with a record of 58-22-5 internationally, and the 1991 Women's World Championship title, having established the United States as the best women's soccer team in the world. His reasons for leaving were all about responsibility to aspects of his life far more important to him than coaching America. He could sense that the landscape of college soccer was changing. He could look over his shoulder and see that the distance between him and his collegiate pursuers simply wasn't so vast anymore. He felt something stirring inside him—that as a coach he was becoming less interested in the chessboard and more interested in the individual pieces. And most importantly he felt guilty about how he'd neglected his duties as a husband and father, lamenting that he'd been married for twenty years and had spent the last eighteen working at least two jobs and often three.

Sure, Dorrance could have hung on to the job and coached the team through the 1995 World Championship and the 1996 Olympics. With his detractors muzzled, he could have continued on a part-time basis, or on whatever terms he chose. But since his days a decade earlier as the regional coach, Dorrance had always preached the value of turnover, of developing new leadership voices, as a means of growing the game.

Dorrance relished the irony two weeks after his resignation when he went public and explained the termination of his tumultuous tenure as the national team coach by stating, "They say the best time to retire is when everybody wants you to stay."

13 | *Selling*

Nothing in this world can take the place of persistence. Talent will not; nothing is more common than unsuccessful men with talent. Genius will not; unrewarded genius is almost a proverb. Education will not; the world is full of educated derelicts. Persistence and determination alone are omnipotent.

—Calvin Coolidge

In the fall of 1974, Anson Dorrance submitted his meager résumé to the Snelling and Snelling employment agency in Chapel Hill. He took an aptitude test, and when the results were examined, Dorrance was pointed to the local branch of Fidelity Union Life Insurance Company. Before starting a job there, Dorrance spent five days attending the Fidelity Union Insurance School at Southfork Ranch in Dallas, the future location for the television show *Dallas.* The school's buzz phrases resonated with him:

> *Everyone's a prospect.*
> *Sell yourself.*
> *Turn negatives into positives.*
> *From the opening line, you are closing.*
> *Be honest.*

Dorrance sold what was called the College Master Plan, cold calling college students as they were preparing to graduate. It's a tough job selling life insurance to twenty-one-year-olds, and Dorrance struggled at first. When telephoning wasn't producing results, he canvassed door to door and realized that people had a tougher time rejecting him in person. He'd drive to his office every Sunday evening and make fifty phone calls. Five of those people would agree to meet him, and if one of them bought a policy, he and M'Liss could survive for another week. "The wonderful lesson I learned as a young man is that success is all about grinding, grinding, grinding," Dorrance says. "It was a job full of stress and doubt, but it was forging because I had to become steeled to adversity and numbed to rejection. I had to develop an unbelievably tough skin and learn about social and verbal agility. If you can sell insurance, you can sell anything."

Because Big Pete was essentially an oil salesman, he took a keen interest in teaching his son the required resiliency of salesmanship. Every month he would send Anson a letter packed with encouraging maxims like *Don't let anyone get the better of you* or *Hard work pays off.* Once, Big Pete enclosed an editorial cartoon featuring a man stoically observing a train derailing off a bridge into a gorge. The caption read simply, "Shit." Anson got the message. Though his work-day might feel like a series of train wrecks, he must keep dialing the next number, ringing the next doorbell. Big Pete also mailed Anson a placard for his desk. On the side that faced out to the customer the placard read, *Illegitimus Non Carborundum.* The side that faced Anson provided the rough translation: *Don't Let the Bastards Grind You Down.*

Ask Dorrance about the single most important element in UNC's success, and he'll answer immediately with one word: *Recruiting.* Dorrance subscribes to the axiom put forth by renowned Oklahoma football coach Barry Switzer, who once said, "It's not the alignment, it's the align*ees.*"

Dorrance has known it ever since he enlisted those kids from the local park to win games in Rainbow or signed up as many McLean Grasshoppers as he could. Good players win games. "If you talk to people who are astute about soccer, they'll tell you that UNC is not doing anything particularly sophisticated on the field, and we never have," Bill Palladino says. "We're successful because of the athletes we have. There's no magic to it. If you gave Anson the players at N.C. State, maybe he could motivate them to play at a higher level, but could they win the national championship? No way."

A few minutes after UNC defeated Tennessee 3–1 in a 2002 NCAA Tourna-ment game at Fetzer Field, Dorrance scanned the crowded bleachers and said to no one in particular, "I wonder if somewhere up there tonight a twelve-year-old girl decided she wanted to be a Tar Heel?"

For some, it starts with a pillowcase. One local company, which devotes itself solely to selling North Carolina women's soccer gear, offers a Carolina blue pil-lowcase with an inscription that reads, *The Dream Starts Here.*

In June of 2003 a letter arrived at the Tar Heel women's soccer office with a drawing of a female stick figure wearing UNC jersey number 15 and some child-ish scribbling:

Dear Mr. Dorrance,

I am eight years old. I would like to play on your team in ten years. I play defense. Me and my friend Cherie are good soccer players. I heard that you won lots of national championships. I live in Florida. I would like to come to North Carolina and kick some dukies. I have a poster of all the years you won.

Sara Winch

At the time, Sara's father, Bob, was coaching at UNC's one-time bitter rival Central Florida.

Dorrance estimates that close to half of the young women who have become Tar Heels have written to him before he ever contacted them. "Recruiting is incredibly fragile, because kids don't really review statistics or do a lot of research to decide where to play," Dorrance says. "When you're a kid you glance up one day and you see Carolina blue, and that's all it takes, and you build on that and decide that's your dream. We want to always be in that glance."

Anne Felts, who was raised in tiny Rolla, Missouri, can still recall an article from the local newspaper when she was ten years old in which she is quoted as saying she wanted to play college soccer at North Carolina. Eleven-year-old Kendall Fletcher was a UNC soccer ballgirl who painted a facsimile of Fetzer Field on her bedroom ceiling, with the overhead light as the center circle. Kristin Acquavella played youth soccer for a team coached by Wendy Gebauer's father, Howard, and one day when Wendy showed up at practice and foot-juggled a softball one hundred times, Acquavella vowed right then to follow Gebauer to UNC. Cindy Parlow was a thirteen-year-old Vanderbilt fan when Dorrance did an autograph signing at a local soccer store in her hometown of Memphis, right after winning the 1991 World Championship. Parlow was too shy to ask for an autograph herself, so she asked her mom to do it while Cindy lingered in the back of the store, watching Dorrance interact with the small throng of girls who had gathered around him. When Josephine Parlow returned with the signed poster, Cindy told her, "Mom, I'm going to play for that man someday." Four years later, Parlow skipped her senior year of high school and joined the Tar Heels without ever visiting the campus or seeing the team play.

Sarah Kate Noftsinger captured the mindset of many Tar Heel prospects in her UNC application essay: *To me Fetzer Field is to soccer like Yankee Stadium is to baseball. It is a place of dreams, legends, and winning. I've dreamed of the day I will step across the line onto Fetzer Field with "TAR HEEL" written in bold across my chest for everyone to see. Some people want to go to the University of North Carolina to win a national championship, but all I want is the chance to fulfill a lifelong reverie. Some people would call it an obsession, but I prefer to call it a dream, a dream I've had for as long as I can recall.*

"There have always been kids who have grown up longing to go to Carolina, and they will want to go there regardless," UCLA coach Jill Ellis says. "If a little girl dreams of Tar Heel blue, other coaches just have to say, 'That's fine. Do what you want to do.'"

Says Santa Clara coach Jerry Smith: "I recently had a recruit leave me a phone message saying, 'I've accepted an offer from the school I've always dreamed of going to . . . UNC.' I've also gotten e-mail messages from recruits whose web addresses are something like *IloveUNC@aol.com.* Gimme a break. How am I supposed to recruit against that?"

While it's ironic that Dorrance, who grew up shy and awkward around teenage women, has spent his career trying to court them to play for him at UNC, it helps that he recruits to a place that bills itself as the Southern Part of Heaven. "It's pretty easy to recruit to Carolina if you ask me, because you have a university that's unbelievable academically in one of the most gorgeous parts of the country, and it's a fun school," Nel Fettig says. "Anson doesn't have a very hard sell. When Anson calls a girl the first time as a recruit, it's the call that a lot of young girls have waited for their whole lives."

The salesman in Dorrance recognizes the inherent advantages of selling an attractive product. Says Dorrance, "I've always thought that if you bring a kid onto the UNC campus in the springtime and she decides to go someplace else, then she is absolutely crazy and we don't want her anyway."

On top of that, Dorrance has parlayed two enormous recruiting advantages in his career. His was the first school in the South and among the first in the country to offer scholarships in women's soccer. And while he was with the national team, he either coached many of the country's elite players before they made their college decisions or was viewed as the most prudent choice as a college coach for those who aspired to that level. Most rival coaches found Dorrance's position as the national team coach to be an unfair recruiting edge. Dorrance argues the advantages gained were balanced out by the recruits he lost because of his time spent training and traveling with the national team, but even he can't point to any specific recruits he lost as evidence.

"I compete with Anson in recruiting, and he's pretty much the god of NCAA soccer," says Tennessee coach Ange Kelly, a Tar Heel alum. "The bottom line is that if Anson really wants a player and is prepared to give her the same scholarship as anybody else, he can get almost any player he wants. I could spend six months on a girl, and he could make one phone call, and all I've done would be nullified."

"Just like Dean Smith, for many years Anson hasn't so much recruited as he's *selected*," Moyer Smith says. "But in order to win all those national titles you still have to make the right selections."

It's a moment. A snapshot. Nothing more. That's what Dorrance is looking for. He's chasing the embodiment of the margin of victory, a quality that separates one player from everybody else on the field. It could be skill or speed or aggression or toughness or passion or a selfish belief that the ball is rightly hers, or it could be a unique combination of the lot. But it happens in the blink of an eye. "In most games, there will come a defining moment for a player that calls for her to do the extraordinary, to achieve a split second of success by sacrificing her body or exploding to a higher energy level," Dorrance says. "Will she take that chance? Will she expose herself to success or failure? Or will she slow up that microsecond that allows her to both look good and still avoid that bone-chilling tackle? The ones who are willing to lay it on the line are the ones I recruit."

Rival coaches wonder why Dorrance watches only snippets of games in a recruiting situation. It is because he is often sold by that single moment, that one burst of greatness. If Dorrance is on the sideline, a prospect can literally earn a scholarship with one stifling slide tackle or one deft touch. He measures a player's competitive potential by watching her in the instant right after her team has either won or lost the ball, that moment of transition where almost every player takes a little break. In the first fifteen seconds of the first game that Dorrance ever saw Mia Hamm play, he noticed that she didn't take that break. He decided he wanted to coach Hamm before he ever saw her touch the ball.

Dorrance often watches a player only once in recruiting, so he'd better have a good eye, and he admits that he honed his instincts largely through making mistakes. He confesses that his poor decisions have all been the result of choosing pure talent over less obvious complementary attributes like competitiveness and self-discipline, the qualities that he believes allow a college coach to truly develop a player.

Dorrance says he looks for women who play like men—more accurately, play like him. Dorrance remembers a moment scouting Libby Guess when she challenged a goalkeeper for a flighted 50-50 ball. "It was a situation where 99 percent of players would have cringed or ducked, but Libby didn't flinch," Dorrance says. "There was a horrific collision, but Libby put the ball in the back of the net as the goalie punched her in the face. It was man-style. I said to myself, 'Yes, *that's* a Tar Heel!'"

Dorrance also seeks out girls with big dreams or big brothers. Ideally both. Dorrance thought Tiffany Roberts might be a Tar Heel when he learned she'd grown up with three older brothers who would regularly stick her in front of their hockey goal and fire slapshots at her. He knew she was a Tar Heel when she told him about being asked in the third grade to draw a picture of the nicest dream she ever had, and she sketched herself winning an Olympic gold medal in soccer, long before soccer was even an Olympic sport.

Dorrance's secret to recruiting is . . . *ssshhhhh* . . . there is no secret.

When he is first asked, he says that his recruiting technique is the one element of his program that he is reluctant to talk about publicly. Fifteen minutes later, with very little prodding, he lays out his entire strategy. He has talked himself into the fact that it is safe to do so because nobody will believe it anyway.

Recruiting is just another war game to Dorrance, and he learned most of what he would need to win it at Fidelity Union Insurance School. Almost everything Dorrance does or says is filtered through the prism of recruiting: the speeches, the clinics, the gear, the memorabilia taped to his office door, even his own autograph, *Anson Dorrance, Coach UNC.* "I always sign with UNC because you never know who you're signing for, and any teenager in the back of the room could be Cindy Parlow," Dorrance says. "I'm always trying to spread the religion of UNC because you never know who might be able to help you. Anyone who walks through my door, I try to treat them like gold." *Everyone's a prospect.*

Dorrance's recruiting is UNC-centric. He abhors negative recruiting, believes it is dishonorable and immoral. The entire focus of his recruiting pitch is how wonderful it is to be a Tar Heel. He lays out all the positive aspects of his school, his players, and his player development. *Sell yourself.* He never talks about UNC in comparison with another program. Meanwhile, he assumes that other schools are negatively recruiting UNC, but he thinks that tactic backfires on them because they are spending time countering the negative attacks they believe he is making against them. Dorrance wants them punching at air.

Because UNC's tradition goes a long way toward selling the program by itself, the most critical part of Dorrance's job in recruiting is to play defense. His challenge is to dispel what he calls "the myths," the counter-recruiting done by other coaches who tell prospects that UNC is an emotionless soccer factory, that Dorrance's system discourages individuality, that UNC offers no full scholarships, that UNC only gives playing time to national team players, that Dorrance is a taskmaster, that Santa Claus and the Tooth Fairy both opted for Duke. Dorrance must first decipher which of these myths are being employed against him for a particular player and then commence *counter*-counter-recruiting. Playing time is usually the biggest concern, and in 2001 when an anxious recruit asked Dorrance about this, he gave her the following response: "If you don't think you can play here then we don't want you, but we wouldn't be recruiting you if we didn't think you could help us. Let me ask you a question. Do you want to be the best? You need to play against the best in practice every day. You need to play with the best in matches and against the best schedule in the sport. Do you want to be the best? If you do, come here. If you don't, you're better off at another school. Are you with me?"

In 2002, an assistant coach at Texas wrote prospect Libby Guess a lengthy letter that focused less on why she should pick Texas than on why she should *not* pick UNC. "She wrote that if I came to UNC, I'd be just another good player in a long line, and I'd get more recognition at Texas," Guess says. "They tried to turn me against UNC, but it had the opposite effect. I wanted to be another player that came to UNC and succeeded and was part of the tradition. What other coaches used to turn me off, really turned me on."

Says Catherine Reddick: "Other coaches play the underdog card. *Wouldn't you rather be the team that beats North Carolina than just be North Carolina?* That's a good ploy. Being the underdog appeals to a lot of girls, but I asked myself, 'Is a team that's never beaten North Carolina going to make me a better player? If so, why haven't they ever beaten UNC? Do I want to be the team that tries to beat North Carolina or do I want to be the team that wins?'"

Says Leslie Gaston: "UNC was my last recruiting visit, and all four of the other schools I visited said, 'We want you to commit to us before you visit North Carolina.' That just made me wonder, 'Why are they so scared of UNC? It must be pretty great there.'"

So sophisticated have rival coaches become at planting doubts in the minds of recruits about UNC that the Tar Heel coaching staff finally compiled a pamphlet called the *Book of Myths* that answers all the anti-UNC propaganda that Tar Heel coaches had gleaned from their players over the years. One Californian whom UNC recruited even mentioned that another college coach had warned her about Chapel Hill's stifling humidity. Ever the salesman, Dorrance found the bright side. *Turn negatives into positives.* "Yes, it is humid here, but you want it to be humid," Dorrance told her. "Someday you want to play on the national team, don't you? Well, they don't get to pick where they play, and they will play in humid places. You want to be ready for anything, don't you?"

The recruit nodded. Dorrance had sold humidity as a positive.

Once he's eliminated the brainwashing, Dorrance can bring his weapons to bear. Because Dorrance acknowledges that the state of North Carolina is a "soccer desert" that produces far fewer players than soccer hotbeds like California, Florida, and Texas, it's critical that UNC somehow attract players from those areas, and no college coach has a better platform from which to scout talent than UNC Girls' Soccer Camp. It is implied that almost everybody who attends UNC's summer camps has at least some interest in becoming a Tar Heel, so it is essentially a mass audition for the 2,000 girls who flock to the camp each summer. For Dorrance it is a chance to set the hook. As the climax of each camp day, Dorrance shares with the entire camp community the story of Mia Hamm's solitary wind sprints or Carla Werden's transformation in 1 v. 1 in a scene reminiscent of a sermon.

Dorrance recruits directly from his camps, and he gets results. Seven of the eleven UNC starters on the 1996 national championship team were former UNC campers. One day at a regional camp in Dallas in 1987, Dorrance said that he would give Tracey Bates's scholarship to anyone who could beat her in a 1 v. 1 drill. Only six-year-old Jordan Walker raised her hand to volunteer, and from that day on Walker never missed a Tar Heel camp and joined the Tar Heels eleven years later. Robin Confer didn't know anything about the Tar Heels' tradition when she first attended a UNC camp as a high school freshman, but she instantly loved the way campers competed, and she kept returning to Chapel Hill each summer until she was sold on playing for Dorrance. Pam Kalinoski can still remember a day as a counselor at a North Carolina camp when Elizabeth Ball announced to her that she would be attending UNC. Since Ball was only twelve years old, it was a bit early for a verbal commitment, but Ball eventually signed with the Tar Heels five years later as one of the top recruits in her class.

Nobody at UNC soccer had ever heard of Katie Brooks when she arrived for camp in the summer of 2003. Brooks was a rising senior who had primarily played lacrosse at Winchester (Massachusetts) High and was being recruited by nobody to play soccer. Then one day her mother, Sue, was checking the Internet for dates for the Duke lacrosse camp when she stumbled upon the UNC soccer web site. She knew Katie had always harbored a desire to play soccer at UNC and had once even written a letter to Dorrance that she never mailed because she thought she wasn't good enough. Sue Brooks encouraged her daughter to chase her dream, so she signed Katie up for a session of UNC soccer camp just two days before it began. As soon as Brooks arrived, she turned heads in camp. Dorrance watched Brooks play in the championship game on the camp's final day and was so impressed that he invited her to his office after the camp. They talked about fate, and Dorrance offered her the chance to attend UNC. Two weeks later, Brooks was a Tar Heel.

Once Dorrance has chosen his targets, the foundation stones of his recruiting pitch are his recruiting letters. Over the course of every year he writes nearly forty letters to potential recruits. They are thorough two-page letters, often painstakingly revised by Dorrance as many as fifteen times before they are sent. Each letter is mailed to about fifty recruits, but it is always subtly targeted at UNC's most prized prospect, the propaganda within chosen specifically for her. They read like newsletters, providing details about UNC's recent games or other news within the program, and they often end with an inspirational anecdote. They are designed to treat Tar Heel recruits as if they are already part of the family. Says Jordan Walker: "It's like getting a letter from a soldier writing home from the war." Randy and Ninalyn Oxenham enjoyed reading Dorrance's letters so much that they waited for four months after their daughter, Gwendolyn, had committed to Duke to inform UNC that it was wasting its postage.

Most players admit that they read only Dorrance's first few letters in their entirety before the sheer volume becomes numbing, and even Dorrance jokes that the strategy behind them is akin to Chinese water torture. Eventually the players skim down through the letter to the personal handwritten note that Dorrance scribbles to some of his most prized recruits at the end of each letter. In March of 1998, he wrote the following at the bottom of a recruiting letter to Susan Bush:

> Susan, I know this was a long letter, but I wanted to share with you how seriously we are going to take your development. I consider players like you a national treasure and I do not want to leave anything to chance. You are special to me and to this country. I will take care of you. Anson

The first time Dorrance telephones a recruit, he is immediately trying to figure out which element of UNC's portfolio will most spark her interest. *From the opening line, you are closing.* He tries to keep the calls as brief as possible, but it is during these phone calls that Dorrance has his only real opportunity to find out if any of the anti-UNC myths have taken hold. It's not easy for Dorrance to connect with every sixteen-year-old, but just as he did in his insurance days, he tries to keep the prospect talking. "Those first moments on the phone with a teenager are like climbing a sheer cliff," Dorrance says. "I'm desperately looking for the slightest toehold to keep climbing and not fall off into oblivion. I know that UNC has a chance if the girl treats me like a human being."

All Dorrance really wants is to eventually lure the girl for a campus visit, confident that once a recruit actually meets him and sees the program for herself, the myths will disappear. For many the recruiting trip to North Carolina is the strangest of all campus visits because there is so little structure. Dorrance completely hands recruits over to his players and lets them do much of the selling, partly because he figures that most women will come to UNC based on how well they like their future teammates, but also because, as he likes to say, "there is nothing more exhausting for me than being polite to people all day." The primary contact that recruits have with Dorrance is what has come to be known affectionately as the "Campus Sprint," when the Tar Heels coach leads a lightning quick forty-five-minute tour of the UNC campus. Dorrance's tours have become more streamlined ever since the day in 1977 when he wanted to show recruit Ricky Marvin and his parents a typical UNC dormitory room, so he walked into Winston dorm and knocked on a random door. A voice inside invited the group to come in, and when Dorrance opened the door, the tour stumbled upon four college boys huddled around a bong.

Dorrance also tends to surprise recruits with his lack of feel-good promises. *Be honest.* It was a lesson Dorrance learned from his first insurance boss, Murray Strawbridge, who repeatedly reminded him about the dangers of "puffing," the sketchy sales practice of making one's product sound a bit better than it actually is. In his early days, Dorrance sold recruits a best-case scenario for playing time, and when that assessment proved overly optimistic, the player held it against him. These days Dorrance errs on the conservative side, deciding it is best to underpromise playing time and then hopefully overdeliver.

During the 2001 season, a recruit met with Dorrance and received the following cautionary pitch:

> *If you want to come, we'd love to have you. Tactically and technically you can hang with our kids. Quickness could be a problem. You're always going to be one of the slower players on our team and that's a dilemma you'll always be fighting here. I can't guarantee that you'll play. I don't want to blow smoke because I always want you to trust me if you come here. So if you want to be guaranteed to play, if soccer is the key part of your life, then don't come here. If you decide to come here, that decision in itself tells me you're going to contribute. You'll love the challenge here. You'll love being a part of this team. You'll love walking across campus with North Carolina on your chest because the girls' soccer team means something here.*

Dorrance never really takes a break from recruiting. Just minutes after UNC defeated George Mason in the 1993 NCAA final at Fetzer Field in Mia Hamm's farewell game, Dorrance promptly gathered his three recruits for a campus sprint. Immediately after winning another title in Greensboro in 1997, Dorrance jumped into his car and drove back to Chapel Hill alone to have dinner with another recruit, Kristin DePlatchett. Each year on the morning of the off day between the NCAA semifinal and final, Dorrance has spent a couple of precious hours scouting recruits at a club tournament staged annually during the Final Four, an investment that has helped net him UNC cornerstones like Leslie Gaston and Kacey White. Even after Dorrance has signed a player, he will often travel to watch her play a game during her senior season, a gesture of appreciation that he calls "showing the love."

Some college coaches scoff at Dorrance's work ethic, implying that he has the pick of the litter, that he is a sort of Pied Piper to whom players flock when they hear his call. "Anson says he works hard in recruiting, but he doesn't compared to a lot of the coaches I see out there," says April Heinrichs, who recruited against Dorrance for nine years as the coach at Maryland and Virginia. "As long as he doesn't completely fall asleep on the job, he's always going to get some of the top kids in the country because kids want to be a part of that success."

Other coaches believe that UNC must be cheating. Once when Tar Heel alum Dawn Crow went to a youth soccer tournament in her hometown of Dallas to visit with some friends, a Connecticut coach thought she was acting as a Tar Heel scout and turned UNC in to the NCAA. When the UNC athletic compliance department contacted Crow about the allegation, she laughed and said, "Do you really think UNC needs my help in recruiting?"

"We hear a lot of ludicrous charges about what we're theoretically doing in recruiting," Dorrance says. "Other coaches don't understand that UNC's a pretty good school, we have a great tradition, and the girls that play here really enjoy it. Why is it a shock when a girl decides she wants to come here? Why does there have to be some sort of conspiracy?"

Still, Dorrance encourages his opponents' paranoid notions. "We want other coaches to believe that we recruit negatively, that we break rules, because we want all of them to have excuses to continue to lose recruits to us," Dorrance says. "We don't want them to think that we're outworking them, because then they might start working harder."

In fact, Dorrance believes he has to outhustle his opponents, because as soon as UNC shows interest in a recruit she will likely be offered a full scholarship by other schools. Meanwhile, to avoid jealousy and bidding wars, UNC offers full scholarships almost exclusively to national team players, and Dorrance's other offers are strictly based on a player's credentials. Since most elite players will therefore have to turn down a full ride somewhere else to come to UNC on a partial scholarship, Dorrance usually has to focus his pitch on elements less tangible than money. Instead he will thumb through a UNC yearbook with pictures of the program's greatest players, and then will ask a recruit what number she'd like to wear and to imagine herself in that Carolina blue jersey with that number on her chest. He asks her to become a Tar Heel in the theater of her mind. He will try to make it her dream. Sometimes he uses a line that he borrowed from Dean Smith. *This is important to you. This is your life. If you were having triple bypass surgery, wouldn't you want to know that it was being performed by someone who had done it successfully more than anybody else?*

"What sets Anson apart from everyone else is his salesmanship ability," Heinrichs says. "He's good at recruiting women because he has always sold more than soccer. He's leading women. He's not begging them to come. Basically he's telling them what they should do, and most of them like that."

Says Palladino: "The balls of some of the things Anson does in recruiting, I couldn't do. He'll go into a household of a kid who's being offered a full scholarship by a dozen other schools without a penny to offer. All he's got is a promise that if you come to North Carolina you'll become a great player. Somehow he can get away with saying something that would sound silly if anybody else were to say it. That's Anson."

Dorrance's philosophy has always been to try to lock up recruits as early as possible, before the myths take hold. Because he gets some early commitments, other coaches assume he is employing a hard sell, when any good salesman knows it is best to soft sell at the outset so as not to scare the prospect off. Jenni Branam wanted to commit to UNC without visiting, but Dorrance convinced her to visit first and make sure she felt comfortable with the school and her teammates. Jena Kluegel can still remember how every rival coach prepared her for Dorrance's high-pressure sales pitch, and then, when he first telephoned, the two spent the entire conversation talking about how he dreaded his wife dragging him to a mall opening. Toward the beginning of his recruiting of Lindsay Tarpley, Dorrance wrote her to tell her that UNC was interested in recruiting one striker, and she was on top of the list. Soon after, Dorrance received a note back from Tarpley in which she wrote, *I'm not sure I'm good enough to be a Tar Heel.* Dorrance incredulously wrote back, *If you're not good enough, would you please suggest someone we can recruit who's better?*

It's only at the culmination of the process that Dorrance's closing instinct kicks in. Libby Guess had never come to UNC camp or worn any Carolina gear or slept on any Carolina pillows. She thought she was going to Texas, because her best friend from her club team had signed there. When Guess came to UNC on an unofficial visit, Dorrance invited Guess and her mother, Page, into his office. Guess was apprehensive because she had never talked to Dorrance before. He pulled out some statistics that listed all of the former UNC players on the national team. He asked Guess what number she'd like to wear. He asked her how she liked the visit. Then he asked his customary closing question. "Libby, do you want to be a Tar Heel?"

Guess said, "I think maybe I would."

The glimmer of a positive response clicked Dorrance into his closing mode. He asked Guess, "What excites you about coming here?"

Guess talked about the tradition, the player development, her future teammates. Suddenly Guess was telling Dorrance why she should commit to UNC.

Then Dorrance said, "All right, what's stopping you from committing right now?"

"Huh?"

"Well, you like the school, you like Chapel Hill, and you want to play here, right?"

"Yeah."

"Well, what's stopping you? Why not commit?"

"Well, I promised Texas I wouldn't commit on this visit. That I would visit Texas first."

"Hell, that's just their way of recruiting against me. Why not commit right now? You want to do it? You want to commit?"

"OK, sure."

Guess's mother blanched. She asked Libby if she shouldn't keep her options open and talk to Texas.

Dorrance said, "Well, you want to be the best, be around the best, don't you, Lib?"

"Yeah."

"Then you're committed?"
"All right, yup, I'm committed."
Dorrance had moved another policy.

They've come for a million different reasons, and they've come for one reason. They all want to be the best. Dorrance got Catherine Reddick to come to UNC by telling her she would be a star, and got Mia Hamm to come by telling her that with so many stars around her she wouldn't have to be the only one. Danielle Borgman and Ange Kelly and Nel Fettig all listened to the counter-recruiting and wondered if they were good enough to play at UNC, so Dorrance appealed to their pride and challenged them to find out. "There were coaches who recruited me who said I was never going to play at Carolina," Kelly says. "If you're dealing with the most competitive women in the country, which is who Anson recruits, that's a very stupid thing to do because reverse psychology pushes them to Carolina even more to prove everybody wrong."

Eventually everyone who becomes a Tar Heel succumbs to her crush on soccer. Some even choose North Carolina over the academic prestige of attending an Ivy League school. Katie Brooks chose UNC over Dartmouth. Maggie Tomecka and Marcia McDermott both spurned Harvard. Tracy Noonan turned down both Harvard and Dartmouth. "I remember sitting in high school homeroom one day with this kid who was a die-hard scholar and really wanted to go to Harvard, and when he found out that I turned them down he was livid," Noonan says. "He said, 'You're turning down Harvard to go to *North Carolina*?' I don't think he could have ever understood the importance of soccer to me. He would've found it shallow, but I just told him, 'UNC is unique.'"

Shannon Higgins grew up just outside Seattle and had every intention of signing with Cal-Berkeley until her father, Ken, asked her to at least visit Chapel Hill. "UNC just felt more 'jock-y' than Berkeley," Higgins says. "UNC felt like home." Tisha Venturini, from Modesto, California, had no desire to leave the West Coast, either. She was unaware of UNC's tradition and thought the school was too far away from home. "But after my trip to UNC I spent two weeks trying to write down on a piece of paper one single thing I didn't like about the school or the team," Venturini says. "I never came up with anything." Dorrance had been 0-for-18 in recruiting Californians before Venturini signed with UNC, opening a pipeline to the Golden State that would produce Keri Sanchez, Tiffany Roberts, Lorrie Fair, and Jenni Branam after that.

Kristine Lilly was another shy kid who didn't want to venture far from her home in Connecticut. During her recruiting visit, Lilly was swayed by a drive from UNC's practice field back to Fetzer Field along serpentine and bucolic Laurel Hill Road, a street that reminded her of her New England hometown and finally made her feel comfortable. Like Hamm and Roberts and Venturini, Lilly was also lured to UNC by her previous connection to Dorrance with the U.S. national team.

Cindy Parlow recalls wetting her thumb and running it over Dorrance's signature on her first recruiting letter. When it smudged, she was officially a Tar Heel. Dorrance got Anne Remy because both of her older sisters went to Duke, where Anne watched them constantly lose to UNC. Alabamian Leslie Gaston, whose father had grown up in North Carolina as a Tar Heel fan, says her decision to come was cemented during her campus sprint when Dorrance walked her through a cemetery at the head of the driveway to Fetzer Field and pointed out a gravestone with the inscription:

> I WAS A TAR HEEL BORN
> AND A TAR HEEL BRED
> AND HERE I LIE
> A TAR HEEL DEAD

For some it began with a chance meeting. Dorrance first learned about Senga Allan, a Scottish immigrant, when she was spotted playing pickup soccer with boys in New York City's Central Park by Alabama A&M coach Tim Hankinson, who then referred Allan to Dorrance for a tryout in 1982. Jessica Maxwell traces her interest in UNC back to the ninth grade at Colleyville Heritage High in Dallas, when her religion teacher, UNC alum Ron Boatwright, gave her a signed UNC soccer poster that she hung on her bedroom wall. Siri Mullinix had narrowed her choices down to UNC and Duke when a local TV sportscaster said to her, "If you want to be the best, why not go to the best school?"

Sometimes it takes a little luck and timing. Emily Pickering wanted to play at Connecticut, where she was offered a scholarship, until Huskies coach Maggie Dunlop suddenly stopped returning her calls. Pickering heard a rumor that Dunlop had been deported—actually she'd been hired at Yale—so Pickering turned to the Tar Heels because UNC assistant athletic director John Lotz was a friend of a coach at her high school. Both of Alyssa Ramsey's parents attended Virginia, and she was committed there until April Heinrichs resigned as the Cavaliers coach just two weeks before Ramsey's signing day. Ramsey settled for her second choice, UNC.

Some are sold by the tradition. "On my recruiting visit I walked into Fetzer Field, and UNC was beating Notre Dame, and I saw all the championship plaques, and the stands were so packed that I couldn't find a place to sit," Branam says. "Fans in the stadium were yelling 'Tar!' and people on the porch of Teague dorm were yelling back 'Heels!' I thought, 'Wow, I'm going to school here!'"

Some even come when the tradition takes a hit. At the postmortem party after UNC's NCAA semifinal loss in 1995, a recruit named Rebekah McDowell shyly approached Dorrance and told him, "I don't know if this is the right time to do this, but I want to commit to the University of North Carolina. I want to help you win it back." All of the other recruits who visited during that weekend, Laurie Schwoy, Lorrie Fair, and Lindsay Stoecker, also committed to UNC and that class did help win the title back the following season.

Some are smitten with Dorrance's slick salesmanship. "He came to my house with these photos, and he started telling stories about each player and about the program for the last twenty years," Jena Kluegel says. "I remember my mom and dad and I sat there for four hours listening to this guy talk. Normally, I'd be thinking, 'Get this over with,' but we were all mesmerized."

Some are smitten by Dorrance's occasionally sloppy salesmanship. "When he came to my house Anson thought he had brought a tape of a Santa Clara game, but it turned out it was Southern Cal," Reddick says. "Then when he left he walked to my dad's car and tried to unlock the door. When he finally found his rental car, he backed it into an oak tree. I really enjoyed that. His ditziness made him more real."

Heather O'Reilly was still debating between Virginia and North Carolina during her visit to UNC in 2002 when she and Dorrance walked out onto the balcony of the McCaskill Soccer Center, overlooking Fetzer Field. Dorrance pointed at the national championship placards and told O'Reilly that there were only a few spots left on the sign, and that if she came to UNC that by the end of her tenure those spots could be filled. "It sounds corny, but he almost made me cry by talking about the things he could teach me in four years," O'Reilly says. "I asked myself, 'Four years from now where is your game going to be?' Anson said he could make me the best, and like everybody else who comes to UNC, that's what I wanted to be."

No, Dorrance doesn't get everybody he recruits. He insists that he only gets his share, though in the same breath he notes that during his long career he has lost just one recruit after offering a larger scholarship than the competition. He still grinds over Julie Foudy.

Ever since Foudy had joined the U.S. national team, Dorrance wanted her to play at UNC because of her extraordinary skill and spirit. When it was permissible to start recruiting her, he phoned her as often as possible at her home in Mission Viejo, California, and when she said she was interested in medical school, he flooded her mailbox with information about UNC's premed program. "Anson was dogged and very convincing," Foudy says. "The energy he gives to recruiting drives a lot of other coaches crazy. It's a big reason why he's so successful, because he dedicates himself to it and it's a lot of work."

Foudy's decision came down to UNC or Stanford. Dorrance offered Foudy a full scholarship. Stanford did not yet have women's soccer scholarships available. Foudy nearly chose to come to Chapel Hill, but eventually opted for Stanford after reading a diary entry she'd written in the second grade, which listed as one of her goals to someday play soccer at Stanford. Even Dorrance couldn't argue with a dream. During her Stanford career, Foudy watched as North Carolina won four national championships.

Michelle Akers chose Central Florida over UNC in 1984 because she was put off by Dorrance's attitude. "When Anson recruited me I didn't like the guy," Akers says. "I was shy back then, and I didn't like talking to coaches on the phone, and Anson would call me all the time and talk about peanut butter sandwiches and how they just won their 150th national championship. I didn't want to hear it. Then I came on my recruiting visit and we watched his team play, and he bragged, 'Have you ever seen soccer played like that?' I was ticked off by him."

Brandi Chastain loved the way women's soccer was respected on the UNC campus, but she couldn't figure out Dorrance when they talked during her visit in 1985. "When I met with Anson I thought, 'My goodness, this guy is very, very confident,'" says Chastain, who attended Cal–Berkeley and later transferred to Santa Clara. "I saw a person who deals with things on his own time line. He had ten minutes to deal with this, ten minutes to deal with that, and ten minutes for me. It was get to the point or get out of the way. He wasn't a mincer of words. For a young kid, I didn't know how to deal with that. I was intrigued and I was overwhelmed at the same time."

"Anson is pretty laid back, and he seems a little disinterested at first, and that's the attitude a lot of girls see," says Abby Wambach, who chose Florida over UNC in 1997. "I was turned off. The thing is, he doesn't have to be interested; he has developed a program that is sold by the players who have played there and the amount of championships that they've won."

All of those players acknowledge that Dorrance wished them well at their school of choice. In fact, Foudy and Dorrance became close friends. After Foudy graduated from Stanford she became the victim of a running joke whenever she saw Dorrance. *Let me see those fingers. Are there any championship rings yet? And by the way, how are those student loan payments going?* A few years ago, Foudy mailed Dorrance a note the day she finally paid off her Stanford student loan. Dorrance later wrote Foudy a recommendation for medical school. "I think that in losing recruits you should lose them gracefully," Dorrance says. "There's a ridiculous arrogance that all of us coaches feel that if a recruit decides not to come to our institution she's not going to be as happy somewhere else. An athlete's happiness is dictated by her."

Dorrance firmly believes that treating Sarah Rafanelli with respect when she chose Stanford over UNC had a huge impact on the decision of Rafanelli's former youth soccer teammate, Tisha Venturini, to pass on Stanford a year later and come to UNC.

While Dorrance handles the rejections honorably, they affect him deeply. "The times when I've been most down in my career are usually after recruiting battles that I've lost," Dorrance says. "The moments when I see the empire tottering are not losing one great player, but losing more than one. Those are moments of peril."

Dorrance is specifically referring to a period in the mid-1990s when he was busy trying to raise money to start a women's professional soccer league. During that time he lost a series of critical recruiting battles to Notre Dame for Cindy Daws, Anne Makinen, Kate Sobrero, and LaKeysia Beene, and to Santa Clara for Aly Wagner and Danielle Slaton.

Dorrance didn't like what was happening to his recruiting. He was receiving more than 600 letters a year from potential recruits, and he was scrambling to reply by hand to every letter. He had no tracking system. His mailing list had over sixty names on it, but he had no idea who most of those players were. His recruiting files had a tendency to get misplaced, and good players mysteriously disappeared off the mailing list. He sent Palladino on a recruiting trip to Florida, and he returned with some good information on prospects, but he dragged his feet on writing a report for weeks and when Dorrance finally insisted he do it, Palladino said he couldn't remember their names anymore. Dorrance found himself relying on a network of former Tar Heels in the coaching ranks to do his scouting for him. One day, Ohio State coach Lori Walker, a Tar Heel alum, phoned Dorrance and said, "What the hell, Anson, you're not recruiting Jena Kluegel?" Turns out Kluegel, a blue-chip prospect, had e-mailed Dorrance dozens of times over the past year, but Dorrance had no idea because he didn't know how to access his e-mail. That's when Dorrance decided he'd better do something.

Dorrance first noticed Chris Ducar when Ducar performed well as a goalkeeper during a Thanksgiving Day pickup soccer game at the UNC practice field in 1994. Ducar, who had been invited into the game by his girlfriend, Tar Heel junior goalkeeper Tracy Noonan, was a former professional goalkeeper nicknamed "Big Bird" because he stood six feet six, with a wingspan that seemed to spread from post to post. Ducar saved everything that came his way that day, including several of Dorrance's shots that the UNC coach was certain were destined for the back of the net. Dorrance was impressed with Ducar's competitive nature. He liked the idea that in a game where winning didn't really matter, Ducar acted as if it did.

Ducar and Noonan had met when both worked as coaches at UNC soccer camp in the summer of 1994. Within weeks Ducar flew back to California and broke off his engagement with his fiancée. He moved to North Carolina with only a car, a computer, and a futon, and barely cobbled together an existence as the part-time goalkeeper coach at UNC–Greensboro and an individual youth coach. When UNC's goalkeeper coach Bill Steffen accepted the head coaching job at Oregon after the 1995 season, Dorrance offered Ducar the opportunity to supplement his income as a part-time UNC assistant coach. "We sent out a player to capture ourselves a goalkeeper coach," Dorrance likes to joke. "Keep in mind that it was Tracy who asked Chris to marry her. That was our master plan."

After two years of shuttling back and forth between Greensboro and Chapel Hill, Ducar was offered a full-time position because Dorrance admired his energy and his organizational skills, two elements that Dorrance was having trouble bringing to UNC's recruiting at the time. The first time Dorrance asked Ducar to evaluate a prospect occurred at a youth tournament during the 1997 Final Four. "I was totally clueless," Ducar recalls. "I didn't have a reference point for what UNC was looking for. I was just out there freezing my ass off. I didn't know what the hell I was doing."

Ducar learned more about how Dorrance thought with every passing recruiting class. He learned to look for the Dorrance indicators of future success, as well as for the girls who were being derailed by the dreaded "Three B's": beers, boys, and beaches. Ducar scouted most of the club tournaments. He did all the grunt work, freeing up Dorrance to do what he does best, close the deal. On Ducar's recommendation, Dorrance offered a scholarship to Maggie Tomecka, a four-year starter at UNC, without ever seeing her play. Ducar stumped for Lindsay Tarpley and Lori Chalupny when many of the nation's coaches didn't think they were the best in their class at their positions, and both earned spots on the U.S. national team as UNC sophomores. But Ducar's proudest achievement occurred when he unearthed Heather O'Reilly well ahead of the competition. Tipped off by O'Reilly's club coach, Charlie Naimo, Ducar watched O'Reilly play at a tournament with no other college coaches around because the players were just tenth graders. O'Reilly didn't score a goal, but Ducar was impressed that when a player stole the ball from her, she exhausted herself to get it back.

As soon as the game ended, Ducar walked over to Naimo and said, "Charlie, that kid is going to be on a full ride to the University of North Carolina."

"Huh?" Naimo said. "She didn't even score."

Ducar replied, "I don't care. *That's* a Tar Heel."

Two years later, as a senior in high school, O'Reilly joined the U.S. national team, and as a freshman at UNC she scored a record eight goals in the NCAA Tournament to lead the Tar Heels to the 2003 national championship.

"I still wouldn't say that I'm completely comfortable as a recruiter, but I think that works to my advantage," Ducar says. "I still have nightmares about Anson saying, 'How the hell did we miss this kid?' I never want to let Anson down. For the first couple of years I'd tell him, 'Anson, you've really got to go watch this player,' and he'd say, 'It's OK, I trust you.' I'm thinking, '*You* trust *me*?!'"

Dorrance says that since he added Ducar as his recruiting coordinator, the Tar Heels have not made a single recruiting mistake. Dorrance has never second-guessed him, never offered a scholarship to a player that Ducar didn't endorse. Ducar has dragged UNC's recruiting into the computer age, and now the program begins compiling files on players as early as the eighth grade. UNC's recruiting is so meticulous that the Tar Heels no longer recruit by position, but can target a specific skill need like a strong attacking header. Ducar has so streamlined Tar Heel recruiting that even though coaches aren't allowed to telephone a high school prospect until July 1 before their senior year, in both the 2001 and 2002 recruiting classes, UNC already had verbal commitments from its entire incoming class before Dorrance was even allowed to phone them.

One night after a game in 1988, Dorrance was sitting in a motel lounge in Clemson, South Carolina, with UNC media coordinator Steve Kirschner, pontificating on the impact of recruiting. "I'm chasing three women who will transcend the game," Dorrance told Kirschner. "If I sign one of them, we'll win the national championship for the next four years. If I sign two of them, we won't lose a game for the next four years. If I sign all three, nobody will come within three goals of us."

The three players were Mia Hamm, Kristine Lilly, and Julie Foudy. Dorrance signed two, and his prognostication was slightly off. In the next four years, UNC lost one game.

14 | *Chaos*

Things which matter most must never be at the mercy of things which matter least.

—Goethe

Ever since Moyer Smith had mistakenly recommended the wrong Anson Dorrance to be Marvin Allen's replacement as the North Carolina men's soccer coach, Smith had taken an understandably keen interest in the real Dorrance's success. This was especially true because Smith had endorsed Dorrance based partly on his managerial skills, which Smith would come to learn, after talking with Dorrance's teammates and Allen, were totally nonexistent. Smith positioned himself as Dorrance's first boss and regularly pointed out to the new soccer coach a placard on Smith's desk that read *Work Smarter, Not Harder.*

Dorrance's first "office" was the corner of a desk occupied by Smith's secretary, Donna Hill. Dorrance would pull up the visitor's chair and reply to his correspondence on the edge of Hill's desk, and Smith couldn't help but notice that the advice on his placard was not sinking in. "The thing that concerned me most about Anson was his lack of organization," Smith says. "He was always thinking about bigger things and overlooking the details, like drawing up a budget each season. Anson is a coach. He is not an administrator."

"Paperwork has never been Anson's strong suit," UNC senior associate athletic director Beth Miller says. "He keeps his life in different piles on his desk, and the stuff that doesn't interest him falls to the bottom. Early in his career there were plenty of days when I had to go to his office and say, 'Anson, we need to go through that stack.' Eventually we realized that if we don't give him some help, it won't ever get done. That's when we moved Delaine."

Delaine Marbry is another Chapel Hill lifer. She was born in Chapel Hill, attended Chapel Hill High, and began working as a part-time secretary at the University of North Carolina while she was still in high school. Marbry first crossed paths with Dorrance in the early 1980s when he taught a few phys ed classes to supplement his meager income as a coach. At the end of every semester, it was Marbry's responsibility to chase down Dorrance for his grade reports. She'd have to ask him over and over for weeks until he finally got it done.

Marbry never much liked Dorrance, but he liked her, and in 1991 he asked the UNC administration if she could be more involved with his program. Dorrance was heeding another piece of advice from Moyer Smith: *Hire people whose strengths are your weaknesses.* Basically Dorrance wanted somebody to do the paperwork he didn't want to do. Marbry began typing up his expense reports and budgets as well as his speeches and recruiting letters. Before long she was ordering him sandwiches, scheduling his dentist appointments, picking up his dry cleaning, and occasionally placing wake-up calls to get him out of bed in the morning.

Through more than twenty years of experience, Marbry knows that the only way to get her boss to do anything is to nag him. Marbry has become jokingly known as Dorrance's "office wife." Mia Hamm describes Marbry as a "saint." Keri Sanchez insists that without Marbry, Dorrance wouldn't know his left from right. "Delaine is basically Anson's guide dog," Tom Sander says. "She's out there in front of him to keep him from running into telephone poles or stepping out in front of traffic. She's also his human Palm Pilot, always reminding him where he needs to go and when."

Dorrance refers to his office as "an archaeological dig." When he is handed a sheet of administrative paperwork he likes to say, "I'll put it in my file." Then he tosses it over his shoulder. Memos he receives in the morning are invariably buried by the afternoon. He usually knows whether or not something is in a pile on his desk, but only that it's in there somewhere among the stuff he had to do yesterday, the stuff he hopes to do before he dies, and the stuff he knows damn well he'll never do. At the bottom of the wreckage are phone messages, player academic transcripts, and random Christmas cards, some of which are three years old or more. On any given day there are also a half-dozen old bank checks submerged on his desk. Sometimes when M'Liss needs money she will sift through the debris, looking for checks to endorse that haven't expired. One day Dorrance received a phone call from a television network asking if he'd received a $10,000 paycheck. He couldn't remember whether or not he'd received it or deposited it, and he couldn't verify it with his checkbook because he doesn't balance it. Dorrance never found the $10,000 check, but while digging through the detritus in search of it, he did turn up a series of other old checks that added up to nearly $7,500.

Other piles on the shelves and floor surrounding his desk include unidentified game tapes, packages of macadamia nuts, and months-old newspapers he plans to read the next chance he gets. He's been known to save an old issue of *Soccer America* for ten years, and when he's asked about it he'll say, "I might need that someday." Dorrance's days are consumed with chiseling down the rubble before more is created. "There's always something buried on my desk that's not going to be done on time, and I'm going to pay some sort of price for it," Dorrance says. "But that's just my nature. I actually do OK in crisis management because it's my life."

Dorrance is a man literally born into chaos, so why wouldn't he be comfortable there? "I think there is something inherently evil about organization," he says. "It interferes with life's flow. It's not natural. I honestly think there's something right about a lack of organization, but I don't want to defend it too much in case it's just one of my character flaws."

When it comes to his administrative responsibilities, the UNC athletic department hierarchy has always viewed Dorrance with trepidation, so they've taken a very hands-off attitude toward the soccer program, an approach that works for both sides. "I always thought about putting a helmet on whenever I went to Anson's office, and I didn't go often because I couldn't stand it," former UNC athletic director John Swofford says. "Order obviously doesn't mean anything to Anson in terms of his day-to-day operation. As a staff we used to laugh about how Anson worked under the philosophy that it's better to ask for forgiveness than permission."

Dorrance never made any secret of the fact that he didn't do his paperwork because he thought it was a waste of time. He endured some dirty looks one day when he went so far as to tease athletic administrators in a meeting by saying, "Just let us coach and let the pencil-pushing be done by everybody else."

"Anson knew it didn't matter whether he got that paperwork done or not," Bill Palladino says. "It may be a rationalization, but one of his best qualities is that he sees through the minutiae to what's really important in the big picture about being successful. Whether you turn in your expense report on time or filled out correctly doesn't have anything to do with your success on the field. That's what infuriated him about the office work. We won so many national championships with very little attention to detail."

In the old days people had trouble leaving phone messages for Dorrance because his voice mail was constantly filled. Eventually Dorrance asked Marbry to clear his answering machine for him daily and take care of the requests that she could handle herself. Every morning Marbry would copy down dozens of messages, killing entire days doing nothing but clearing Dorrance's machine. So when the soccer staff moved into the McCaskill Soccer Center in 1999, Marbry strategically refused to allow Dorrance to install voice mail. If Dorrance is out of his office, phone calls to him ring endlessly. He recently got a cell phone that does include voice mail, but he checks it only sporadically. Danielle Borgman once got a return call two months after she'd left Dorrance a message.

On those rare occasions when Dorrance answers his office phone and the call is not for him, he has no idea how to transfer the call. He has no business cards. He sometimes can't get into McCaskill because he doesn't know the combination to the door. Dorrance had received over 2,000 e-mails before he realized he even *had* e-mail. While he has learned to access his e-mail in the office, there are still times when he can't open his e-mail on the road, because he can't remember his password. Other than e-mail he has no idea how to operate his computer. Years ago, Dorrance's daughter Michelle installed a goofy screensaver photo of her father and Mia Hamm from the late 1980s, and it has remained there ever since, at least partially because Dorrance doesn't possess the computer skills to remove it. Because he is so computer-phobic, Dorrance still writes out his pregames, his goal-setting conference notes, and his recruiting letters in longhand on a white legal pad. Whenever he finds himself befuddled by modern technology, he'll exclaim, "I was born into the wrong century!"

With the help of Marbry, Tom Sander, and Chris Ducar, Dorrance has managed to winnow his office duties down to returning phone calls and e-mail, writing recruiting letters, and clearing his desk. Still, the UNC soccer office is hardly a model of efficiency. "It's like Romper Room, like a bunch of kids milling around a playroom," Sander says. "They'll pick up some toy and play with it for ten minutes and then get tired of it, and then it's snack time. There's no real schedule involved. It's so disorganized that you wonder what happened before Anson had help. How did he get this far when nothing gets done? How did he keep track of who he's recruiting? How did the players stay eligible? I still haven't figured that out."

One day when the chaos became almost unbearable, Sander found a roll of masking tape and taped an "X" on his office window, mimicking what Agent Mulder did on the *X Files* when he was in trouble and needed help. Everybody knows that the only way to maintain sanity in the soccer office is to retain a sense of humor. As a Christmas gift in 2002, Sander gave Dorrance a placard, which barely peeks out from beneath the rubble on the front edge of Dorrance's desk. It features a quote from Albert Einstein, another disorganized genius in his field: *If a cluttered desk is a sign of a cluttered mind, of what then is an empty desk?*

One of the first road trips Dr. Bill Prentice ever took with the UNC women's soccer team was a visit to the University of Connecticut in October of 1981, riding in the ancient Blue Goose with the men's team on the bus as well. With food stops and bathroom breaks, the drive lasted nearly fifteen hours before the bus rolled into Storrs, Connecticut, late one night. Stopped at an intersection, the bus driver turned around to the UNC coaches and asked, "OK guys, which hotel are you staying at?" Dorrance looked at Palladino. Palladino looked at Geoff Griffin. Griffin looked back at Dorrance. At the same time, they all said, "I thought *you* made the reservation."

"Here we are with sixty people on this bus in the middle of nowhere in the middle of the night and we had no place to sleep," Prentice says. "I'm sitting there thinking, 'What the fuck am I doing with these yahoos?'"

Prentice could never have imagined the road pandemonium he would experience over the next twenty-five years. There was the time when Dorrance and Palladino were both away, recruiting in different cities and planning to hook up with the team at the start of a road trip in California. That day both coaches suddenly realized that neither of them would be in Chapel Hill to accompany the team on the flight to the West Coast. With only a few hours to spare, Dorrance phoned Prentice and told him to pick up the airline tickets and get the girls to the airport to fly to San Francisco. When Prentice asked what hotel they were staying at, Dorrance said, "You'll have to find one." When Prentice asked about food, Dorrance said, "Take them to a supermarket with a credit card and buy them some fruit."

While a head count is regularly performed during road trips, many Tar Heel players have stories about the time they were left behind. No abandonment story is as alarming as that of Stacey Enos, who made the mistake of lingering a little too long in a rest-stop bathroom on Interstate 85 at three o'clock in the morning on the way home from a road trip to George Mason. When Enos emerged from the restroom, she discovered that the UNC vans had left without her. Her van drove ten miles down the highway and back before recovering Enos in a confused state of anger and relief.

Whenever a player is left behind the first time, she learns the general rule of thumb to prevent it. Keep an eye on Tom. Wherever Sander is, the team is sure to follow . . . except when Sander is left behind. He was once stranded at a hotel in Houston when the team left for a game. The Tar Heels realized it when they arrived at the field with no uniforms, soccer balls, or team managers.

Nothing is more slapstick than UNC's mad dashes to the airport after games, involving a caravan of three vans snaking through highway traffic at eighty-five miles per hour. Once the Tar Heels were playing a game in Florida and the players didn't have time to change afterward, so they rode home on the plane in their uniforms, some of them still wearing cleats. Always pushing the envelope, UNC in the old days often left rental vans at the airport curb with the keys still in the ignition. One time a UNC rental van got a flat tire on the way to the airport, so the players in that van squeezed into the team's other van as if it were a clown car at the circus, and the disabled van was deserted on the shoulder. Another time, one Tar Heel van rear-ended another car during the ride to the airport. The UNC vehicle was the only one damaged, so the team left it in the rental lot with a smashed front end and a note to bill UNC. "I remember a time when we were playing in a tournament in Houston, and Duke was there too," says Anson's brother Pete, who came along on the trip. "We're running through the airport like O.J. in the old Hertz commercials with sweat pouring down our foreheads. Meanwhile, Duke is on the same flight, and they've been there for an hour, and they're all composed sitting at the gate. I looked at the Duke coach, and he had this look on his face that said, 'I can't believe these idiots win.'"

In more contemporary security-conscious times, when abandoning a van at the airport curb no longer works, the Tar Heels have perfected a series of stalling techniques so that everybody can make the flight. The coaches drop the players off at the curb and return the vans to the rental lot. To stall for time, the players proceed at a leisurely pace through security, two at a time at regular intervals. Once, coming home from a road trip in Dallas, when the players were all seated on the plane and the coaches were nowhere to be seen, a UNC student manager, Croft Young, waited at the gate for the coaches, assuring the gate attendants the coaches were just around the corner. When the coaches didn't arrive, the attendants insisted that Young board the flight because it was ready to take off. Young walked halfway down the jetway and sat down, knowing that the plane couldn't leave without him, but that it would take a little while to figure out that he hadn't boarded. Minutes later Young was discovered, and just as security was summoned to halt his sit-in, the UNC coaches showed up at the gate.

Another time after a game in Dallas, Palladino wanted to stop at his favorite hamburger joint on the way to the airport. "So then it becomes this ninety-mile-an-hour drive to catch our flight," Tracy Noonan says. "I'm in Anson's van, and we're driving along at breakneck speed in the fast lane, and some slowpoke is in front of us and we can't get by him. Anson passed this guy on the shoulder, on the dirt, and we're all screaming, 'We're going to die!' We get to the airport, and the players get out at the curb, and Anson and Dino return the vans. I remember we were using all of our stalling techniques, pissing everybody off by doing whatever we could to delay the flight taking off for five, ten, fifteen minutes. Finally Dino strolls onto the plane with a Diet Coke in his hand. And we're all thinking, '*You stopped to get a COKE!!*'"

The golden rule of travel at UNC is that it's not a road trip without a U-Turn. For years, Palladino was the team's primary navigator until it became painfully obvious that he had no sense of direction. Palladino's idea of directions was usually to look for stadium lights, which is akin to navigating by the North Star. "What always amazed me was that Dino had been on these road trips to the other ACC schools a million times, yet he still never knew where he was going," Jena Kluegel says. "I always wondered, 'Why is this such a mystery? Why are we lost?'"

Once, on the forty-five-minute trip to a game at Elon College, one of the two team vans got lost. Everybody in the van that arrived on time started the game. The "starters" wore a variety of T-shirts because the uniforms were in the lost van, which didn't arrive until fifteen minutes into the game. Says Dorrance: "For us, winning the game is sometimes less of an achievement than finding the stadium."

Poor navigation is not the only reason the Tar Heels are chronically late. No matter how short the trip, Palladino always likes to stop at a convenience store on the way to pick up what is affectionately known as a "little diddy," a soda, chips and salsa, beef jerky, whatever. Other times, UNC's tardiness is an honest mistake. On a road trip to Maryland in 2001, Palladino thought the game started at 7:30 when it actually started at 7. Panicked Tar Heel parents at the stadium phoned their daughters on the bus as they watched the warmup clock run out. The UNC bus rolled up to the field at 7:15. The Maryland coach, former Tar Heel Shannon Higgins, couldn't help but laugh and chalked it up to traveling on DinoTime. Palladino's excuse was that he didn't have a schedule, which would have been more credible had not Palladino *arranged* the schedule himself.

One of the most screwed-up of all UNC trips occurred on October 10, 2002, on a theoretically simple twenty-mile drive to N.C. State. It was a rainy evening, and UNC didn't allow enough time for the bumper-to-bumper traffic on Interstate 40. Despite driving on shoulders and even without a stop for a little diddy, the trip took seventy minutes, and the vans didn't arrive at the field until three minutes before the start of the game. It was still pouring rain on the ride home, and when the vans pulled back into the McCaskill lot that night they discovered that someone had been left behind. They'd forgotten Dorrance.

In Bill Steffen's second year as UNC's goalkeeper coach in 1994, he traveled to Portland, Oregon, for his first Final Four with the Tar Heels outside of Chapel Hill. UNC scheduled a light practice on the off day between the semifinals and the championship game at a practice field visible from the hotel where the team was staying. On a dank, rainy day, the team divided into three vans for the ride to practice. Two of the vans got off the highway at the exit for the field, but the other van was nowhere to be found. After waiting ten minutes, the two vans reloaded and drove to an alternate practice site at the University of Portland. After a twenty-five-minute drive to the other site, they found the other van, but were informed that they were indeed supposed to practice at the original site near the hotel. So all three vans reloaded and took off north, back up Interstate 5. Palladino was driving the lead van, Prentice was driving the middle van, and Steffen followed in the third van. Palladino missed the exit for the practice field and kept driving north on I-5, where he actually drove out of Oregon and into Washington before he realized his mistake and made a U-turn south back toward Portland. The other vans continued following him. When Palladino missed the exit for the field, once again driving southbound, Steffen decided to exit. Fifteen more minutes would pass before the other two vans finally showed up at the correct field. The entire trip to a field less than a mile from the hotel lasted more than an hour. "If you put yourself in the position of one of those players, and you've been sitting in the van for an hour watching these clowns drive all over the Pacific Northwest, you'd think they'd be antsy or nervous," Steffen says. "But it was like nothing happened. There was absolutely no difference from if we'd driven directly to the field. They trained in the mud and slop as if we hadn't been through the whole escapade. The players' tolerance level for stress is very high. It comes from how Anson runs the program. They're used to it."

During that odyssey through Oregon it struck Steffen that there's a stress in creating structure, there's a stress in adhering to structure, there's a stress in restructuring when the structure doesn't work, and that UNC coaches had eliminated all that by eliminating the structure. "That's when Bill learned how adjusted the girls are," Sander says. "He was sitting there freaking out because we're late getting to the practice field, it's pouring rain, Anson and Dino aren't there, we don't have the balls, our timetable's shot, and everything's out of whack. Meanwhile, the girls are sitting in the van listening to music, joking around, laughing. It didn't faze them at all. That's what the program is all about. Go with the flow, because you never know what's going to happen next."

Steffen, who is finishing his Ph.D. in exercise and sports science at UNC–Greensboro, was so fascinated by the experience in Oregon that he is writing his dissertation on the subject of the benefits of chaos. His paper is titled "Slice Of A Dynasty," and Steffen's conclusion is that UNC doesn't win despite the chaos, but partly *because* of it. "The chaos has proven to be a happy set of circumstances," Steffen says. "If it didn't work, if this program hadn't ascended to the heights to which it has, would Anson and Dino have changed? We'll never know, because what they're doing works. Is it intentional? I don't think so. They just went about it this way and the system worked, and so no one questioned it."

The transformation of the Tar Heels is extraordinary to watch. Walking through the stadium gate is like Alice returning from her journey through Wonderland. The conversion occurs when the players take their seats for the pregame talk, and

Dorrance pointedly asks them all to put their feet on the floor. Only then are they grounded.

"At first, getting to games made me so nervous it drove me crazy," Mia Hamm says. "I spent four years trying to create a routine, which our coaches made impossible. But once we stepped into the locker room, suddenly the chaos was gone and we became this organized team. Everything magically fell into place."

Says Kristine Lilly: "Somehow the coaches were never stressed even if we were arriving twenty minutes before the start of a game. Anson always had a calm about him that rubbed off on us in the game. It's a 'nothing can stop us' attitude."

For Dorrance it's about building a firewall between his players' lives on and off the field. He acknowledges that almost anybody else who lived a day in the chaos of his program would do so in what he calls a "sphincter-tightening panic." But he is always looking for ways to take the outside pressure to be perfect off of his players, and it doesn't hurt to prove to them daily that the UNC program is imperfect. Dorrance hates team meetings. Other than practices and games, he doesn't like to structure his players' time. In fact, he barely sees them. "We don't want them to worry about anything, and we convey that because we don't worry about anything," Dorrance says. "It's not an act. We're relaxed about chaos and our players can handle it. Once the pregame starts, that's the line of demarcation, that's when comfort comes from structure, because it's in the games when players fear the unknown."

Once a UNC pregame begins, all is calm. It's like one of those light-switch decisions. Set pieces are rehearsed ad nauseum. Dorrance is scribbling plenty of Xs and Os for attack and defense, box organization, and corner kicks, like the meticulous kid with his little metal soldiers. The Tar Heels' warmup for a game is run with a Teutonic precision, the competitive cauldron bubbling, asses suddenly ceasing to be grabbed, game faces appearing as easily as pulling on a mask. The whistle blows and *shit happens*.

"When you first get there you have this perception that as this elite program Carolina must run like clockwork, but before long you're saying to yourself, 'Wow, this is really how it's done here?'" Susan Bush says. "It's good in a way because nobody's uptight. You become immune to it. You stop worrying about the little things. We've got enough pressure to deal with in the demands of the games."

Says Sander: "Any good consultant would be aghast at our business model. When I first started I assumed these girls went out like in the Army and did their drills, and then went to the games and played and that's it. But that's only 10 percent of the program. The other 90 percent is total chaos. Nobody sees that, and they don't have any clue because the image we present at games is very regimented, very professional. If they ever did a Tar Heels reality TV show and followed us around with a camera, nobody would ever believe it. They'd say it was staged, because it's so different from what you'd expect. People expect a soccer machine churning out soccer robots, when really it's just ordinary people doing extraordinary things."

Dorrance admits that any fringe benefit to the chaos is not premeditated. It is a stroke of luck, and not a pattern of behavior that anybody at UNC really thought about until Steffen brought it to their attention. In fact, coming from a disciplined research science background, Palladino was initially surprised by the chaos, but realized it sprang from Dorrance's lifestyle, and that nobody was going to change that. So Palladino, and everyone else who has followed him, just went along with it. "Our program goes against the way most people think it should be run," Palladino says. "There was once an article in *Fortune* magazine where we were included among the models for team management along with the Navy Seals. *The Navy Seals?* We might be the Navy Seals on the field, but we're the Keystone Kops getting there."

There is history to suggest that Dorrance not only disdains organization, but sabotages it. He not only welcomes chaos, he works to create it. In his senior year at UNC, Dorrance chafed at the way his roommate, Mark Berson, anally lined up his pencils in parallel lines on his desk. "His immaculate pencils were unfathomable to me," Dorrance says. "On more than one occasion I took it upon myself to set his pencils free." One time after Dorrance liberated the pencils, Berson returned to the room and saw his pencils scattered all over his desk, and he looked over at Dorrance in his bed squelching a demonic grin.

"I do believe Anson seeks out the chaos," M'Liss says. "He loves the chase. He doesn't mind the race to beat the clock. It stresses out other people, but to him it's another competition. *Let's see if we can do this.* It's an adrenaline rush. He'd rather be late than an hour early because he hates waiting. He's a procrastinator because he knows he's at his best if the pressure is on."

Dorrance, whose pulse rate is so astoundingly low that doctors often double-check it during his physicals, breeds players who evolve to share his love of the unknown because they ultimately have no other choice. "I was so stressed when I first joined the program," Leslie Gaston says. "But I honestly feel like being a part of something that's so crazy all the time makes you cool about everything. You learn to roll with the punches. You can't always control everything that happens in your life. As a senior I'd purposely wait until midnight to write a six-page paper for the next morning because I learned to work better on deadline."

After a game on September 29, 2002, when the Tar Heels headed to the Portland airport with four hours to spare before an 11:45 p.m. red-eye flight home to North Carolina, it was Gaston who asked Dorrance if the team could go see a movie. Dorrance loved the idea. Gaston, a proud native of Montgomery, Alabama, phoned her roommate in Chapel Hill, who quickly scoured the Internet for a theater near the airport that was showing *Sweet Home Alabama.* The team dropped off its bags at the airport, gassed up the vans, and then went to the 8:55 show. At 11:05 the team was still in the theater. With the movie just reaching its climax, Dorrance looked at his watch and announced, "All right, we're outta here!" With just forty minutes until takeoff and a ten-mile drive to the airport, the rest of the trip became the usual eighty-five-mile-per-hour white-knuckle van ride in the pouring rain, possibly running a red light here or there, followed by the customary running up airport escalators and a final windsprint to the gate. The Tar Heels made the flight with seconds to spare, giggling as usual at their folly.

So for those patrons at the Century 16 Eastport movieplex that Sunday night who wondered why twenty-five people stood up at once and dashed out of *Sweet Home Alabama* with just five minutes left in the film, understand this: it isn't that they disliked the movie, it's just that they had a plane to catch.

"Maturity"

15 | *Growing Up*

Our generation plants the trees; another gets the shade.

—Chinese proverb

At a soccer coaches' convention back in the early 1980s, Anson Dorrance and his colleagues were each handed an index card and asked to write down a mission statement for their sport. When one of the coaches was asked to share his statement, he said, "For soccer to be the most popular sport in America." One coach after another echoed that sentiment, touting the vast growth potential of men's soccer in the United States. When Dorrance was asked to share his mission statement, he stood up and said, "For soccer to be the most popular *female* sport in America." *Huh? Women's soccer? Popular?* Dorrance was the rebel, as usual, the only one on the other side of the fence. He had a vision for women's soccer in the theater of his mind. Everyone else in the room thought he'd lost his mind.

Dorrance often detested coaching men. There were plenty of times when he was the coach of the UNC men's soccer team that he fumed as he watched one of his players dogging it or bailing out on a physical challenge. Like his mentor, Marvin Allen, Dorrance hated nothing more than when his team lacked balls. It didn't help that back in his early days as the Tar Heels' coach, Dorrance wasn't much older than his players and knew that he could still compete at their level. "One of my fantasies as a coach back then was to sub in ten of me and just crush the opponent," Dorrance says. "I would sit there and think, 'Could I win this game if I just subbed in one of me? Or would it have to be four? How many *mes* would it take?'"

While most of his female players were academically responsible, he disliked how many of his men tested the boundaries of eligibility. While his women responded to his motivational talks, some of the men tuned him out. While the women approached his competitive cauldron with an honorable spirit, the men spent their energy trying to figure out ways to cheat the system, fouling so excessively in drills that Dorrance would have needed a referee to police each duel. He appreciated that despite his women's team's success, they still respected all of their opponents and remained remarkably humble, but as soon as the men enjoyed any hint of success they developed an unjustified hubris and got beaten by inferior competition. "My men's team was much less coachable," Dorrance says. "It was always a battle between our male egos. The fighting got tedious. I started thinking, 'Why should I have to get up every morning and convince an eighteen-year-old that I know more than him?' I hated their cocky attitudes, and it made me want to kick their ass."

Dorrance never hesitated to jump into a drill and prove to his players that he could still be the best player on the field, at least until 1981 when he recruited Billy Hartman, the first player Dorrance knew was clearly better than him.

"Because Anson was such a young coach there was a credibility issue with players, who would ask, 'What the hell do you know?,'" says Geoff Griffin, Dorrance's men's assistant coach. "They were butting heads all the time. Meanwhile, the women didn't have any frame of reference. They just sucked it up and played."

Clearly, when Dorrance first started coaching both teams, the men were his primary concern. Those were the games that mattered in those days. Those were the results that he thought would determine his coaching future. As much as he loathed the men sometimes, at least he felt like those were the players he understood, because he'd been there. "I think that if you look back at his playing days, Anson is instinctively a leader of men," Griffin says. "His ability to work with women was a learned experience that didn't sink in until the mid-eighties. Before that it was like trying to teach two different classes back to back. It was hard to switch gears, and it took him a while to figure out that you couldn't be the Great Santini to both."

The longer Dorrance coached the women, the more he started to believe that his personality was better suited to them. "His natural approach is verbal and analytical, and while guys don't find those to be positive coaching qualities, it's very helpful with women," Bill Palladino says. "The more four-letter words you use with guys, the better off you are, but Anson preferred sarcasm, and because women take everything so personally that was a huge motivator that delved right into their hearts."

It didn't take long before Dorrance realized that he was stretched too thin between two teams. There were simply too many players to coach. For years he manipulated the men's and women's schedules so that he could coach both teams, but sometimes when the schedules conflicted he had to make difficult decisions about which team to coach. "Bouncing back and forth so much, we all questioned, 'Can he really do both?,'" Griffin says. "With his personality he was able to spin plates and juggle balls and produce two very good programs, and I don't think very many people could have done that, but clearly that's not the best formula or more schools would have done it."

In the mid-1980s, as Dorrance focused more of his attention on the women's team, he began farming out the men's recruiting responsibilities to Griffin. He let Griffin deliver the men's pregame talks. He let Griffin run the men's practices, and sometimes Dorrance didn't show up at all, leaving the players to wonder who was really making the decisions. By the time Griffin resigned and Elmar Bolowich took over as Dorrance's lead men's assistant in 1987, Dorrance had basically deeded the team to his assistant. "You can compare it to the English system," Bolowich says. "With the men's team, Anson was the manager, I was the coach. With the women, he was the manager and the coach. He just seemed a little more passionate about the women's program, probably because he started it and he was instantly very successful and proud of that. The women had become his identity."

On top of that, Dorrance's men's team was never competing on a level playing field. In the 1980s, men's soccer was far deeper and more competitive than the women's game, and the ACC was the strongest conference in the country, but Dorrance operated with a lower budget and fewer scholarships than his league rivals. Many of those schools featured excellent coaches like Bruce Arena at Virginia, I.M. Ibrahim at Clemson, and John Rennie at Duke, all of whom were only coaching men. On the recruiting trail, Dorrance was often asked the same nagging question, "Are you a men's coach or a women's coach?"

Much of Dorrance's tenure as the UNC men's soccer coach mirrored Allen's in that there were plenty of victories, but mostly disappointment in the big games, except in 1987 when the Tar Heels won the inaugural ACC Tournament and reached the Final Four in the NCAA Tournament. The team began 1988 ranked No. 1 in the preseason, but started that year 4-6-1 because of a combination of hubris and overscheduling before rallying to finish 14-9-1 and earn the team's second straight NCAA bid. "Anson didn't have as many great athletes coming to play for his men's team at UNC," April Heinrichs says. "If he had men who were superior athletes like his women, might he have won ten national championships at North Carolina in men's soccer? I think so. The success of the women pushed him towards them, and then he translated anecdotal situations into fact and decided that he's better at coaching women."

As seasons passed, Dorrance eventually noticed that he kept comparing his men to his women, and he liked everything better about the women. When the two teams played in doubleheaders and the men would lose in the opener, the women's team almost always won and acted as his therapy. When both teams reached the postseason and the schedules conflicted, he would coach the women because they were always further along in their tournament. It was becoming too much. All along he wanted to coach only one team, but over the course of the 1980s that team changed, and he knew that the sacrifices he was making were never fair to the men's team.

Dorrance was also looking at a bigger picture. The men's game on the national level was an old boys' network. There was little room to grow. The women's game was less established, and once he accepted the women's national team coaching job in 1986, there was never any question which way Dorrance had plotted his future. That year Dorrance first approached UNC athletic director John Swofford to ask if the two Tar Heel soccer programs could be split and he could go with the women, but the idea was rejected because the athletic department couldn't afford the extra cost of running the programs independently. The split wouldn't actually occur until 1989, when Dorrance eliminated any extra cost by agreeing to split the soccer budget in half. Dorrance resigned as the UNC men's coach after twelve seasons with a total of 172 wins, two fewer than Marvin Allen. He passed the coaching reins to Bolowich and set his sights on what he could do with the women's game.

Says Griffin: "Anson ultimately asked himself, 'What business am I going to be in where I can really have an impact? Should I try to develop the women's game? Or should I try to compete with the rest of the ACC in the men's game?' Building the women's game became the most interesting challenge. He saw his opening to have an impact not just on one team, but on the entire women's game. He saw an opportunity to basically invent a sport. How many people ever get that chance?"

Anson Dorrance was hardly the most likely torchbearer for women's soccer in America. He didn't grow up loving soccer more than any other sport. It had been just one of the sports he played at the Villa; he was barely competent enough to continue playing at St. Mary's; and when he came to UNC, only the fact that it was still a low-profile soccer program permitted him to try out. Dorrance never picked soccer as much as soccer kept stubbornly picking him.

During college, when Dorrance summered at his parents' home in Greenwich, Connecticut, he organized soccer leagues there, cutting and lining the fields and scheduling the practices, because that was the only way he could find a game. Eventually he became a player-coach of the Chapel Hill Soccer Club and founder of the North Carolina Soccer League, the North Carolina Senior Soccer Association, and the North Carolina Youth Soccer Association. Dorrance organized the team he played on, organized the league it played in, and organized the association it played under.

On the wall in his apartment he posted a map of the state of North Carolina and covered it with yellow pins indicating that a town had an active club, and green pins indicating that someone in that town might be interested in starting a club. Then, each summer, Dorrance and Palladino drove all around the state and the country in an old RV conducting soccer clinics. Says Dorrance, "When I began to promote the game, began to sell all the game's great qualities, in a way my evangelism sold me on the game."

The growth of Dorrance's career mirrors the evolution of women's soccer in the United States. While women's college soccer was born at Brown University in the fall of 1972 when Karen Stevenson, daughter of that school's men's soccer coach, Cliff Stevenson, talked her father into starting a women's soccer club, UNC women's soccer is generally viewed as the sport's time line. "Anson Dorrance is the Christopher Columbus of his sport," U.S. women's national team media coordinator Aaron Heifetz says. "Anson had vision, and he was always ahead of the game. He figured out this women's soccer thing way before anyone else. He got a head start on everybody."

What Dorrance had understood ever since that day he shared his mission statement at the coaches' convention was the potential for a sport that hadn't already been claimed by the rest of the world. "I saw women's soccer in America as a sleeping giant, and my goal was to wake it up," Dorrance says. "I don't think UNC alone started the boom, but I do think we were a beacon for it, because we didn't want to just win, we wanted to win attractively."

Dorrance decided that in order to get Americans excited about his sport, he would have to play the most fan-friendly style he could dream up. He would play "the beautiful game" the way it was intended. He would play the 3-4-3, he would encourage his players to duel 1 v. 1, and he would push them to score goals at the genuine risk of having goals scored against them. That would sell the game.

Dorrance also recognized the need for positive exposure. When his team won the 1981 AIAW national tournament he choreographed some photos with his team posed in front of a clump of fans, so it looked like the game was played in front of a huge crowd when actually there were fewer than 4,000 spectators in UNC's cavernous football stadium. That sort of publicity lured the NCAA to sanction the tournament the following year. Only twenty-five varsity teams existed to compete for that first NCAA title in 1982. That number would more than double to fifty-four programs by 1985, and again to 103 in 1992. By 1997 women's programs outnumbered men's programs in Division 1. In 2005 there were 301 Division 1 women's soccer programs and a total of 920 in all divisions.

Attendance followed a similar gradual progression. In the late 1980s it wasn't uncommon for a UNC regular season game to draw fewer than a hundred fans, but attendance spiked after the 1991 World Championship. Since the early 1990s the Tar Heels have averaged 2,000 fans for regular-season home games and 5,000 for NCAA games. Of the top twenty-seven crowds ever to watch a college women's soccer game, twenty-two of those games have involved UNC. Meanwhile, NCAA Tournament attendance has continued to rise steadily throughout the years, from 1,000 at the 1982 championship game and 3,061 combined for the entire tournament, to a peak in 2003, when there was a sold-out crowd of 10,042 fans at the final and 59,410 overall.

As early as 1990 Dorrance was already lobbying the USSF to authorize a women's professional soccer league to continue player development beyond the college level. When no action was ever taken, Dorrance in 1996 dedicated much of his own time to trying to start the National Soccer Alliance, a league designed to take advantage of the momentum created by the United States' gold medal in the 1996 Olympics. Dorrance's league never gained the crucial support of the USSF and was scuttled, but as soon as plans for the Women's United Soccer Association commenced in 1999, Dorrance tracked down his NSA sponsors and was among the first to drum up financial support. When the WUSA launched in 2001, Dorrance was hired as the league's enthusiastic television color commentator, a responsibility that forced him to miss UNC's 2002 exhibition opener against Notre Dame. After that he said, "It's bad when I can't seem to squeeze my real job into my schedule."

There are an estimated 18 million soccer players in the United States, half of which are women, and the average age of female players is fifteen. Participation in girls' youth soccer has doubled over the past decade, while youth participation in all other sports has dropped. It's the same story at the high school level, where participation in women's sports like basketball and volleyball has leveled off in recent years, while the percentage of high school girls who play soccer has increased significantly. The number of high schools fielding a girls' soccer team has doubled in the last ten years, and there are more women playing soccer in college than any other sport. "Anson has helped develop the game that is so ingrained in our society now," April Heinrichs says. "If you don't play, your niece plays or your daughter plays. It reminds me of that play *Six Degrees of Separation*. Everybody in America is one or two degrees of separation away from the game of women's soccer."

"Anson's made women's soccer hip," Heifetz says. "A teenage women's soccer player is a cool thing to be. Soccer players are the most popular girls, the prettiest girls, the most social, the most athletic, and all of that started in Chapel Hill. Our sport needed a Chicago Bulls, and that was UNC, and we needed a Michael Jordan and that was Mia Hamm. Anson created all that."

One of the proudest moments of Dorrance's life was the 1999 World Cup final, played before 90,185 fans at the Rose Bowl and 40 million television viewers, the largest American television audience ever for a soccer game. The U.S. women's national team was featured on the covers of *Time, Newsweek, Sports Illustrated,* and *People,* all in the same week. "I believe that afternoon was the seminal moment for women's athletics around the world," Dorrance says, "and to see the sport of women's soccer leading the charge for credibility was wonderful."

After the 1999 World Cup, FIFA president Sepp Blatter even went so far as to proclaim, "The future of football is feminine." To a large extent, that's due to Dorrance. If it wasn't for the North Carolina program or his early national teams, that level of excitement would never have been generated so quickly. *Who's crazy now?*

"Very few men would have made Anson's level of commitment to the women's game because of their own egos," Geoff Griffin says. "Anson has a relentless willingness to make a difference in the game and not be afraid to take any risk to grow it. If you had to say who's been the most influential person in the development of women's soccer, you'd be hard-pressed to put somebody ahead of him. I see women's soccer as this massive ocean liner. Anson captained the ship for a while, but he probably takes more pride in being its architect."

"Anson sees things expansively and encourages everyone around him to expand what they think is possible," Marcia McDermott says. "He pushes the boundaries. He's out in front saying we can do this and we can do that, and people chuckle at his dreams at first, and then they've come true. They haven't come true just because of Anson, but you need someone to boldly say what is possible before anyone else considers it possible."

Says Carin Jennings: "I think if you'd asked all of us in the American women's soccer community back in 1990, 'Can you see two world championships and two Olympic gold medals and three hundred Division 1 women's college programs?' Anson would have been the only one of us who would have said, 'Yes, it can happen.' He believed in it, and he brought us all along with him on the ride."

Dorrance saw himself as a proud papa when he attended the first WUSA championship game in 2001. Two of his former players, Cindy Parlow and Tisha Venturini, scored goals in the game as he sat in a luxury box at Foxboro Stadium with women who have come to be known as the sport's "Founding Players": Michelle Akers, Julie Foudy, Mia Hamm, Kristine Lilly, and Carla Werden. Dorrance thought back exactly one decade to 1991 and to the World Championship victory in China that he believes laid the groundwork for that day. "That was when we showed FIFA that we were a worthy game for them," Dorrance says. "That U.S. team attacked with flair and countered all the negative aspects of the men's game. Before that World Championship I think FIFA looked at the women's game and thought, 'Why the hell are we going all the way to China?' Then all of sudden they were saying, 'My gosh, these women can play.' That one tournament doubled the population of the sport by adding women into the mix. They realized that the United States could be a soccer nation."

Toward the end of that WUSA title game, Dorrance told the group his favorite story about the arrival of women's soccer in America. He said that he once met NFL quarterback Doug Flutie, who'd told him that he and his daughter, Alexa, had recently watched a television commercial that featured Michael Jordan and Mia Hamm. Alexa turned to her father and asked, "Daddy, who's that guy with Mia Hamm?"

Dorrance's soccer philosophy isn't really Dorrance's philosophy at all. It's stolen, pilfered, borrowed, lifted. Call it what you want. He doesn't hide it. Dorrance believes that every elite coach is part innovator and part imitator, and by his own admission hardly anything that he does as a coach is something he thought up. He learned a lot of his principles for the attacking box while scouting during a Canadian national team clinic. He learned his seams finishing drill from a Russian national coach. After being dismayed at his team's lack of stamina during the 1991 World Championship final, Dorrance implemented a new fitness regimen that he learned from Michelle Akers, and he's used that workout ever since. When he heard about how Clemson coach I.M. Ibrahim spent 50 percent of his practices working on a half-dozen different plays off corner kicks and then played a style to create more corners, Dorrance incorporated that. And after watching Florida execute a creative play off a free kick during a 2004 match against UNC, Dorrance taught his team the very same formation in his next practice. He has adapted coaching leadership principles from books he's read about John Wooden, Vince Lombardi, and Phil Jackson. And then there's all the stuff he stole from Dean Smith. "One of Anson's greatest strengths is that he's always learning, always reading, always trying to improve himself," Janet Rayfield says. "He's not ashamed to say he learned something from watching somebody else. He doesn't insist that all his theories be his own."

Says Shannon Higgins: "Anson claims to have learned something from every player that he's coached, and that's what makes him grow. He sees a special quality in a player, whether it's April Heinrichs' mentality or Birthe Hegstad's ability to touch the ball away from defenders with her back to pressure, and he says, 'Wow, that's good. Let's see if we can teach all of our players that.' He evolved as a coach by watching great players play. You can either take it and learn from it or just watch it in awe. He took it."

"There are certain professions where a quest for knowledge is fundamental to the job, but soccer coach isn't one of them," Colleen Hacker says. "Anson's endless curiosity is particularly unusual for someone so successful, but for me that separates the wannabe greats from the truly greats. Certain critics disparage him by saying, 'Oh, he stole that from the Germans and that from some coach in Brazil.' I think that's the sign of a good scholar, but you also have to have a broad mind that can see all these scattered Lego pieces and put them together to make a dump truck, a better dump truck than anything that we've ever thought of before."

For the last twenty-five years, Dorrance has been a virtual clearinghouse of soccer ideas, from the brilliant to the cockamamie. It's all part of his strategy to grow the sport. He has culled what he thinks are the best ideas and has laid out his blueprint hundreds of times in clinics he's hosted all across the country. Every UNC practice is open to anybody who wishes to watch, and there are often unidentified strangers wandering the sideline. He spends an inordinate amount of time, including two weeks at team camps each summer and at every coaches' convention, trying to sell his colleagues on adopting the 3-4-3 system. After Rutgers suffered a narrow 2–1 loss to the Tar Heels in the 2001 NCAA Tournament, Scarlet Knights coach Glenn Crooks admitted that part of his game plan was devised from his days as a young coach listening to Dorrance speak at the national coaching conventions.

Some members of Dorrance's own staff question whether he should be so forthcoming. "With us there is no mystery," Bill Palladino says. "Hell, all Anson does is go out there and tell people what we do. I don't agree with that, but it's a luxury that we have because if our system and training regimen is all that mattered, then somebody with half a brain would listen to Anson speak and turn his team into the same sort of powerhouse. It doesn't happen. It won't happen. The key ingredients they are missing are the incredibly talented players and Anson's motivational skill. It's the synergy between those two elements that is hard to replicate."

Says Cindy Parlow: "There is no secret to our success. Anson's showing everybody what we're doing and how we're doing it, but for some reason nobody's copying it. Either they're very stupid or it's not an easy thing to do. You can't just say, 'OK, we're going to kick each other's asses in practice and still have good team chemistry today.'"

Dorrance will never duck a question about why his team succeeds. At a summer team camp in 2003, one college coach kiddingly asked, "So, what is the best way to beat UNC's three-back defense?" Dorrance spent the next ten minutes comprehensively diagramming how to beat his team, including all the Xs and Os. Having no secrets is all part of UNC's image of absolute power. "You can know their system and you can dissect them any way you want, but you've still got to face their players," N.C. State coach Laura Kerrigan says. "That's the amazing thing about Anson. He tells everybody, 'These are the strengths of my system, and these are the weaknesses that we practice to prevent. OK, come and try to beat us now.'"

"We are the pioneers, and sharing is part of lifting up soccer," Dorrance says. "Stealing from other coaches makes me better, and hopefully I make them better and we're going to compete on a higher level nationally and internationally. At the end of my coaching clinics people come up to me all the time and ask, 'Aren't you worried about sharing all of your ideas?' I don't understand that kind of paranoia. This isn't the Manhattan Project. I'm stunned at the arrogance of soccer coaches who feel they have secrets that are important enough to hide."

It starts with that color. It's not blue. It's *Carolina* blue. There is no such thing as Connecticut blue or UCLA blue or Duke blue. There is no Ohio State red or Florida orange, even Notre Dame green. No other school in the nation dresses in the same shade of blue. "It's a unique color, and that's fitting because this is a unique program that's accomplished unique things," Catherine Reddick says. "Not many people get to wear this color. You've got to earn it. It's a compliment. Wearing Carolina blue means you're something special as a soccer player, and it looks really cool, too."

Moments before an NCAA Tournament game in 2001, UNC volunteer coach Kalli Kamholz watched the Tar Heels take the field and said, "I love when we wear blue instead of white. It reminds the other team why they hate us so much."

At Fetzer Field, visitors are assaulted by that blue from every direction. The scoreboard is Carolina blue. The track that winds around the field is Carolina blue. The sign that reads WOMEN'S SOCCER NCAA CHAMPIONS, strategically placed to greet visiting teams as they enter, includes eighteen different Carolina blue championship tiles. Even the trash can liners are Carolina blue. And of course the sky is often Carolina blue as well.

It's all part of what has become known around Chapel Hill as the "mystique." Before every home game the warmup tape includes Chairmen of the Board's song "Carolina Girls (Best in the World)." A popular T-shirt on campus features a list of all the years in which UNC has won national championships, and for the seasons when championships were not won, it just says *Oops.* "Clearly there is an aura of winning around our program," Palladino says. "We don't stress it much because most of the players come in with it, but the mystique helps to perpetuate it."

Ange Kelly calls it a *righteousness,* as if UNC winning is right and any other team winning is not. Like Kelly, former Maryland coach and UNC alum Shannon Higgins understands the confidence that attitude inspires as a Tar Heel player and the doubt that causes when you coach against them. "When you walk out on the field as a Tar Heel you have half the battle won because you know what's been done before, and you carry that with you," Higgins says. "If my UNC teams were down in the final minutes of a game, we weren't thinking, 'Oh no, we're going to lose.' We were thinking, 'We don't lose. We're Carolina. It's unacceptable. How are we going to win?' That's the fear in playing against them."

Says former Florida striker Abby Wambach: "UNC has a sense of confidence whenever they step on the field, and their opponents have a sense of 'Holy Cow! It's Carolina.'"

During the postgame press conference after Duke's second round loss to UNC in the 2001 NCAA Tournament, Blue Devil senior Sara Pickens said, "UNC has a psychological edge. You don't just play the team, you play the dynasty."

Says Michelle Akers: "I remember when I was a freshman at Central Florida my teammates were all nervous about playing UNC because they thought of them like they were superwomen, like their players couldn't have the crap beaten out of them. I didn't understand it. I thought, 'UNC? Yeah, so what?' But if you're playing a team with a lot of confidence and you can't match their confidence, you're going to lose."

The biggest hurdle for coaches facing UNC is how to avoid losing the game before it ever begins. Says Santa Clara coach Jerry Smith: "If you look at the winning streaks they've put together and the record they have overall, it's really, really intimidating; so my advice to anyone playing them is to ignore those numbers. If you buy into the numbers, you won't beat them."

"When you play Carolina you play against the mystique," says Texas A&M coach G. Guerrieri. "You have to prove to your players that they are actually human and that they drink water like the rest of us, and not some magic potion."

For many opposing players, just getting the opportunity to play against the Tar Heels is the pinnacle of their career. When High Point came to Chapel Hill for the NCAA Tournament opener in 2003, the Panthers arrived at Fetzer Field early to take photographs of themselves on the field and then visited the UNC student bookstore, where many of them bought Carolina soccer T-shirts and gear. After her team's 8–0 loss, Panthers coach Tracie Foels, a UNC graduate school alum who'd once been recruited by Dorrance, had to talk her players out of asking the Tar Heels for autographs.

Before facing the Tar Heels later in the 2003 NCAA Tournament, Purdue coach Rob Klatte compared the challenge of beating UNC in Chapel Hill to climbing Mount Everest, which isn't exactly accurate because many more people have successfully scaled Everest. One of Klatte's players, Annette Kent, who had attended a Final Four in Chapel Hill as a kid and gathered newspaper clippings about the Tar Heels that she turned into a collage tacked to her bedroom wall, wrote a column on the Purdue web site about the upcoming game: *No one could smother the excitement or happiness I have right now. I don't wanna play Portland, Santa Clara, UConn, UCLA or any other top-10 team. I want North Carolina. I know the field; I can even see the players. The stadium is dark with only the frost of overhead lights to set the mood. It's their kickoff as they bob up and down in their Carolina blue awaiting the start of the game. I stand on the other side of the line that divides legacy and desire.* Purdue lost 7–0.

After Penn State senior defender Bonnie Young had UNC's second goal deflect off her body in the Nittany Lions' 2–1 loss to the Tar Heels in the 2001

NCAA quarterfinal, she said, "In a way I lived a dream tonight. I scored a goal at Fetzer Field in my final game . . . and it was a game-winner."

Dorrance believes the mystique feeds on itself, because it lures opposing coaches into finding excuses for why their teams lose to UNC. Early on it was that UNC was among the first varsities and then among the first programs with scholarships. Then it was his national team connections. He loves to hear the excuses from other coaches and backs them up wholeheartedly whenever he can. Dorrance believes one of the reasons his teams win is that he's eliminated all of UNC's excuses not to. "It's like the famous story of Cortés landing in the Americas and getting all of his troops on shore and then burning their ships," Dorrance says. "That's a defiant statement. *Guess what? We're here and we're not leaving. There's the group we have to fight through if we want to stay alive.* When you burn every excuse for losing, you empower yourself."

Naturally, as UNC's mystique has grown over the years, each Tar Heel team's responsibility grows along with it. Despite what UNC opponents may believe, mystique has never scored a goal or made a save. There are times when it can become a cross to bear. "Wearing Carolina on my shirt didn't give me the feeling that we could just show up and win," Mia Hamm says. "In contrast, it made me feel like we had to play harder because every game we played could make our opponent's season. It gave us a responsibility to respect the game. It was an honor, and anything that feels that special is not handed to you, you have to earn it every day."

Like so many others, this UNC match looked like a *mis*match. On September 21, 2003, the undefeated and No. 1–ranked Tar Heels faced Richmond, with a record of 1-3-1 and coming into the game off of three straight shutout defeats. Spiders coach Peter Albright understandably feared a drubbing. On the eve of the game, Albright met with his center back Meghan Ogilvie at the team hotel and gave her a pep talk. *Tomorrow you'll be playing against the best player on the best team in the country. You're playing against some of the best players you will ever see. You better bring your "A" game.* "I could just see Meghan get taller," Albright said. "The challenge of playing Carolina will bring out the best in you. It became personal for her, and that's when athletes rise. Also, in the back of your mind, you don't want to be embarrassed. You don't want to lose 9–0."

The following afternoon an inspired Richmond team limited UNC to just two shots in the game's first forty minutes and went into halftime tied 0–0. UNC finally broke the scoreless tie at the 68:59 mark and then added another goal in the eighty-fourth minute for a hard-fought 2–0 win.

"That was the best game we've played in a long time," Albright said afterward. "Playing Carolina helps you find eleven players who are willing rip a lung out to win a soccer game. We gave a good account of ourselves, and that is what a lot of teams hope to do against Carolina. I'm not sure that's good. You should be playing to win. The aura around their program is a tremendous obstacle to overcome, but I'd play them again tomorrow if I had the chance. It was awesome."

"I almost feel bad for Carolina sometimes because I know that every team that plays them is going to give them their best game," Ogilvie said. "Everyone's looking to take them down, and that kind of sucks for them. Even if your team is struggling you play them relaxed because you're thinking, 'What do we have to lose?' We all grew up seeing Carolina everywhere, and it gets to a point when you're older when you say, 'Screw Carolina. I don't want to be Mia Hamm. I want to kick their asses.'"

North Carolina is the biggest game of everybody else's season. The game circled on everybody's calendar. The game when opposing teams wear their lucky uniforms. The game that all their parents want to come to. Even as early as 1982, a year after Boston College had been drubbed at home by UNC 8–1, Tar Heel midfielder Laurie Gregg recalls walking past a Boston College practice and hearing the team chanting, *'North Carolina! North Carolina!'* as a means of psyching themselves up. In recent years Wake Forest players have engaged in a drinking game with Gatorade on the night before facing UNC. The game is called *Fuck the Heels.*

In 2003 Navy coach Carin Jennings, the MVP of the 1991 World Championship, asked Dorrance to bring his Tar Heels to Annapolis to help market her program. She showed her appreciation by organizing a promotion that set the NCAA attendance record, 6,527 rabid Midshipmen screaming their guts out for UNC to lose, and the Tar Heels barely escaped with a 1–0 victory. After the game, when asked to describe in one word what playing UNC adds to its opponents, Navy senior Stacy Finley said, "Oomph."

Every elite college program sees Carolina as its Moby Dick. But it makes sense that while UNC is everybody else's biggest game, they all can't be UNC's biggest game. On the day that a regular-season tournament was beginning in Houston in 2003, Heather O'Reilly was riding on a hotel elevator with two Texas Longhorn players on their way to a game. "Who are you playing today?" O'Reilly asked.

The two players looked at each other incredulously and said, "You."

"Oh," O'Reilly said, "well, good luck."

The two Longhorns were so aghast that they told their coach Chris Petrucelli about it, and he used the story in his pregame remarks to fire up his troops. Texas still lost to UNC 1–0 in overtime.

Not only does everybody want to beat UNC, they want *anybody* to beat UNC. Santa Clara boosters wear T-shirts that read: *My two favorite teams are Santa Clara and Whoever is Playing North Carolina.* "Everyone wants UNC to lose," former Florida All-American Heather Mitts says. "We all root against them. Even when you go to the Final Four and your school's not in it, you root for any of the three teams other than UNC. You just want the underdog to win, and everybody except UNC is the underdog."

Says former Notre Dame goalkeeper LaKeysia Beene: "I have to admit that it's fun for me when any team upsets North Carolina. It doesn't have to be your school. I'm happy when *anybody* beats them. I look at it as Carolina versus everybody else."

Around the country the vengeance has assumed its own acronym, *ABC. Anybody But Carolina.* "It's us against the world, and our players have to understand that every time they step on the field," Dorrance says. "Every team we play measures themselves against us, so we're going to get their best shot. If a team is ranked fiftieth in the nation, we elevate them forty places, but does their coach ever send us a thank-you note for raising their level? *Noooooo.*"

Coaches tell players that if they beat North Carolina they'll be on the front page of the sports section the next day. Every game against UNC is a chance to do something that only twenty-two college teams and just sixteen different programs have done in more than a quarter century. With Rutgers ahead of UNC 1–0 at halftime in a 2001 NCAA game, midfielder Shannon Evans walked into her Scarlet Knights huddle and yelled, "Forty-five minutes to make some fucking history!"

Higgins recalls that her pregame talks before her Maryland team's matchups with UNC were the easiest motivational speeches she ever made. "The reason it's fun to play against UNC is because you're supposed to lose," she says. "So I'd tell them, 'Go out and have fun and play without fear.' Playing the Tar Heels is an opportunity to face the best, and if Maryland ever beats them I can guarantee all of the players will want to run through College Park in their uniforms screaming their heads off. It's a 'What if . . .' game, and every player lives for those."

Says former Notre Dame All-American Kate Sobrero: "I wasn't recruited by Anson, and everyone like me felt like they wanted to beat him because he didn't think we were good enough to go to UNC. I always had that little bit of anger in me, and that's how 90 percent of my teammates felt. You wanted to kill his team, and you wanted to beat him, and you wanted him to think that he made a mistake. At the same time you had to respect someone you wanted to beat that badly."

The mystique is why so many girls go to UNC, and the chance to tarnish it is why more and more girls are going everywhere else. The attitude started way back in 1983 when Carin Jennings chose to stay close to home and play at Cal–Santa Barbara instead of playing at UNC, the school that had won the first two national championships. "I asked myself, 'Do I want to go to a program where they're going to win with or without me, or do I want to stick around and maybe help establish a program?'"

Today that notion is one of the prime selling points for almost every coach recruiting against Dorrance. Whenever Florida coach Becky Burleigh makes a home visit she asks a recruit the same question. *There are people who want to be UNC and people who want to beat UNC. Which are you?*

"There are more players today that don't want to be just another piece of the UNC puzzle," Clemson coach Todd Bramble says. "There are great players at UNC who get lost in the shuffle because they are such a soccer machine. We can sell players on the idea of being a catalyst in a program that can beat North Carolina."

Abby Wambach knew all about the UNC tradition. She had grown up a rabid UNC fan, wearing a Carolina T-shirt and hat as part of her daily ensemble.

Wambach took a campus visit to UNC in 1997 and received a partial scholarship offer, but by that time she says she identified herself more in the underdog role. She chose to attend Florida on a full scholarship. "One day I got to a point where I said, 'I want to beat the best because there's something more special about that.' Only seven teams have been able to do that in the NCAAs. You want to beat the team that's unbeatable, and Carolina was always that unbeatable team."

Danielle Fotopolous nearly transferred to UNC from Southern Methodist in 1996. She had worked UNC soccer camps and admired Dorrance, but in the end, she too picked Florida, where she would have an opportunity to slay the dragon. She and her teammate Erin Baxter both suffered through a 9–0 defeat against UNC in 1996, a game they both call the most humiliating beating of their soccer careers. "They came out and killed us," Fotopolous says. "That one game drove Erin and me for the rest of our careers, and I think a lot of college players who've been crushed by Carolina would say the same thing. I was still upset about that game when we played them for the national championship."

Fotopolous, Baxter, Wambach, and Mitts were all a part of the Florida team that defeated UNC 1–0 in the 1998 NCAA championship game. "We had the advantage over Carolina because we went out there to have a blast," Fotopolous says. "We thought, 'What's the worst that can happen? We lose 9–0 again? So what?' Nobody thinks we can win, and that makes teams more dangerous. I remember at the end of the game I didn't believe what had happened. My husband kept shaking me and telling me, 'You won. You beat Carolina. You won the national championship!' I kept saying, 'We won?'"

Wambach admits it took five months for that win to sink in. Mitts says she didn't really believe what had happened until she returned to Gainesville and watched the game on videotape. "I got chills when the clock ran out and I saw that we actually won," Mitts says. "I never thought we could be one of those rare teams to beat UNC in the NCAAs. It's definitely something I brag about. These days when I introduce myself at a clinic, I'll always say, 'I'm Heather Mitts, blah, blah, blah, and I was on a team that beat UNC for the national championship!'"

Aly Wagner and Danielle Slaton were both waffling between UNC and Santa Clara when they traveled from California to Chapel Hill together for their recruiting trip in 1997. "Before I visited UNC I didn't think I was going to go there," Wagner says. "But on the way home I was convinced that I would. It was an amazing visit, overwhelming, to be honest. You get caught up in the mystique when you're there. I remember on the plane ride home to California I turned to Danielle and I said to her, 'How could we turn this down? How could we not go to UNC?'"

For both players, the trip to UNC was their first campus visit, and by the time they'd seen the rest of the schools, they were persuaded that they'd rather try to establish a new soccer tradition closer to home at Santa Clara. "I'd grown up watching Santa Clara lose and lose and lose to UNC and thinking, 'God, can't we just beat them once?'" Slaton says. "I wanted to prove that Santa Clara wasn't cursed against them."

Slaton and Wagner would come to represent a new breed of players who turned down UNC and came back to haunt the Tar Heels. In the 2001 NCAA championship game, Slaton's staunch defense stifled the UNC attack, and Wagner scored the game's only goal on a brilliant, bending shot into the upper left corner of the Tar Heels' net. "After that game was over I was not excited, just relieved," Wagner says. "It was a letdown. I thought, 'Is this what it's supposed to feel like?' Sure, someday I can tell my kids that my childhood dream was always to beat UNC in the national final and I achieved it, but it's strange when I think back on it. I guess my dream wasn't really to win a national championship, it was to not lose to UNC."

The tipping point is clear. Something changed after UNC's 5–0 win over Notre Dame in the 1994 national championship game. While nobody else realized it at the time, part of the reason Dorrance felt compelled to resign from the U.S. national team in 1994 can be chalked up to the tidal wave of women's soccer talent that he had helped to foster, which was making it increasingly difficult to win national titles at UNC. It only started to become apparent on the first day of December in 1995, when the Tar Heels lost 1–0 to Notre Dame in the NCAA semifinals at Fetzer Field, just the second home loss in the history of the UNC program.

While the Tar Heels had won the previous five NCAA title games by a combined margin of 29–2, suddenly championship games would become competitive. UNC defeated Notre Dame in the 1996 championship on a goal in the second overtime. The Tar Heels defeated UConn 2–0 in a tense battle in 1997, scoring the clinching goal only in the final two minutes. Then UNC lost in the 1998 final to Florida. After winning 2–0 over Notre Dame in the 1999 final, UNC lost three games during the 2000 season and had to scramble from behind in both games of the Final Four to eke out its seventeenth national championship. The following year, UNC lost 1–0 to Wagner and Slaton and Santa Clara in the NCAA championship game, and in 2002 the Tar Heels lost to the Broncos again, 2–1, in the NCAA semifinals, the first time the Tar Heels had ever failed to win the national title in consecutive seasons. UNC championships no longer seemed predestined. Rival soccer coaches anxiously began using the word *parity*.

"When April or Mia played here we often just rolled the ball out on the field and we won the game, but opposing players and coaches are getting better, and it's getting more precarious every year," Dorrance says. "It seems like there are more and more teams out there who can beat us when they're at their best and we're not at ours."

Says Bill Palladino: "The playing field is getting more level. It used to be that when North Carolina had a good recruiting year, then nobody else did. Now we can have a good recruiting year and so can two or three other schools. The player pool is getting bigger and bigger. Now there are twenty good players that are all about the same. Pretty soon there will be thirty. We're going to be getting some, but so will a lot of other schools. That's where the parity thing is coming in to play."

Dorrance acknowledges that it's becoming increasingly difficult to pry recruits out of far-flung soccer hotbeds like Texas and California, and along with the growing recruiting pool and the lure for players to beat UNC, fear of Title IX has prompted more schools to increase funding and attract more experienced coaches. Suddenly Dorrance is living the phenomenon he prepared for all those early years as a coach, the day when his program would begin to be preyed upon by the monster it created.

"When I first got to UNC in 1999 we had great players like Lorrie Fair and Laurie Schwoy, and I thought, 'If I'm in awe of them, what must our opponents be thinking?'" Leslie Gaston says. "It seems like we were beating teams 5–0, 6–0, 9–0 regularly. Back then we expected to win a national title, but by the time I became a senior I didn't necessarily expect it. When I first got there it was like teams were scared to play us. By the time I graduated they were fired up to play us."

Ask opposing coaches how to beat UNC and they'll say to capitalize on your limited chances on offense, try to combat their depth with your depth and to possess the ball for as long as possible to keep it away from the Tar Heels. But the ultimate key is to somehow take UNC out of its rhythm, to discomfort a team whose game plan is based on discomforting you. Florida beat UNC in the 1998 final by disrupting UNC's fluid tempo with physically intimidating play. Duke in 1994 and Notre Dame in 1995 both upset the Tar Heels by employing a pressuring three-front, essentially beating UNC at its own game, but few coaches have the hangin' kind to try that.

"For years we viewed the Final Four as the Tar Heel Invitational, but when Santa Clara finally started beating them we showed that the Tar Heels are not invincible anymore," says Broncos coach Jerry Smith, who has four wins against UNC, more than any other college coach. "You have to destroy that psychological barrier. You have to break your own four-minute mile. You've got to watch the movie *Hoosiers* and ask yourself, 'How do *they* do it?' You have to believe in miracles."

It's so hard for coaches to convince their players that they can actually beat UNC because there is so little positive history upon which to draw. Desperate for a psychological edge before Florida State met UNC in the 2003 ACC Tournament final, the school's web site jokingly boasted that while FSU owned a 1-14 overall record against the Tar Heels, the Seminoles had never previously lost to UNC in the ACC title game on the day after a lunar eclipse. Maryland had been outscored 100–1 in its first eighteen meetings with UNC when the Terrapins came to Chapel Hill in 2002 and forged a 1–1 tie. "This means a lot as far as our progress as a program," Higgins said after the game. "In years past, we didn't score any goals against Carolina, and we didn't even touch the ball much. We were just chasing the whole time. To know we can tie Carolina makes me think they are seeming more and more human."

With any loss, or even any tie, UNC must deal with the inevitable forecasts that the empire is crumbling. Taped to a cabinet door above Tom Sander's desk is a newspaper story from the Raleigh *News & Observer* that carries the headline *The End Of The North Carolina Women's Dynasty Foretold.* The column concludes with the line, "It certainly looks as if the end of the North Carolina dynasty is at hand." The story was printed on December 26, 1994. UNC won two of the next three and four of the next six NCAA titles.

Both sides of the argument over parity can basically be summed up in the Tar Heels' final results during the 2003, 2004, and 2005 seasons. In 2003 UNC achieved its first undefeated and untied season since 1993. The Tar Heels broke the NCAA Tournament scoring record by ten goals and registered six straight shutouts for the first time in tournament history. In the final, UNC scored more goals than UConn took shots, and the Huskies did not manage a single shot on goal. For the season, UNC ranked first in goals and goals against average, while outscoring its opponents 113–11, the widest margin since that of the celebrated 1992 team. Because of the acknowledged increase in the level of competition across the sport, it was arguably the greatest season in UNC history. Then, in 2004, the Tar Heels entered the NCAA Tournament as the nation's only undefeated team, but lost in the third round to Santa Clara 1–0 in overtime, and in 2005, UNC lost just once before being eliminated by Florida State in the fourth round of the NCAAs in a penalty-kick shootout. The fact that the 2004 and 2005 seasons represent the first two seasons in which UNC has ever failed to reach the Final Four would seem to provide a compelling case for parity. However, the Tar Heels can claim in response that in the two NCAA games in which they were eliminated, they outshot their two opponents by a combined margin of 50–12 and that over the course of the three seasons from 2003 to 2005, UNC lost only two games, while no other Division 1 team lost fewer than seven.

Santa Clara's Smith believes that any UNC loss is a victory for women's college soccer. "UNC's dominance hasn't been healthy for our sport at all," Smith says. "It certainly brought us some attention initially, and that was beneficial, but I think it's no longer something that needs to exist for us to survive as a sport."

Apparently the debate over whether parity is good or bad for the game depends on whether or not you are affiliated with UNC. Nothing stirs up the Tar Heel coaching staff like the suggestion that UNC losing is a boost for college soccer. "When we lose, other coaches like to sympathize with us by telling us how it's good for the game," Chris Ducar says. "That's bullshit. Have we been bad for the game up to this point? Is setting a high standard a bad thing? UNC losing is good for *them*."

Says Dorrance: "There's a feeling out there that our dominance has choked the sport. I don't believe that. Look at the Yankees. You either love them or you hate them, but they are frigging driving the game. It's the same way with us. You either love the Tar Heels or you hate them, but it makes for a spirited argument."

What everybody can agree upon is that simply by chasing North Carolina, many of its rival programs have improved significantly. "Anson hasn't sacrificed his program for the sake of parity," says former UNC assistant and Oregon head coach Bill Steffen. "Anson doesn't fear parity, but he has always refused to regress to the mean. He wants other programs to catch up to his. By maintaining his lofty standards the rising tide has allowed other boats to float higher."

The man who worked so diligently for more than two decades to grow the game is now the most obvious casualty of his success. Dorrance will publicly back any opposing coach or player who asserts that parity has arrived in women's college soccer, but it's all part of his psychological gamesmanship. Privately he will not acknowledge the existence of parity until his program no longer dominates the soccer landscape on a regular basis. But whether or not parity is inevitable isn't really important to Dorrance. The competition is what he has always craved. For years in the 1980s and early 1990s he stood at the podium after winning another championship, brazenly challenging his expanding horde of rivals like that little kid on the Ethiopian playground, daring them to try harder, not only because that would be more fun for him, but because he knew that his dream for soccer to become America's most popular female sport depended upon coaches of programs all across the country deciding they wanted to kick his ass. "Anson's career mission has always been to grow the sport of women's soccer," Ducar says. "History will say, *He was a champion*, but he'd prefer that it say, *He was a champion for the game*."

16 | *Losing*

When I fall on my face from time to time, I try not to worry because I'm still going forward.

—Linda Aucoin

On the day before Mia Hamm's wedding in December of 1994, Hamm and her guests, who included a bevy of elite athletes, were all looking for a way to blow off some nervous energy. Hamm suggested a game of roller hockey, so two dozen wedding guests took to a set of abandoned tennis courts near the UNC campus. Hardly anybody knew how to skate, so the players giddily fell on their butts, crashed into each other, and executed headers entirely different from the kind they had once been taught by Anson Dorrance. Dorrance enjoyed the game so much that he has been playing roller hockey ever since. Three times a week, Dorrance, Bill Palladino, and Chris Ducar skate with a motley crew ranging from former college ice hockey players to local sexagenarian businessmen with a death wish.

During the spring when the NCAA prohibits Dorrance from training his full team on the soccer field, he invites his players to try roller hockey . . . at their own risk. "The first time I ever skated I saw Anson coming at me, and I thought, 'He's not really going to hit me while I'm standing here vulnerable on these skates,'" Lorrie Fair says. "But he kept coming, and all of sudden I'm on the ground with these scrapes on my knees and elbows, and he's just skating away. The next time I pummeled him before he pummeled me, and he smiled at me and said, 'OK, that's what I wanted.'"

"Playing roller hockey with Anson, you see how competitive a person he is," Keri Sanchez says. "Even at the beginning when he couldn't skate and couldn't stop, he was still barking at everybody, telling them where to go as he's detaching his face from the chain-link fence."

Dorrance's fellow skaters say that he brings an intensity to the hockey game that disappears whenever he's not there. "Hockey games without Anson just aren't as competitive," says Dan London, a regular in the pickup game. "I can understand how he brings out the best in his soccer players, because when I'm on his hockey team I want to skate harder, better, faster. Anson has taught me to never underestimate the power of being the one who cares the most."

Dorrance has been known to tailor his entire daily schedule around roller hockey and claims it is the most stimulating part of his day. "The competition is still what I love about sport the most," he says. "There's something incredibly fun and satisfying about trying hard against someone else who is trying hard. That's the essence of all of us who like to compete. But it's not always a personal duel against another individual; it's also against that part of yourself that wants to be comfortable. You have to continuously win that victory against yourself. *Hey, I'm not dead yet.* That's why I'm so happy I can still do this at my age and feel like I'm alive."

If it's not roller hockey, it's golf or squash or Monopoly. Dorrance plays paintball with his son, Donovan, with the same military zeal that he once invested in Capture the Flag at the Villa Saint-Jean. "The essence of Anson's personality has always been his competitiveness," says former UNC soccer teammate Mark Berson. "There always has to be a challenge there for him. It's like a nervous twitch. He always wants another competition to be coming around the bend to get excited about, and he still thrives on being in the arena."

Dorrance always wants to match himself against the best player on the opposition and would prefer to play for the team expected to lose rather than the favorite, because it gives him a reason to try harder. The underdog spirit that still simmers in Dorrance from his childhood helped spawn a friendship with UNC's longtime wrestling coach Bill Lam. Dorrance once bought a T-shirt for Lam, whose heritage is part Native American, depicting an outnumbered brood of Indians attacking a battalion of soldiers with a caption reading, *I WILL GO TO WAR.* "Anson said that it reminded him so much of my competitive spirit that he had to buy it for me," Lam says. "I think he sees that in me because he has that in himself."

"Anson is the most intense competitor I've ever met," says Jack Simmons, the former Teague dorm intramural manager. "It's like they say about Michael Jordan. You have to kill him to beat him. Anson has that same quality. You might think you've killed him, but you better stomp on him and then light him on fire or he'll keep coming after you."

When Dorrance arrived at UNC from St. Mary's and waited out a redshirt year away from competitive soccer, he helped fuel his athletic fire with rugby. Even though he was repeatedly reminded by teammates that they weren't supposed to hit each other too hard in practice, Dorrance just couldn't resist the contact. "Anson had one great failing in rugby," teammate Joe Patterson recalls. "As a scrum half you're supposed to stand behind the scrum and wait for the ball to pop out and start the attack. But Anson liked to dive into the scrum. He had no fear of running into players twice his size. I had a certain amount of enlightened self-interest. I would pass the ball before I got hit. Anson never would."

While staying with his family in Greenwich during the summer before his senior year at UNC, Dorrance was playing rugby for a club team in New York City when he was tackled onto a manhole with its cover ajar. Dorrance's shoulder muscles were detached from his sternum. Eventually he would spend three hours at the emergency room waiting for treatment behind gunshot victims simply because their bleeding was *external*, but not until after he'd finished the game. To this day, M'Liss tells friends that the rugby injury explains why her husband is lopsided.

Dorrance is a man in his fifties, with no ACL in his right knee, who still runs through many of his off-season soccer practices when he's short on players and still firmly believes he could earn a starting spot on his own team, without any preferential treatment from the coach. He's a man who has had both of his front teeth knocked out by assistant coaches; one was accidentally removed during a heated racquetball game with Geoff Griffin, and the other was detached during a playful wrestling match with a former goalkeeper coach named Bruce Talbot. He's a man so competitive that when his sister Maggie visits his home for Christmas, and she and Anson sit down to play cards, M'Liss will refuse to join them because the game is too cutthroat. UNC men's soccer coach Elmar Bolowich recalls one day when he showed Dorrance his hunting bow. Dorrance took the bow and shot a few arrows, and before long the two soccer coaches would remain at the field after soccer practices, hunting trash cans. The loser had to empty the trash.

"Anson is so well-educated and well-spoken that a lot of people don't know what a fierce competitor he really is, but if you compete against him it's so vivid you can't miss it," Lam says. "Earlier in our coaching careers we would run together, but it would always be with other people, because there are some head-to-head competitions you just don't get into, and that's about as big a compliment as I can pay him. We'd have started running away from campus and I know I'd never have said it's time to turn around, and Anson would have died before he said it. We'd still be running."

A cruel woman. That's what Dorrance calls soccer. In this sport more than others, the better team doesn't necessarily win. Because it is so difficult to score, games are often decided by the capricious bounce of a ball that, while round, can be surprisingly unpredictable. UNC suffered a 1–0 loss in the NCAA final against Florida in 1998 despite dominating the Gators 21–6 in shots and 9–2 in corner kicks. In 1995, UNC outscored its twenty-six opponents by a total of 108–6, but lost 1–0 in the national semifinal to Notre Dame on an own goal off the head of Cindy Parlow, while outshooting the Irish 15–5. In fact, in the twenty defeats that North Carolina has endured since beginning its run of national championships in 1981, the Tar Heels have been outshot in only *three* of those games. Dorrance likes to joke that he is a man who dropped out of law school to coach a sport with no justice, but he doesn't look at any of those losses with malice. They are part of the game. Part of *his* game.

When it comes to soccer Dorrance is a realist, and nothing ticks him off more than the assumption that UNC's success has been easy or preordained in some way. "I never think we can't lose a game, because every soccer coach has lost games they deserved to win," Dorrance says. "I'm always puzzled when one of my players says after a game that she knew we were going to win. How can you know that? Are you a wizard? There are so many elements involved in victory that are absolutely out of your control. Luck is such a factor, and the absence of bad luck is a factor. You're dealing with twenty-year-olds that live on emotional teeter-totters, and if one of your players is at her low ebb at the same moment when the girl she's playing against is hitting her apogee, then the ball is in the back of your net and you lose."

Dorrance psychologically prepares to lose every UNC game. Before each match, he reviews the mental state he expects both he and his team will be in should they lose. "I think losing requires a rehearsal because it's a sign of weakness to be destroyed by defeat," Dorrance says. "Because I think some players' psyches are fragile, I can't talk about the losing scenario to my team, or they might read the wrong message into it, but I am always playing out how a UNC defeat impacts the balance of soccer power in the collegiate universe. If we're going to drop the scepter there are some programs I wouldn't mind picking it up, while there are others who would delight in beating us to a bloody pulp with it."

Whenever UNC is trailing with ten minutes left in a game, Dorrance begins composing his concession speech in his head. By doing so, he is already experiencing the loss emotionally, which relaxes him and helps him calm his players when they might otherwise panic. On those rare occasions when the Tar Heels do wind up losing, Dorrance is in homeostasis because he has already lost the game in his mind.

Dorrance prides himself on losing graciously, a reaction that stems back to the Boystown softball team in Singapore who praised the little guy for doing the impossible, because isn't that precisely what everybody thinks whenever anyone beats UNC? Another formative moment occurred in 1987 when Dorrance's U.S. national team defeated an injury-depleted Norwegian national team 3–0, and after the game Norway coach Even Pellerud shook Dorrance's hand and detailed all of the ingredients of the United States' success. "Pellerud had every right to mention his team's injuries as an excuse to mollify his loss, but he didn't, and I've never forgotten that," Dorrance says. "I remember thinking to myself, 'What a strong and tough sonofabitch. This guy isn't going to whine, he's going to address his team's weaknesses against us, fix them, and come after us.' That attitude scared the shit out of me."

Dorrance has since employed a similar postgame approach after losses. He always makes a point to praise the opposing coach on the area where his team performed most effectively against UNC. Then he'll walk up to every opposing player who he thinks was critical in defeating the Tar Heels and tell her why. In the postgame press conference, Dorrance will never offer up excuses, even if he believes his team deserved to win the game. He will never say, *What if?* Instead, Dorrance's public statement is always the same: *Bummer.*

"Sometimes I wonder, how does such a competitive person accept losing so stoically?" Jena Kluegel says. "Everyone else that I know who's that competitive absolutely hates to lose. You know he's got to be disappointed, but he's so forward-thinking that he never dwells on it with the team. It's done. That's how his brain works."

Says April Heinrichs: "Make no mistake, Anson Dorrance wants to win more than any other human being on Planet Earth, but losing is not an emotional moment for him, and he prides himself in appearing macho about setbacks."

"When Anson loses he understands the code of conduct, and he reacts with a lot of class, but it's a cover-up," Berson says. "He is seething inside. It's been that way since he was a player. He's dying to play that team again after a five-minute water break and crush them in the rematch."

Says Dorrance: "One of the things I've never been able to accept about sports is that one team has to lose, and yet I'm very good at arranging for other teams to lose. There's something wrong with that philosophically, don't you think? On the other hand, I am not a sore loser, but when my team loses I am teed off. It irritates me that I'm teed off, so why don't I sever that part of my personality? Is it because I don't want to? Is it just winning that I'm after?"

If Dorrance sounds conflicted about his reaction to losing, it's because he is. He remembers his losses so much more clearly than his victories, and his public reaction to defeat sometimes clashes with his private soul-searching. On August 31, 1986, in Chapel Hill, Dorrance's men's team lost 2–1 in overtime to Central Florida, and then his women's team tied UCF 1–1. Back at home after the double-header, Dorrance's six-year-old daughter Michelle asked her father to play a game of Chutes & Ladders. Anson rolled the dice and moved his piece around the board, totally preoccupied by the results of the day's soccer games. Finally, Michelle won the game and burst into tears. "Michelle, what's wrong?" Anson asked.

"Daddy, I just wanted you to win something today."

Look behind the scenes and it's clear that Dorrance grinds over losses much more than he reveals, even to his own players. Back in the early 1980s, M'Liss used to buy her husband Pepto-Bismol by the case. Anson would toss and turn all night after a loss, dropping as much as four pounds overnight and then wake up feeling like he hadn't slept at all. M'Liss worried he would develop an ulcer. "He'll always be very gracious with the press, but he comes home from any loss deflatedly replaying the game over and over in his head and very frustrated with the players who didn't try hard enough," M'Liss says. "That really depresses him because he feels like he didn't prepare them right. He'll always find a way to blame himself."

Says Dorrance: "I'm not one of those coaches who has a Pollyanna attitude toward losing. It is never a positive experience. After a loss, I just can't help thinking, 'Will we ever win again?' Obviously, that's ludicrous, but I swear that's exactly what goes through my mind. Fortunately, that attitude contributes in a positive way because it gives me permission to question everything I'm doing. 'What's our best forward line? Should I change the goalkeeper? Was it bad scheduling?' I'm the captain of a plane in a nosedive, and I'm doing everything I can to pull us out of it."

Dorrance doesn't reflexively attempt to gild every loss as a wake-up call for his team. He believes that only in hindsight at season's end can he evaluate whether a loss ultimately inspired or damaged the Tar Heels, but he is certain that every single UNC defeat causes some crisis of confidence for himself and his players. He revealed his method of privately reconstructing himself in a note to goalkeeper Tracy Noonan shortly after the Tar Heels lost the 1995 NCAA semifinal with Noonan in goal.

Tracy,

One day when my father was obviously very frustrated with me he told me I was the most confident person without any talent he had ever met. I considered that a wonderful compliment, which caused him to throw up his hands in despair. I am not always confident but you will never see when I am not. Rest assured I will eventually get there because I always try my best. Part of the game is to pretend you are something you are not and it is amazing how often you will become what you are trying to be. I also don't sweat my failures . . . I just get back to work. Hard work, persistence, fearlessness always win out in the end. You and I are both wonderful testaments to it. Don't forget what you have done . . . you are an amazing woman.

Your friend,
Anson

Dorrance recognizes that part of his power as a leader is to appear invulnerable, when in fact he is only human. "In the course of a day, even the most confident people live on an invisible emotional rollercoaster," Dorrance says. "No one else can see this ride, but tiny things affect where you are on this rollercoaster in terms of your confidence. You are always trying to maintain an equilibrium, but when you lose you're now looking at all of your tragic flaws, and if you're cerebral and thorough, you're going to come up with so many different ways you screwed up that it's unforgivable. I've read all these biographies of great leaders, and when you know all the things they've done to be successful you can list all of the millions of things that you've never done. What you're cataloging after a loss is this unbelievably bleak list of all of the areas where you've failed your team. And then what I'm thinking is, 'What incredible luck that I've lasted this long.'"

He said it in 1985. He said it in 1995. He said it in 2005. Dorrance says it at the end of every season that UNC finishes with a defeat. *I wouldn't trade anybody in this room for anybody on the other team.* The words are spoken with a mixture of sweetness and defiance to remind his girls that win or lose, UNC soccer is always about more than numbers on a scoreboard. The line is meant to get his players to look around the room at each other and feel a connection beyond the game.

At the press conference following UNC's loss to Florida in the 1998 NCAA final, reporters asked Tar Heel seniors Tiffany Roberts, Siri Mullinix, and Cindy Parlow to describe their heartbreak. Parlow chewed on a sandwich throughout the discussion. Roberts couldn't stop smiling even when she was talking about how bummed out she was. Mullinix kept whispering in Parlow's ear and cracking her up. "Obviously we're disappointed that we lost the national championship, but there's a lot more to a Carolina women's soccer team than winning national championships," Parlow said that day. "We're a family, and I'm very proud of everyone that I've had the honor of knowing. I'll never be disappointed about being a Tar Heel."

When Roberts was asked why she was smiling she replied, "Because I've played on a team that's very special and I'm part of a program that's unbelievable. I didn't go out with a national championship this year, but I'm going out with twenty-six best friends."

Then Mullinix added, "We all agreed that we would trade the rings we would have gotten today for the friends we've made and the coaching staff we have."

Later, when Dorrance entered the interview room, he was asked to explain his players' sanguine reaction. "To hear that's what they're saying makes me feel wonderful," Dorrance said. "There's no way in athletics you can guarantee consistent championship seasons, but what you can create in athletic teams is the bond our players are articulating."

Years later, Parlow is still amused and incredulous about the scene that day. "We were laughing and joking with the media because no matter how many different ways we tried to explain how we felt, they had no concept," Parlow says. "Sure, losing sucks and it hurts and it's no fun, but it's not the end of the world. The reporters were wondering, 'Why aren't you crying? Why aren't you upset? Why aren't you busting up the locker room?' Everyone was so surprised that we weren't suicidal, and I thought, 'You people just don't get it.' It isn't all about the soccer. Did we want to win this game? Yeah. Are we going to sulk for two months? No. I knew that disappointing moment would pass, but those friendships would last forever."

The day after the press conference, Dr. Bill Prentice read a newspaper column about one reporter's amazement over the response of the Tar Heels to their defeat. Prentice tacked the story up on his bulletin board, the only piece of soccer memorabilia in his office. As with so many in the program, Prentice's fondest memory of his time at UNC occurred after a loss, because these are the sore thumbs that stick out in the program, when the team's true character is revealed. Prentice still chokes up when he talks about the moments after UNC's NCAA Tournament loss in 1995. "We were clearly the better team that day, so it was a frigging nightmare, an extremely painful game to lose," Prentice says. "I remember a little while after the game Amy Roberts came up to Anson with tears streaming down her face, and she said, 'I am so sorry that we let you down.' Anson just hugged her, chuckled, and said, 'Don't worry about it. It's just a soccer game.' I get emotional just thinking about it. I thought that that's what this whole program is really all about. They want to win, they want to continue the tradition, but in the big picture, winning doesn't mean a damn thing."

One day shortly after Delaine Marbry joined Dorrance's staff as his secretary, she tracked him down and said that he had to return an urgent business call. After returning the call, Dorrance asked Marbry to come into his office. "Delaine, I'm a soccer coach," Dorrance told her. "How could I possibly have an urgent call?"

To ultimately understand Dorrance's attitude toward the significance of winning and losing, one has to understand his perspective on athletics. It's another thing he learned from Dean Smith, who was often quoted as dismissing the value of basketball in the real world. Whenever Smith needed to straighten out a reporter who was treating college basketball like a conflict in the Middle East, he would sigh and say; "It's just a basketball game." Listen to Dorrance. He says it all the time. *It's just a soccer game.*

"There's little about athletics that elevates you as a human being," Dorrance says. "If there were, there wouldn't be so many frigging assholes in athletics that I've lost count. I don't think athletics is anything more than people running around, breaking a sweat, and having a good time. It's frivolous. We're not finding a cure for cancer. We're not taking serial killers and turning them into nuns. Our underlying theme has always got to be that there are a billion people in China who don't even know we're playing soccer today, so let's relax and enjoy ourselves because this isn't the end of the world."

Dorrance says this as if he's reminding himself. He knows that his women don't need him to tell them it's just a soccer game. It's another difference he sees between men and women. "In our society women value relationships, while men tend to measure their lives by athletic success and failure," Dorrance says. "That's why you see movies of the old high school star quarterback pumping gas somewhere, and the message is that he had a great arm, but it didn't make him a great man."

Anyone looking for a symbol of the UNC women's soccer mindset need look no further than a closet door inside the McCaskill Soccer Center. The door is decorated as a shrine of NCAA awards and lacquered newspaper articles, but from beneath the door protrudes a rubber novelty foot. Whenever Dorrance is shepherding a group of visitors through the UNC soccer office, the tour inevitably screeches to halt when a young girl shrieks at the sight of the foot and asks, "What's *that*?!" The coach's well-rehearsed response is, "That is the last Tar Heel who didn't pass fitness."

Says former assistant coach Bill Steffen, "When people ask me, 'What do you remember most about working at UNC?' The first word that comes to my mind isn't *winning* or *training* or *tradition*, it is *fun.*"

At the end of almost every UNC soccer practice, Bill Palladino looks expectantly at Tom Sander and asks, "Do we have cake?" One of Sander's duties is to procure a preponderance of cakes for various occasions, everything from a player's birthday to an anomalous cake for the last day of fitness each season to a cake because they haven't had a cake in a while. The cakes are always ceremoniously cut with one of Dr. Prentice's tongue depressors and consumed by the fistful.

In order to satisfy the players' sugar fix during games, the program developed what is very affectionately known as "the candy bag." Since 1992, before each game, Sander has filled a plastic grocery bag with candy, from Sweet Tarts to Jawbreakers to Pixy Stix, a sugary smorgasbord that he firmly believes is a lucky talisman as well as a fattening one. The candy bag was briefly banned in 1994 by Dorrance after one reserve player, who was slightly above her ideal playing weight, drained the bag during a game. Two days later, the Tar Heels tied Notre Dame, snapping a long unbeaten streak. Two weeks after that, when UNC lost at Fetzer Field for the first time ever, Sander was convinced it was "the curse of the candy bag." He surreptitiously reinstituted the candy, and it has been on the Tar Heels bench ever since. UNC players stash Starbursts in the lining of their shorts for "energy." Dorrance eats a handful of Gummi Worms before every game. Palladino favors Tootsie Rolls. Even game officials have been known to occasionally forage into the candy bag. Sander figured out that each season the Tar Heels consume an average of 155 pounds of candy, and Robin Confer swears that her massive sugar intake led to a series of root canals shortly after she graduated. "Whenever I dug into our candy bag and there weren't any Sour Gummi Worms left, then all hell broke loose," Danielle Borgman says. "That keeps everything in perspective. What other team argues over the supply of Sour Gummi Worms?"

Dorrance balances the intensity of the competitive cauldron in practice with games of pickup kickball and drills that pit blondes versus brunettes, after which the losers are punished by standing "butts up" in the goal while the winners pelt them with penalty kicks. At practice on the day before each game the Tar Heels traditionally dress in the school colors of their upcoming opponent, and on Halloween the players all arrive in costume, from Catwoman to a Parisian hooker to Anson Dorrance. In 2003, Dorrance even rescheduled a home game with Florida State from November 1 to October 31 so that his players could enjoy the full fruits of Halloween, a huge party night in Chapel Hill.

On the eve of the 2001 NCAA Final Four in Dallas, Palladino improvised "Dino's Tour of Christmas Lights," a wildly meandering van tour through a ritzy neighborhood, with passengers trying to guess which house belonged to Cowboys owner Jerry Jones. Later that night, there was a thirty-minute drive, including multiple U-turns, to a Baskin-Robbins located no more than a mile from the hotel. Along the way, the Tar Heels sang along with Christmas carols on the radio and discussed how one can watch the movie *The Wizard of Oz* with Pink Floyd's *Dark Side of the Moon* as its soundtrack. After returning from their ice cream run, the best collegiate women's soccer players in America skipped up and down the hotel hallway giddily pantsing each other.

Every UNC game is an unscripted sitcom. Before Dorrance arrives for his pregame talk, players sometimes indulge in an X-rated game of Hangman on the blackboard. Just before the pregame of the 2003 ACC tourney opener, Carmen Watley read a love poem written by one of her teammates' boyfriends, who was posing as the fictional secret admirer of another player, a provocative revision of Keats's "Ode on a Grecian Urn." Then there was the time that Anne Remy went AWOL during one pregame because she'd been stopped for speeding on the way to the field. After she called Dorrance to inform him, Dorrance conducted a poll of Remy's teammates to decide if she cried her way out of the ticket. Remy arrived in tears with a ticket in hand and couldn't help but laugh when she noticed the poll numbers significantly supported her amnesty.

For a game against Guilford in 2002, Dorrance loaned Quakers coach Eric Lewis a necktie because he didn't have one, and then he loaned Lewis his daughter Natalie as an assistant coach because Lewis didn't have one of those either. Before another game, Rakel Karvelsson's UNC teammates goaded her into singing the national anthem. Trouble was, Karvelsson, a native of Iceland, was not at all familiar with the words.

On the bench during a game, Palladino has been known to tell the reserve players that if the coaches forget to sub them into a game at the appointed moment, they should throw a Tootsie Roll at him, which might just be the easiest way for him to get a Tootsie Roll. During one lopsided win at Maryland, Dorrance couldn't decide whom to sub in at the end of the game, so he told his reserves to rock/paper/scissors for it. Other times he has made lineup changes based on suggestions phoned in from former players in the stands. Perhaps it was Dorrance's whimsical substituting that led Staci Wilson, who was tired of being subbed out early in blowouts, to show up at the bench before one game carrying a paper bag. Dorrance opened the bag to find a plastic skull with a dagger stuck in it, and a note that read, *Anson, if you take me out of the game, this is going to be you.* Wilson played the full ninety minutes.

During another blowout win, when backup goalkeeper Merridee Proost took the concept of leadership on the field a tad too far by subbing herself into the game without orders to do so, Dorrance devised a multiple choice for punishment:

A) Run the Cooper again
B) Wear an extra small uniform
C) Become your backup's slave for a day

Much to her eventual regret, Proost chose C.

There have been times during comfortable victories when the UNC coaches perhaps had too much time on their hands. During the second half of a 7–0 win against Virginia in 1992, when Tar Heel alum Laurie Gregg was the Cavaliers' coach, Dorrance and Palladino got hungry and decided to order food and have it delivered to the sideline. Palladino looked over to Gregg and said, "Laurie, we're getting some pizza, would you guys like some?" Gregg replied, "Yeah, what the hell. Might as well."

Before the 1994 NCAA championship game, the UNC coaches bought themselves chicken fingers and potato wedges and stashed them under the bench during the game. As they watched the Tar Heels defeat Notre Dame 5–0, the UNC coaches passed chicken up and down the bench. "Other coaches would look at that and be horrified," Palladino says. "Winning allows us to behave this way. If we were doing that and we were losing there would be hell to pay. Somebody would see that, and they'd laugh us right out of our jobs."

Says Prentice: "I've been around athletics all my life, and I have never seen any other situation like this. I used to sit there and think, 'How the hell do these guys get away with this?' Then one day you realize that maybe everybody else is doing it wrong. A lot of the other coaches have forgotten that it's supposed to be fun. Maybe Anson and Dino have figured out that one of the keys to being successful is to treat the sport the way it was intended to be played. It is just a frigging *game*."

On the day before a UNC home game against Alabama in 1997, Dorrance invited Crimson Tide coach Don Staley to play golf, and the two coaches made a bet that the loser would buy the winner lunch during the next day's game. Dorrance lost, and as his student manager presented Staley with a hot dog at halftime, the UNC coach watched the ceremony out of the corner of his eye, stewing as he saw Staley's players laughing and congratulating their coach. The Tar Heels defeated Alabama 6–0 that day, but that revenge did not satisfy Dorrance. After the game he huddled with Wilson and told her, "Staci, you were a shark out there, and now you've got to do me a favor. Their coach beat me in golf yesterday, and I've got to get him back somehow."

On Dorrance's instructions, Wilson walked over to Staley and said, "Coach, I can never tell if Anson is just doing this to motivate me or not, but he told me before the game that the girl I was marking was the daughter of the Grand Wizard of the Ku Klux Klan. Is that true?"

"Nooo, Staci, noooo," said Staley, clearly upset at the notion. "That's not true at all."

"Oh, OK," Wilson said matter-of-factly. Wilson then started walking off the field, winked at Dorrance and said, "Anson, we got him."

It is Dorrance's sense of humor and his healthy perspective which ultimately help him dull the pain of his rare defeats. He recalls showing up for a UNC booster club appearance after the 1998 season with nothing prepared to say. Dorrance listened as UNC field hockey coach Karen Shelton thanked the Tar Heel fans for their support, talked about her team's season, and concluded by saying, "I'm most proud of the fact that our kids had the highest GPA we've ever had." After some polite applause, Dorrance then stood up for his remarks. "I was also really proud of my girls for having the highest GPA we've ever had, but then we lost the national championship game," Dorrance told the audience, "so I say, *'Bring back the dumb ones!'"*

17 | *Ascension*

What lies behind us and what lies before us are tiny matters compared to what lies within us.

—Ralph Waldo Emerson

Anson Dorrance has adapted his philosophy of life from a *Calvin and Hobbes* comic strip. In the strip, Calvin is a boy philosopher and Hobbes is a tiger who acts as Calvin's sidekick, alter ego, and counterpoint. Dorrance's defining strip is a Sunday comic which features Calvin and Hobbes pulling a child's wagon up a hill, across a plateau and then riding in the wagon together as it careens downhill and finally off a cliff. The dialogue is as follows:

Calvin (walking): *My life could be a lot better than it is. I'm happy but it's not like I'm ecstatic.*

(climbing) *Life is like topography, Hobbes. There are summits of happiness and success . . .*

(on the plateau) *. . . Flat stretches of boring routine . . .*

(riding downhill) *. . . And valleys of frustration and failure.*

But I'm dedicating myself to experiencing only peaks! I want my life to be one of never-ending ascension!

Each minute of every day should bring me greater joy than the previous minute!

I should always be saying, 'My life is better than I ever imagined it would be. And it's only going to improve.'

I'm just going to jump from peak to peak! I'm (off the cliff) . . . whoops.

(As the two tumble down into a chasm)

Hobbes: *At least with flat places you don't have so far to go down.*

Calvin: *Only losers go down! For me it's only going to be up and up!*

"I love that comic because it represents life," Dorrance says. "I love that regardless of the topography, Calvin's got this indomitable spirit. I want myself and my players to construct ourselves with this attitude of a never-ending ascension. I love the fact that even when Calvin is cascading downhill and into the gorge, he is still talking about ascending, because to live a life of never-ending ascension you have to be the eternal optimist, even as you fall into the abyss. That's the foundation of character."

Many of Dorrance's players and staff say he is the most optimistic person they have ever met. Not only is Dorrance's glass always half full, he's expecting a refill any second now. Dorrance traces his attitude back to his youth spent reading inspirational books about war heroes and successful salespeople. He has since read articles which have informed him that his attitude can be determined by what his mind tells him to feel. So Dorrance believes he can choose to be content.

Dorrance doesn't so much believe in overcoming adversity as in dismissing it entirely. When the wind chill dipped to minus 18 degrees on the morning of the 1988 NCAA final at the University of Massachusetts, Dorrance noticed his players huddled forlornly in their vans as they prepared to leave the team hotel. Dorrance walked out of the lobby and began stripping off layers, until he was naked above the waist. He paraded around the vans chirping, "It's not cold out here; it's like a tropical island." By the time the team arrived at the field everyone had joined in the spirit. Lori Henry marched around the locker room singing, "We're having a heat wave, a tropical heat wave." UNC won the game 1–0, though Dorrance likes to joke that he did sacrifice his left nipple to frostbite for the cause.

"What I like about Anson the most, and I'm still just in awe of, is how he's always overwhelmingly positive," Tracy Noonan says. "I've never seen him in a bad mood. I've never seen him slam a door. How can you never get upset? It's like he doesn't have that anger emotion in him."

Back when Dorrance was just a twelve-year-old kid, Big Pete defined it as *insouciance*. When Anson asked his father what the word meant, Big Pete said, "Well, Mr. Insouciant, look it up."

"I remember reading the definition and thinking, 'Dad's got something here,'" Anson says. "*Insouciant* describes a kind of oblivion, and I've always had a kind of oblivion about reality."

Michelle Akers calls it "airheadedness." Lorrie Fair refers to Dorrance as an "absent-minded professor." By any definition, Dorrance is pretty clueless. He once bumped into an old friend from Louisburg at a Chapel Hill restaurant, sat down to join him for lunch, and didn't realize until after he'd returned to the soccer office and checked his desk calendar that he had actually been participating in a previously scheduled lunch meeting. The first time Dorrance had dinner with Mia Hamm and her future husband, the All-Star baseball player Nomar Garciaparra, Dorrance had no idea who Garciaparra was. Then there was the time he tried to pay for a team meal at McDonald's with a personal check. When the cashier told him they don't accept checks, he said, "Well, then you aren't going to get paid because that's all I have." Eventually, McDonald's took the check. Another time Dorrance was narrating a summer camp demonstration when some ominous clouds started brewing behind him as the campers anxiously pointed and whispered to each other about the approaching storm. Finally, when a lightning bolt struck the field behind Dorrance, most of the kids jumped up and started fleeing toward the parking lot, but Dorrance kept rambling on about attacking box organization to the few campers who were more afraid of deserting him than they were of electrocution.

Take a close look on any given day, and it's likely that Dorrance is wearing his soccer shorts on backward. "Other than coaching soccer, everything else is extraneous to him," Betsy Johnson says. "Anson subscribes to the theory that you don't sweat the small stuff, and almost everything is small to him."

"People are told that UNC is a soccer factory and that I'm a tyrant who's going to make you train nine hours a day," Dorrance says. "Then they come here and find out I don't even know what time the games start."

When either M'Liss or Delaine Marbry needs information about Anson's schedule, they will bypass him and call each other, a system that is hardly foolproof. One day before a practice, M'Liss showed up at the field to bring her husband a cold drink only to discover that he wasn't there. "Where's Anson?" M'Liss asked the players.

The girls looked at each other sheepishly until one of them said, "He's in South Carolina with the men's team."

On the eve of the 2002 ACC Tournament, Dorrance was teeing off on the first hole of a round of golf when he received a call on his cell phone from M'Liss's brother, Mark, asking for M'Liss's cell number. Anson couldn't remember the number, and he casually asked Mark why he was looking for her. Mark told him it was M'Liss's birthday. Anson was stunned, but not too stunned to keep from finishing the round. Dorrance regularly forgets his wife's and kids' birthdays, which tends to improve the quality of gifts they eventually receive.

Almost every time he and M'Liss get in the car to go anywhere, Anson reflexively drives toward the soccer office before she straightens him out. M'Liss says that the first five years of marriage to Anson were the hardest, before it dawned on her that her husband was never going to change. "Anson is very intellectual, but you expect intellectuals to be very organized and ordered," M'Liss says. "The normal things that most people feel obligated to he finds dispensable, and so he goes along on his merry way forgetting half the things he's supposed to be doing that day. It's unintentional. He's flaky in that regard. It's almost as if he's chosen not to care about these things because he can't remember them anyway."

Dorrance cannot identify his players by their numbers because he never bothers to learn them, and he isn't too sharp with names, either. Tired of Dorrance calling her *Carolyn,* Caroline McLaughlin started wearing a T-shirt to practice that featured her name spelled out phonetically. Throughout most of Shanna Caldwell's freshman year, Dorrance called her *Shannon,* until the day Caldwell told him, "It sounds like *banana,*" which didn't help Dorrance, but did prompt Caldwell's teammates to start calling her *Banana.* Even though he consults a UNC roster when writing letters to parents so that he won't spell their child's name wrong, halfway through goalkeeper Aly Winget's sophomore season, Dorrance was still spelling her name *Wingate.* He spelled Lindsay Tarpley's first name *Lindsey* for months in recruiting letters until Lindsay's mother phoned to tell Dorrance that he might have a better chance to sign her daughter if he began spelling her name right. There are some players whose names he forgets entirely. His fallback for any of these players is *whatshername.* Often he'll turn to Tom Sander and say, "Get me *whatshername.*" To which Sander then responds, "Which *whatshername?*"

Dorrance is essentially a cartoon character whose seconds scurry around him, handling him, putting out fires, preventing him from falling through trap doors, so that his obliviousness can be preserved. "Sometimes Anson will ask Chris or Delaine or me to do something that really doesn't need to be done, and we'll just play along," Sander says. "He thinks it's getting done, so he's happy, and what he doesn't know won't kill him. We'll pretend that we're in Anson's world, but we always try to keep that rope of reality around us so we can find our way out of the labyrinth."

Perhaps the biggest challenge for those around Dorrance is to try to gain and maintain his full attention. "If I'm babbling away I can tell instantly when Anson stops listening to me," brother Pete says. "He starts saying, 'Uh-huh, uh-huh, uh-huh,' and his mind is a million miles away. I could start speaking French and he'd still be saying, 'Uh-huh, uh-huh, uh-huh.' He has the ability to plug himself in and out of a conversation."

"I think Anson's always got his to-do list running on a continuous loop in his head," Wendy Gebauer says. "I like to call him out. *Anson, this is your friend Wendy back on Earth.*"

When the UNC players perform skits at the team's annual season-ending banquet, nobody wants to sit next to Dorrance because he has trouble following the plots. "He doesn't get any of the jokes, and he'll sit there and ask you the whole time, 'What's going on?'" Jenni Branam says. "You feel like telling him, 'You had to be there.' But he *was* there."

As he has aged, Dorrance has begun relying on the term "senior moment" to explain his lapses. Perhaps his most legendary senior moment occurred on a Sunday in 1996 when he asked the team's academic counselor Brian Davis if he could borrow a key to UNC's Academic Center to conduct a coaching clinic there. Dorrance arrived at the academic center and tried to unlock the door over and over with no success. Finally, he phoned Davis, who drove twenty minutes to meet him. Davis looked at the key in Dorrance's hand and told him, "That isn't the key I gave you." Dorrance then looked at the key and responded, "You know, you're right. That's my house key."

Shortly thereafter when Davis ran into Mia Hamm before a national team game and told her the key story, Hamm shook her head and said, "How the hell do we win so many games?"

One day in 1976, Dorrance was selling life insurance door-to-door when he stumbled upon another group of solicitors. Dorrance asked them, "What are you guys selling?" One of the two men dressed in matching white shirts and dark slacks replied, "Let's make an appointment and I'll tell you."

A few days later, the two men showed up at Dorrance's home, and he invited them in before he'd even learned what they were angling to sell. The pair were Mormon missionaries, and while Dorrance wasn't necessarily looking for a new religion, he agreed to hear them out, while M'Liss sequestered herself to the bedroom. Dorrance asked aggressive questions of these men, as he had of the

Jehovah's Witnesses, the Krishnas and anyone else who showed up at his door. As someone who had endured the catechism and a childhood of Catholic schooling, Dorrance harbored some gripes against Catholicism. He hated the way his Catholic faith self-righteously condemned the Hindu nanny he'd adored as a boy in India, as well as basically everybody he'd come in contact with on the African continent. At the Villa Saint-Jean he found himself regularly embroiled in raging debates about Catholicism with teachers who encouraged him to question it in hopes of improving his understanding.

When the Mormons sat in his living room, Dorrance treated their appearance like one of those classes at the Villa. After a few missionary visits, M'Liss eventually joined in the discussions with a more spiritual curiosity than her husband. The longer M'Liss listened, the more she felt connected. Anson merely enjoyed the debate. "I wore out these missionaries, and the church kept sending new ones," Anson says. "Finally, after six sets, they finally sent this stocky Midwestern redneck, and he says, 'All right, you guys have to be baptized. I just have a feeling that it has to be done now. This is important.'" M'Liss was spiritually moved, while the salesman in Anson couldn't deny that it was a compelling close.

The following afternoon, the Dorrances were baptized Mormon. Just three days later, M'Liss's mother, father, and sister all tragically perished in a late-night fire at their Virginia home, and Anson was relieved to have the support structure of their new faith behind them.

Shortly thereafter, Anson and M'Liss had a second wedding in the Mormon Temple in Washington, D.C., a union that is seen by the faith as an eternal marriage, not broken by death. They decided to raise their children Mormon. Dorrance tithes 10 percent of his gross income to the church, though he has never been able to bring himself to actually sign the sizable checks, so M'Liss always forges his signature. Observing church doctrine, Dorrance gave up drinking alcohol, so when the rest of his roller hockey group sits down for postgame beers, Dorrance is presented with a Gatorade, which he calls "Mormon beer." He even forgoes hockey games on Sundays because his religion preaches Sunday as a day of rest and reflection, though he is compelled to coach his team regularly on that day during the season and in the NCAA championship game. While he has also sworn off caffeine and tea, he has, against the church's wishes, never given up cursing. He considers cursing to be more of a venial than a mortal sin, though his own children have regularly condemned him for swearing ever since the day that ten-year-old Natalie was a ballgirl at a UNC match and was stunned to hear her father's language on the sideline. Otherwise, Dorrance is so dedicated to his religion that he once turned down an invitation to play golf at Pebble Beach because he was asked to deliver a speech that day at church. "I just hope that God understands the magnitude of my sacrifice," Dorrance jokes. "If Hell is arranged in tiers, I just hope that I'm at one of the higher levels."

It is an example of the dichotomy of Dorrance that he describes himself as "not a particularly spiritual person" and has often told his players that he subscribes to Karl Marx's theory that "religion is the opiate of the masses," yet he is a regular Sunday school teacher. It is an example of the dichotomy of Dorrance that this learned man who has built much of his coaching philosophy through reading the philosophical tomes of Aristotle and Kierkegaard and Viktor Frankl sees his approach to life in a Sunday comic taped to his office door. He is a relentless optimist who loses one game and wonders if he will ever win again. He is a self-described alpha male who took ballet classes from M'Liss one summer for fun. He is a man who wears sweats to the office almost every day, but wears a tie for every game to honor his former coach Marvin Allen. He is a man who lets his NCAA trophies collect dust but won't let his wife throw away his boarding school yearbooks. He is a man who forty years later can still recall by heart the Singapore television network's daily sign-on in Chinese, but he can't remember his wife's birthday. He is a man so distrusting of doctors that he once super-glued one of his false front teeth back into his gum rather than visit his dentist, yet he submitted to acupuncture treatment one day in his office from a total stranger who guaranteed it as a cure for tendonitis. He is a compelling public speaker who despises public speaking. He is an inveterate teaser who, his players lament, is impervious to ribbing about his short shorts, his poofy hair, his garish sneakers, or his bug-eyed sunglasses, but who privately admits that he dislikes his first name Albert so much that he uses the initial A on most official documents. He is a man who admits to leading a life of chaos, yet he is still such a rigid perfectionist that when he was asked to throw out the first pitch at a UNC softball game, he wasn't satisfied with the accuracy of his first effort. Or his second. So Dorrance actually threw out the first *three* pitches.

He is a coach with a lucrative Nike sponsorship deal who has such indifference toward money that he doesn't even carry a wallet, and drives a 1990 Saab with 129,000 miles on it that has a dent in the passenger door and smells like the inside of a hockey glove, a car he has stubbornly resisted trading in despite his doctor's concern that carbon monoxide fumes from the engine cause him vertigo. He is a self-avowed patriot who has fervently defended America and its democracy against a hostile majority throughout his life, but has never once voted in an election. "He's doesn't vote because he feels like one vote can't make a difference, yet that mentality runs completely against his coaching philosophy," daughter Michelle says. "That's like saying that one individual on a team can't make a difference. Also, he calls himself a Republican, but preaches the liberal idea that you're only as strong as your weakest link. He's a complete enigma to me sometimes."

Of those closest to Dorrance, some say he couldn't be more basic, while others insist he couldn't be more complicated, which likely lends credibility to the latter. Dorrance finds himself very ordinary. "My life is pretty simple," he says. "It's always been about family, friends, sports, and books. That's about it."

Big Pete Dorrance always made restless noises in his sleep, but Peggy had never heard a groan like this before. Something was not right. She turned toward her husband on this August night in 1984 and noticed that he looked terribly pale.

Big Pete had suffered a massive heart attack. He was dead before they could get him to the hospital. Gone, just like that, at 61. Sure, Big Pete had done everything in his power to kill himself, smoking and drinking too much along with his type AAA personality, but he still looked plenty fit and strong, and his family just assumed the Great Santini was too frigging stubborn to ever give in to death.

Peggy first called her son Pete with the news. Pete called M'Liss. M'Liss could barely bring herself to phone Anson, who was away coaching at a national youth camp in Michigan. M'Liss wept, and Anson tried to comfort her as best he could over the phone. Anson didn't cry. He just said, "I'll be home on the next flight out." First thing the next morning, Dorrance called a team meeting and choked up as he told his youth team that his father had passed away.

Anson requested to deliver the eulogy at his father's funeral because he thought his public expression of affection for Big Pete would be cathartic. He saw the speech as a last chance to talk to his dad, to say goodbye and to thank him. He delivered the eulogy in a strong voice, pausing a few times to steel himself. Anson spoke about how Big Pete had desperately wanted him to become his corporate lawyer and had initially scoffed at his decision to coach soccer instead, but how when Big Pete and Peggy had moved to Chapel Hill in 1983, and Big Pete finally watched his son coach a soccer game at UNC, father had walked up to son afterward and said, "Now I know why you chose this." Anson then said that his young daughter Michelle would grow up understanding the meaning of the phrase "indefatigable human spirit," because she had learned it from her grandfather. He concluded with a humorous story about the night Big Pete made an impatient exit from a party by announcing, "N.R. Dorrance is leaving!" right before slipping on a patch of ice and falling on his butt in a fit of self-deprecating laughter.

Anson chose to view his father's life in only the most positive terms, and even two decades later when he speaks about Big Pete, he still refers to him in the present tense. "Anson's done so much to keep Dad alive for all of us in telling his stories, and quite frankly he might be gilding some of them," brother Pete says. "It's like he's building this persona that I didn't see all the time. Anson's always being generous in his portrayal, almost as a way of giving back to Dad in a mythical sort of way. Anson sees the best in people, and I've always appreciated that he had the quality in him to do that."

In fact, Big Pete had worked tirelessly for the last twenty years of his life trying to realize his dream of starting his own oil refining business, sometimes at the expense of his own family. Big Pete spent weeks at a time away from his wife and children, and literally bet the farm on his company when he mortgaged the Nutbush plantation in Louisburg as collateral. Several times he came within a day of signing papers with a bank to secure financing for the first refinery, but the deal would mysteriously fall apart overnight, and bankers with whom he'd been getting along famously suddenly wouldn't return his phone calls. Gradually it began to dawn on Big Pete that the ideal scenario from the standpoint of the major oil companies was that his refineries were never built, but he still kept fighting to build them until the day Carolina Refining & Distributing died with him.

"Initially when you lose someone, you think about all the incredible things about them, but Anson eventually came to recognize the sacrifices his dad made to chase his dreams," M'Liss says. "Big Pete had the same optimism and drive that Anson had, but he became so entrenched in those that he couldn't recognize the downside. You have to decide how far it's worth it to go before you risk damaging your family or your marriage. Anson began to realize how there has to be a balance in your life."

With the loss of his father, suddenly the women in Dorrance's life became the dominant influences. The man who had spent much of his first twenty years around virtually no females would now spend the rest of his days surrounded almost exclusively by women, from his mother, his wife, and his daughters, to his female soccer players. While Dorrance's optimism came naturally to him, dredging up the female side of his personality required a push. Dorrance's transformation, which had begun with his realization that women behave differently than men and should be trained differently, was finally ripe to blossom.

The metamorphosis of Dorrance began on the surface. He had never cared about his personal appearance until one day in the mid-1980s when one of his players mentioned that his looks could actually affect his recruiting. "We all knew that seventeen-to-twenty-one-year-old women are the most critical human beings you could ever be around," Shannon Higgins says. "We were all very proud of Anson as a coach, and we didn't want him to look like such a dork. He finally realized that not being a dork would be appealing to women, and they might actually listen to him more."

Many UNC players took an interest in Dorrance's prolonged makeover, and he once gave Mia Hamm his credit card to go out and buy some stylish clothes for him. The changes began when Dorrance branched out in his practice attire from wearing all white to *black* and white. Before long the guy who once refused to cut his moptop suddenly knew what kind of conditioner was best for making his hair more manageable and even started moussing. Suddenly at games his dress shirts actually matched his slacks. When he started doing some television commentary, Dorrance even began checking himself out in the mirror now and then. "Anson really got into applying his own makeup," confides Beth Mowins, Dorrance's former WUSA television partner. "He once asked me, 'Do you think my skin tone is fall or spring?'"

The woman's touch also started to penetrate beneath the surface. "At the beginning I think women's soccer was more of a project for Anson," Michelle Akers says. "He treated it more like a challenge. *Let's see if I can cultivate these women to play.* Eventually he gained more of an appreciation and a respect for what he's doing. It became more personal."

In the early 1980s, Dorrance made a point never to touch any of his players because he felt that helped create a dividing line between them. He rarely even left the bench when one of his women suffered an injury. Then during one practice in 1984, Diane Beatty crashed to the ground holding her injured leg. Dorrance jogged onto the field and put his hand on her back. There was an audible gasp from the rest of the team because it was the first time he'd ever touched one of them. That sort of gesture was still notable when Tracey Bates suffered a knee injury that would end her college career during a game against N.C. State in 1989. Bill Prentice helped Bates off the field into a van, and Dorrance ignored the ongoing game to comfort his injured player. Bates was crying. Dorrance didn't know what to say. "I remember the crushing disappointment in his face and saw how what had happened to me was tugging on his heart," Bates says. "He hugged me like I was his daughter."

Hamm, who sat out that N.C. State game with her own injury, was surprised to see her coach cry for the first time. "For Anson, it was no longer about being Tracey's coach, but about being her friend and about being a father figure," Hamm says. "Tracey's sadness and the impact that it had on Anson was what touched me the most. His reaction meant the world to her. Sometimes we picture Anson as this huge soccer icon and forget that he is human. For us as players, you're always waiting to see that side, and that moment made me reevaluate why I went to Carolina. You invest in it because you care about each other, and if you don't the experience isn't going to be as meaningful or as fun. Over the course of each season there are hundreds of small successes and failures, and all of these at the college level are melodramatic because it's such an impressionable time in your life. Anson's learned to be more sensitive to these moments and much more open with his feelings. I hope he doesn't think of it as a sign of weakness, because for all of us it makes us love him even more. It also makes him a better coach because his players can relate to him on a level beyond soccer. A stoic, unemotional person asking you to be emotional about the game just doesn't carry the same weight."

In 1984, when Dorrance told his national youth team that his father had just died, it was the first time he had ever choked up in front of any of his players. He also teared up when he told his Tar Heels he would be leaving them behind to coach at the 1991 World Championship. When senior Tiffany Roberts was excused from the room with the other seniors before the 1998 NCAA final, Dorrance drew an enormous heart around a diagram of a soccer field on the blackboard and told the team that that's the size of Roberts's heart, as tears streamed down his cheeks. "The first time or two that I saw him cry in front of the team I was really stunned because it took a long time for that to happen," M'Liss says. "Becoming empathetic was like learning another language for him, but the longer he's worked with women, the more he's understood the significance of people's emotions and the more emotional he's become."

Dorrance admits to being influenced by a story he once read in *Time* magazine about a person's "emotional IQ." The thrust of the article was that the more emotional you are, the more evolved you are as a human being. The story suggested that a person's intelligence and emotional threshold are tied together, so Dorrance decided that women were more highly developed creatures. Suddenly Dorrance didn't see women as such psychos anymore. He stopped trying to turn them into men, and he started admitting that when conflicts occurred it might be *his* fault.

Bettina Bernardi couldn't do anything right during one spring scrimmage in 1986, and whenever Bernardi mistouched the ball, Dorrance bellowed *"Unnnnnnnbelievable!"* in a decidedly uncomplimentary fashion. After about forty-five minutes, Bernardi couldn't stand it anymore, and she walked off the field in tears. When Palladino asked her what was wrong, she said, "I can't take it. Anson is being an absolute asshole. If I stay here any longer I'm going to say something that'll get me in trouble. So I'm just leaving."

The next day in the weight room, Dorrance walked up to Bernardi and said, "I'm really sorry for being such an ass yesterday."

Dorrance ascribes his transformation to being "coachable." He has come to see his players as part of his family, and he tries to figure out which ones need a pep talk after a rough day in practice.

"If you're going to coach women, you need to plug in and understand their sensitivity, and that's helped Anson as a coach," Ange Kelly says. "I think it was always in him, but being brought up in his household with his father, he had to be very strong. Now he realizes that he's in an environment where it's OK to be a little exposed, be vulnerable by telling people that he cares about them, and appreciate people for who they are beyond the soccer field. He's become a great ear for his players."

"There was a time when if a girl cried, Anson thought it was because she just wasn't tough, so he was callous and just dismissed it," M'Liss says. "He no longer tries to be strong enough not to be affected by it. Having lost his dad and watching me go through losing half my family, having those tests of faith and loyalty, he's realized that personal relationships are the most important part of your life. He used to be more self-sufficient, but now he enjoys people's company more."

M'Liss thinks that her husband's increased accessibility has occasionally even prompted an emotional attachment that she believes is natural whenever a group of young women are working with a male authority figure. "I used to tease Anson about how some of the girls must have a crush on him, and he'd say, 'No way, I intimidate them too much,'" M'Liss says. "He was oblivious, as usual."

On the wall in his office Dorrance once posted a note that featured the quote, *People don't know how much you know until they know how much you care.* "As a young coach I thought these women were toy soldiers with different factors of strength that I could move around the field," he says. "Now I appreciate the players more as people, and there's a human element in all of my decisions. I've realized that I'm not hired at UNC to win soccer games. I'm hired to develop human beings, and we sort of do this national championship thing on the side."

In a 1987 game against George Mason, Carla Werden made an ill-advised backpass to her goalkeeper that resulted in a Patriots goal. Dorrance noticed Werden crying about the mistake afterward, so the next day he invited Werden to his house to eat pizza with his family. This began a tradition of inviting psychologically or physically wounded players to dine with him for what Dorrance calls *Dinners for People Whose Lives Have Been Struck by Lightning.* Unlike in years past, these days he'll think about finding a few minutes of playing time for a benchwarmer whom he respects, or one whose parents have shown up for a par-ticular game. He even admits that his favorite moments of the office day are the drop-in visits from his players. "I think he cares more about what the players think of him than he used to, but he hates to admit that because he's a guy," Delaine Marbry says. "More and more every year, he really wants the girls to like him."

"I've learned more from my women than I've taught them," Dorrance says. "Coaching women has made me a better husband, a better father, and a better coach. They've changed me. They've taught me how to relate better as a human being, and I've taught them how to compete. They've given me one of the great gifts that women possess, and I've given them one of the great gifts that men possess, and I am clearly the victor in that exchange."

18 *Defense*

To fly, we have to have resistance.

—Maya Lin

In a September 1992 recruiting letter to Debbie Keller confirming her decision to attend UNC, Anson Dorrance scribbled his customary personal message at the bottom: *Chase your dreams. I always have and I have loved every impossible thing that has happened to me.*

When Keller arrived at UNC in the fall of 1993 as the program's top-ranked freshman, Dorrance recognized immediately that she was not blessed with superior speed, agility, or athleticism, but that she overcame her deficiencies with a tenacious work ethic. Keller was that rare player who sprinted to arrive first at every practice huddle because she burned to be good at soccer. He also noticed that her bubbly personality masked a lack of self-esteem. Over the next four years, Keller would show up at Dorrance's office regularly to talk, and through dozens of confidence-building conversations she eventually transformed herself into an effective leader. The Tar Heel coach would come to view Keller as a model success story, and toward the end of her career, Dorrance had privately begun referring to her among his favorite players ever at UNC. "I loved coaching Debbie Keller," Dorrance says. "She wasn't the most skilled player, but she was as coachable as anybody I've ever had, and she drove herself into becoming one of the greatest players in our history."

Dorrance also admired Keller for her academic responsibility, her kindness, her ambition, her passion, and, above all, her intense loyalty. She was one of the Tar Heel players who babysat his son, Donovan, and she spent enough time at the Dorrance home that M'Liss told her husband, "she's like another daughter to us." Keller once showed her coach a poster she had tacked to her dorm room wall that featured a motivational poem called "To Achieve Your Dreams." The poem's upbeat lyrics reminded Dorrance of Keller, and he asked her to copy down the poetry for him. Dorrance framed the lyrics and hung them in his teenage daughter Michelle's bedroom because, as he often told Michelle, "I'd like you to be just like Debbie."

Keller was the finest recruiter among all the players Dorrance had ever coached. No other Tar Heel ever closed recruits like Deb, because she loved UNC and its soccer program, lived and breathed it, bought into the legend of what Dorrance had created as absolutely as anyone ever did. Ten times Dorrance paired Keller with a recruit on an official visit to UNC. Ten times the prospect signed on to become a Tar Heel.

Along with her devotion to the program, Keller possessed the other critical ingredient coaches seek in a recruiter: she could dominate on the soccer field. Keller completed her UNC career ranked fifth overall in points, sixth in goals, and second in assists, behind only Mia Hamm, while playing more games than any other Tar Heel. In her final UNC match against Notre Dame in the 1996 NCAA title game, Keller slashed her way to the rebound of a redirected cross from teammate Rakel Karvelsson in the second overtime of a scoreless game and headed the ball into the net for the game-winning goal. It was a typical Keller goal, unspectacular but tactical, the reward for a player in the right place at the right time. Keller's last goal marked the most glorious farewell in Tar Heel history, especially because she had fought her way back to top form after off-season foot surgery to play the full 120 minutes of the national final. All told, Keller scored sixteen game-winning goals during her career and won three national championships. Two weeks after her final game, she was featured as one of the "Faces in the Crowd" in *Sports Illustrated,* and a month later, Keller was honored as the 1996 National Player of the Year.

Six years later in 2002, the Tar Heel soccer program printed a promotional poster to be sold at summer camps and on the school's athletic web site that featured UNC's Players of the Year. It is a human time line of Tar Heel royalty, from April Heinrichs bulling her way upfield, to a determined and mud-covered Kristine Lilly, to an imperial Mia Hamm, to Staci Wilson in full fury, to Meredith Florance with the ball dancing at her feet. But look closely between Tisha Venturini and Robin Confer. One player is missing.

Debbie Keller.

She knew it was coming. M'Liss just didn't know when. Day after day for more than two weeks that August, she would toss and turn in bed until 4 a.m. waiting to hear the morning newspaper land in her driveway. She would rise in the dark, shuffle to the curb in her robe and slippers, open the paper to the front page, and then quickly flip to the sports section. She was waiting for everybody else to learn what she already knew, and she was dreading it.

Then, on the morning of August 21, 1998, Anson was flying home from a soccer clinic in England when M'Liss received a package with a draft of an impending lawsuit against her husband. The UNC chancellor's office had hastily scheduled a strategy session for that afternoon about how to react to the suit, so when Anson arrived at his house he promptly took a shower while his wife sat in their bathroom reading to him. M'Liss methodically read through the twenty-six-page lawsuit levied against Anson by Debbie Keller and another former UNC soccer player, Melissa Jennings, claiming sexual harassment, assault, battery, and invasion of privacy among other allegations. The suit specifically alleged that on more than one occasion Dorrance made an "uninvited sexual advance" toward Keller, and that at other times he made "uninvited physical contact" with her by putting "his arm and hands on her body." It also alleged that Dorrance would "constantly interrogate" his players about their personal sexual relationships. Keller also alleged that Dorrance forced her to come back from a 1995 foot injury too soon and without a custom-made shoe that would have aided her rehabilitation. The suit also claimed that Dorrance encouraged Jennings to drink alcohol while she was a minor and cut her from the team with two years of eligibility remaining, as retaliation against her for complaints made by her family on her behalf to UNC administrators.

Other soccer staff named as defendants in the suit were assistant coaches Bill Palladino and Chris Ducar, volunteer coach Tracy Noonan, who was a teammate of Keller's on the U.S. women's national team, and trainer Bill Prentice. The list of defendants also included UNC chancellor Michael Hooker, the school's two most recent athletic directors, John Swofford and Dick Baddour, senior associate athletic director Beth Miller, and assistant to the chancellor Susan Ehringhaus. All of Dorrance's co-defendants were cited on the grounds that they either failed to report Dorrance's actions or were subsequently made aware of them and neglected to take any action. Keller and Jennings sought $12 million, including $1 million each in compensatory damages and $10 million in punitive damages, along with an injunction barring Dorrance from coaching the UNC soccer team.

At the August 21 meeting, held in the UNC vice chancellor's office, Chancellor Hooker turned to Dorrance and pointedly asked him, "If the university defends you, is it going to be embarrassed?"

Dorrance responded with a definitive, "No way."

UNC's lawyers then proposed that Dorrance adhere to university policy and say nothing to the press about the lawsuit, but the school's publicity staff, led by media coordinator Steve Kirschner, argued vehemently that Dorrance should be allowed to speak on his own behalf. "If you don't believe him, fire him," Kirschner told everyone in the office that day. "If you do, let him talk. You've either got to let him go or let him defend himself."

On August 25, just two days before the opening game of the 1998 Tar Heel women's soccer season, UNC was notified that the lawsuit was officially being filed. While Dorrance and his players were posing for their annual team picture, he was informed that the university would be hosting a press conference in less than two hours to reveal the existence of the suit against him, which had remained so secret to that point that none of the local reporters had any idea what they were about to hear. The university chose to conduct the session in a meeting room at the Carolina Inn, a strategically chosen off-campus venue, and Dorrance was accompanied at the podium by Baddour and Kirschner, and supported by M'Liss, his two teenage daughters, and his brother Pete.

Dorrance began the press conference by reading the following statement: "I am shocked and saddened by these allegations. I intend to vigorously defend myself and this program's integrity. The allegations of sexual harassment are not true. I have never and would never abuse my position in any way. I've respected every player I have coached, both as an individual and as a member of my teams.

Those of you who know me understand that I would love to be able to stand here and address this completely today, but our attorneys have advised me not to respond to specific details. I look forward to resolving this matter and concentrating on my duties coaching the team."

Then, joined by his family and while holding his wife's hand and choking up, Dorrance followed his prepared remarks by saying, "This is obviously humiliating and embarrassing. I'll say this for my family, they are a powerful collection of people, and I've appreciated all their support in this."

During the press conference the university also issued a statement from Baddour:

The University has found absolutely no evidence that Coach Anson Dorrance used his position to make uninvited, sexually explicit comments to the plaintiffs, or that suggested that he engaged in inappropriate physical conduct with or made a sexual advance toward them, or that there was any retaliation against the plaintiffs for any reason. . . . Although we found no evidence of misconduct, we did conclude that his conduct fell short of the standards of good judgment that we expect of University officials.

As soon as the press conference ended, a group of UNC players announced to reporters that they also had something to say. Outside the ballroom in the hotel hallway, all twenty-six players on the 1998 Tar Heel roster locked arms and formed a semicircle around junior Beth Sheppard, who read a statement that concluded, "We find this situation deplorable and are hurt by these accusations, which, to our knowledge, are false. We insist that our unequivocal endorsement for all parties involved, particularly Anson Dorrance, be acknowledged. Our program has been and will continue to be something very special."

After the statement, several players agreed to be interviewed. "We're all so hurt by it," said Tiffany Roberts, a former Keller teammate and roommate. "I think it's ridiculous. You can tell how hurt he is by it. We are all totally behind Anson."

"This is so misguided," said Sheppard, another former Keller teammate and roommate. "We all want to know what the motivation is. We have no idea where all this came from. No one on the team has seen anything indicative of improper conduct. We all feel betrayed right now, but anger is starting to enter into it."

Later that evening Dorrance took his entire family out to dinner at Aurora, a restaurant in Chapel Hill, a clear statement in his mind that he had no intention of hiding from the public eye during the lawsuit. Back at home that night, daughter Michelle put on a Ben Harper CD and played the song "I'll Rise," repeating it over and over until the Dorrances could sing it together. Natalie typed out the song's defiant lyrics, written by poet Maya Angelou, and Anson posted them on the wall. *You may write me down in history/With your bitter twisted lies/You may trod me down in the very dirt/And still like the dust I'll rise.*

That night Dorrance also phoned all of his committed high school recruits and followed up with a note to each of them, which read similarly to this one he sent to Susan Bush:

Dear Susan,

I enjoyed my opportunity to talk to you. I wanted to be able to speak to you before you saw it in the press. All of us are shocked and rest assured the accusations are driven by ulterior motives and are not true.

I have enclosed a team phone list for you. Please call anyone to be assured the team is unified, loyal, and excited about the season. Nothing in our great tradition will be affected and we can't wait to see you on campus.

A few weeks later, on September 23, 1998, a group of UNC soccer alums released a letter signed by more than one hundred current and former Tar Heels. It was the first public comment from many of UNC's established stars, including Shannon Higgins, Tisha Venturini, and Mia Hamm. *We are confident that the recent allegations are unfounded . . . We have no reservations about our own daughters someday playing soccer under the remarkable leadership of Anson Dorrance.*

He didn't know it was coming. Maybe it was the optimist in Dorrance. Maybe it was his obliviousness. Bill Palladino had first sensed a disturbing side to Debbie Keller during her freshman year, and by the end of her junior season he had begun warning Dorrance regularly that trouble was brewing behind his back. But Dorrance kept brushing him off by saying, "Deb and I are fine."

"When Anson misses a read on somebody, it's a surprise to him that it's even an issue," Palladino says. "He's not really as concerned about where the players are coming from as much as he wants them to buy into where he's coming from."

"If Anson has a blind spot, it's that he's a very trusting person, and so if you come up to him and you present a positive persona, he'll accept that," brother Pete says. "If you're really a backstabber, he'll first believe whatever you want him to believe."

Some former Tar Heels say that Dorrance is guilty of seeing people through what they call "Anson glasses," that he searches diligently for a person's concealed positives, all the while screening out the far more obvious negatives. "When it comes to reading people, Anson is definitely too optimistic," Chris Ducar says. "He tries to will everybody to be better people. He struggles to accept that anybody is just an asshole. It may be Utopian to hope for the best in people, but is that a flaw? Should he be punished for that?"

Dorrance admits that he had no idea how dramatically his relationship with Keller had begun to deteriorate in the fall of 1995. At that time, Adidas, UNC's shoe sponsor, had come out with a new soccer cleat, and Keller wanted to wear the new model. Unfortunately, she would gradually discover that her feet were too wide for the cleats, and she developed an injury to her left heel that began hampering her play toward the end of that season. In the off-season, Keller decided to undergo foot surgery, after which she would require a custom shoe to relieve pressure on the injured heel. Dorrance asked Adidas to build a special shoe for Keller. When those shoes didn't alleviate her pain, Dorrance then contacted

Nike with a similar request, but he says the process was slow to develop through bureaucratic red tape. Eventually Keller's mother, Judy, began phoning Nike herself to ask about the progress of the shoe, and when Dorrance suggested that Judy be more patient, she thought that Dorrance might be conspiring against her daughter, more concerned about his shoe sponsorship leverage than Debbie's health. Judy told Debbie that Dorrance was sabotaging the process.

The next season, after a UNC game on October 20, 1996, in Houston, an angry Judy Keller ambushed Dorrance and began yelling at him in front of his players and a group of fans. She accused him of causing Debbie's injury. She accused him of not finding a shoe to fix the problem. She accused him of not promoting her daughter in the press as much as he did sophomore Cindy Parlow, and she accused him of deliberately neglecting to nominate Debbie for the Missouri Athletic Club Player of the Year award. Dorrance returned to the UNC van both troubled and puzzled by the confrontation. He turned to Palladino and asked, "What is she talking about? All of a sudden Judy Keller is accusing me of everything but the Kennedy assassination."

Coincidentally, just a year earlier, Dorrance had received a recommendation from Judy, an Illinois high school women's soccer coach, about a goalkeeper prospect she'd seen named Melissa Jennings. Jennings had no high school soccer experience, having twice been cut from her varsity team, but Dorrance recruited her anyway as a reserve keeper without ever seeing her play because he trusted Judy's eye for talent. Naturally, Dorrance was surprised when he asked Debbie to host Jennings during her recruiting visit to UNC, and Keller politely declined saying that she didn't like Jennings. It was the only time Keller ever begged out of a recruiting assignment.

Jennings arrived at UNC in 1996, and during her first preseason she immediately earned a poor reputation with her new coaches because of her entitled attitude and the fact that she wasn't fit. At one practice, Jennings dove to block a shot, and when she hit the ground, candy sprung out of her pants pockets. The UNC coaches also noticed that she often left empty Twinkie and Ho Ho wrappers on the dashboard of her car.

Before Jennings's second game as a Tar Heel on September 7, 1996, in the aftermath of Hurricane Fran, Dorrance was in the midst of his pregame team meeting when he was informed that the storm had knocked out access to water at Fetzer Field. He asked for a volunteer among his reserve players to go buy some Gatorade for the game. Jennings raised her hand.

Later that season, UNC athletic director John Swofford received a note from Jennings's father, Craig, complaining that Dorrance borrowed money from his daughter for the Gatorade and about how Melissa had been served alcohol on her recruiting visit.

At that point, Dorrance had already begun to view Melissa Jennings as a malcontent, and though he could remember cutting only three players in his career, he realized that like those previous cast-offs, Jennings was contributing nothing to his team athletically, academically, or socially. Dorrance received a flurry of negative reports from Jennings's position coach, Chris Ducar. "I evaluated that kid and I hated her after the second week," Ducar says. "I talked to Anson about cutting her as a freshman, and then in her second year I got down on my knees and begged him, but he kept going to the seniors for their input, and of course they're reluctant to vote to cut a girl. They would feel bad."

Finally, before the 1997 NCAA Tournament, the UNC senior leadership did vote to cut Jennings, but Dorrance overruled them, deciding to give Jennings one last chance to prove herself the following spring. In essence, Dorrance had protected Jennings from his own staff and her teammates who wanted her gone. Finally, after spring workouts in 1998, during which Jennings finished dead last in the team's annual peer evaluations, Dorrance concluded that Jennings was "unsaveable." During Jennings' year-end goal-setting meeting with Dorrance on May 5, 1998, she was cut from the Tar Heels, having played in only three games in her career.

Says Ducar: "The only mistake Anson made was the timing. He cut her during final exams, so that gave her the ammo to say it was malicious. It wasn't. That's when all the players have their meetings with him, and her departure was in the works for a long, long time."

Threats of a lawsuit began almost immediately after Jennings was removed from the team. A few weeks earlier, Baddour had asked Dorrance to meet with Keller to seek some closure over her parents' complaints about the foot surgery, the custom shoes, and some medical bills. Dorrance met with Keller on the morning of April 21 at a bagel shop in downtown Chapel Hill and asked her if she backed the claims that her parents were making against him. To his surprise, Keller said that she did. There was still no mention of any sexual harassment charges.

On May 13, the university received a phone call from her father, Ron, during which he raised the prospect of sexual harassment charges for the first time, a delay that Keller's lawyer, Louis Varchetto, would later chalk up to "embarrassment" on Debbie's part. At that same time, the UNC athletic department received a letter from Craig Jennings containing similar harassment allegations against Dorrance.

It was a particularly awkward predicament for recently promoted UNC athletic director Dick Baddour because Keller was dating Chris Hill, a former UNC tennis player whose parents are among the Baddours' closest friends. In fact, just a month earlier at the NCAA men's basketball Final Four in San Antonio, the Baddours had shared a dinner with the Hills, along with Chris and Debbie.

On June 9, 1998, Dorrance and Baddour cosigned a letter to Craig Jennings which acknowledged that the UNC coach "participated in group discussions of a jesting or a teasing nature," conversations that he admitted were "inappropriate," but insisted that he had never discussed sex during individual meetings. Dorrance also indicated that he "understands that alcoholic beverages must not be allowed at any activity involving team members," apologized for using "poor judgment" in asking to borrow money from Jennings, and acknowledged that Jennings's dismissal from the team during final exams was "ill-timed." However, in that same letter, Baddour also noted Dorrance's record and wrote that he was "committed" to keeping the coach in his job.

Meanwhile Jennings and her family had approached Keller about the possibility of joining a lawsuit. Varchetto said that his clients decided to file suit because they felt that the university had not responded sufficiently to their complaints about Dorrance. Debbie Keller was particularly incredulous about what Baddour termed his university's "thorough investigation" of the allegations. Says Keller: "How thorough could it have been if nobody at UNC ever bothered to talk to me?"

Seven days before the public revelation of the sexual harassment lawsuit against Dorrance, President Bill Clinton appeared on national television to admit that he had covered up the truth about the extent of his relationship with former White House intern Monica Lewinsky. "After the President of the United States admits that he's been lying for months in a similar situation, how is a soccer coach going to have any credibility?" Steve Kirschner says. "I don't think Anson could have survived professionally if he hadn't come out publicly and denied everything."

The press conference at the Carolina Inn was the last time that Dorrance would speak publicly about the case. His lawyers instructed him to remain silent after that, but while Dorrance repeatedly refused comment, his players had no such gag order.

Public opinion anxiously waited to see if there would be any other Tar Heels rallying to the cause of Keller and Jennings. None did. In fact, none of Keller's teammates had any inkling of the anguish she claimed to be suffering during the end of her UNC career.

"I was shocked, and I think all of my teammates from that time were shocked by the lawsuit," says Siri Mullinix, a goalkeeper at UNC from 1995 to 1998. "My philosophy is that if you feel that threatened by someone you don't associate with him, and Keller hung around Anson a lot. And Jennings was cut on ability and should have been cut, and claimed that she shouldn't have been. I knew both of those players well, and the combination of the two together was suspicious. A lot of their claims had no credibility with me."

As a reserve goalkeeper, Jennings had little contact with Dorrance outside of team meetings, but Keller and Dorrance spoke regularly on the field and in his office, and many of her teammates marveled at the dynamics of their relationship. "I got to know Debbie, and she had this big friendship with Anson and I feel like she had him kind of snowed," says Staci Wilson, another Keller teammate. "He didn't see through her to see how she's not that great of a person. Her teammates saw it before him. We were thinking, 'Why does he think she's such a sweet, nice person? She's not sweet and nice. She's got two faces.'"

"For most of her career, Debbie and Anson had a great relationship," says Jana Withrow, a former UNC field hockey player who was Keller's closest friend and her roommate in 1995–96. "It was strange sometimes. It seemed to me like she had a crush on him. She loved getting attention from him. She loved to go to lunch with him. She loved to visit him in his office. Then everything changed when the shoe thing happened. All of a sudden she was convinced she'd been wronged by him, and eventually she turned on him."

"It hurts me to see a player do something like that after Anson supported her," says Robin Confer, who played alongside Keller on the Tar Heel front line. "Debbie never said anything to me. She went in to talk to him a lot, and he was there for her. Then so much time passed between when everything allegedly happened and when the lawsuit came out. It was like Debbie used that time to gather information on how she could nail Anson."

"Debbie's clearly delusional," says Charlotte Mitchell, another Keller teammate. "Her parents put a lot of pressure on her. It's sad. Sexual harassment is a gray area, and if someone wants to portray something in a certain light, they can do that, but it's not the truth. When all this stuff hit the fan, the press was trying to dig up the dirt on Anson, and nobody in the program said anything bad about him, because while you may be pissed off that he sat you on the bench for four years, everybody acknowledges that he's a good person, a good man."

As soon as the news of the lawsuit disseminated through the Tar Heel ranks, the alumni mobilized. Betsy Johnson and about a dozen other Tar Heel soccer alums telephoned Dorrance that night to check on him. Lisa Duffy organized a letter-writing campaign to shower Dorrance with thank-you notes from former players. Tom Castelloe, whose daughter, Keath, played for Dorrance in the mid-1980s, wrote a check to the UNC women's soccer program for $100,000 as his family's statement of support. At an alumni reunion the following spring there was an outpouring of emotion toward the coach. "We laughed, we cried, and a lot of players got up and took the microphone," Wendy Gebauer says. "Everybody was telling Anson how much we love him and how much we appreciate every day what he's done for us."

One of the few alums who remained silent and didn't publicly back Dorrance was Kristine Lilly, who at the time of the lawsuit was dating Debbie Keller's older brother, Steve. April Heinrichs, who coached Virginia at the time, cautiously refused to declare her allegiance to either side. "My first reaction to the suit was 'Don't answer the phone,'" Heinrichs says. "As a female role model I had a responsibility to withhold judgment because only the people involved know what happened, yet there were a million people chiming in with opinions. I know some of Anson's former players said it wasn't possible, and if it weren't for loyalty in life there'd be a lot of disloyalty, and the world would be a miserable place, so I had no issues with them."

Elsewhere around the university, Chancellor Hooker, a codefendant in the lawsuit, publicly displayed his support for Dorrance by continuing to attend women's soccer games with his wife, Carmen. In the interest of appearances, the UNC media relations department pulled a photograph from the 1998 media guide of Dorrance hugging a jubilant Sarah Dacey and replaced it with a photo of Dorrance standing by himself. Privately, the university was also concerned about the impression left by the fact that both of Dorrance's assistant coaches were romantically involved with former Tar Heel players—Ducar was married to former

Tar Heel goalkeeper Tracy Noonan, and Palladino was dating Wendy Gebauer—although it should be noted that the situation is not uncommon in the insular women's soccer world. Both Julie Foudy and Brandi Chastain are married to their former coaches.

Outside of the UNC universe, the reaction was understandably guarded. Michelle Akers, one of Keller's teammates on the U.S. national team and Dorrance's former player, wrote letters of support to both parties. Most of Dorrance's coaching colleagues refused to comment on the lawsuit at all. Just before the 1998 Final Four, however, Santa Clara coach Jerry Smith was quoted in *Sports Illustrated* as saying, "I don't know the truth, but the thing I come back to is, Why would Debbie go through this if it's not true? If it is true, maybe it can't be proven. She has everything to lose and nothing to gain."

Moments after UNC lost in the 1998 NCAA final, Dorrance crossed paths with Smith. The Tar Heel coach mimicked a knife in his back and said, "Jerry, can you help me pull this thing out? I can't quite reach it and it's killing me." Smith sat there stunned in Dorrance's wake.

Over the course of the lawsuit, Dorrance concerned himself primarily with how it was affecting his family. Less than a month after the suit went public, his mother, Peggy, developed bleeding ulcers. His two daughters, Michelle and Natalie, each received harassing phone calls. M'Liss says she never asked her husband about any of the charges because she never doubted her husband's innocence, but she did grow frustrated with him for his lack of anger, so she got mad enough for both of them. She implored the university to debunk every negative newspaper article. She even encouraged her husband to countersue. "Anson never had any personal animosity toward the two girls, while I wanted to make voodoo dolls of both of them," M'Liss says. "I'm not normally combative, but when someone comes after one of my own, I felt like a protective mother bear. Anson had done nothing but support Debbie, so I thought, 'How dare you try to ruin our lives?'"

Says brother Pete: "I remember Anson once telling me, 'I'd love to take this on myself because I know what I did and didn't do, and I know how mentally tough I am, and I know I can get through this, but the thing I can't do is shield my family.' He definitely has feelings that a lot of people don't believe he has, but he'll be strong for others first. He might be hurting, but he'll pull everybody else through."

Dorrance acknowledges that he was initially embarrassed by the lawsuit because of the negative publicity that it generated for the university. He was disappointed because he believed that Keller and Jennings had fallen prey to the victim feminism that he often decries, and the competitor in him chafed at the fact that he couldn't immediately tell his side of the story. He says his own emotional reaction to the lawsuit evolved over the years. "At first it was shocking and stressful, but eventually I became calloused to it," Dorrance says. "I can't believe you could ever get used to something like that, but it's just something that you adapt to."

Says Ducar: "Anson kept his emotional control even when the real shit was hitting the fan. We were all devastated, but the rest of us were just footnotes. This man's whole life was being eviscerated in front of the world."

As usual, Dorrance steeled himself with his sense of humor. After a victory over Virginia in October of 1998, he approached Rakel Karvelsson and said, "Great game, Rakel. I'd hug you, but I'd get in trouble." In more recent years, Dorrance chose to keep the lawsuit completely separate from his players. When Dorrance disappeared for a week toward the end of the 2003 season while attending depositions in Chicago, chaos being the rule at UNC, none of the players even bothered to ask where he had gone.

"A lot of people don't understand that he's just a man, and when you're being attacked in your own mind unjustly you still have to get up every day and do your job," former UNC wrestling coach Bill Lam says. "To me that showed his grit that he fought through that, he didn't cower from it and still kept doing the things he had to do to keep his program on top. I don't know many people who could do that."

"Anson knows about psychology, and he knows that the only possible response is to not give it any credence, but it ate him up that someone questioned his integrity," his old friend Jack Simmons says. "He prides himself on fairness, and this was not fair. How could he fight it? When I spoke to him about it I heard anger, I heard defiance, and I heard the hurt of a man who felt that his trust had been betrayed. He told me, 'The bastards aren't going to grind me down!'" *Illegitimus non Carborundum.*

For a man who values loyalty above all else, what could be a more painful dagger to endure than that someone he once counted among his most faithful had accused him of *this?* Dorrance admits there was one moment during the suit when his resolve was shaken. On October 13, 2002, he was sitting alone at the airport in Greenville, South Carolina, during the early hours of a rainy Sunday morning, with his flight delayed for the foreseeable future. M'Liss phoned him and read him that day's front-page story from the local newspaper in which Keller detailed her allegations against him for the first time publicly, saying she was "embarrassed" and "almost repulsed" by Dorrance's conduct. The article provided little more than Dorrance's mandated *no comment* in his defense. When M'Liss finished reading there was a prolonged silence on the other end of the line, before her husband finally said, "How is that permissible? How can a collection of people just make something up that is obviously designed to defame you, and why is there a system that supports it? Why am I still coaching? Is it worth it? Why should we make ourselves targets? Why would anyone?"

M'Liss didn't know what to say.

"My wife never hears me asking those kinds of questions, so it shocked her," Dorrance recalls. "But she knew that I still loved coaching, so eventually she said, 'Don't worry about it, honey. It'll be all right. Press on.' It wasn't a Shakespearean sonnet, but it was the clear support I needed."

The bomb dropped in the first week of December of 1998, just two days before the Tar Heels were to play in the NCAA Tournament semifinal. As soon as the *Sports Illustrated* story was released, a UNC media representative walked a copy of it the few hundred yards from the Dean Smith Center to the parking lot where Dorrance was playing roller hockey. Dorrance skated out of the game, read the ten faxed pages, and skated back into the fray without a hint of emotion.

He later admitted he was disappointed at what he perceived to be a distinct bias toward Keller in the article, but he was even more dismayed that she had used heartfelt letters he'd sent to build her confidence as propaganda against him. The magazine printed four of a series of letters from Dorrance to Keller, letters that suggested to many readers a bond beyond that of a typical coach/player relationship. The most personal letter published was one written by Dorrance to Keller while she was away training with the national team during her sophomore year on March 3, 1995:

Dear Debbie,

Thank you for your wonderful letter. The things you shared were so personal and sweet you made me feel very special. It's funny, you told me once how difficult it was for you to share your feelings and yet this letter is filled with intimate detail and so very warm. You are so thoughtful and nice to me.

I called your mom and thanked her for the calendar. She is very considerate and looking through the pictures made me miss you even more. Our team is not the same without you and seeing you in those group shots was nostalgic . . . I found myself trying to find you in each picture . . .

I know what you mean about simple pleasures. In the past my life has been a whirlwind of complication and there were so many things I always felt pressured to do . . . clinics, speeches, national team . . . it always seemed so important to do everything and I never turned anything down. I lived in an airplane and I gave so many speeches to so many people I didn't even know I felt distanced from everyone and even the people like you that I genuinely liked and wanted to get close to I never had time for . . .

Well, I have learned many things. I learned that kind of slavery was not making me happy. Do you know that I was not even happy after we won the World Championship? . . . I want you to know I loved last fall: Seeing us deal with adversity, climb new heights after each setback and play so brilliantly in the national final. I compare my feeling that day with my feeling that day with the World Cup and they are total contrasts. And the best part of that amazing day was when we were walking off the field and I put my arm around your shoulders and pulled you close so I could whisper in your ear. I told you that you were wonderful and that I wanted to talk to you about building a new team from the graduation ashes of our ten seniors and I wanted to build it around your sweet spirit, your big heart and your indomitable will.

I care for you.

Anson

"I think to many people in the outside world the letters seemed creepy," Kirschner says. "Society didn't know how to react to a good-looking middle-aged coach relating on a personal level with a young female player. They weren't ready for a male coach whose female players talk to him about their personal lives. Well, society needs to understand that that stuff affects their performance on the field."

Dorrance says he was surprised and somewhat incredulous at how miserable Keller sounded in the *Sports Illustrated* story and in subsequent interviews. Once, when Keller was asked about her best moment as a Tar Heel player, she said, "I don't have any good memories of my time with UNC soccer. Even when I scored the goal to win the championship in 1996, I only felt relieved because I couldn't wait for my career to be over."

Keller said that for years she was in denial about what she thought was going on between her and Dorrance, and she avoided any conflict just in case she was mis-reading it. She said she considered transferring, but she loved UNC and didn't want to leave her friends in Chapel Hill. She said she was reluctant to complain to university athletic officials about Dorrance's behavior while she was still in school because she believed it could drive a wedge between her and her teammates, but as soon as her parents learned of her feelings, they wrote the university to complain.

Meanwhile, Dorrance believed he had already apologized for his mistakes. He told his lawyers that the sexual harassment charges were lies and that the lawsuit ultimately revolved around issues over which he did not have total control. Judging from the confrontation with Judy Keller in Houston, he believed that the Kellers were annoyed that as a senior, Debbie wasn't receiving the same media attention as younger Tar Heel stars like Cindy Parlow and Lorrie Fair, but Dorrance wondered how he could influence whom the newspapers chose to write about. After incurring Judy Keller's wrath over the MAC Player of the Year award nomination, Dorrance later explained to her that he had in fact nominated Debbie, only to watch her candidacy killed by the votes of rival coaches for different players, but that he'd subsequently lobbied successfully to get Debbie added to the list of nominees. He knew the Kellers were upset about the custom shoe issue, but thought that he had done everything in his power to acquire them for Debbie. And he knew the Kellers blamed his close relationship with U.S. national team coach Tony DiCicco, Dorrance's former assistant, for keeping Debbie off the 1999 World Cup roster after the lawsuit came out, even though DiCicco had stated that his decision had nothing to do with his connection to Dorrance. DiCicco said that he didn't think Keller deserved a spot on a roster filled with talented strikers like Mia Hamm, Tiffeny Milbrett, Shannon MacMillan, Danielle Fotopolous, and Parlow, although he did acknowledge that the lawsuit created "chemistry issues" on a team stocked with Tar Heels who clearly supported Dorrance.

Over the years, prosecution lawyers repeatedly hinted that more of Dorrance's former players would testify against him in trial. Keller said that she expected to be supported by teammates like Tisha Venturini and Nel Fettig, but they refused to speak out against their former coach. In her complaint, Jennings mentioned Sarah Dacey, Aubrey Falk, and Fettig as potential corroborating witnesses, but each subsequently wrote a letter to plaintiffs' lawyers in full support of Dorrance and even hired lawyers to help them dodge subpoenas. Only one former UNC player, Amy Steelman, a walk-on goalkeeper who never played in a game during her career with the Tar Heels in 1995 and 1996, agreed to be interviewed by plaintiffs' lawyers in support of their allegations. "Basically it boils down to a classic case of he said/she said," Keller acknowledged in the summer of 2003. "Of course I wish some of my friends had stood by me, but I certainly can't blame them for being afraid of the backlash."

Dorrance's defense team began to sense some desperation among the plaintiffs when their charges were embellished each time a new motion was filed or a new deposition was taken in the case. Dorrance's lawyers repeatedly filed motions to dismiss the case on lack of evidence for a harassment charge. Meanwhile, the plaintiffs floated several offers to settle the case, but the university's legal team remained incredulous over the dearth of evidence implicating Dorrance of harassment.

In 2002 all of the defendants except for Dorrance and Palladino were dropped from the suit. Then, early in 2003, the plaintiffs' lawyers abandoned the case, and the suit essentially split between Keller and Jennings, who each retained separate legal counsel.

Finally, on June 13, 2003, inside a Raleigh conference room, Keller and Dorrance saw each other for the first time in five years, as Keller gave her deposition. Based on Keller's sworn testimony that day, her sexual harassment allegations no longer involved anything that Dorrance had actually said or done to either Keller or Jennings, but instead centered primarily on an incident of "girl talk" before a UNC practice in 1996, during which Dorrance commented sarcastically about the promiscuity of another Tar Heel player. After the deposition, Dorrance was encouraged because he felt Keller's testimony was by far the most truthful of those given by his accusers and might actually aid in his defense. He disagreed with Keller only when she stated that he'd harbored romantic feelings for her that had compelled him to try to distance Debbie from her mother's allegations. Leaving the conference room that day, one of Dorrance's lawyers, Doug Kingsbery, turned to his client and whispered, "That was like being stoned to death by popcorn."

When the settlement of the Keller portion of the lawsuit was released to the public late on the afternoon of March 23, 2004, Dorrance was standing on the South Lawn of the White House with President George W. Bush, celebrating UNC's 2003 national championship, basking in the most prominent public acknowledgment ever of his success. Meanwhile, Keller was at the David Wade Salon in Raleigh, another Tuesday of work as a hairdresser.

The next morning the local newspapers buried the details of the Tar Heels' visit to the White House, if it was mentioned at all. The lawsuit headline was above the fold in every paper.

When the Keller suit was finally settled after five years and seven months, so much time had passed that one of the original defendants, UNC chancellor Michael Hooker, had been diagnosed with cancer, fought the disease, and passed away, all while the suit languished in legal limbo. It had endured for so long that several of the younger players on UNC's 2003 team were totally unaware of the case, and a majority of the rest assumed it had concluded years ago.

Like most of Dorrance's former players, Susan Ellis disagreed with his settling the case because the decision appeared to belie the fighter that she knew as her coach. "Shortly after the settlement, I was substitute teaching, and my class started talking about UNC soccer," Ellis recalls. "One of the kids said, 'They're good, but that's the school where the coach molested the players.' That's what frustrates me so much. I want Anson's name completely cleared. He's like a part of my family and I want it all to be made right."

Ultimately, the UNC administration had reasoned that if the school were to be found guilty on even one minor count, it would have been liable for all of the court costs, which could have amounted to as much as $500,000 or more, so a settlement was in UNC's best financial interests. Surprisingly, however, Dorrance was even more committed to settling the case than his bosses. Even armed with The Force, the former law student believed he was part of a judicial system he simply could not trust enough to allow his case brought to trial. This time a Dorrance laid down his sword so as not to risk having his head lopped off with it.

"I love a fight, but it has to be fair," Dorrance says. "I understand that a jury trial is a crapshoot. It isn't necessarily about the facts. There could be two girls crying on the witness stand, and the whole thing could be viewed as two underdogs against the system. What is innocent in reality could appear as salacious when spun by their lawyers. The way I see it, you have to really understand how our soccer program works. Our athletic culture is unique. Someone in that jury box might come out to practice and hear what I say to these girls and while it's not wrong, they just wouldn't understand it out of context."

Dorrance realized that with a settlement the most damaging part of the lawsuit could be concluded with one last burst of negative publicity instead of weeks of enduring his program being dragged through the mud in court. He also felt that a verdict wouldn't ultimately alter anybody's mindset toward the case. "People who always supported and believed in me will continue to believe I'm innocent in all this, and people who want to believe that I'm a sexual deviant are going to think that no matter what," he says. "With a settlement, nothing was going to change in either camp, but I could keep recruiting, keep doing my job, and the program could move forward."

The settlement called for the university to pay Keller $70,000 in damages and required Dorrance to participate in annual education on UNC's sexual harassment policy and in yearly sensitivity training through the year 2012. Dorrance provided a settlement statement that read:

> *I acknowledge that prior to June 1998, I participated with members of the UNC–CH women's soccer team in group discussions of those team*

members' sexual activities or relationships with men. While my participa-
tion in such discussions was in a jesting or teasing nature and was not in-
tended to be offensive, I now realize that my comments offended Debbie
Keller. I understand that my participation in those discussions was alto-
gether inappropriate and unacceptable. I apologize to Debbie Keller and
her family, as well as any other member of the soccer team who I offended.

After nearly six years of legal wrangling, Dorrance had given essentially the
same statement of contrition that he had in his letter to Craig Jennings before
the suit came out, and again at the Carolina Inn on the day the lawsuit went public in 1998.

Keller, who would turn twenty-nine the day after the settlement was announced, was hardly the same young woman who had filed the lawsuit as a twenty-
three-year-old, though she was still the fierce competitor whom Dorrance had
trained in his own image to go nose-to-nose with an opponent he could have never
imagined would someday be himself. Keller had battled to exhaustion, just as the
defendant had trained her to do, and then she'd asked out when she could bear to
fight no longer. Though the settlement recouped only a fraction of the money
she had spent on legal fees, Keller said that the lawsuit was never about money,
but about the principles in the policy of sexual harassment. She insisted that the
time and effort spent was worth it, and that her satisfaction had little to do with
Dorrance's apology. It was not so much in what he said, but in what she said.

"This case was all about how schools, including UNC, must take their responsibility seriously to ensure such offensive actions do not occur," Keller said
after the settlement. "I just wanted UNC and the soccer program to take some
responsibility so this sort of thing might never happen to another girl in the
future."

In her settlement statement Keller wrote:

Anson Dorrance made multiple overt sexual comments that were unin-
vited and that, in my opinion, were offensive. As a result, I personally felt
very uncomfortable around him. Neither Anson Dorrance nor any mem-
ber of the coaching staff for the UNC–CH women's soccer team made an
overt pass at me or asked for a sexual relationship.

After the settlement, one source in the Keller family described Debbie as "relieved" and said that the entire lawsuit could have been avoided had only the university been more receptive to the Kellers' initial complaints. The source also
said that once the suit was filed it could have been settled much sooner, but that
the Jennings family was the driving force for bringing it to trial.

Seven months later, on October 27, 2004, the Jennings portion of the lawsuit
was dismissed in summary judgment for lack of sufficient evidence just five days
before the trial was scheduled to begin. That night Dorrance symbolically took his
family out to dinner, just as he had on the night the suit first went public, at Aurora.

The letters. Debbie Keller's lawsuit always hinged on letters, but not necessarily the letters that everyone suspected. Sure, there were the letters that everybody read, but what about the letters that nobody read?

The letters in *Sports Illustrated* caused a firestorm when they were published, but what that article neglected to point out is that Dorrance had written similar letters to other players. "When I read those letters to Debbie Keller I shrugged," April Heinrichs says. "Other people were shocked, but for me they were no different than his letters to Shannon Higgins or Tracey Bates or Julie Guarnotta or thirty other players. I think those letters were read out of context."

After the *SI* story came out, many former Tar Heels began digging through their hope chests for the first time in years, searching for letters to offer to Dorrance as evidence in his defense. While Dorrance was touched, he told all of them that he didn't want to use any of their letters. Dorrance felt secure in the knowledge that game tapes showed Debbie Keller had giddily jumped into his arms after the national championship game in 1996, that she posed for dozens of snapshots after that game smiling with Dorrance and his family, and that the Kellers had sent the Dorrances a Christmas gift that year. He was further buoyed by the fact that Keller had spent much of the spring of 1998 training with the Tar Heels, during which she appeared in an instructional video praising Dorrance's coaching, just three months before the lawsuit was filed. And besides, if Dorrance needed any letters to support his defense, he already had them. Looking through the case files, the most potentially damaging evidence to Keller's case is her own correspondence, including a series of e-mails, postcards, and notes that she sent to Dorrance during the critical period from 1996 to 1998. As Keller prepared to leave for a trip to Australia in the summer of 1997, she wrote:

June 11, 1997

Dear Anson,

Hi! Just wanted to thank you for the sweet note you sent me back in May. I just got it, my mail was sent to my old roommate's new house. I'm sorry I never responded or thanked you. I've been busy getting ready for Australia. I leave on July 13, so things are a little hectic. I didn't forget about you. I'd tried to call, but you were out of town. Just in case I don't see you, best of luck this season. I'll be thinking about the team and cheering for you guys. I should have e-mail when I get there so I'll be in touch.

Thanks again and hope to see you soon.

Love,
Debbie

For the six years of the lawsuit during many of his monthly visits to George at the Tar Heel Barber Shop, Dorrance would stare at a Carolina blue laminated sign directly in front of the barber chair. It featured a series of quotes, including one from the author Margaret Mitchell: *Until you've lost your reputation, you never realize what a burden it was.*

Dorrance found some comfort in that particular quote because it reminded him once again never to take himself too seriously. "I realized that your reputation really doesn't matter at all," Dorrance says. "It'll never change with the people you're close to, and those are the people who already remind you daily that you're the same shiftless individual they've known all along. I have to look at the lawsuit that way, because even though I didn't do anything wrong, the stain is there forever. It's part of my obituary."

Indeed while the lawsuit became a national story when it was filed, very few newspapers outside of North Carolina even bothered to publish any news of its conclusion. "The damage is done," Betsy Johnson says. "Is ESPN ever going to vindicate Anson? Is *Sports Illustrated* going to vindicate him? A lot of people will never know that he didn't do what Debbie originally said and when his name comes up they'll say, 'Isn't he the one who sexually harassed that girl?'"

There is a school of thought in the college soccer world that what Dorrance has endured is actually an instructive cautionary tale. "I think the lawsuit produced a great dialogue and raised consciousness," Heinrichs says. "I once heard another college soccer coach say that the scary thing is that all the male coaches now have to be a little more careful about what they say and I'm thinking, 'Why is that so scary?' If you're really worried as a coach, then you better reevaluate your technique. It was a red flag for everybody."

On the other hand, some of Dorrance's male coaching colleagues admit that fear of a similar lawsuit has forced them to act less compassionately toward their players. After the Keller suit, Santa Clara coach Jerry Smith changed his policy on individual contact with players. All meetings in his office are conducted with his door open, and on road trips he no longer meets with players in his hotel room, but instead in the lobby. Smith recalls one road trip to Texas A&M shortly after the lawsuit came out when he criticized a player who was having a poor practice, and she phoned him at the hotel later that day and asked to see him. "In the past we would have met in my room, but this time I said, 'We're meeting in the lobby with lots of people around us,'" Smith recalls. "The poor kid was crying. I felt so sorry for her. But that lawsuit made me think, 'You better have a system of checks and balances in place because you're in a very vulnerable position.'"

In hindsight, Dorrance takes full responsibility for opening the door to the lawsuit. Convinced that the suit was more a product of overzealous parents than disgruntled players, he says he's learned that he can't just coach young women, he must also coach their parents. At the 2005 NSCAA convention, Dorrance told his coaching peers that he'd erred by not sharing enough information with parents. He told the coaches about how he has since begun to mail more stats and fitness information from the competitive cauldron to his players' parents so they can see what he sees on a daily basis, to disarm them of ammunition they might later use against him and hopefully to encourage them to challenge their daughters as he does.

Dorrance admits that as a result of the suit he is now more likely to cut a marginal player with a detrimental attitude before she becomes a problem. He has also made a more conscious effort to start photocopying all of his personal letters, creating a paper trail to prove he has nothing to hide. In the past, whenever the Tar Heel players were kidding a teammate about her sexual promiscuity, Dorrance couldn't resist adding his own commentary to bolster an argument against the idea. Today, while he still feels just as strongly about mentoring his players, he resists, or at least tones down, his opinions on their personal lives and has even asked his staff to alert him if they think he is ever crossing the line.

For a while after the lawsuit, Dorrance stopped having closed-door meetings with his players, until he realized that many of his players were less comfortable with the door open than closed. He still sometimes hesitates for a moment whenever he lays his hand on a player's shoulder to make a point, but he stubbornly refuses to back off at all on being an emotional safety net for his team. In a hallway beside the press room in Dallas just moments after UNC's loss in the 2001 NCAA final, Dorrance hugged a distraught Anne Remy, the forward whose offside erased UNC's tying goal late in the second half, telling her that he and her teammates still respected and cared for her no matter what had taken place on the field.

Dorrance's decision to stick with the foundation of his coaching philosophy can be traced back at least in part to a day on the practice field not long after the lawsuit went public when Carmen Hooker, wife of the UNC chancellor, visited the team and pleaded, "Don't ever change the things that set you guys apart." Dorrance's alums have also encouraged him to remain as involved in the lives of his current and future players as he was in theirs. "The atmosphere on our team has always been very casual, very open, very personal and gossipy, and that's one of the reasons we are so successful," Robin Confer says. "We're not serious all the time. We integrate our personal lives with soccer. Lots of people on the team are always going in and talking to Anson about their relationships, but he'd never interrogate you. It would just take away some stress because you knew you always had someone there to talk to."

Dorrance asserts that the fact that his players feel comfortable enough to discuss their most intimate stories with him should only serve as proof of how much they trust him. Says Janet Rayfield: "I know that me and most of the alums value the genuine, personal interaction with Anson, and there's a sentiment that we don't want him to change that because of the lawsuit. I told Anson, 'I hope it doesn't affect your ability to write a caring note to me. I'd miss that.'"

Dorrance's Exhibit A in support of his approach is an e-mail from Jena Kluegel's mother, Sue, written during the season the lawsuit was filed in 1998:

To: Anson
From: The Sue Kluegel For-What-It's-Worth-Department
   I just finished reading the article about you and the team in the Nov. 21
Raleigh News & Observer. You know, it's ironic, but the issues that you

are being criticized for are exactly the reasons I wanted Jena to go to UNC. Really.

The photos in the media guides with you and a player embracing or your arm around a player were the ones I liked the best in all of the media guides and helped convince me that UNC and Anson Dorrance were the right choice for Jena. The roses you give to the seniors is one of the nicest things a coach ever did for his players.

Your joking with the players about their dating lives, etc. That's one of the first things that Jena mentioned after her visit to UNC. I know it makes her feel less like a piece of meat playing for a college team and more like a person whose coach is interested in her life.

And as for those who might criticize your encouraging the feeling that the soccer team is a family, all I can think of is that they are jealous. That family feeling is what makes your team so special. I don't know of many coaches who would visit a new kid in her dorm room when she's sick, share his family holiday with the team, or invite 20 million friends and family to his house for a party. The ease with which the players, coaches, and family members interact is incredible. There is a chemistry and caring attitude among the group that runs directly from them to you like a bolt of lightning. And I, for one, hope you don't change your "personal approach."

With the Keller lawsuit behind him, Dorrance is going about the business of repairing the collateral damage. While Kristine Lilly is no longer dating Steve Keller, the wedge driven between Dorrance and one of his greatest players over the suit has yet to be completely removed. "Our relationship grew very distant, but it is much less so as time passes," Lilly says. "I know if I needed anything, he'd be there for me."

Dorrance is convinced he will eventually fully reconnect with Lilly, and he says that if either Jennings or Keller showed up at his office door he would welcome them in to talk. Jennings, who transferred out of UNC in 1999, is now a teacher and youth soccer coach after three seasons as the head women's soccer coach at Waubonsee Community College in Sugar Grove, Illinois. Keller married Chris Hill in 2001, and the couple lives in Raleigh just twenty miles from the UNC campus. Keller is a mother of a young son and still works at the hair salon one day a week. She still has friends in Chapel Hill, but from the UNC soccer community only Amy Roberts, Keller's former high school and college teammate, attended her wedding. Keller says that she feels uncomfortable on those occasions when she attends a football or basketball game at UNC. "The lawsuit was a long, frustrating ordeal, but I believe it was worth it in the end," Keller says. "It was a great learning experience and I have no regrets. I fought for a cause and I'm proud of that, and now it's time to move on with the rest of my life. I don't think Anson and I will ever truly settle this between us, but I'm proud of what I did for UNC women's soccer, and I'm still a fan of the program. I'm just not an Anson Dorrance fan."

At the McCaskill Soccer Center, Keller's retired number 8 jersey and her biographical plaque have always remained hanging in the hallway amidst the rest of UNC's Players of the Year as if the lawsuit never happened. Dorrance steadfastly refused all overtures to remove Keller's memorabilia, believing that history should not be rewritten under any circumstances. In fact, just four months after the settlement, Dorrance extended an invitation to Keller through intermediaries to appear on UNC's next Player of the Year poster. Keller initially expressed interest, but eventually turned down the offer after consulting with her mother. "In my mind, Debbie never separated from the program," Dorrance says. "I think the lawsuit polarized her and then she actually started believing what she told the press."

Throughout the case, Dorrance couldn't help but marvel at the irony that the path he had chosen back in the mid-1980s to start treating his women differently from his men had won him everything and could have lost him everything as well. How could he ever have imagined that choosing to be the kinder, gentler Anson could land him in a mess that the Great Santini never would have risked?

Ever the optimist, Dorrance points out that at least the lawsuit didn't disable his program or even hamper his recruiting in any tangible way. Personally he sees a bright side even in this latest impossible thing that has happened to him. "Some good came out of all this," Dorrance says. "Obviously my players rallying around me was very enriching, but it's also a wonderful inoculation. We're born with all these extraordinary insecurities, and our life experiences inoculate us against those fears one by one, until if you live long enough, you're fearless. This has inoculated me against the court of public opinion. I'm no longer afraid of that. In fact, I feel OK about the whole lawsuit. If you like who you are, why would you ever change anything that has happened to you?"

19 *The Dark Side*

It is not the critic who counts, not the man who points out how the strong man stumbles, or where the doer of deeds could have done them better. The credit belongs to the man in the arena, whose face is marred by dust and sweat and blood, who strives valiantly . . . who knows the great enthusiasms, the great devotions, who spends himself in a worthy cause, who at best knows in the end the triumph of high achievement, and who at the worst, if he fails, at least fails while daring greatly, so that his place shall never be with those cold and timid souls who know neither victory nor defeat.

— Theodore Roosevelt

Anson Dorrance has a big head. Literally. He discovered this one day in 1991 when M'Liss phoned him in a panic and asked, "Anson, what's your hat size?" Their son, Donovan, was just two weeks old and at the pediatrician's office for a checkup. The doctors were concerned that the baby's abnormally large head measured in the top one percentile, which could have indicated some problem with his brain. Anson didn't know his hat size, so he scrambled around the Hut searching for a tape measure. Eventually he turned up string and a yardstick, recorded the circumference of his cranium, and called his wife. Anson overheard M'Liss report his head size to the doctor, followed by an audible sigh of relief. M'Liss told Anson not to worry because his head also ranked in the top one percentile, to which Anson responded, "No wonder I was such a good header."

Brandi Chastain calls it the "A-word." It is the adjective that she, and almost anybody else who knows Dorrance, reflexively blurts out when asked to describe him. *Arrogant.* Chastain noticed it when as a teenager she first met Dorrance and didn't receive the same unqualified praise she heard from other coaches. When Dorrance recruited Tiffeny Milbrett she didn't much like it when she asked him why she should choose UNC and the Tar Heel coach joked, "Can't you tell by the number of titles we have?" After Michelle Akers visited UNC, she called Dorrance "the master of arrogance" and set off for Central Florida as part of a small but significant legion of players who ventured elsewhere, burning with the expressed desire to stick it to that cocky bastard in Chapel Hill. Even one of Dorrance's own players, Carla Werden, accused him of conceit when as a Duke assistant coach in 1992 she endured UNC's 9–1 thumping of the Blue Devils in the NCAA final and believed Dorrance ran up the score. Former U.S. men's national team coach Bruce

Arena, who coached against Dorrance's men's team while at Virginia, once said, "I thought I was the most arrogant person in the world until I met Anson Dorrance."

Maybe it's because Dorrance still maintains a hint of the British accent he picked up in his colonial days, so he says the word "victory" in two syllables, *victree*, the way Churchill once did. Or maybe it's because during warmups before every UNC game, Dorrance's team sprints in a formation known as the "Big V," a perceived reference to victory. Or maybe it's the 9–0 Rule, which some opponents interpret as more demeaning than sportsmanlike, because both teams know the Tar Heels could score more yet choose not to. Maybe it's something as simple as Dorrance's office chair, which is leather, tall-backed, and plush like that of a corporate CEO. Or it could be his unique stride, upright and regal like that of a monarch during a coronation ceremony, the same lilting gait that once reduced his Villa Saint-Jean soccer teammates to giggles.

Sometimes there's a fine line between arrogance and insouciance. For instance, as time ran out on UNC's 3–0 win over Villanova in 2003, Dorrance received a cell phone call informing him that Tar Heel defender Catherine Reddick, who was on loan to the U.S. national team, had just scored a goal in the Women's World Cup. Dorrance was still distractedly chatting on the phone during the postgame handshake with Wildcats coach Ann Clifton. Sometimes it's hard to distinguish arrogance from irreverence, like the time during the annual UNC coaches recruiting test when Dorrance was asked by assistant athletic director Larry Gallo to explain why a volunteer soccer coach was there that day taking the exam. Dorrance jokingly announced to Gallo in front of the entire UNC coaching contingent, "Well, we need *somebody* on our staff who knows the rules." Sometimes it's hard to distinguish between arrogance and innocence. During a UNC men's soccer game at Connecticut in 1981, North Carolina striker Tony Johnson received a red card disqualification for a retaliatory tackle during a game the Tar Heels eventually lost 1–0. Following the game a reporter from the *Hartford Courant* asked Dorrance for his opinion of the referee's call, and despite assurances he was speaking off the record, Dorrance was quoted saying, "It's a good thing I didn't have a pistol in my hand."

Sometimes, although playing for laughs, Dorrance comes off as just plain arrogant. When Dorrance was disappointed with what he believed was an unfair NCAA Tournament draw in 2003, he told the press that the first question he would ask the selection committee is, "Have you ever seen a soccer game?" He is far less diplomatic with game officials. He once barked at a referee, "Come here, Art, you conehead with glasses, I want to bring your game up a level." During another game he yelled out loud enough for the whole stadium to hear, "Ref, you're getting nothing right. What's your address? I'll send you the tape!" He cursed at the officials so enthusiastically during the 1996 NCAA final that he got suspended from the first game of the 1997 tournament. During one game against N.C. State when Dorrance was suffering from laryngitis, the insults he asked Bill Palladino to voice to the referee got Palladino tossed out of the game.

Dorrance explains his outbursts by saying, "It's an effort to demonstrate to my players that I'm behind them. Accepting all the injustice in the world might get you to Buddhist nirvana, but it doesn't help your soccer team win."

The UNC coach admits that his favorite emotion is "righteous indignation." He always says what he thinks and believes that what he thinks is right. And he's never averse to using The Force. Says Bettina Bernardi, "Anson thinks there's only one right way to do it. *His* way. Getting him to listen to another suggestion is like pulling teeth."

Says Chris Ducar: "There's an old joke about a guy who says, 'I am never wrong. Actually, I was wrong once. At least I thought I was wrong, but I was right.' That's Anson."

"Because of Anson's success, most of the time when he gets up in front of a group and starts talking, everybody's jaw drops and it's assumed whatever he says is gospel," Palladino says. "The environment that has been created around him is a charmed place to be because so few people question what's he doing."

Maybe it goes back to his youth, when he was attended by a fleet of servants, but there are times when Dorrance assumes that everybody is completely at his beck and call. When the Tar Heels are eating out on road trips he's been known to huddle up the waitresses and explain to them how to serve his team more efficiently. He has even ventured into a kitchen to coach the cook. Once the Tar Heels were staying in a hotel in Houston, and Dorrance wanted a greaseboard and markers for a pregame talk. Tom Sander reported that the desk would charge the team $150 for the supplies. Dorrance told Sander, "OK, go back and tell them that we will never come back and stay in this fucking stinkhole again if they don't give it to us for free."

"Anson really wanted me to say that," Sander says, still incredulous. "So, I just went back to my room and didn't worry about it. When he asked me later where the stuff was, I told him that the hotel wouldn't budge. I've learned never to say to Anson, 'That can't be done.' Instead I'll say, 'It's not feasible.' Because he won't accept that anything can't be done."

Dorrance's staff jokingly calls him *Batman*, poking fun at the fact that he sincerely believes that any wrong can be righted, perhaps because he has experienced so little evidence to the contrary. "Once you're around Anson and you work with him, you realize that he is arrogant, but it's not something that interferes," Delaine Marbry says. "He grows on you. I laugh at his arrogance and I just tell myself, 'That's Anson!' I say that every day."

Dorrance has come to view his program the way he once viewed himself. To him UNC women's soccer is the underdog in a world of far more celebrated sports. It's an athletic Napoleon Complex, and Dorrance will fight to make sure his Tar Heels are never disrespected. On a rainy day back in the early 1980s, UNC football coach Dick Crum brought his team to practice on Fetzer Field so his players wouldn't tear up their own practice field. Dorrance was training his players on a nearby intramural field so they wouldn't damage Fetzer, and when he saw the football players on his game field he charged over there headlong into a football coach who attempted to debate him on the matter. "Don't even pretend you can do verbal battle with me," Dorrance told him. The football team left, but Dorrance spent a forced detention in the athletic director's office the next day.

"Early on there were some people in UNC's athletic department who found Anson cocky and threatening," says former UNC wrestling coach Bill Lam. "I remember when I worked at Oklahoma, our football coach Barry Switzer used to say, 'If I'm losing, I could walk down Main Street with St. Peter and my ass is outta here. If I'm winning, I could fuck a cow on Main Street and I'm fine.' Anson coaches with that same belief that his is the sport that really counts at UNC."

In fact, whenever Dorrance is asked about his latest dustup with a game official or a colleague, he begins his response by saying, "Well, it's not like UNC's going to fire me . . ."

Dorrance calls it the Dark Side. It is a land where a mostly silent majority of the American women's soccer universe resides. "A lot of people in the soccer community don't like Anson," former Oregon coach Bill Steffen says. "They're pissed off at the guy because he wins and wins and wins. Who doesn't hate someone who wins all the time? And he wins with a little arrogance, so people are going to hate him even more."

Says Michelle Akers: "Sometimes Anson doesn't even realize when he puts people off. It's not just what he says but how he carries himself, how he expresses himself. Some people don't understand it and say, 'What a jerk!' Most of Anson's arrogance is his sense of humor, but people miss that because they are too wrapped up in themselves. There are only two camps in the women's soccer community: people who love Anson Dorrance and people who hate him."

Dorrance approaches his critics with a sort of bunker mentality. He has convinced himself that outside of the boundaries of Chapel Hill, the anti-UNC propaganda is nearly pervasive. "There's such an animosity towards us out there that coaches can't help but get caught up in it," Dorrance says. "Even coaches who once played at UNC are surrounded by so many people trashing us that they feel like they have to convert in a way, or they're looked at disparagingly by their colleagues as *too Carolina*."

Florida coach Becky Burleigh still stews about a home game when she was a player at Division III Methodist College in 1988. Dorrance's team arrived typically late for the game, and as the Tar Heels were quick-changing in their vans, Burleigh overheard Dorrance announce that the first eleven players dressed would play. She resented the implication that UNC could win with any eleven players, even if it was true. "Anson is that arrogant little intellectual nerd who thinks he's smarter than everybody else in class," Burleigh says. "There have been times when I've been really upset with him and times when I've hated him. I remember coaching a game against him that my Florida team would lose 9–0, and some of his players were reading magazines on the bench in the second half. That pissed me off. A coach is responsible for how his team behaves, and that's not right. With Anson you have to get past the dislike to respect him."

Most college coaches won't criticize Dorrance publicly because he is viewed as a sort of godfather of the women's game, and you don't take sides against the family. Coaches do, however, openly criticize Dorrance's system. One of the pet peeves about UNC is that the Tar Heels' style of play is too direct, that they don't build possessions, but just blast the ball over the opponent's back line and sprint onto it to score goals. The system is negatively referred to around the collegiate soccer world as *Kick & Run.* "The Carolina way is to get the ball to their goalkeeper and punt a sixty-yard airball up to the frontrunners and then chase it, play smashmouth high pressure, win the ball, and then serve it into the box to prearranged routes, which is ugly to watch," says Massachusetts coach Jim Rudy, who previously coached Central Florida from 1981 to 1987. "It's all physical and psychological, not skillful and tactical. Every young girl wants to be the next Mia Hamm, but the truth is that Mia wasn't that technical, she could only beat you on the run. If America keeps churning out nothing but Carolina clones, then I'm a little scared for our future."

There is also carping about how UNC plays only one system. "Anson believes in his direct 3-4-3 system, do or die, and sometimes I think that can hurt him," UCLA coach Jill Ellis says. "Most coaches play a system that fits their players. Anson recruits players that fit his system."

Says Santa Clara coach Jerry Smith, "I talk to many coaches around the country who complain that UNC doesn't possess the ball, they just kick it and chase it. I tell them, 'Well, you've got to beat them to force a change.' Until then, why would Anson do anything different?"

"People say UNC doesn't have enough combination play, and a lot of times that's all about looking pretty, but pretty soccer doesn't necessarily win games," Catherine Reddick says. "What we do produces goals. Some coaches complain that we play only one system. Well, that *works.* Some coaches complain that we're all about 1 v. 1. That *works.* Some coaches say we're too direct and all we do is play boomball. That *works.* So shut up."

"A coach criticizing our style of play is just a recruiting gimmick that collapses under the scrutiny of reality," Dorrance says. "We bring in potential recruits and we show them game tapes of us playing against other top programs, and they're shocked to see that our pressure suffocates their possessional game so much that we actually play the more attractive style."

The complaints about Dorrance's system could be construed as a cover-up for the fact that rival college coaches and players simply don't understand or appreciate Dorrance's presentation. "Anson's bravado drove me crazy for years," says Santa Clara alum Brandi Chastain. "He made me feel like an outsider. It's like in junior high school when you're either part of the 'in' crowd or you're not. When you've played at Santa Clara, then you're on the outside looking in, and you notice a lot of these arrogant moments that you otherwise wouldn't. UNC players might say, 'What are you talking about?' Well, step out here with me and you'll see."

"Anson's success breeds resentment, and his arrogance breeds controversy," former U.S. national team coach Tony DiCicco says. "Anson carries a lot of political baggage with him. He's not welcome in every soccer conversation, but I think most of that is unfounded. When you're on top, people are going to want to take a shot at you, and he's been on top for a long time, so he's had to become bulletproof."

"I've found that if you have lunch with Anson he's a very accommodating man who speaks to you as an equal," William & Mary coach John Daly says. "But at game time there's an aloofness in the way he sticks his nose in the air and struts to his bench when he's essentially telling his opponent, 'Look at me and be afraid.'"

Those closest to Dorrance sense that his arrogance is partly an act. "Look at the way Anson carries himself walking across the field," brother Pete says. "If that's not a picture of arrogance, what is? That's his public persona, and that's what he wants coaches to see when they coach against him, and it's what he wants his kids to feed off of. I don't know how much of it is manufactured for the moment, but I think that he knows that's part of what makes him and his players great. To a degree it's calculated, and to a degree it's natural."

Says Dorrance: "I've never been big on swagger, but calling me arrogant is probably a reaction to how my success makes others feel. Arrogance is a feeling of innate superiority, and I don't see myself that way. I hate arrogance. If I sense it in someone else, then I want to kick their ass. If only the other coaches knew that what's running through my mind before every game is a litany of doubts about our weaknesses that usually leaves me thinking, 'How the fuck are we going to win this game?'"

Dorrance will acknowledge that when he stands before a room of his coaching peers at a clinic or a convention, he sees himself as a teacher and feels he must project an air of authority vital to that position. Even Chastain has come to understand one reason Dorrance behaves the way he does. "It's like the difference between me waking up the day of the 1999 World Cup final and waking up the day after," Chastain says. "Nobody cared about my opinion on July tenth, but all of a sudden everybody cares about my opinion on the eleventh. Sometimes you start to believe that you have all the answers when you're really the same person you were the day before, when you didn't know a dang thing. It's hard when everybody in the soccer world thinks that Anson knows all the answers because he has to come across as being a know-it-all, or he'll lose half his audience right away. To get things done at times you have to be arrogant, but *arrogant* and *confident* and *strong* can be synonymous."

Akers, who disliked Dorrance before she played for him on the U.S. national team, says that most of the people she knows who condemn Dorrance have never actually had a conversation with him. Georgia coach Patrick Baker is one example of how attitudes toward Dorrance sometimes change when you spend time with him. "There was a moment early in our coaching relationship when Anson brushed past me like we'd never met and I thought he was an arrogant SOB like everybody else, but the more I got to know him and got a better understanding of who he was, the more we forged a good bond," Baker says. "If all you know of Anson comes from reading articles about him, seeing him on TV at the Final

Four every year and from his seminars at soccer conventions, he seems arrogant. But now when someone says that about him, I ask, 'What if you were in his shoes? How would you act? Wouldn't you be proud of what you've done?' C'mon, it's awesome."

Says Heather O'Reilly: "Before I got to UNC I'd been told that Anson is the cockiest sonofabitch you'll ever meet. Then I got there and I had to laugh. I saw his junky car. I saw the trophies he uses as doorstoppers. The sign congratulating Anson on his 500th win is sitting in the locker room shower. How special could that 500th win have been to him if it's in the shower right now?"

"I think people misunderstand Anson as a person," Julie Foudy says. "He reminds me somewhat of Mia Hamm, where he's very introverted in a sense, very private. He's got a wonderful personality, but he doesn't necessarily have to walk through a room and start shaking hands and chit-chatting with everyone just because he's Anson. I like that about him, but other people who don't know him might find that arrogant."

People who support Dorrance believe the common thread connecting those on the Dark Side is professional jealousy. "There are lots of people in the soccer community who despise Anson," says former Florida defender Erin Baxter. "But it's probably not a coincidence that every single one of those people wish they were in his shoes."

On August 19, 2002, Dorrance submitted to a colonoscopy between UNC's two-a-day preseason practices. The colonoscopy became a prolific source of mirth for Dorrance's staff, because he is so relentlessly positive that he can even make a colonoscopy sound fun, as well as for his players because each had endured a verbal colonoscopy from him at some point in their careers. After the procedure, Dorrance joked, "For one day in my life, I'm not full of shit."

"Anson is the world class emperor of bullshit," Bill Prentice says. "He's a master at it. He knows how to use the bullshit to his advantage. That is really part of why he has been so successful. He is able to convince people that whatever he is thinking and saying is absolutely right."

Says Foudy: "A lot of Anson's b.s. is just in jest and fun, but when it came to soccer it really helped. I used to always say that he could feed you shit and you'd think it was chocolate and you'd eat it all up."

At UNC they've invented a G-rated term for Dorrance's b.s. The players call it *blowing sunshine*. "I love the sunshine that Anson blows," Susan Ellis says. "It makes you confident. When he needs a certain player to perform, then he performs."

Ellis recalls a time when her UNC team was doing a fitness drill that included a sprint up a hill. Ellis's teammate Amy Machin had bad knees, so she skipped the hill and then blew her teammates away in the ensuing sprint. Says Ellis: "I remember Anson said, 'Oh, Amy, you're awesome. You're getting so much faster, you're kicking everyone's ass.' And we're all sitting there pissed off. But Amy needed that stroking. It was the right motivation for her."

There is a running joke at UNC soccer summer camps that Dorrance will tell campers at a particular station that they are being coached by his best instructors. Then he will say the exact same thing at another station. "That's the trouble with bullshit," Bill Palladino says. "If you say too much of it, you can't remember what you've said."

The red flag warning at UNC is something that Nel Fettig once had printed on the back of a sorority T-shirt. *Don't ever let a fool kiss you . . . or a kiss fool you.* UNC players have learned to look for the caution signs, and many are wary of Dorrance's sunshine. "Sometimes you just want an honest opinion, and I don't think Anson gives it to you all the time," Catherine Reddick says. "Normally he'll never sugarcoat what he thinks, but he hides it every once in a while if he's afraid it will hurt your confidence. I think he should always tell the truth, because then you'd know exactly what frustrates him about your game and why you're sitting on the bench. Maybe he thinks that some girls are too sensitive to handle it. Maybe we are. Maybe if he said what he really thought we'd go home crying. But I don't think it would hurt us if we went home crying sometimes."

The danger in blowing sunshine is the division it can create within the team. For years, some UNC players have felt that Dorrance went out of his way to heap praise upon certain players to massage their fragile egos. "When I first came to UNC I got the feeling that other girls on the team thought he favored me," Susan Bush says. "I thought he placed me on a pedestal. He always told me that if I ever had any confidence issues to come see him and he would tell me all these wonderful things about me. He told me what I wanted to hear. For some people that's good and for others it's bad. Some people want honesty; other people need to feel like they're awesome all the time."

During the team's editorial skits at the season-ending banquet that year, Bush's teammates targeted her over the sunshine issue. Laurie Schwoy impersonated Bush, wearing a shirt with a big "S" emblazoned upon it, which Schwoy announced stood for *SuperSusan*. On the back it read, *Susan Saves the Year*. Bush says it was hard on her because she couldn't control how Dorrance acted toward her, and then in her junior year, when he stopped blowing sunshine, she wasn't emotionally prepared for the transition, and her confidence plummeted.

If there is a Dark Side among the players whom Dorrance has coached, it's among those who, as the term suggests, feel they've been unfairly denied Dorrance's sunshine. "It sucks that there's one class of soccer players with such fragile egos that they have to be worshiped like queens, and then you've got the rest of us proletariat who actually do all the grunt tasks like train, lift weights, practice hard every day, and pass fitness," says Charlotte Mitchell, a UNC walk-on who played from 1996 to 1999. "There were days when I wanted to shoot myself when X, Y, and Z are running themselves ragged, and he's focused only on A, putting her on a pedestal. That takes a toll on that person, and it pisses off the rest of the team. I'm sure Anson knows that, but you've got to do a cost-benefit analysis. As a soccer coach he has one responsibility, and as a person who influences young women's lives, he has another. The humanist coach may be an oxymoron. Can that exist?"

"Anson tends to b.s. the big-name players, the national teamers, and that creates a hierarchy," Alyssa Ramsey says. "The people he bullshits go out there and play well for him because they want to play well for him. The people like me who weren't his favorites went out there and played well in spite of him."

Blowing sunshine is the most controversial issue in team dynamics that Dorrance has confronted during his career. Even Palladino believes that Dorrance overuses the tactic. "Anson calls it 'protecting' them," Palladino says. "What Anson doesn't realize is how obvious it is to everybody else. Players get frustrated because they see some players who screw up and aren't held accountable. I'll tell him when there's a problem, but he'll usually defend his decision, and then it's up to me to placate the angry ones with as little upheaval as possible."

Dorrance says there are fewer than a dozen players in his career who have received full-blown sunshine, and while he acknowledges the inherent conflict with his insistence on holding players accountable, he feels it is justified in certain cases. "I will treat that rare someone differently if she is the margin of victory," Dorrance says. "If you have a game-breaker, you protect her from any self-doubt that you can. I will push whatever button I can to protect her and empower her because I need her to win. Teammates who complain that those players aren't held accountable don't realize that those players are responsible for us winning and losing games, which makes them accountable in a different way. Sometimes you have to make decisions that benefit the overall success of the organization even if it ticks off some of the individuals."

Robin Confer benefits from having viewed the process of blowing sunshine as a UNC player and now as an assistant coach at Georgia. "Some players will be on the pedestal in every program, and if you have a player of that caliber, of course, you want to insulate her," Confer says. "At UNC I had teammates who dodged fitness, and it drove some people crazy, but I always thought, 'Why spend four years pouting about not getting enough attention?' I always thought it would be uncomfortable on the pedestal because I knew what the rest of the team would think."

Says Reddick: "It's inevitable for a coach to play favorites, and it definitely helps to be on Anson's good side. You don't want coaches to play favorites because it's unfair and people see that, but what's neat about Anson is that he doesn't care. He's going to do it his way, and that bothers a lot of his players. They all want him to like them most."

"I get so pissed when people bitch that Anson isn't nice enough to them," Jordan Walker says. "This is a business. He's paid to win. He's invested in these girls by helping them get their college educations, and he deserves some production and some loyalty in return. He shouldn't have to coddle them to get it."

For all he's learned about women during his coaching career, there are still some instances when Dorrance's players believe that maybe some legally mandated sensitivity training isn't such a bad idea. Leslie Gaston recalls a game against Texas when she thought she heard her goalkeeper call for a ball, so she ducked a potential clearing header, and the ball bounced over the keeper's head and into the goal. After UNC won the game 3–2, Dorrance approached Gaston and barked, *If you can clear the ball, clear the frigging ball! Take responsibility!* "He really lit into me," Gaston says. "I just looked at him and started crying, and then I just completely closed off. I couldn't believe he was saying that to me, and it broke my heart. If I learned one thing about this program going through it for four years, it's that it develops character. We are put through trials, and you have to find a way to get through them."

Other players believe that Dorrance simply doesn't understand when he's taken his sarcasm too far. During most of Jenni Branam's freshman year, Dorrance called her "China Doll" because she was often injured. "He'd call me that like fifty times in one practice," Branam says. "It went from being funny to being mean. You start to think, 'Holy crap, I thought this coach cared about me and now he's just making fun of me. This is like sixth grade all over again.'"

Dorrance can be particularly tough on his flank midfielders, who play within earshot of their coach, directly in front of the team bench. During the 1999 season, outside midfielders Jena Kluegel and Raven McDonald were occasionally driven to tears on the field during the half when they were subject to Dorrance's caustic asides. "Raven and I had our own personal coach," Kluegel says. "*Trap it! Turn! Pass it to someone in blue!* I always felt like telling Anson to shut up, but he said it was like therapy for him to rib us. He'd always joke with us that it's a good thing he didn't have a loaded weapon on the bench because he'd probably shoot us both. I told him, 'It *is* a good thing, because I'd probably shoot you first.'"

Dorrance tends to push hardest on the players with the most potential, and that included Kluegel. But after two seasons at UNC, Kluegel became so weary of Dorrance's sarcasm that during her junior year, she marched into his office and told him to cease and desist. Kluegel actually considered buying earplugs for her opposite flank midfielder, Sara Randolph, when Randolph arrived as a freshman in 2001.

"Nothing Anson says is premeditated, and if a player is pushed too far, he has no clue," Palladino says. "He tells the players that the more he criticizes them, the more he respects them, so when he hears afterward that a comment blew a girl away, he's shocked because he's usually just trying to be funny."

Dorrance gets in trouble when he expects all of his women to react to teasing as he once did with his father. It takes him a while to grasp that his banter simply doesn't work on some players. "At times I don't think Anson realizes how much he hurts people," Maggie Tomecka says. "Honestly, I think I would have played much better if he hadn't pointed out every single mistake I ever made, because that made me nervous and thinking, 'I can't make another mistake.' And so, of course, I'd make another mistake, because the whole time I'm thinking about making another mistake."

"Anson goes too far sometimes and says hurtful things without thinking twice about it," Carmen Watley says. "In the end, he was so for the greater cause that you almost felt sorry for him thinking that the way he treated people was justified when it wasn't. I wondered sometimes, 'What's going on in your mind?' I didn't hate him, but I didn't really like him when I played there. I tolerated him."

Says Susan Bush: "Lots of his players misread Anson's humor. When he's sarcastic to them they don't take it as constructive criticism, they take it as a personal attack. His comments are amusing to the rest of the team, but they can be upsetting sometimes to the player he's criticizing if she's sensitive. He claims he knows women really well, but I don't think any man can really know the female psyche. He thinks he knows who can take it and who can't, but he'd be surprised. He doesn't."

Amy Machin once grew so frustrated with Dorrance's shtick that after a game in 1984 she walked up to her coach with her jersey, socks and cleats in hand, and a threat. *I've heard enough of your shit, Anson, and if you want to keep crossing that line because you think it's pissing me off to play better, I'm prepared to walk away.* "If I had been a weaker person, I would have left my stuff right there at his feet," Machin says. "I sometimes wonder if maybe he knew exactly how far he could push me? In the end how clever was he? He got me mad enough at him to produce, and isn't that what all coaches are looking for? Looking back on it, I don't think he should have done that to me, but maybe you've got to be willing to take some steps down dark paths to get where you need to be."

Nobody acts as Dorrance's whistleblower more than April Heinrichs, one of his greatest players ever and the protégée who has advanced the furthest in the coaching ranks. "I know Anson well, and my rose-colored glasses are off," Heinrichs says. "I am one of Anson's biggest fans and one of his biggest critics. When you get out from under his spell I think you come to realize that he's human, and he has his flaws and his moments when you wish he wouldn't have said something to you because it hurt your feelings. He can be insensitive at times, and he can be self-absorbed at times."

Chastain saw Dorrance's insensitive side when he once informed her that she was cut from the U.S. national team roster by way of a message left with her husband, Santa Clara coach Jerry Smith, while he and Smith were on the phone scheduling a game. "I was so angry that I couldn't see straight because Anson didn't have the courage to call me and do his own dirty work," Chastain says. "I wrote a letter to him and called him a coward and said that he had lost all my respect."

In Dorrance's mind he was just multi-tasking, but he sent a letter back to Chastain saying that if she trained with the kind of passion contained in her letter that he would invite her back to national team camp, which he eventually did.

No player ever clashed with Dorrance as much as Tiffeny Milbrett, who was part of his national team pool from 1991 until he resigned as coach in 1994. Milbrett had grown up reflexively wanting to play for Dorrance at UNC but chose Portland instead after becoming disillusioned with Dorrance during her camp stints with the national team. Like Chastain, Milbrett didn't meet Dorrance's standards of fitness or defensive intensity, the two areas he feels every player can control. "It was a major struggle to play the game through his philosophy," Milbrett says. "Everybody has a different coaching style, and I'm not saying his is wrong, but it was wrong for me, and I know I'm not alone in thinking that. There were times when he was very cruel to me, and I felt I was treated unfairly, more harshly than other players. He tried to motivate me by saying mean things, and I didn't appreciate that kind of motivation."

In one conversation with a former UNC player, Milbrett explained that she held Dorrance responsible for some of the most trying times in her soccer career. She revealed her most visceral feelings toward Dorrance when she said, "Anson is the most evil person I have ever known."

They don't know about the hot dogs. Most of Dorrance's critics don't know that every winter the entire UNC women's soccer team works in a concession stand at Tar Heel men's basketball games. They don't know that Dorrance himself is often working the mustard. While the negligible profits are sprinkled into the soccer budget, Dorrance's real objective is to remind his players about the importance of humility and giving back to their university. For the players, it's a concession to a mission larger than themselves. "I remember the basketball game in 1992 when I first saw the soccer team working that booth in the Smith Center," UNC media coordinator Steve Kirschner remembers. "I thought, 'What are they doing? Here's the best women's soccer coach and the best female athletes in the world, and they're selling *hot dogs*?'"

Most of the coaches and players on the Dark Side don't hear Dorrance regularly laugh off his coaching success as the product of "smoke and mirrors." They don't recall that during the postgame of the 1991 World Championship triumph he said, "I think it's a fitting slogan my grandfather told me: *Luck is better than skill.*" They don't know about the halftime meeting at the 2001 ACC Tournament semifinal when Leslie Gaston, tired of her coach's sarcasm, told him, "I've got to stop listening to you and just play," and how before the final Dorrance responded by joking, "I just want to thank you, Leslie, for your halftime commentary the other night, because I need to be reminded every once in a while that basically all I do for a living is pick up my paycheck."

They don't know that Dorrance coaches without a contract and has never once considered asking his athletic director for a long-term deal. They don't know that he has never requested an extra penny for his skimpy operating budget, even though it ranks thirteenth among sports at UNC behind women's lacrosse and rowing, is the lowest among all ACC women's soccer programs, and is dwarfed by what the University of Nebraska allocates for its *bowling team*. They don't know that on recruiting trips he's been known to sleep on the hotel room floor of a coaching colleague with a larger budget, or that on UNC road trips his team often eats at Denny's, where he requests the players all drink water with their meals to save a few bucks, or that in the early days, when the budget was even tighter, he would sometimes agree to give a speech just to pay for travel to the next game. They don't know that for the Tar Heels to function each season, Dorrance secretly pays about $30,000 out of his own pocket just to cover his budget shortfall.

They don't know that he answers his own office phone with no idea who is on the other end, and thus often talks to overzealous soccer moms for an hour about their nine-year-old daughters' heading deficiencies. They don't know that whenever Dorrance votes for a colleague as the National Coach of the Year, he photocopies his ballot and mails it to his chosen candidate before the results come out so whether or not he or she wins, that coach can see how much Dorrance respected the job they did. They don't know that after he won a 2001 Coach of the Year award, Dorrance sent the certificate to Tennessee coach Ange Kelly because he felt she deserved it more. They don't know that after playing Rutgers in the 2001 NCAA Tournament, Dorrance complimented Scarlet Knights coach Glenn Crooks for his game plan during the press conference and then mailed Crooks the local newspaper clippings the next morning.

They don't know that a tie hangs on the closet door in his office, given to him by the widow of John Lotz, one of his early mentors at UNC, a tie Dorrance wears for one game each season to honor his former colleague. They don't know that he upholds the tradition of UNC's "Big V" pregame sprint, not as any reference to victory, but as a tribute to the spirit of Tar Heel casualties like Vanessa Rubio, whose career-ending knee injury in 1996 first spawned the "Big V."

They don't know that Dorrance rejects the notion of hierarchy so fiercely that nobody calls him "Coach," and the only three people left in his world who don't call him "Anson" call him "Dad." They don't know how much Dorrance enjoys the moments when one of his assistant coaches walks up to him and asks if he combed his hair with a shoe, or how he waited until the last possible minute to invite those coaches to his induction ceremony for the North Carolina Sports Hall of Fame in 2001, so they would not feel obligated to attend. They don't know that he has never once, after any of UNC's eighteen national titles, appeared in his team's championship photo.

They don't see Dorrance's satisfaction, because he won't let them. He has never been much for celebration. Not as a player or as a coach. In fact, Dorrance remains as stoic as possible after every victory because he feels that any sort of outward celebration could be viewed as insulting to his opponents, like dancing on their graves, so he prefers to stand back and observe the joy in his women. As his players dog-piled moments after UNC's double overtime victory in the 1996 NCAA final, Dorrance calmly walked over to Notre Dame coach Chris Petrucelli and said, "Congratulations, your team played great." By ten o'clock that night, the UNC coach was in his pajamas reading a book in his hotel bed. "Wins like that are hugely fulfilling for me, but maybe not in the same way that other people enjoy them," Dorrance says. "Each season for me is part of a larger cycle, so my goal is never just to win one game. I can't celebrate anything yet, because the cycle's not over."

"Anson doesn't need to have people slap him on the back when he wins," M'Liss says. "He'd rather sit quietly by himself and bask in the feeling. That's his reward."

Those closest to Dorrance confide that there were some instances early in his career when he was an unexpectedly vulnerable target for the Dark Side. Says brother Pete: "Some soccer coaches who have taken potshots at him in the press probably think, 'How can we hurt this guy who doesn't have any feelings?' But they left their mark."

In recent years, however, whether Dorrance is being showered with praise or sliced to ribbons, he has followed Big Pete's example never to take his success or failure too seriously. He believes he developed a thicker skin deflecting criticism as the national team coach, and a virtual suit of armor during the six years of negative publicity surrounding the Debbie Keller lawsuit. These days he ignores his detractors, describing criticism toward him as an insect landing on a rhinoceros. He just doesn't really care anymore. He answers Chastain or Milbrett or Watley or any player he's offended in the same way. "In a good coach/player relationship there should be a tension," Dorrance says. "It's my job to bring them to their potential, and that's never entirely comfortable for them. Maybe some of them don't like the way I push them. Bummer. There may be times when I'm driving a player when all she's hearing is, 'I don't like you' or 'I don't respect you,' but I obviously respected her game enough to pick her to play for me. My players don't have to like me for me to like them. You have to coach through your own personality, so I'm never going to be their fairy godmother. I'm going to get after them, because that's who I am and who I've always been."

Dorrance's favorite poem, Rudyard Kipling's "If," sums up his reaction to anyone who ventures to the Dark Side. He has memorized the poem, which is posted on the back of his office door, and he delights in reciting a couple of stanzas off the cuff to visiting reporters who ask him about his critics.

> *If you can keep your head when all about you*
> *Are losing theirs and blaming it on you,*
> *If you can trust yourself when all men doubt you*
> *But make allowance for their doubting too,*
> *If you can wait and not be tired by waiting,*
> *Or being lied about, don't deal in lies*
> *Or being hated, don't give way to hating,*
> *And yet don't look too good, nor talk too wise:*
>
> *If you can talk with crowds and keep your virtue,*
> *Or walk with kings—nor lose the common touch,*
> *If neither foes nor loving friends can hurt you;*
> *If all men count with you, but none too much;*
> *If you can fill the unforgiving minute*
> *With sixty seconds' worth of distance run,*
> *Yours is the Earth and everything that's in it,*
> *And—which is more—you'll be a Man, my son!*

20 | *Circles*

No man is an island, entire of itself; every man is a piece of the continent, a
part of the main . . . any man's death diminishes me, because I am involved
in mankind, and therefore never send to know for whom the bell tolls; it
tolls for thee.

—John Donne

*F*reshman class,

The reason we are gathered here tonight is for your initiation ceremony
into the Carolina tradition which you have been part of now for one week.
What lies ahead of you this evening will be a night you will never forget.
Not so much for obvious reasons like the act of your initiation, but for the
most part because it symbolizes the beginning of your membership to the
University of North Carolina women's soccer team. Tonight you will complete the circle you see before you. As the circle is a half now, tonight it will
become whole, bonded by the pride, courage, dedication, support through
friendship, and ambition for the future that each of you possess. This
evening all of you will prove yourselves worthy of this membership.

Please don't take the honor lightly. Before you stand the best friends
you will ever know. We will be here for you whenever you need us. We will
support you both on and off the field. Look to us for anything just as long as
you have given everything you have. We will not let you down.

The history of this team is known to you all. Great players have gone
before and many more will follow, but every player who has worn Carolina
blue is a member of the circle known as Tar Heel women's soccer. The
traditions set by the players before is one of grace, courage, and, above all,
excellence. These former wearers of Carolina blue set this great standard
and we invite you all to take pride in keeping the tradition alive.

Every time you step foot on the field, you carry the name of the University of North Carolina with you. Records have been set and others are to be
made, but the records are not important. It is the people who stand before
you that are. What's important is the bond that each of you form with us
and us with you. This bond is important because without it no records would
be worth setting. Look around at your teammates. We will each carry someone else present tonight at some time this year. Be it on the field or off.
That is the most valuable asset about this circle. Remember that always.

No one knows as well as we do the power of friendship—for it carries us in everything we do. This evening not only symbolizes the beginning of your membership in this group, but it is also a symbol of everything we mean to each other. By playing for each other we will not be defeated. We will always be a success. In order to succeed tonight, you must work together as you do on the field. There is no room for those who find themselves superior. We are all equal. We will be waiting to welcome you at the end of this evening to complete the circle that is Carolina Soccer. Then we will be one.

UNC women's soccer is about circles. No player is more important than another. All are necessary to complete the shape. For many years, the Tar Heels met at the center circle at Fetzer Field a week or so into the preseason for the team's initiation ceremony.

While the script was edited from year to year, the basic premise remained the same. The team's incoming freshmen were summoned to a designated location and blindfolded with soccer socks by the upperclassmen, who were dressed in dark sweatsuits and sunglasses. They were led to the center circle at Fetzer Field, where their blindfolds were removed and they stood facing their peers, who had formed a semicircle. The upperclassmen lit candles, and one of them solemnly read the initiation speech.

At the end of the speech, the freshmen were told that they should collect as much toilet paper as they could swipe from campus buildings and use it to T.P. the Hut. Then the recruits were compelled to consume an unsavory meal of sardines, celery soda, and pink coconut Sno-Balls. Many of the different hazing rituals were named after UNC practice drills. When two freshmen were told to consume the same banana from either end, it was called "1 v. 1 to the cone." Eventually the freshmen were told to wear their underwear on the outside of their clothes, put diapers on their heads, and parade through campus double-file, chanting,

We are peons, yes we are,
We don't know where the hell we are,
We kiss upperclassmen's ass
Because we are the freshman class

Then, in the early morning hours after an evening in town collecting signatures from bar bouncers on their stomachs and elsewhere, the freshmen were once again blindfolded and driven to a house on the outskirts of town. They were unceremoniously dumped on the doorstep with some incriminating toilet paper in their possession, and after the doorbell was rung, the initiators sped off. Eventually the door was opened, and a yawning Anson Dorrance said, "Hello, freshmen, welcome to the UNC family."

April 12, 1991

I just wanted you all to know how much I appreciated the time you took to make my fortieth birthday memorable. I know it is hard to notice if

*anything registers with me. Kristine Lilly commented that she did see a
flicker of surprise and wonderment when I walked in and all of you screamed
in unison. Don't be deceived. The individual gestures of affection each of
you share with me or each other register and run very deep. None of you
will ever know how much I enjoy my experience with you and how much I
respect and admire how hard you work and the things you do for your teammates and staff. Sometimes it might be hard to tell. I know abrasive sarcasm and editorial humor don't reinforce an impression that I like each of
you unconditionally, but I do. I have to walk a precarious tightrope of caring for you and challenging you at the same time. Too much of one side or
the other are not the best for you . . .*

*So fortunately or unfortunately I will praise, criticize, soothe, tease and
joke, be sarcastic at times, be in awe of you amazing people and care about
each one of you every step of the way.*

*Thanks again for your wonderful concern. To quote Laura Boone off my
birthday card, yesterday was, "just another step in my never-ending ascension." I could take that as my own type of sarcasm being played back for
me, but I don't. My life does ascend every day because of each one of you.
Thank you for being who you are.*

Anson

At the end of the afternoon in 1966 when Peggy Dorrance dropped off her son
Anson at the Villa Saint-Jean for the first time, he was deeply engaged in a foosball
game as she prepared to leave. When Peggy said goodbye, Anson grunted and
never looked up from the table. Peggy was heartbroken when she realized that her
fourteen-year-old son was already so fiercely independent that he would suffer far
less anxiety over their separation than she would. Anson thought it was a compliment. Don't successful parents produce children who feel confident without them?

Anson was never much for sentimentality. Growing up he considered his relationships mostly disposable. He had few close friends and rarely even attended
the same school with any of his siblings. "We didn't have a normal brotherly relationship," Pete says. "We were never sleeping in bunk beds in the same room,
and to me it always felt like Anson was a guest in our house. He had an odd childhood, and now it's like his first eighteen years have faded away because those
years of his life weren't reinforced. You don't remember the trees you climbed as
a kid when you never go back to see them."

Other than his immediate family and M'Liss, Dorrance no longer has any relationships that date back before college. Even some of the people to whom he is
now closest don't claim to know him well. Though they have known each other
for more than thirty years, Dorrance rarely socializes with Bill Palladino outside
of work. Their relationship is based as much on mutual respect as on genuine
affection. Says Palladino: "Those of us who are around Anson on a regular basis
are able to connect with him, but does that mean that I know everything about
him? No. There are tiers. He does have a distance, but it's not because of his
position. It's natural. That's who he is."

"I think Anson is a very distant person for the most part," Bill Prentice says. "He is a very, very difficult person to get to know. Even after all the time that we've spent together, I don't totally understand him."

Members of his staff say that Dorrance is easy to talk to, but that he is much more comfortable conversing about soccer than about his personal life. "He is very guarded," Chris Ducar says. "That's part of his life philosophy. We all have problems. Deal with them and move on. I think whenever he's in trouble his instinct is to solve it on his own. If Anson was caught in a bear trap, he'd chew his own leg off, hop out of the woods, bring the leg with him, and stitch it back on himself."

Even Pete says that he sometimes has trouble making small talk with his older brother and that Anson requires his quiet time. "I wouldn't say he's a loner because his whole life is about interacting with people, but he can be in a large group of people and still be alone," Pete says. "It's just the way he's wired. He has a quality of going inside himself. It's not a meditative state, it's more active than that, but you can tell when he's in his own world."

Dorrance's players say that they've learned the most about him through the notes and letters he's written to them, a distance from which he feels more comfortable expressing his feelings. "He doesn't let you get to know him easily, but the more you're around him the more you see that his heart is in the right place," Michelle Akers says. "I know he'll be ticked that I'm revealing his secret, but I think the real Anson is soft-hearted, like a little boy on the inside. He can't show that side to many people because he'd be eaten alive. All of that has to be filtered through the professional Anson that most people see."

Among all of his former players, Marcia McDermott has experienced more personal discussions with Dorrance over the years than anybody else, but she rarely induces Dorrance to talk about himself as much as he inquires about her. "Like all coaches, Anson is honed to try and impact everybody else around him," McDermott says. "There are times when I'm having a conversation with him and I think he's just there as 'Coach,' and there are other times when he seems to be more of a friend, and I never know which I'm going to get. But there's been a consistency to the man—loyalty, confidence, and a surprising humility, that he has presented steadfastly over the years. After twenty years of presentation, is that truth? I don't know. That's the mystery of Anson."

Dec. 10, 2001

Dear Anson,

I just watched the NCAA championship game on TV, as I always do. I'm sure you are disappointed and I'm not sure how you are feeling now. I hope you keep things in perspective. You have had unparalleled, mind-boggling success. But the true measure of your success, Anson, I believe, is the love and loyalty of your players. From the superstar to the so-called "scrub," you are loved and respected. As Julie Foudy said in her TV commentary, you have built a family. So consider yourself hugged, the way you hugged me after the loss in 1985. I am grateful for the experiences I had at Carolina and the continued connection I feel to you and the program. You are doing something very right. Don't lose sight of that.

Love,
Nancy Slocum

For the longest time, Dorrance defined the word *community* as "a neighborhood of houses." Then he read M. Scott Peck's book *The Different Drum,* and he began to develop a new definition for the word. In the book's opening chapter, Peck describes how he once attended an elite New England boarding school where students divided into cliques based on their looks, grades, and sophistication, and everyone struggled to be accepted among the "in" crowd. Then Peck transferred to a Quaker school where differences among the students were celebrated, and a community formed without any outcasts. Dorrance considered how he could inject that idea of community into his team. "One of the hardest things to do in competitive athletics is to construct a community, because every team is made up of hierarchies: starters and reserves, piano players and piano carriers, people that work hard and people who don't, nice people and assholes," Dorrance says. "It's exposed daily in practice, and that can create tremendous divisions."

Dorrance has come to define the word *community* as "any gathering of people with a shared bond." Acceptance into the UNC community is earned simply by surviving the program. The baptism of fire as a freshman. The competitive cauldron. The chaos. The "touch of a billy goat" remarks. "When you're working your ass off so hard next to somebody else, there's a weird connection that bonds you with them," Heather O'Reilly says. "When I came to UNC I thought that I would have a 'soccer life' and a 'college life,' but they definitely meshed together more than I thought they were going to. My teammates became my best friends."

UNC women's soccer is its own sorority, so much so that most of the players never consider rushing a real one. In fact, every August on sorority Bid Night, a group of Tar Heel soccer players gathers uptown to witness the sorority girls giddily stampeding to their new houses, a ritual the soccer players mockingly call "the Running of the Boobs."

The UNC soccer sisterhood endures beyond graduation. A decade after Carolyn Springer left the UNC program, she says her three closest friends are all former Tar Heel teammates: Paige Coley, Danielle Egan, and Roz Santana. Though Springer lives in Boston, Coley in Atlanta, Egan in England, and Santana in Germany, Springer phones each of them at least once a week, and the four gather for a reunion every summer. Cindy Parlow says she is still in contact with almost every player on her 1998 team, and she considers many of them among her most faithful confidantes. "I remember after one WUSA game talking to a player on the other team who went to UNC, and she said, 'Oh my gosh, I think I'm going to get in trouble because my coach sees me talking to you,'" Parlow recalls. "I was dumbfounded. I said, 'What? I consider you family. Are you not allowed to talk to family after a game?' She just looked at me and said, 'I guess you're right.' So we just sat out there on the field and chatted like sisters for the next fifteen minutes."

The community can sometimes even span an entire generation. When Leslie Gaston, class of '02, was rehabbing a knee injury, she received regular "Get Well" e-mails from Janet Rayfield, class of '82. "In the community I see myself as the grandmother, and I get a sense of respect from all the younger players," Rayfield says. "It's understood that everybody had a part to play in teams that came after them. That's the thread that holds the community together. It's the tie that binds us."

Says Gaston: "There's an amazing connection among all of us that has changed my life. Being a part of the UNC program is so much more than just soccer. It's not about winning a national championship; it's deeper, and you can't really understand it unless you're a part of it. Maybe that's the real mystique of the program."

Evidence of the power of the community can reveal itself in many forms. It occurred during a game against Florida International in the 2002 season when seven Tar Heel soccer alums in the stands improvised their own chant that had Dorrance and Palladino doubled over laughing on the bench:

> *A L U–M N I*
> *Tar Heel players never say die*
> *Alumni, alumni, go Heels*
> *A L U–M N I*
> *Because of us, the Tar Heels fly,*
> *Alumni, alumni, go Heels*
> *A L U–M N I*
> *Send us up a pizza pie*
> *Alumni, alumni, go Heels*

It was evident on a United States Navy ship in the middle of the Persian Gulf in 1998 when Kristin Acquavella was stationed there during Operation Desert Fox. One night she turned on the television in her stateroom and saw her friend and former teammate Mia Hamm in a shampoo commercial, and suddenly felt at home 7,000 miles away from Chapel Hill. It was evident after the NCAA Tournament loss in 2001 when senior Danielle Borgman's mother, Sue, approached Dorrance with tears streaming down her face and said, "I just want to give you a hug. I don't even know if it's appropriate, but I don't care."

Unlike in many college programs, players' parents are welcome in the UNC community. Few other college coaches encourage parents to sit in on a pregame meeting or to dine with the team on road trips. Dorrance also embraces UNC soccer's two "groupies," Art and Ray. Ray Jefferies, age 80, a former UNC assistant dean of students, is the program's unofficial publicist, who photocopies local newspaper stories about the team, stuffs envelopes with recruiting letters, and will rattle on for twenty minutes about UNC soccer when asked, "How are you?" Art Halpern, age 81, a retired accountant who refers to himself as UNC's assistant ballboy, shags balls in practice, takes team photos with his Instamatic camera, and offers Dorrance unsolicited advice on UNC's box organization. Art and Ray are the unofficial leaders of a group of Tar Heel soccer zealots known as the Heeligans.

Dorrance stages regular alumni reunions, hoping to reestablish a dialogue with players who have lost touch with the program, like the notoriously selfish little clod of ailments, Dawn Crow, who graduated without ever buying into his message. He even tries to reintegrate the few players who have transferred away from UNC. Two of those transfers, Shanna Caldwell and Amy Burns, have since become mainstays as counselors at UNC summer camps, and Dorrance attended Burns's wedding, one of more than thirty alumni weddings he has witnessed over the years. Tisha Venturini says one of the highlights of her wedding day came when she stumbled upon Dorrance, Palladino, and their wives scrambling into the church fifteen minutes late because they had stopped on the way for a little diddy at Taco Bell. Because Tracey Bates's father had passed away before she married in 1992, Bates asked Dorrance to walk her down the aisle. "Of all the accolades and honors and awards and tributes that have been paid to me as a coach, that is absolutely the greatest one," Dorrance says. "I used to hate weddings, but then when my players started getting married I found them very life-affirming, very rich, connective moments."

This is the final piece of Dorrance's personal transformation. His players have helped him realize what is really valuable about his job. He has suspected it ever since he sat beside Keri Sanchez for a campus radio interview in 1995. When Sanchez, who had recently graduated, was asked about her greatest memories of playing for UNC, she instantly replied, "The friends I met along the way mean the most. The national titles are great, but the people you meet being a part of the Carolina program are what make it so memorable."

In fact, ask any Tar Heel about her most memorable moment in the program, and most will talk about an instance *off* the field. Elizabeth Ball says hers occurred during a road trip to California when Alyssa Ramsey piggybacked her six blocks to a convenience store for ice cream because Ball had loaned her shoes to a teammate. Acquavella treasures most the day when she and fellow freshmen Hamm, Julie Carter, Rita Tower, and Sarah Ludington decided to embark on an impromptu camping trip without a tent and were eventually saved by a troop of Boy Scouts. "Ten years later, you really don't remember the soccer," Acquavella says. "I was part of four national championships, and I don't have a single ring to show for it. I gave them all away. What makes Carolina special are the personal relationships."

Dorrance has come to understand that whenever his UNC teams play in an NCAA semifinal, they want to win the game mostly so they can spend two more days together, and that the players actually enjoy the off days on road trips more than the game days. He noticed the power of player camaraderie one year when he tried to make his team's practice warmup more efficient by eliminating the opening ten minutes when the girls chat and giggle while aimlessly jogging around the field. Team morale plummeted after the change, and Dorrance felt compelled to reinstate the old warmup a few weeks later. "There is nothing they do in those minutes that is warming any of them up, but it is the most critical part of practice because of their connection," Dorrance says. "That reminded me why they play. They don't play soccer to win championships. They're on this team because they love each other's company."

That's why Dorrance invents any excuse for his community to gather. He regularly invites the players to his home for team dinners, including a last supper for his seniors each spring. The team celebrates every Thanksgiving together at a restaurant that Pete Dorrance owns in Chapel Hill, parents and alums included. The UNC coach clearly relishes being the hub that connects all these women. "The more I understood this idea of community," Dorrance says, "the more I realized that I needed it for my own happiness as well."

Dorrance's outlook is influenced by a conversation he had with McDermott when she was the soccer coach at Northwestern in the late 1990s. McDermott told Dorrance about the Wildcats men's basketball coach, Ricky Byrdsong, a man plugged in to the community around him, who always took the time to acknowledge McDermott's players on their successes. Byrdsong's coaching record was just 34–78 over four seasons at Northwestern when he was fired in 1997. Two years later, he was shot to death. McDermott attended Byrdsong's funeral and said that it clarified for her the value of having an effect on people through relationships rather than winning. "I told Anson how the funeral was packed with people and players whose lives Ricky had touched," McDermott says. "It became very clear to me how much more important it was that everybody regarded him as a good man, even though not everybody thought he was a good coach. There's something about that story that really moves Anson."

Dorrance describes his reaction to Byrdsong's story as a sort of Scrooge-like wake-up call. "What every coach debates in their own mind is, 'Do I really want to get into work at dawn and leave at 10 p.m. and construct my soccer empire?'" Dorrance says. "My guess is that Ricky Byrdsong could have been a lot more 'successful' in terms of the way we would judge him as a coach, but what would he have sacrificed in his responsibility to the human race? Would his life truly have been the victory it was? I think about success off the field a lot more lately. Are we a good community? Do we fully accept each other for all of our faults, and do we embrace everyone? It's funny that when you're young a community doesn't have great significance, but when you get older and sort out that this is an incredibly lonely world we live in, a group of people who accept you unconditionally is priceless."

Dec. 20, 2000

Anson,

   I wanted to wish you and your family a most wonderful holiday season! I cannot begin to tell you how much I miss UNC soccer and everything it

stands for. You truly are an amazing coach and leader! I have utmost re-
spect for you and can only hope that I will be half as successful as you have
been! Please keep your fingers crossed for me! I have decided to keep both
the soccer avenue and career avenue open and pursue whichever comes first.
I feel that there is something rooted deeply within my heart and soul that is
untapped waiting for me to discover. I'm confident I'll sort things out. Af-
ter all, you helped me tremendously in developing my confidence. You've
been a great mentor for me. You more so than anyone has prepared me for
this unpredictable and cutthroat world in which we live. I am forever in-
debted to you. Not so much for what you taught me on the field but for
what you taught me about life. I honestly feel I can achieve whatever I set
my mind to! So thank you, thank you, thank you, for a most wonderful 4
years that I will always hold dear.

With love,
Raven McDonald

Amy Machin once told Dorrance she couldn't run the Cooper because she
was in love. Mary Eubanks returned to school one preseason in poor physical
condition, and when Dorrance inquired about her summer fitness regimen, she
told him it consisted of "long walks on the beach with my mother." Jena Kluegel
thought she couldn't play well unless she ate her pregame meal *exactly* four hours
before gametime. Jordan Walker shaved her legs before every game to help her
run faster. Whenever Helen Lawler screwed up during her freshman season, she
told Dorrance, "I don't know why I'm this bad. I was great in high school."

The Tar Heels have spent long van rides predicting everything from the order
in which teammates would be engaged to the order of which remaining Tar Heel
virgins would lose their virginity. During a 2003 preseason trip to Europe, Alyssa
Ramsey and Laura Winslow bet who would be the first to kiss an Englishman. In
1993 Ange Kelly and Tisha Venturini started wearing a ring of white athletic tape
around their left pinkies for team bonding, and the current Tar Heels are still
superstitiously wearing the pinkie tape more than a decade later.

Agnes Allan changed her name to Senga (*Agnes* spelled backward) because
she thought that sounded "cooler." Carolyn Springer changed her name to
Ntozake Zola, which she translated as "to carry love," secretly married an African-American classmate, painted anti-apartheid slogans on her dorm room wall,
and absolutely freaked out whenever anyone touched her pillow.

OK, so there is some odd female behavior that even *Cosmo* can't explain, but
these women are all a part of Dorrance's community, so he has to keep trying to
figure them out. While he may not be totally comfortable talking about his own
personal life, he is readily available to discuss anybody else's issues, the same way
Dean Smith has always shepherded his community. Dorrance will never force his
counsel on a player. They know where to find him. Some come. Some never come.
"His door would always be open if you wanted to talk to him," Kristine Lilly says.
"He would hang up the phone immediately for any player that came in, and that

was a huge thing. Whether you wanted to talk about soccer or how much you hate school, he was always there, and I dropped by a lot just to bounce stuff off of him."

Says Leslie Gaston: "I'd go into his office to talk about once a week. I'd talk to him about my boyfriend, my family, my friends, a lot of things outside of soccer. I really valued his opinion a lot. He's very knowledgeable, and he has a different perspective from anyone else I've met. Everything he says is backed by a sound argument."

"Anson helped me grow up," Machin says. "I needed to learn that the world didn't revolve around me. *Winning not whining.* It's amazing how much shit he had to put up with. Sometimes I'm surprised he didn't just drown all of us. He helped a lot of girls grow into women. The older you get the more you realize that game-winning goals are meaningless. Those and a quarter won't get you a cup of coffee. The personal growth is what matters."

Many of Dorrance's players treat him as a psychologist whose couch they visit regularly. He also answers an average of five phone calls and twenty e-mails a week from former players for whom he acts as everything from a marriage counselor to a legal advisor to a job placement service. "I e-mail back and forth with Anson ten times a year," Meredith Florance says. "Whenever I'm frustrated with my career and I need advice or encouragement, he's still always there to give it to me. Lots of former UNC players still look to him as a father figure."

Mia Hamm has taken that designation more seriously than anybody else. Hamm, an Air Force brat who had grown up all over the world, felt a special bond with her coach whose childhood story mirrored her own. Dorrance identified with this girl who viewed a soccer field as the closest place to a real home, and when Hamm matriculated at Chapel Hill at age seventeen, the eighth move of her young life, and then her parents moved to Italy, Hamm chose Dorrance to be her legal guardian. Hamm spoke with Dorrance often and studied how he related to people, how he conducted interviews, how he prepared for a game. Hamm says that aside from her late brother, Garrett, Dorrance has been the most influential person in her life. It meant a lot to Dorrance when during the 1999 World Cup, years after Hamm had moved away from North Carolina, she still listed Chapel Hill as her hometown on the national team roster. "Because of my relationship with Anson, of all the places I've lived, I grew up the most there," Hamm says. "At the beginning he can be sort of an intimidating person to get to know, but he'll show glimpses of himself that reassure you. He lives to invest in us."

Raven McDonald once asked Dorrance to talk to her boyfriend about proposing to her. Bettina Bernardi can remember breaking up with a boyfriend, retreating to Dorrance's office, crying her eyes out, and having Dorrance bluntly tell her, "Don't worry, he's not good enough for you." During one practice, Dorrance noticed that Julie Carter looked miserable, and when he inquired about the last time she'd eaten, she admitted it was two days earlier. After practice, Dorrance drove Carter to a bagel shop, and Carter opened up to him about a breakup with her girlfriend. The pair talked for three hours, during which

Dorrance told Carter about some of the unrequited crushes he'd had as a young man, and the two cried together for so long that Dorrance became dehydrated.

Dorrance once spent an hour over lunch before a game at Virginia talking with Anne Remy about Milan Kundera's *The Unbearable Lightness of Being,* which led into a discussion about an impending marriage proposal from Remy's boyfriend. Says Tom Sander: "Anson told Anne to ask some questions of herself. *Are you in it for the love? Or the sex? Or the money? Are you ready? How many kids do you both want?* More and more girls started gathering around them until eventually it looked like Jesus and his disciples. He may have been talking to one person, but the life lesson was for everyone."

These lessons can come at any time. Staci Wilson remembers a long van ride during her freshman year when she, Dorrance, and some of Wilson's teammates launched into a discussion inspired by a plot on *Melrose Place* in which a husband was caught on tape sleeping with a prostitute. Wilson recalls saying, "Gosh, I hope my husband loves me enough not to do something like that." Wilson's teammates nodded their agreement. Dorrance then replied, "You don't want a man who loves you enough that he won't do that. You want a man who won't do that because it's not the right thing to do. There are going to be good times, and there are going to be bad times, and there are going to be times when he feels like he doesn't love you very much. What should he do then?"

"For something that's a basic little concept, on a certain level it was profound," Wilson says. "I still think about what he said all the time with decision-making. I may want to do something, but then it doesn't appeal to me because it's the wrong thing to do."

Ever since Dorrance moved into his first office, a glorified closet behind the men's lacrosse office where he overheard regular boasting from players about their one-night stands, he became determined to counsel his women about the evils of associating with lacrosse players. Naturally, that virtually guaranteed that most of them would date a lacrosse player at some point in college. When Amy Burns began dating a lacrosse player in 1994, she approached Dorrance in the weight room one afternoon and said, 'Anson, guess what my boyfriend gave me?" Without missing a beat, Dorrance replied, "AIDS?"

Says Emily Rice: "I remember Anson would always tell us, 'Don't sacrifice yourself for some undergraduate dirtbag! You are more ambitious than just wanting to be somebody's wife.' I didn't know if he was right, but he sure knew how to get through to a twenty year old."

Whatever issues have confronted Dorrance's players, whether it is homosexuality or eating disorders, he has devoured every book he can find to become more educated on the subject. "I remember when Anson called me once to ask about anorexia," sports psychologist Colleen Hacker says. "He asked me to list every book he could read and then for some suggestions about how to combat it. Everybody wants the problem solved, they want to affect change in people, but they don't want to do the work to solve it. Where is the magic in that? Anson's willing to do the work."

"In this collegiate environment our players' emotions are spinning all over the place, there are life issues, sexuality issues, independence issues, parental issues," Chris Ducar says. "Anson's getting them at a pretty volatile time in their lives. What people eventually come to realize is how much he cares. Even the pains in the asses, he extended a hand to them."

In her first two years at UNC, Libby Guess fought problems with poor grades and subpar fitness. Dorrance reacted by enrolling in one of Guess's classes and attending it regularly to motivate her academically. He also personally confiscated Guess's dorm refrigerator to help her stay fit, and invited her to his house for dinner to advise her about nutrition. "Coming to UNC I would never have expected so much support," Guess says. "He gets in your head, and if you allow him to he can make a total positive impact on your life. He motivated me to work harder in school, to stop eating huge meals at four in the morning, to drink less beer, to change my lifestyle. He motivated me to motivate myself. No other coach ever knew how to talk to me without preaching to me."

Ever since Emily Pickering flatly rejected his no-swearing dictum in 1982, Dorrance has ruled without rules. At UNC there are no curfews, and there is no prohibition on drinking forty-eight hours before a game, two rules that are prevalent at other college programs. Dorrance doesn't want to be a policeman or a babysitter, because he never wants to stand in judgment of his players based on his conception of what is right and wrong. He asks only that his players show up on time and dress better than he does on the road, both of which are made easier by the fact that Dorrance is often late and dressed in sweats. It's all about responsibility. The good news is that when a Tar Heel arrives late for practice she is rarely disciplined, only lampooned by Dorrance saying, "Nice of you to mosey by." The bad news is that when a Tar Heel is given her airline ticket on a road trip and loses it, she is on her own to find her way back to Chapel Hill.

Dorrance doesn't want the players to see him as some sort of Orwellian Big Brother. He is one of the few coaches who gives his team Saturdays off between games on Friday and Sunday. He usually plays golf on those Saturdays and doesn't see his players at all, believing both sides can use the break. "In a weird way, it's part of the Carolina tradition that the girls are left on their own," Pete says. "They're not as nurtured as they might be in another program. They're treated as adults."

Dorrance's leniency exists partly because, given his own decadent college behavior, any other approach would smack of hypocrisy, and partly because he believes it is best to learn from your own mistakes as he once did. Dorrance had never endured rules. Not at the Villa. Not from Marvin Allen. How could a guy who went out drinking on nights before his own soccer games deny his players that right? If they can play through it, great. If they can't, they sit on the bench and learn a lesson. Dorrance believes that regulations often become more restrictive on coaches than players. "Why create all these ridiculous rules to entrap your players?" Dorrance says. "That just forces coaches into this melodramatic self-flagellation over whether to enforce their own rules or bench their best players. Do rules in life really construct you? I want to create a culture of correct behavior in which the players monitor themselves and you can trust them. Is it better to order people to do the right thing or to hope they choose it for themselves? The latter, I think, because then it's their own."

"Anson wasn't the cleanest-living college kid himself, but he learned from his experience and realized that's not the direction he wanted to go," Susan Ellis says. "He wanted us to ask ourselves the same question. Do you want to be a drughead or do you want to do something with your life? He didn't give us a list of things we needed to do to be a good human being, he let us stumble upon them, and we loved that."

"Anson wants his players to have the complete college experience, so he let us be responsible for ourselves rather than rebel against authority," Susan Bush says. "I made bad decisions all the time, and I learned from them. I remember the day before the N.C. State game my senior year I'd been out late drinking the night before, and I woke up at 2:30 for a 2:30 practice. It was a brain cramp. It was a miserable day of practice, and I vowed right then never to let that happen again. You screw up, you grow up."

"My dad treats his players the same way he's treated his kids," Michelle Dorrance says. "He never got angry with me. Anger inspires more anger. He'd be disappointed, and that is more powerful, more personal. He had expectations that you'd make the right decisions, and you wanted to live up to his trust."

"One of my first memories of Anson was when I got hired by the national team about a year before the '96 Olympics," Hacker says. "He said, 'You've got some of my kids there. Take good care of them.' I kind of gulped, but it wasn't like a threat. In essence he was saying, 'You've got something precious, something special.' I thought, 'Wow. His players are never out of sight. They may think they are, but he watches and he cares and he's aware. How beautiful is that?'"

During the 2003 season, sophomore Amy Steadman came to Dorrance's office and tearfully announced that she felt she needed to undergo knee surgery as soon as possible. Although Steadman was still mobile enough to give the Tar Heels quality minutes, Dorrance told her to have the surgery if that gave her peace of mind. "Anson let me know that my soccer life wasn't as important as my personal happiness, and I was really relieved," Steadman says. "I must have thanked him fifteen different times, and as I stood up to leave I gave him a huge hug as if I hadn't seen him in ten years. That moment really showed me what I had known all along, that this arrogant asshole, as so many refer to him, cares about me like no one I have ever met outside of my parents."

Dorrance felt confident in thinking big picture with Steadman because he'd been there before. Back in 1990, freshman Ange Kelly had broken her leg in the final scrimmage before the season opener. Dorrance visited Kelly at the hospital late that night, and they talked for more than an hour. Before leaving, Dorrance told Kelly, "Sometimes things in life don't always make sense, but they all happen for a reason. You might not realize the reason immediately, but maybe the reason is that you're supposed to hang out with me for an extra year."

Four years later as a redshirt senior, Kelly scored UNC's first goal in the Tar Heels' 5–0 win over Notre Dame in the 1994 NCAA championship game. "Late in that game I was having so much fun, and I remember stopping for a second to soak in the moment," Kelly says. "I looked over at Anson, and I remembered back to that time in the hospital and I thought, 'Anson, you were right. This all happened for a reason.'"

March 4, 2001
Anson,

I was sitting in my room the other day reflecting upon all the things I have grown to love in Chapel Hill. The classes, the restaurants, the beautiful scenery, the soccer team . . . and I stumbled across something a bit unusual . . . something I know I will miss more than I realize . . . sitting across the desk from you, chatting about soccer, chatting about our futures, and chatting about life. That occasional hour of banter has found a special place in my routine, and it is something that keeps me sane. In a hectic world of indecisive college students, many floating through their experience without passion and without purpose, I am sometimes tempted to join them, tempted to settle for being like everyone else, tempted to produce what is expected and nothing more. However, the sound of your voice and the words you say (and sometimes the words you don't say) remind me how short I will fall if I don't take the risk of failing or succeeding, the risk of attempting something excellent.

While I am confident in my own ability, the support and endorsement you give to me means so much more than you or anyone else realizes. I want to fulfill your every expectation, and I want to surpass them. Anson, I never realized that what I would be gaining from soccer was a window to success, but somehow that is what has happened. I have many acquaintances in Chapel Hill but only a few friends, as my friendship is not something I easily give. You have won my friendship and my respect, and I am so thankful to have two more years to straighten out my life with your instruction and watchful eye. Thank you for your time, your encouragement, and please always expect the best from me.

Jordan Walker

It's a few minutes before four o'clock on a chilly late October afternoon when Heather O'Reilly and Libby Guess, two wonderfully blank freshman canvases, wander into Dorrance's office wearing Asian sun hats that they have just bought in town for their Halloween costumes and it is the first day of their first Fall Break and there is no practice today, so it is a time to be free, and the girls are both away from home for the first time and don't know what to do with themselves, and so they put their feet up and Anson leans back in his chair and ignores the many growing piles on his desk, and they talk in stream of consciousness the way teenagers do about the *The Cruel Sea,* the first great book Dorrance ever read, and how it turned him onto reading and how O'Reilly should start reading more than *Cosmo* and romance novels, and he shares a quote he has just read, *College is about books, which are for broadening your mastery of one or more important subjects that will go on deepening your understanding of the world, yourself, and the people around you,* and while he's reading Guess copies down quotes from his quote book and asks about self-discipline, and Dorrance says to follow O'Reilly's example, prompting O'Reilly to ask if leaders are born or can be bred, and Dorrance replies by asking 'What do you think?,' and she says she doesn't see herself as a born leader, and Dorrance tells her to study some of Guess's leadership qualities and tells her to ask Guess, a more sophisticated reader, for a potential book list while she's at it, and O'Reilly asks about living a fuller life, and Dorrance recites a quote from a Pat Conroy book about how there should be "two lives apportioned to every man and every woman" so people wouldn't have to miss out on so much, which is something he wants them both to know, and Guess volunteers her newly discovered passion for kung fu movies, and they talk about whether study hall is really how two hours can best be spent and what GPA is required to escape it and about which cereal is better, Raisin Bran or Cocoa Krispies, and they talk about climbing Mount Everest and dating and dieting, and about how even the most inane geography class can be valuable if seen from a broader world view, and then just about life for a while and about that Conroy guy and Kerouac and Capote, and Dorrance urges these girls not to make the same dumb mistakes he did as a college kid, and he shares some examples of his three years wasted, while Guess sends Dorrance a text message on his cell phone, *Yo Dawg,* to see if he can respond to it and, of course, he can't, and O'Reilly asks about ambition, to which Dorrance says that even the most perfect person should want to be perfecter, and during the whole time they are together Dorrance is subtly trying to instill O'Reilly's discipline into Guess and Guess's intellectual curiosity into O'Reilly, using the strengths of those around them to fill in their weaknesses, investing in them the way Big Pete once did with him, investing in their futures and his own in a way, and before they all know it they have dorked off for more than two hours, none of the three uttering a single word about soccer, until Dorrance realizes he's ten minutes late for roller hockey and he leaves the girls behind, still wearing those silly hats, to lock up as he proudly struts out the door of McCaskill and says, "*That* is why I coach."

June 17, 2003

Hey everyone,

I hope you are all having a good summer. I can't believe it's going to be my senior year. I feel so old! My college years and seasons have really flown by. But I am writing to you all because I don't want this season to pass like last year's or the one from the year before. I'm sick of this 2nd and 3rd place bullshit.

I just wanted to remind you of how it felt to walk off that field in Texas last year. I mean, we didn't even make the finals. And, we got knocked out by Santa Clara . . . for the SECOND time. I'm so sick of getting that far and then losing. We are better than that; we deserve more.

This season is still a month and a half away, but I wanted to write to you all now, because I know how important it is to prepare in advance. If passing fitness motivates you to run, that's great, but that has never motivated me. What motivates me is the potential to get to that final game, and seeing my defender bent over, with her hands on her knees, and me cruising by her. And then the second thing that motivates me is taking back our National Championship. That's why we are working hard right now. Because the trophy belongs to us, and we need to get it back this year. The potential of our team this year is incredible. I want us to totally dominate like Carolina used to, back in the day. I want to go into the tournament knowing that without a doubt we are the best team there. But that can only happen if we put on a show from the beginning. We need to work hard and get shit done this summer.

This isn't some bullshit school. We are the University of North Carolina. Don't forget that.

Maggie Tomecka

They are bound by a common crucible, a burden for some, which is never discussed among them. Not among the players. Not among the coaches. Heck, you can't escape the history, but it is only referenced when reporters come calling, because the question is so deliciously compelling. How could they not ask? *What does the pressure feel like to try to maintain a dynasty?*

"We've all felt the huge weight of the tradition on our shoulders," Alyssa Ramsey says. "That's the deal with the devil you make when you pull on a Carolina uniform."

Says Carmen Watley: "Even my friends who didn't follow soccer would ask me after the season, 'Hey, did you guys win the national championship again this year?' When I said we didn't, they were like, '*What happened?!*' Whenever anybody loses to us they say, 'Big deal. Everybody loses to UNC.' But anytime we lose, then people immediately say the dynasty is dead. It's like we're not allowed to lose."

Dorrance laughs at the antiquated notion that if he doesn't win the national championship every season he should be fired. "At the end of every championship season I tell myself, 'Now would be a good time to die,' but unfortunately I keep surviving and then I have to try to do it again," Dorrance says. "How many programs are good enough to claim a national championship as the only road to success? I want each UNC team to fulfill its own destiny and not be saddled with a tradition that can be oppressive, but we understand there's a wonderful underlying pressure that we all live with."

"You can't help but feel the burden of our tradition," Heather O'Reilly says. "When I was being recruited I thought, 'Holy shit, do I want to risk being a part of UNC's downfall? Do I want to risk being a part of a losing streak? I'm not going to lie. It was a little scary to be the only team that really has anything to lose, but it's thrilling as well."

"Anson recruits players who enjoy pressure, players who want to take a penalty kick in front of ten thousand people to win or lose an NCAA championship, players who aren't bothered that their mistakes make headlines in the newspaper," former UNC assistant coach Bill Steffen says. "You have to enjoy that pressure because you're going to be subjected to that at UNC, and if they can't handle it they're going to crumble."

UNC doesn't get to celebrate most wins like everybody else. Any victory before the NCAA title game is viewed as merely a means to an end. "It's like we're not permitted to celebrate until we win the national title, until we've proven our point," Jena Kluegel says. "Otherwise, we're just expected to win every game. *OK, that one's done. Next?*"

Even winning the ultimate game is sometimes viewed as more of a relief than an opportunity for exultation, because the Tar Heels are always viewed as the tournament favorite. "It's a little sad for them that they're expected to win it all every year," former Santa Clara midfielder Aly Wagner says. "UNC winning a national championship should still be an amazing accomplishment, but no one looks at it that way, and that's wrong."

UNC players come to understand that because they lose so rarely, every game is potentially a part of history, every game is a potential crack in the mystique. Every generation of players is responsible for the torch passed on by the previous one. "When we lost the first game at Fetzer ever, it was sickening because it felt like we let down all the alumni," Ange Kelly says. "We felt like we didn't fulfill the obligation that everybody prior to us filled. We disappointed a lot of former Tar Heels, and that's what really sucked."

Says Watley: "There's a whole nation of alumni out there that's expecting us to win every game, and when we lose you wonder, 'What are they going to think now? What are they going to start saying about us?'"

At a UNC soccer reunion in 1989, April Heinrichs broke down sobbing at the podium while recalling her memories of losing the NCAA championship game four years earlier. At an alumni gathering following UNC's NCAA defeat in 1995, Staci Wilson recalls choking up repeatedly because she felt so guilty. The only alumni who could console Wilson were the players who had endured the Tar Heels' only other NCAA Tournament loss a decade before.

Wendy Gebauer and Susan Ellis still attend almost every UNC game, and dozens more Tar Heel alums show up for the Final Fours. Suzy Cobb's Internet home page is the UNC women's soccer web site. After Maggie Tomecka graduated in 2004, she followed live play-by-play of UNC games on the Internet from her medical school apartment on the Caribbean island of Dominica, becoming one of many former Tar Heels who track the team closely on the web. "The alumni are more fanatical about Carolina soccer than the current players because they appreciate the tradition more and don't want it to end," Lorrie Fair says. "I remember when I was a freshman at the Final Four and I met Rita Tower, and she grabbed me by my shirt, got in my face and said, 'You better win this fucking championship!' I didn't understand what she was doing until I was the alum looking around for someone to yell at."

At UNC soccer reunions the players who won four national titles tease the ones who won only three. The players who have won fewer than three view themselves as untouchables. "Our alumni have unrealistic expectations," Tom Sander says. "They can be very critical, and it's intimidating to have Mia Hamm and Cindy Parlow and the others sitting in the stands. They've all won so much. They think they were perfect, and some of them were."

There is a general suspicion among the alums that the more contemporary players are too soft. "In 1995 when we came back for the ten-year reunion of our championships and we watched UNC lose, we were all saying, 'I wonder what that would feel like?' Amy Machin says. "We were in disbelief. They were losing the national semifinal and their jerseys were still clean. That's not acceptable."

"I sure as hell hope that winning the national title means as much to the modern player as it did to me," Gebauer says. "I was petrified not to carry on the tradition. I didn't want to let the program down. I didn't want to let the alumni down. It was my turn, our turn, to carry that responsibility. Winning national championships is why you're here. It's your job. It would piss me off if I ever sensed that it wasn't important to somebody at UNC, because there are hundreds of kids out there dying to be in their position."

Catherine Reddick, who completed her career in 2003, believes it's unreasonable for the UNC alumni to hold the more recent Tar Heel teams to the same standards because the competition is much fiercer. "It's a little unfair that the alumni still expected us to win every game," she says. "We didn't want to disappoint them because we know they did so much for us, but it was tough when you saw a former Tar Heel and she'd ask, 'Are y'all going to win it this year?' You could see in her eyes that we had better win, that she was expecting us to win, that maybe she believed that she shouldn't even need to ask that question."

Says Chris Ducar: "I respect every player who comes to UNC, because of the awesome responsibility. I can't believe the pressure that these girls play with. The fallacy is that you show up in Chapel Hill and you're anointed a national champion, so people dismiss the dedication of our girls. Our players are bonded together by this mission. They are always defending the castle."

12/4/03

anson,

well it's almost midnight. can't get to sleep yet. felt like e-mailing you. i was remembering the 1997 final four. i had so many emotions flying through my body that weekend. i knew that dec. 8th would be the very last time i would play soccer competitively, and with all my best friends in the entire world. it was a strange feeling knowing that soccer, something that has been a part of my everyday life for as long as I had memory, was going to forever be changed. rereading that sentence makes it seem so dramatic! but it was . . . it still is. it wasn't just the soccer of course. it was knowing that i wouldn't be going out to practice at 2:30 with my girls to hang out. you know . . . it really was just hanging out with friends. practicing and kicking each other's asses for 90 minutes was just something we did while we were there. i won't lie . . . i never would've thought of practices in that way while i was at UNC. no player in their right frickin' mind would. but i do now, and damn do i miss those days! i remember times like these and i have to tell myself, "dude, move on, get out of the glory days" but you know what? i can't remember one bad moment during my time playing for carolina. well, let me rephrase that. i CAN remember a lot of shitty moments . . . times where i thought my lungs would burst, or my legs would buckle. times where my heart was torn or my feelings hurt b/c you yelled one of your horrible famous insults in front of everyone which gave me visions of making a voodoo doll of you and sticking pins in it! I DO remember all these shitty moments, but i have a big fat smile on my face when i think of them!

i am so proud to see us go to another final four. from what i hear, this is one of the best teams to go through carolina. the girls should know they can just close their eyes and feel the strength, courage and pride of 22 years worth of champions on the field with them. opposing teams can feel it too!

thanks for listening Anson . . . be thinking of you and the girls all this weekend!

aubrey falk (aubs)

It began as a group hug, basically, because nobody ever sets out to start a tradition. The Tar Heel alums in attendance at the 1998 Final Four gathered together at the postgame party for a toast with the seniors who had just completed their careers. By the time it became clear that this ceremony would take place annually on the night of UNC's final game, this makeshift reunion had been dubbed the "Alumni Club."

About the same time that the university began to outlaw the traditional season-opening initiation hazing rituals, the Alumni Club was born, one sacred ritual replacing another. The original inspiration behind the club was Wendy Gebauer, who is the closest person UNC has to an alumni coordinator. "Win or lose, we wanted our seniors not to suffer a letdown," Gebauer says. "Suddenly their careers are over and they don't want to accept that they're done. We want them to know that no matter if they are a superstar or they never played a second, we are one big family. It's hard to hold back the tears because we have more appreciation for what they go through each season, and sharing that with them is very emotional. Alumni Club is a lot more fun when we win the championship, but it may be more impactful when we don't."

Just past 1 a.m. on the night of UNC's 2002 NCAA semifinal loss to Santa Clara in Austin, Texas, Gebauer placed a cell phone call to Cindy Parlow, who immediately phoned Ange Kelly and Kristine Lilly and Mia Hamm, and within thirty minutes a Mount Rushmore of UNC soccer gathered at the TGI Friday's bar in the Austin Radisson. Just before last call, the five Tar Heel alums bought shots for themselves and the three seniors, Jenni Branam, Susan Bush, and Leslie Gaston, all of whom had stubbornly refused to shed their uniforms. It seemed appropriate that Southern Comfort was the drink of choice as the group of eight moved off to a secluded corner of the restaurant and formed a circle for the toast.

Gebauer: *I guess I'll start. We know you all are disappointed about what happened tonight, but we're here to tell you that as alumni we are so proud of how you played and how you represented UNC. You guys had a great season, and losing that game doesn't take away from that. It's been fun watching you guys play and watching you guys grow up, and we hope you keep coming back to watch the next generations play and grow. I think I speak for all the alums when I say thank you for all you've done for UNC soccer the last four years.*

Parlow: *I remember this tradition started back in 1998 when we lost the national championship. We were all bummed, and I remember how the alums rallied around us and showed us that whether or not you win or lose, the most important thing you get at Carolina are the close friends you make and being a part of this unbelievably close family of players. Don't ever forget that.*

Kelly: *To follow up on what Cindy said, while I may be the coach at Tennessee now, in my heart I will always be a Tar Heel. That special feeling never leaves you. We are all incredibly lucky to be able to have called this program home, and it will remain your home no matter where you go in your lives. Long after we've all forgotten what happened on the field tonight, you'll still have that.*

Lilly: *Keep in mind that playing is just the first phase of the UNC experience. I know this feels like an ending, but it is also a beginning, the beginning of your lives as UNC alums. You should be happy about that because we're all here to tell you that in some ways that is the most fun time of all. Welcome to the other side.*

Hamm: *Anson always talks about community and that's really why we're all here tonight. Each of you is one of us. Only those lucky few of us who have had the honor of wearing a Carolina uniform can understand this feeling and be part of a community that you will come to understand has this unbelievable value in your life. We are all here for you now and we always will be and we know you'll always be there for us. Cherish that.*

Now, as we always say at the end of these things. . . . It's better to be a has-been than a never-was.

Eight glasses clinked, and the Tar Heels huddled together in an even tighter circle.

A Day in September

Every young man needs an old man. Because getting older is like climbing a mountain. Each year the older you get, the higher you are, the more distance you can see. You can warn the people below you what you see so they don't run up against things.

—Ann Iverson describing her son Allen's
relationship with coach Larry Brown

Although he did not know it yet, this was a day that Anson Dorrance had been waiting for his entire adult life. He had a tee time set for 8 a.m. at UNC's Finley Golf Course. It was supposed to be a twosome, Dorrance and former UNC basketball coach Bill Guthridge.

Dorrance's alarm clock sounded at 7:30, and he awoke to find M'Liss suffering from the first migraine headache she had ever experienced. Dorrance fetched his wife some aspirin and a cool washcloth for her forehead, all the time hoping that in the darkness she wouldn't notice he was dressed in golf clothes.

He arrived at the golf course at 8:04, a potentially calamitous faux pas in the world of UNC basketball, where watches are always precisely synchronized. "You're late," Guthridge said with a teasing smile. "You'll have to do sprints, and you won't be allowed to dress for our next game."

Dorrance grinned sheepishly at Guthridge who was sitting in a golf cart with his golf bag strapped to the back. A second cart was parked directly behind it with another golf bag attached. Dorrance peeked over toward the practice putting green and spotted an unmistakable silhouette. Dean Smith.

For years, Dorrance had dreamed about the day he might play golf with UNC's basketball coaching icon. Dorrance openly refers to Smith, who retired in 1997, as his "earthly mentor" even while admitting that the two men never shared so much as a substantive conversation in the twenty-five years they worked in the same athletic department. Everything that Dorrance has gleaned from Smith has come from watching him on the bench, reading every newspaper article and book written about him, studying his every move. His admiration for Smith is almost childlike. Dozens of times during the last two decades, Dorrance had wondered what it would be like to someday be invited into Smith's exclusive inner sanctum. Over the years, the two coaches had chatted a few times about their mutual obsession with golf and talked about playing a round together. But Dorrance had vowed that he would never telephone Smith about it, never put the reclusive man in a position where he might feel cornered. He'd wait for Smith to call. Or not call.

A few months before that September morning, Dorrance speculated about the possibility when he said, "I know Dean is incredibly uncomfortable being revered, and I would never put him in a position that makes him feel uncomfortable, but if I'm ever in a golf cart with him, I'll ask him all the questions I've always wanted to. Who knows if I'm going to learn any more than I've already stolen from him, or even if I have to? But I know I'm going to get something."

As Dorrance strapped his bag onto Smith's cart that morning, he realized to his chagrin that his golf spikes were not in his bag. He had played golf the day before and arrived so late to soccer practice that he'd worn his golf shoes during training. After practice he had forgotten to put the shoes back into his bag. He would have to play the round with Smith and Guthridge in sneakers. As the threesome drove to the first tee, Dorrance was thinking, "Oh my gosh, these men are going to think that I'm an absolute clown." Sure enough, the first comment out of Smith's mouth was a wry dig at Dorrance's footwear.

On the first tee, Smith spent a few moments laying out the rules for competition, as he always does when he plays with somebody new. Gimmes must be inside the leather, winter rules in the fairway, one mulligan on the first tee. Dorrance loved Smith's guidelines, because it was exactly the way he always structures sports in his own mind. Dorrance wanted rules governing the competition that eliminated all the social graces that he might normally extend to people in positions of respect like Smith or Guthridge, leaving only the pure contest. The trio agreed on a small stakes wager. Unbeknownst to his playing partners, Dorrance, who hadn't expected to bet, had only six bucks in his pocket.

After Dorrance's first putt on the opening green, he laid down his putter and discovered that part of his ball reached the edge of the leather. Smith ruled that he would have to putt it out. Dorrance immediately embraced Smith's competitiveness. Just as Dorrance had suspected, he and Smith were kindred spirits.

In the ninth fairway, just as Dorrance was beginning to feel comfortable, a maintenance man on a lawn mower approached the threesome.

"Did you hear?" the man asked.

"Hear what?" Smith said.

"A plane hit the World Trade Center."

"What?" Smith said. "Are you sure?"

Smith asked the man for more information, but he didn't know any details. The three coaches assumed it was a prop plane. Shortly thereafter, M'Liss and Chris Ducar each attempted to call Dorrance on his cell phone to inform him about the day's tragic events, but he had left his phone in the car.

During the four-hour round, Smith and Dorrance never once talked about coaching. They talked about their daughters, who had become friends over the years. They talked about Bill Palladino, whom Smith had watched grow up in Chapel Hill. They talked about their longtime colleague, UNC assistant athletic director John Lotz, who had passed away a few months before. At one point on the back nine, Smith turned to Guthridge and told him a story about the day when Lotz's daughter, Laci, married Jake McDowell, the brother of two girls who played soccer for Dorrance at UNC. The wedding reception was located at a home down a narrow, winding road on the outskirts of Chapel Hill, and the guests drove there in a violent thunderstorm, during which Dorrance stood in the soaking rain, acting as a volunteer traffic cop. "Anson," Smith told Guthridge, "was the hero of the wedding."

As the three coaches completed their round of golf that day, they had no idea about the scale of the catastrophe that morning. They could never have imagined the Twin Towers collapsing or another jet crashing into the Pentagon. What they did notice was that as the morning passed, fewer and fewer golfers were on the course. Once, when Guthridge mishit a shot, he said, "I was wondering about that plane."

Smith responded, "We all are."

Guthridge took copious notes on his scorecard throughout the round, meticulously compiling the scores and the points for the bet. For the first time he could ever remember in any round of golf, Dorrance did not keep his own score. At the end of the round as Guthridge tallied up the results, Smith turned to Dorrance and whispered, "We can trust Bill. He was a math major."

Dorrance shot an 88, right on his handicap. He beat Smith and lost to Guthridge. Finishing in the middle was exactly where he wanted to be. As he began devising a precautionary payment plan in which he would drive to his bank directly from the golf course and drop off his gambling debt at the Dean Smith Center, he was informed that he'd broken even. As Guthridge and Dorrance loaded their golf clubs into their cars, Smith returned from the clubhouse and said, "I've just seen what happened. We'll remember this day forever."

By the time Dorrance returned to his office a mile from the golf course, the round with his earthly mentor had been largely forgotten. None of his staff would learn for several days that he'd just lived out one of his adult fantasies by playing a round of golf with his coaching idol. Ducar walked into Dorrance's office, sat down, and turned on the television that hangs from the ceiling in the corner opposite Dorrance's desk. Jordan Walker showed up in search of company and took the other chair. Tom Sander stood in the doorway. Dorrance said, "Can you believe this is happening?" Then the four fell silent for almost an hour. "Anson was speechless," Sander says. "I had never seen him speechless."

Dorrance found himself profoundly moved by the powerful confluence of his bonding with the coach he most respected in the world and the ghastly images playing out on the television in front of him. The distressing events sparked a flashback to his youth in Singapore, where his family regularly practiced emergency drills, dashing into a bomb shelter in their front yard.

The silence in the soccer office was finally broken by a phone call from M'Liss saying that Anson's mother, Peggy, had received a brief phone call from their daughter Michelle in New York City to say that she was safe and would call back again later in the day. Dorrance, Ducar, and Walker drove to lunch and talked about who could have masterminded the attack and then returned to the soccer office and clicked on the television again. It was the first time in his coaching career that Dorrance had ever prepared to go to practice with the television on. He sat there still speechless, pondering a speech. "Eventually the performer came out in him," Sander says. "He always says that the team takes on the character of its coach, and he wanted them to feel as defiant as he did."

As Dorrance approached the practice field at 2:30 that afternoon, his players instinctively set off on their pre-practice jog. Dorrance stopped them and waved them in. He consciously repositioned his players so that their backs were to the sun, the late summer glare shining into his own eyes, an old coaching tactic. He wanted his players to be able to look at him without squinting as he spoke.

I was born and raised overseas, and there's a love/hate relationship between everyone that lives abroad and the United States. What we saw today was an example of the hate. What everyone out there who hates us wants us to do is to be affected by this, and there is no way we're going to give them that satisfaction. They want us to change our lives, they want us to never fly again, never build a building over twenty stories. They want us not to practice today, and we won't let them win. We're going to train today and tomorrow and the day after that as if none of this ever happened. We won't be affected by this. Obviously if someone has a relative or a friend in New York we'll be sensitive to that. My daughter called from there. She's fine. So for this, we don't change our lives. That's evil, and that's what they want you to do, and the way to combat it is not to change anything. In a much smaller way, the only way you give satisfaction to a thug is when they smack you and you're writhing around on the ground. If you get smacked by one of these thugs, it's going to hurt, but the best way to combat that is to pretend like it doesn't. What we do as a soccer team really has no significance. Athletics itself has no intrinsic value. If it has any value, it's in what you bring to it. The value you bring to it is your humanity, and the value in this context is our connection. I value the richness of my experiences the last twenty years coaching this team. That has value. There is no better context to review the importance of those connections than this day when this horrific, insensitive killing of your fellow man has taken place. If we cherish something from all of this, it's that we care for each other and that there is a connection between all of us. Let this be a positive reminder, not a negative one. Are you with me?

Dorrance realized immediately that his tone and his words on the relative importance of athletics were both borrowed directly from Dean Smith. As the September 11 practice unfolded, there was no evidence that anything unusual had occurred that day. It was one of the most competitive training sessions of the season. "One of Anson's axioms is, 'Never let your players see your stress,'" Ducar says. "He was giving them permission to be soccer players for that hour and a half, and they blasted through it."

When Dorrance returned home that night after practice, he and M'Liss watched more coverage of the attack on television. Every few minutes, M'Liss instinctively pressed the redial button on the cordless phone, hoping to hear her daughter Michelle's voice, but instead she got a recording that informed her that all the circuits were busy. M'Liss kept thinking about a Muslim houseboy her family had once employed in Ethiopia and the demeaning teasing he endured from the African servants whenever he prayed. Anson experienced the same patriotic ardor he'd felt as a scorned little white boy in Addis Ababa in the late 1950s, or when he horsewhipped a neophyte U.S. national soccer team to the 1991 World Championship in communist China. "Anson told me, 'You have to understand the self-righteousness with which we were attacked and understand how the terrorists irrationally yet passionately believe that as Americans we are all the devil,'" M'Liss recalls. "I was stunned and overwhelmed by what had taken place, but Anson was much more philosophical, trying to put an astronomically hateful act into some context that would make sense to me."

Anson, who usually goes to bed by 10 p.m., stayed up with M'Liss watching the news reports until 1 a.m. As they finally walked upstairs to bed, the phone rang. It was Michelle. She told her parents that she was OK. She said that when the attack occurred she was at the library reading Sir Thomas More's *Utopia,* and that she planned to spend part of the following day, her twenty-second birthday, donating blood.

As the Dorrances lay in bed, Anson told M'Liss about the two times in his life when he thought he was going to die on an airplane. Twice he'd been on flights when the pilot informed the passengers that the landing gear wasn't functional and asked them to prepare for a crash landing. While both disabled planes eventually coaxed down their wheels and landed safely, Anson told his wife that those moments were particularly poignant for him, because his uncle, his namesake, had died in a plane crash on D-Day. "What all of us should want to do, is die well," he told M'Liss. "You don't want to have the plane going down and you screaming, '*I DON'T WANT TO DIE!!*' You want to have some dignity. There are ways to die well. There's a great scene in the movie *Braveheart* when Mel Gibson's character is about to be led out of his prison cell for his public execution. A visitor comes into his cell and asks him, 'Are you afraid of dying?' He says, 'No, I'm not afraid of dying, I'm afraid of dying badly.' That's a great statement."

How could Dorrance have ever imagined these would be his final thoughts on September 11, 2001? On this day when, by his own definition, so many fellow Americans had perished so bravely, died so well, he thought about the irony of a morning on the golf course spent talking about keeping score, about trust, about heroes, and about rules at a time when so many rules had been shattered.

As Dorrance turned off the light beside his bed, he reviewed this day and wondered if it was all real or had he merely dreamt it and he had a tee time in a few hours with Bill Guthridge. He thought about Dean Smith, and he thought back to sitting at his desk over lunch, fingering through his quote book to recall the words of Ann Iverson. He thought about looking into the eyes of his players with the sun at their backs at practice that afternoon, and he realized he was becoming that old man climbing the mountain, seeing farther and farther into the distance, and how it was up to him to keep warning his young women so they wouldn't run up against things.

22 | *Emanating Rings*

What do you do when your real life exceeds your dreams?

—from the movie *Broadcast News*

*In the beginning . . . there was women's soccer at Carolina.
And from it emanated women's soccer throughout the southeast.
And the Tar Heels looked back at what they begat, and they were pleased.*

Call it foresight. Call it prophecy. Or call it a lucky guess. In the September 12, 1979, edition of the *Daily Tar Heel,* previewing UNC women's soccer's first-ever varsity game, staff writer Marjo Rankin's poetic lead predicted the future. Later in the brief story on page 9, UNC's coach, Anson Dorrance, told Rankin about his aspirations for the new program.

As word gets out that we have a women's varsity other schools will try to follow suit. It's very inexpensive to maintain, so we feel schools will have no qualms about starting it . . . We're very confident about playing anyone. We look forward to playing a match we'll lose or barely win because our great fear is that we won't have competition. Our concern is not so much win or lose as it is developing the game. Our function is trying to encourage other schools to establish varsity teams . . . I see nothing but benefits. Because we're the first, we'll try to stay on top. We'll encourage people in the state and in the East to come here.

Teams came from the state. They came from the East. They eventually came from the West and North and South. Same thing kept happening. Not many of them provided UNC much competition. Still don't.

In the program's first twenty-seven seasons, Dorrance's North Carolina teams posted a record of 602-27-18, a winning percentage of .944, averaging exactly one loss per season against the toughest annual schedule in the country. During the program's history, the Tar Heels have outscored their opponents 2,725–303. They have averaged 4.2 goals per game, and, despite playing the riskiest defensive system in the sport, have allowed only .47 goals per game. They have shut out their opponents in 428 of 647 total games, while being held scoreless just 18 times.

The longest losing "streak" in UNC history is two games. Against college competition, the Tar Heels have never lost by more than two goals, have never even trailed by more than two goals during a game, and have lost only three games by more than one goal. After falling 2–0 to George Mason in the 1985 NCAA final, they have not lost a game, more than 500 in a row and counting, by more than one goal since. Since the Tar Heels established their championship tradition in 1981, the team has never allowed more than three goals in a game, and has allowed more than two goals only eight times.

The Tar Heels have won eighteen of the twenty-five national championships ever contested. Notre Dame and Portland have each won two. No other team has more than one. No coach other than Dorrance has won more than one title, and while UNC has reached twenty-two of twenty-four NCAA Final Fours, no other team has gone to more than Santa Clara's ten. While UNC has made twenty appearances in the national championship game, no other program has reached more than five. Overall, the Tar Heels have won eighty-six NCAA Tournament games against seven defeats, losing in the finals three times, the semifinals twice, and once each in the third round and fourth rounds, and when Dorrance is asked about it, he says, "We're still pissed that we lost those seven."

"Gosh, I wish I had those numbers," Santa Clara coach Jerry Smith says. "It's ridiculous, impossible, inconceivable. Nobody should win that much. I try not to look at the numbers because I'm so embarrassed. Holy Toledo, what are the rest of us doing?"

Says Colorado coach Bill Hempen: "I've been coaching for twenty years now, and I've been hearing about how other schools are catching up to Carolina since I started. Seems like other college coaches are always saying, 'Give it five more years.' Then after five years, 'Give it five more years.' There's Carolina, and then there's everybody else. The only parity in our game is among the rest of us from No. 2 on down."

UNC's late chancellor Michael Hooker once referred to Tar Heel women's soccer as "a species with no other members." Marcia McDermott has noticed in her travels as a coach that journalists around the country have utilized the UNC soccer program as a metaphor for success.

"It's funny, but the notion of winning and losing was never really a part of our mindset," Ange Kelly says. "We never thought about our winning streaks. It wasn't like, 'Good job ladies, that's ninety in a row, let's keep the streak going.' We just kept playing, and all we ever cared about was that in each game nobody got the better of us."

Says Julie Foudy: "I am just in awe of how Anson's been able to consistently win and win and win without any lulls. It goes against the logic of soccer. That's not just luck. It's not because he goes to church every Sunday. It's *him*. He's the common denominator in all those years."

Many in the soccer world argue that UNC's abundance of victories is actually less remarkable than its scarcity of defeats. "The most amazing thing to me about UNC is not that they've won all those championships, but that they've been upset so few times when every team in the country is looking to play their best game against them," N.C. State coach Laura Kerrigan says. "The soccer record books are full of upsets, because it's not always the team with the most national team players that wins. Sometimes it's the team who has fought hardest to win that day. UNC wins both ways. A lot of people could coach Anson's teams and win a lot of games, but would those coaches' teams get upset more? Yes."

Says Florida coach Becky Burleigh: "What strikes me most about Anson is that coaching UNC really is not an enviable job. He's got so little budget, no players nearby to recruit, he has to share his field with the lacrosse team, and yet he still wins and defends national championships year after year, which I know from experience is unbelievably hard to do."

Dorrance says that his favorite compliment to the UNC soccer program occurred the day after Dean Smith won his first NCAA basketball championship in 1982. Smith stepped out of his office in Carmichael Auditorium and crossed paths with Dorrance, who had won his first national title four months earlier. As Dorrance began to congratulate Smith, the older coach gently cut him off and said, "Anson, all we do around here is try to keep up with women's soccer."

Smith's acknowledgment wouldn't go public until fifteen years later at a press conference in the summer of 1997, when he was questioned by a sportswriter about the Tar Heels' preseason No. 1 ranking in football. *What's it like for a sport other than basketball to be in the spotlight at UNC?* Smith famously responded, "This is a women's soccer school. We're just trying to keep up with them."

By that time, these were validating words from history's winningest college basketball coach to history's winningest college soccer coach. For years, Dorrance has given Smith much of the credit for teaching him how to coach and said that he used the consistent success of Smith's basketball program, which won twenty games or more for twenty-seven straight seasons, as a model for his own. "I'm pleased that maybe Anson has picked up something from watching me, but he's given me way too much credit," Smith says. "Anson's a talented leader. This didn't just happen accidentally. I admire very much what he's done. It's hard to compare to anything, anywhere."

Dorrance says one must only examine his coaching career to realize the importance of his mentor, because he swears he's been making this up as he goes along. "To have something like this fall into my lap is an incredible stroke of fortune, and I'll never pretend it's anything more than that," Dorrance says. "I was just a boy, really, who happened to be sitting on the crest of this tidal wave that would impact an entire sport. I am frigging stunned because I never really planned for all this success, but then all of a sudden you look back and something good has happened."

Former UNC athletic director Bill Cobey calls Dorrance "a good hire," laughing at the understatement. "Twenty-five years ago I saw the ingredients of a very successful program, but there's a difference between seeing and actually doing it," Cobey says. "Anson grasped the little vision that I had and took it beyond my wildest imagination. I asked him to run the 100-yard dash in under ten seconds, and then I watched him do it year after year. How could you possibly expect someone to produce those results? It's like that movie, *The Natural*. Anson was born to coach, he was in the right place at the right time, and the rest is history."

The only dynasty that Dorrance has ever acknowledged is right there outside his office window. Not on Fetzer Field. Beyond that. Across the track. Past the tote board with all the Carolina blue championship tiles. Up the hill to the dormitory. To Teague. He can see his old room. It also overlooks the soccer field.

Years later, the men of Teague banded together for one last intramural cause. It began with a casual remark from Dorrance to Jack Simmons, and then the old intramural director picked up the ball. He staged a reunion that brought back boys from all of Teague's seventeen straight intramural championships, most of whom had never met and had little in common besides the same college dorm address. Together they helped build a monument to a dynasty. There was no megabucks donor among the seventy-five Teague alums who chipped in, just a team effort like there had always been. Down a staircase from Dorrance's office in the plush McCaskill Soccer Center, which opened in 1999, there is a plaque facing out toward Teague that reads:

> Teague Dorm (perennial residence hall intramural champions from 1970–87) would like to recognize another athletic dynasty, the UNC women's soccer team, as well as former Teague alumnus Anson Dorrance for his role in both dynasties . . . With each passing year our memories become less trustworthy and our accomplishments become accordingly more heroic. Our wish is that our memories continue to decline and our accomplishments continue to rise, thereby justifying our self-proclaimed legendary status.

It makes sense, this plaque affixed to this building, because in many ways the dynasty Dorrance acknowledges and the one he does not are one and the same. Says Simmons, "One of the reasons Anson's so fond of Teague is that he once told me, 'I teach my women how to play like we did in intramurals. We played hard, we played together, we had the killer instinct, and we really cared about each other.' Like Teague, UNC soccer hasn't just won a series of championships. You go past series, all the way to dynasty."

The word *dynasty* started cropping up in newspaper articles about UNC women's soccer as early as 1983. At the 1987 Final Four, Massachusetts coach Jim Rudy said, "Carolina women's soccer will be bigger than UCLA basketball. They will be the biggest dynasty forever in any sport."

Still, for twenty years, it was the one question Dorrance never knew how to answer. *Is UNC women's soccer a dynasty?* No matter how Dorrance responded, it sounded like the kind of hubris he never wanted his fellow coaches to hear. "If people want to consider us a dynasty," Dorrance would say, "let them understand it is a dynasty of hard work, a dynasty of year-round play, and a dynasty of commitment to being the best."

Then, following the 2003 NCAA championship, Wendy Gebauer forwarded Dorrance an e-mail she had received from a friend. It provided Dorrance with his new and improved response to the dynasty question. The e-mail read, *Now that we've watched the Tar Heels for nearly ten years, the thing that stands out the most is how fragile it all is. Somehow the coaches and the players have kept this program balanced on the high wire for decades. The use of the word "dynasty" to describe it is completely misleading. A dynasty involves people born to*

a station who hold their position whether they deserve it or not. In total con-
trast, this program earns its position every game. Nothing is given. There is no
birthright, only attitude and effort. The games all start even. Past success guar-
antees nothing. The fall from the high wire could come at any moment. I can tell
you this, if we thought there was some kind of guarantee, it would be a lot less
interesting to watch.

Of course, Dorrance won't quibble if the press wants to label his program a
dynasty. He was humbled in the fall of 2003 when *Sports Illustrated* labeled his
Tar Heels "the greatest college sports program ever," better even than the extraordinary achievements of programs like Arkansas track, Iowa wrestling, Division III Kenyon College swimming and, most notably, UCLA's run of ten NCAA
men's basketball titles in twelve seasons from 1964 to 1975 under coach John
Wooden.

What's indisputable is that UNC has won more national titles than any other
NCAA Division I women's program in the nation, but, like Dean Smith, Dorrance
is concerned only that people realize his success is built entirely on his players.
There could be no purer symbolism than the foundation of the McCaskill Soccer
Center. The building, which has become known as "The Castle," would never
have been built without the players whose names are etched onto the bricks that
literally hold the place up, more than two decades of names that support the
program itself:

EMILY J. PICKERING 1981–84 THANK YOU SWEET MEMORIES!
APRIL HEINRICHS CLASS OF 86 KEEP KICKING
ANNE E. SHEROW CLASS OF 89 GO HEELS
THE TRADITION WILL CONTINUE RITA TOWER 89–94

Dorrance will acknowledge that he views his program's stature much like that
of the New York Yankees, a team with some inherent advantages and some ludicrous expectations. "I remember when Janet Rayfield came to my office before
the 1981 season and I told her about my vision that we were going to be awesome . . . in 1981 . . . not for 20 years," Dorrance says. "Unless you're an idiot, you
don't have that kind of long-term vision. Each summer I've thought, 'We're going to be pretty good next year.' We'd lose Rayfield and replace her with Heinrichs
and then Higgins and then Hamm and then Venturini and Confer and Parlow,
and at some point, whatever you want to call it, they'd created a tradition here
that didn't permit anything less than a national championship."

Geoff Griffin: *How does Anson do it? Sometimes I just chuckle over how*
people are just awed by Carolina. All this stuff is not that complicated. It's just a
game with a round ball played between four lines. It's all about Anson's passion.
Back in the beginning he created an environment where his women could share
his passion.

Liz Crowley: *I think Anson's greatest strength is communication. He's in-*
credibly articulate. He teaches. I once said at an alumni function that Anson is

the best teacher I've ever had. That's how he made the Dinosaurs into the dynasty. He understands the notion that a soccer coach doesn't coach on game day. He teaches you what you need to know to play as an individual and as a team. There's no magic to it. He shows you how to play and then you do it.

Patrick Baker: *I think Anson likes close games that actually force him to make coaching decisions. He gets overlooked tactically because his players are so talented and the system doesn't change, but he has a lot of options within his system: possessional passes, overlapping runs, unbalancing runs, sophisticated balls in behind your defense—and he's a master at knowing when to use each style.*

Julie Foudy: *Maybe because he's coached such great players, his greatest strength is not teaching a player how to strike a long ball that bends toward the far post or how to juggle and trap a ball properly. He was always more interested in figuring out how to organize you and mentally drive you in a way that's going to win games. Anson nurtured in all of us the quality to kick ass.*

Carin Jennings: *Anson motivates individual players better than any coach I've ever had or known. I don't know how he does it. It's an innate ability. It's an intangible. It's not something you can describe or something that comes with instructions. It's a gift.*

Brandi Chastain: *I think Anson was one of the very first individuals, male or female, to be able to motivate women to combine physical activity with emotion. He's had the best athletes, and that obviously helped, but he's also able to get them to amp themselves up, not into a frenzy, but into a desire that I don't think most people understand. It could be USA or UNC or two ballboys at practice. He could literally ask who's going to chase down the most balls and have their side ready to play faster than the other guy. He somehow can make you feel like everything is a race, everything is a competition, and how are you going to be the best?*

Freddie Kiger: *Anson possesses some of those traits that only a select few have to be the President of the United States or to be on the cutting edge of invention. He has the drive, the energy, and the sense of purpose that 99 percent of us can't even begin to grasp. That's why he wins the championships. That's why people want to play for him even though he may piss them off. He'll get the most out of them somehow, some way. It's a marvelous thing to watch.*

Bill Steffen: *The UNC players have got the brains and they've got the talent, but it's important to understand that they are still overachievers. They work harder than any other team in the country. That's where Anson deserves the credit.*

Mia Hamm: *Anson taught us at a young age that we never had to apologize for wanting to be the best, and if anything it's the players around you who don't help you, who are the ones who should be apologizing. He makes it your responsibility by putting you in an environment that stretches you physically, tactically, emotionally, and you get stronger by fighting through that.*

Kristine Lilly: *He brought a group of people together that included a lot of great players and also a lot of walk-ons and he created a "team." He made players* work for each other, believe in each other, and play for each other. We were always winning it for someone else. You're never winning it for yourself.

Staci Wilson: *It is a combination of a bunch of things. Anson's very smart tactically. He's got a high IQ. He has a special spirit. He's a great motivator. He had good timing, and he's got his shit together.*

Jerry Smith: *Anson works his butt off. Most coaches would never admit this, but sometimes when I'm sitting in my office I'm thinking, "Anson Dorrance is out there somewhere outworking me." He's just grinding harder, writing more letters to recruits, talking tirelessly to his players about how to maximize their potential, just doing a little better job than the rest of us coaches, and you have to respect that.*

Colleen Hacker: *There is no simple explanation for Anson's success. It's not a Soccer for Dummies approach. You can't sit with him for an hour, turn on a tape recorder, and ask, "What makes you great?" It's extraordinarily more complex than that. It is said that the greatest soccer players think three passes ahead, and in terms of leadership, Anson thinks three passes ahead. It's not just a single conversation with a player, it's a ripple effect, like a pebble thrown in the water that has ring after ring emanating from it. It's a beautiful balance of a few core principles that don't change over time and a charisma that rejuvenates itself to the moment and encourages, almost demands, that his players shun mediocrity, pursue excellence to the nth degree, and then even more miraculously, sustain that year after year. Anson doesn't just say it's a great idea to go to California; he's driving the car and mapping the route. A dreamer without actions is a mad scientist, but he's done it with more than 200 different players over the course of more than twenty-five years. He has orchestrated, he has cultivated, he has motivated, and, I dare say, he has willed into existence a dynasty.*

The ceremony took place away from the television cameras, away from the national championship trophy, tucked in a corner of the field as far away from the spotlight as possible. In the moments immediately after securing the 2003 national title, Dorrance, Bill Palladino, Chris Ducar, and Bill Prentice huddled up in a corner of the field and convened their own private awards ceremony.

First, Dorrance turned to Prentice. "Bill, I'm thrilled to bestow upon you the National Trainer of the Year award."

"Aw, shucks," Prentice said. "Me again? I can't believe you picked me."

"And Chris," Dorrance continued. "You have won the National Goalkeeper Coach of the Year Award."

"You're kidding?" Ducar said. "I was just happy to be nominated."

"And Dino, my dear friend, yes, you are the National Assistant Head Coach of the Year."

Palladino playfully buried his head in Dorrance's shoulder and pretended to cry. Palladino then cleared his throat and said, "Anson, against all odds, you have won the National Coach of the Year award."

"No, it can't be me," Dorrance said, overacting. "It shouldn't be me. It should be some coach we crushed along the way."

And so it goes after every UNC championship season.

"After our silly awards ceremony we have a group hug, and we turn into four idiots jumping up and down, and we absolutely love it," Dorrance says. "That's our moment together. That's the part of the championship celebration that is special to me. Of all the things we do all year, I enjoy that moment as much as anything else."

It's more Tar Heel kitsch, sarcasm designed to poke fun at the postseason awards that so often overlook the UNC players and coaches because their success is expected and sometimes begrudged. The idea for the ritual stems from a line in the movie *Rob Roy*, when the title character explains to his son, *Honor is what no man can give you and none can take away. Honor is a man's gift to himself.* "This is how we honor ourselves," Palladino says. "It's like everything we do in that there's a slight hint of honesty as we poke fun at the politics of soccer."

Dorrance has actually won the women's collegiate National Coach of the Year Award only three times. Back in the mid-1990s, he stopped even bothering to attend the presentation at the annual NSCAA convention and therefore was a no-show when he finally did win for the third time in 2003. "Awards and accolades have never been important to Anson," Ange Kelly says. "People are jealous of him, and they don't want to give him that recognition because he's already won too many times already. Where does it say in the rulebook that if you've won this many times that you're not deserving anymore?"

Dorrance never wears championship rings. The first five he won were all stolen from his desk drawer in the late 1980s. After that, he began giving them away to his mother, his siblings, his daughters. M'Liss wears one as a charm on a necklace. He is a man who is leery of looking backward long enough even to appreciate the dynasty he's built. "I don't want any relics of the past," Dorrance says. "I love living in the present, and I love planning the future. I never want us to rest on our laurels."

Predictably, Dorrance has never had much interest in trophies either. In the Hut, national championship trophies were used as bookends or paperweights, or stashed haphazardly under desks. Three NCAA championship trophies were discovered behind a door just minutes before the Hut was destroyed. When the Tar Heels arrived back at Raleigh-Durham Airport after winning the 1996 national title, they were picked up by a bus for the ride back to campus. Alas, they left that championship trophy sitting on the curb.

Finally, convinced of the potential recruiting value, Dorrance acquiesced to a modest trophy case in the McCaskill Soccer Center, where the program's national championship hardware is crammed. Other than that, the tradition is largely overlooked. The "UNC Women's Soccer Museum" is a beat-up cardboard box mushed onto a shelf above Tom Sander's desk. It contains everything from the 1981 AIAW national tournament program to a sheet of September 26, 1985, practice stats, to the 1997 pregame notes for the national title game, to various ticket stubs and posters, to random dog-eared newspaper articles, to 8 x 10 glossies of Mia Hamm before she became *Mia!,* to a sign from 1992 that reads *Parity means teams can now take a lead on North Carolina before the Tar Heels win a championship,* to the infamous bedsheet from 1984 with the slogan *UNC Women Love the Smell of NAPALM in the afternoon: NCAA Champs.* Most of it is water-stained, having been belatedly rescued from a flood during Hurricane Floyd in 1998.

After more than twenty-five years as the UNC coach, Dorrance's name is still mispronounced, *Dor-RANCE,* during the introductions before road games by most of the public address announcers in his own conference, much to the quiet delight of his players. It took Dorrance eighteen national championships before his UNC team was finally invited to the White House. When Dorrance, who scored only eight college goals, was surprisingly honored as one of the top fifty men's soccer players in ACC history, he was teased mercilessly by his staff for days until he finally responded by sheepishly saying, "You can't quantify fury. Poetry can be written about it, but you can't quantify the human spirit with statistics." He then vowed to write a note of apology to whoever finished fifty-first.

Dorrance still laughs about how his daughter Natalie got upset with him when he quit as the U.S. national team coach because, she said, he wasn't going to be famous anymore. *Anymore?* Dorrance neither believes he is a celebrity, nor is impressed by celebrity. "I'm not one of these people who is starstruck," he says. "If I was hungry and Madonna walked into the room, I'd still go get a sandwich."

Maybe the closest Dorrance ever came to gaining a measure of fame occurred after the 1991 World Championship, when he was approached about consulting on a movie about his life. The film never attracted a producer, and the project was eventually scrapped, which was fine with Dorrance because the Hollywood suits were considering casting Pierce Brosnan to play him. Dorrance found Brosnan too effeminate, joking that he should be portrayed by either Robert De Niro or Robert Duvall, two of the actors whose movie lines he has coopted.

While two of Dorrance's UNC players, April Heinrichs and Shannon Higgins, are already enshrined in the National Soccer Hall of Fame, Dorrance is not. He doesn't even know if he is eligible. Dorrance understands that rings, trophies, even a Hall of Fame bust, are not his legacy. His legacy can be seen in the enduring effect of his program.

It can be seen in his alums. One afternoon during a Tar Heel practice in the fall of 1995, just three months after giving birth to her son, Jackson, and nine months before the 1996 Olympics, U.S. national team captain Carla Werden Overbeck walked into the UNC practice facility, propped up her baby inside a diaper bag and then laid out a series of cones for an hour of exhausting sprinting. Periodically, Werden would see her son topple over, and she'd jog over to wedge Jackson back into the bag and then resume running. At one point, Dorrance stopped UNC's practice, asked his players to watch Werden for a moment, and then said, "So what is our excuse for being out of shape?"

Dorrance's legacy can be seen in his team's name recognition. UNC women's soccer is the top women's sports brand in the world. There is a special section devoted to the program in the Eurosport catalog, making it the only American college soccer gear, men's or women's, sold by the company. Kristin Acquavella experienced the reach of the brand when she wanted to try out for the All-Navy soccer team. "I called the coach and introduced myself, and he said, 'Well, we've already been training for two weeks, we're really good, really fit, we don't really have a place for you,'" Acquavella recalls. "Just before we hung up he asked if I'd played in college, and I told him I played at UNC, and he said, 'Well, we've only been training for two weeks, we're not that good, not that fit. When can you start?'"

The legacy can be seen at his school, where his program has collected more than half of the national titles ever won at UNC. "If this dynasty had never happened, the name University of North Carolina wouldn't pop up so much in the newspapers and on TV," UNC senior associate athletic director Beth Miller says. "When you're watching a soccer game and you hear this girl is from the University of North Carolina and that girl is from the University of North Carolina, it gets in your head. The chancellor's going to appreciate that."

Dorrance's legacy can also be seen in other college soccer programs. After Florida State defeated UNC in 2000, Seminoles coach Patrick Baker walked up to Dorrance and said, "You make me want to be a better coach." Three years later, Baker hired Tar Heel alum Robin Confer as an assistant coach, hoping to make his program, as he puts it, "more Carolina-ish." College programs are all aspiring to be mentioned in the same sentence with UNC. "When I first started in college coaching, I looked at Carolina and I was jealous," Virginia coach Steve Swanson says. "But as I matured I began to accept the challenge that Anson and his program pose. It forces me to be good at what I do or be embarrassed. I *must* be good. I *must* recruit well. My team *must* compete hard. If there's any legacy that should be left in Anson's name, it's that there's no way you can go halfway and beat him at anything, and that can do nothing but improve our sport."

Says Santa Clara's Jerry Smith: "When I review film of my team, what I'm looking for are the things that aren't good enough to beat UNC. They are the only standard to which I aspire. I wouldn't want UNC ever to be less of a program. I want mine to be better."

Dorrance's legacy can be seen in all of the women he's coached, including a total of sixty-two All-Americans. Among those are thirteen National Players of the Year, all of whose numbers had been retired until they were unretired before the 2006 season to keep future Tar Heels out of jersey numbers in the triple digits. It can be seen on the U.S. national team, where a total of forty-three Tar Heels have earned caps, including five of the top eleven goal-scorers in team history. Fourteen different Tar Heels have won a World Championship. Ten have earned an Olympic gold medal. At least one player from UNC has started every national team game in its history. Tiffany Roberts played nine years with the U.S. national team and eventually lived that dream she had sketched as a third grader when she won an Olympic gold medal in 1996. When the United States competed in the 2003 World Cup, more than a decade after Dorrance had resigned as the national team coach, six of the team's twenty players were Tar Heels. The head coach and assistant were Tar Heels. The color commentator was a Tar Heel. Even the sideline reporter was a Tar Heel.

"A lot of players he's coached have been the most important and influential players in the country," says Aaron Heifetz, the U.S. women's national team media coordinator. "These are the players who have been winning all the games, doing all the interviews, getting all the endorsements, helping to keep pushing our sport along."

But the only legacy that really matters to Dorrance is that whenever Julie Foudy speaks to youth soccer players, she always quotes her favorite line from Dorrance: "I respect talent, but I admire courage." It matters to him that in the introduction to her autobiography *Go For The Goal,* Hamm used the quote, *The vision of a champion is someone who is bent over, drenched in sweat, at the point of exhaustion when no one else is watching.* It matters that after initially despising Dorrance's personality, Michelle Akers asked him to introduce her at her Hall of Fame induction and later presented him with a national team jersey upon which she had written, *To Anson . . . Thanks for setting the standard for greatness.* It matters that Brandi Chastain eventually became the player Dorrance always believed she could be. "As much as Anson drives me crazy, he taught me a good lesson that you'll get what you deserve if you keep on working for it," Chastain says. "Anson is all about those types of mental exercises. Some people call them head games. How are you going to deal with a situation that either you're really happy with or really not happy with? Do you come out on the winning side, or do you come out on the losing end? Anson helped me learn a lot about myself."

These days, whenever Dorrance is asked at the end of a season if he considers it a success, whether UNC has won a national championship or not, he'll say that it's too soon to know. Borrowing a line from legendary University of Chicago coach Amos Alonzo Stagg, Dorrance says, "I'll let you know in twenty years."

"Anson's pride comes from inviting someone onto his team and giving her the tools to succeed in her life well into the future," Lindsay Stoecker says. "I'll face a challenge in my present life and it's not as scary because I'll think, 'If I could survive Anson's program, I can do this!'"

In 2004, when ESPN named Dorrance among the twenty-five best coaches in all sports in the last twenty-five years, the only soccer coach on the list, Dorrance was asked about his legacy. "Our program has been a wonderful role model for women's soccer in America," he said. "What I'm especially proud of is that we've taken a sport that had no profile and by developing women to play it with reckless abandon, we've laid to rest the insult, 'You play like a girl.'"

In February of 2003 Dorrance traveled back to Ethiopia for the first time in forty-two years, accepting an invitation to train the fledgling Ethiopian women's national team. Invited by one of his former UNC men's team goalkeepers, Lee Horton, Dorrance went as a volunteer to preach the religion of soccer, once again playing the evangelist. Dorrance brought candy and soccer videotapes, and fulfilled a desperate need for sports bras. He also brought hope. He trained the top Ethiopian coaches, and a year later, in every region of the country, those who attended the Anson Dorrance Coaching Initiative were granted coaching positions for their regional teams.

In March of 2006, German men's national team coach Juergen Klinsmann shocked the European soccer community by inviting Dorrance to Germany during his team's preparation for the World Cup to pick the UNC coach's brain about the "competitive cauldron," an act considered heresy in Europe. What could Klinsmann possibly learn from an American . . . who coaches college . . . and *women?!*

Dorrance's impact is both macro and micro. Southern Cal football coach Pete Carroll says he incorporated the competitive cauldron into the Trojans' practice routine during the summer of 2003, right before his team won back-to-back national titles and thirty-four straight games. Meanwhile, Scott Weldon e-mailed Dorrance to tell him he'd instituted a scaled-down version of the cauldron with his Under-11 girls' soccer team in New Hampshire. Ashu Saxena, who brought his club team to UNC soccer camp three times, transformed a bunch of kids from the Fairfax, Virginia, area into a two-time state club champion, and twenty-five of the twenty-seven kids from Saxena's club who have graduated from high school have gone on to play college soccer. Another club coach, Jim Wain, recalls the day at a 1997 tournament when his team trailed 1–0 at the half, and Dorrance stopped by to say hello. He started chatting with Wain's players, and before Wain could stop him, Dorrance started teaching them the 3-4-3 and convinced them to try it in the second half. Wain's team came back and won the game 3–1. "I couldn't believe he was doing this, but who's going to say 'no' to Anson Dorrance?" Wain asks. "After the game, he told me he couldn't attend our next game, so he invited me to dinner and taught me the rest of the 3-4-3 during the meal."

In his first season at Louisville's Sacred Heart Academy, coach Dave Griffiths implemented Dorrance's 3-4-3 system, and ordered his players to run 120s and shuttle run to Carolina blue-painted cones, and his team improved from 8-6-1 to 27-1 and won a state championship. After reading about Dorrance's training methods, coach Mike Lagow led Florida's Gulf Breeze High Lady Dolphins to three straight state championship games and two state titles, and became the highest-scoring team in the state. Coach Jim Bruno's Good Counsel High team from Wheaton, Maryland, switched to the 3-4-3 after learning it at a UNC team camp and won three of the next four conference titles. In this era of caller ID and phone screening, Dorrance responds to every phone call and e-mail he receives from every coach at any level in any sport, including pleas for advice from Chrissy Lynch, the assistant junior varsity soccer coach at Cincinnati's Sycamore High, and from Craig Case, the assistant women's volleyball coach at Northern State University in Aberdeen, South Dakota. "I remember when I had a question about the midfield and Anson called me right back," Bruno says. "He's actually accessible. Most college coaches won't give you the time of day, even when they're recruiting one of your players."

Coach Bob Barnes took over the program at Division III Ohio Wesleyan in 1997 and immediately installed the 3-4-3 that he'd learned from listening to Dorrance's lectures at NSCAA conventions and attending UNC team camps over the summer. Barnes was jokingly branded by fellow conference coaches as "the Anson Dorrance of Ohio." OWU, which had never won an NCAA Tournament game and had no winning tradition before Barnes arrived, won forty-five games in a row and the Division III championship in 2001 and 2002. Says Barnes: "Is it a coincidence? I don't think so. I owe our success 100 percent to Anson. It's a microcosm of all the things that happened at UNC. The records, the streaks, the championships, even the opposing coaches making all the same excuses."

In 2003 Barnes's team ceded the Division III national championship to the College at Oneonta, coached by Tracey Ranieri, who studied under Dorrance at two national coaching diploma courses. Ranieri, who has hung a photo of Dorrance beside one of her diplomas in her office, sent a note to her mentor shortly after winning her school's first team title in any sport in 114 years. In the note she wrote: *I know our success is a direct result of the coaching knowledge and education you have given me. Thank you.*

During many of his pregame talks, Dorrance will preface a tactical question to his players with the phrase, "OK, all you future coaches of America . . ."

It's another benefit of the Socratic method. UNC players don't just play the game; they must be able to explain it. They don't just learn how. They learn why. Dorrance coaches his players to be coaches by teaching them to *see* the game, and he believes no player ever saw it better than Shannon Higgins, whose keen eye Dorrance attributes partly to her hearing deficiency. In the ultimate display of respect for a player, Dorrance says that he stopped coaching Higgins during her sophomore season and began consulting her instead, because she was the most tactically advanced player that he has ever encountered. In fact, when Higgins landed the Maryland coaching job in 1999, Dorrance told her, "If I die today, soccer won't really lose that much, because everything I know is in your brain."

Dorrance estimates that more than half of his former players have gone on to coach soccer at some level. Eleven of Dorrance's former players are currently college head coaches, including Ange Kelly at Tennessee, Lori Walker at Ohio State, Chris Huston at Rice, and Janet Rayfield, who not only coaches at Illinois but is also the president of the NSCAA. Amy Burns, who once transferred away from UNC in part because of stress over the competitive cauldron, subjects her players to many of those same statistical tests as the coach at Wofford. When Amy Machin accepted a job at Regis University in 1992, she became the first-ever female coach of a men's college soccer team.

Marcia McDermott, who coached Northwestern for seven seasons and then the WUSA's Carolina Courage, says that she grew up aspiring to be a lawyer, very skeptical about the value of being a soccer coach until Dorrance convinced her otherwise. "I became a coach because of Anson," she says. "He really is a great spokesperson for the career because he once had the same doubts I had. He told me that if the job was just about winning and losing then it's not particularly interesting, but that you get to have an impact on people's lives."

Dorrance encourages all of his players to give back to the game as coaches. Schools around the country have treated recommendations from "the Godfather" as offers they can't refuse. Bill Steffen was hired as the coach at Oregon in 1996 without any head coaching experience, and Tracy Noonan was hired by Greensboro (North Carolina) College in 2004 with no coaching experience at all. Tom Sander has compiled a list of all former Tar Heels who aspire to be college coaches, and whenever an athletic director contacts Dorrance about a coaching opening, he scans the list and plays matchmaker, writing and rewriting the recommendation until he has all but guaranteed the outcome.

To watch Kelly lead her Tennessee team through a warmup is to understand Dorrance's influence. She runs many of the same drills and speaks in a similar cadence with a similar soccer lexicon, parroting Dorrance phrases like, "Let's talk about this," "Solve it," and "Good enough!" Kelly even admits to stealing some of Dorrance's core value stories and replacing him in the story with herself. "We'd all be very, very stupid not to use the things that Anson has taught us," Kelly says. "I'm not an Anson clone, but do I motivate in a lot of the same ways he does? Yes. Do I wish to cultivate competitiveness the same way? Yes. If those weren't the answers, I would be an idiot. The man's won eighteen national championships."

For every Tar Heel who is coaching in the U.S. national team system or in the college ranks, there's another who's coaching kids. Susan Ellis created a high school powerhouse at Ursuline Academy in Dallas, where she produced an unathletic tactical overachiever protegée in Jordan Walker. Emily Pickering, Diane Beatty, and Suzy Cobb each coach their daughter's club teams. Emily Rice is a teacher and soccer coach at T.C. Williams High School in Alexandria, Virginia, and she credits Dorrance with leading her toward her career as a way to "pay it forward." Sarah Dacey is coaching soccer at Babson College. "I want to be a positive role model and pass along the soccer knowledge and the life lessons I took away from being a part of the Tar Heels," Dacey says. "I always appreciated Anson and Dino for looking at the person first and the soccer player second, and I try to pass that on to my players."

Dorrance admits that he derives the most satisfaction from the Tar Heel alums who followed in his coaching footsteps against all odds. "A significant percentage of my problem children have ended up as coaches," Dorrance says. "Justice for each of them is coaching someone just like themselves."

When the question of coaching was raised in Pam Kalinoski's final goal-setting meeting in 1991, she had absolutely no interest. "I thought, 'I didn't go to college just so I could be a *soccer coach*,'" Kalinoski recalls. "Four years later, I went to Anson and said, 'The real world is overrated. I want to be a soccer coach now.' In 2001 Kalinoski became the women's coach at the University of San Francisco, where, inspired by Dorrance, she now has seven journals full of inspirational quotes that she sprinkles into her pregame talks.

Lori Walker once told Dorrance that she didn't need to be fit to play goal-keeper and stubbornly defended her opinion throughout her career until, claiming she was burned out on soccer, Walker left the UNC program after her junior season. Two years later, after becoming an assistant coach at Maryland, Walker wrote Dorrance a note that read, *I now understand what you went through coaching me because I'm now coaching girls like me and it's driving me nuts. I apologize for everything I ever did to you.* It was also Walker who provided Dorrance with the definitive George Bernard Shaw quote about being "a force of fortune instead of a feverish, selfish little clod of ailments" that he's used to try to rehabilitate his other malcontents ever since.

Dorrance was never more surprised than the day in 2002 when he received a letter from the Duquesne women's soccer coach:

Dear Anson,

This probably has to be the most long overdue letter in the history of the Carolina program, and the biggest reason for writing it is to give a long overdue thank you. I find myself here at Duquesne using a lot of what I learned from you. One thing I had to get used to in coaching is my kids have said, "This isn't Carolina." I know it is not, but why settle. No matter where you go it is still a part of you. I could never separate me as a soccer player from me as a person. I defined myself by what I did on the field and how I was in the rankings that were posted. I think I didn't get what I could have out of my college experience and for a long time I blamed you. Boy did I need to grow up. Now I have this view where I love getting up in the morning and attacking the day. The force of fortune quote you made me memorize my freshman year — the one you thought didn't work — it just took me longer. I believe I am a student of the game and of life and they do have a great deal in common. I really want to go to grad school to get my masters in leadership. I think this is something I gained appreciation for at Carolina.

Hope you didn't mind me writing, but it was time to get this off my chest. I really just needed you to know that I do appreciate everything you and Dino did for me while I was at UNC. I know how you are about quotes and I think this one fits me to a tee with the learning stuff and it is shorter than the one by Mr. Shaw. "We actually live two lives, we live the life we learn with and then the life we choose to live after."

Respectfully yours,
Dawn Crow

They didn't all become coaches, but many of the Tar Heel soccer alums who left the game behind say their lives have still been touched in some way by crossing paths with Dorrance. Dianne Beatty, an insurance sales executive, is convinced that every step of her career path has been shaped by the woman she became at UNC. "I believe that I landed my first job out of college because my employer saw me as a *champion*," Beatty says. "I believe that many of my client relation-ships today were started because the owner of the business liked doing business with a champion. Being a champion has opened so many doors for me."

Kristin Acquavella redshirted one season at UNC because she was the battal-ion commander of her ROTC unit and she credits Dorrance with encouraging her to pursue her interest in the military, where she is now a lieutenant commander in the Navy. Charlotte Mitchell is working toward her law degree in the same building where Dorrance once studied, and she thanks her former coach for help-ing forge in her the persistence to get the degree that he didn't have the desire to earn. Wendy Gebauer, one of the shyest women ever recruited to the UNC pro-gram, is now a part-time television commentator. "At UNC we were always learn-ing about crisis management in different ways, and I know that's helped me a ton," Gebauer says. "There is no huge crisis in my life. I know everything will be OK. I'm around a lot of people in the working world, and it's just not that way with them, and I swear it's my training in the program. We have an edge."

Aubrey Falk says that Dorrance's words still ring in her ears. "My mom died three years ago, and I swear on her sweet soul that the reason I was able to get through that horrible period in my life was because of my experience as a player for Anson," Falk says. "I remembered him saying, 'Get up! This is a contact sport, not fucking badminton!' So the day after my mom died, I got up."

Shelley Finger, who once buried a dog that Dorrance ran over during a road trip to Virginia, is now a veterinarian. Julia Marslender, who followed her sister Eliza-beth to UNC, took the leadership skills she learned from Dorrance and translated them into a job at the Pentagon. Donna Rigley, who ran one of the best Coopers ever after guzzling a 32-ounce beer, is now an elite marathoner.

These Tar Heels are all connected somehow. Chris Ducar married Tracy Noonan in 1997. Bill Palladino married Gebauer in 2001. Amy Machin is married to Kip Ward's younger brother, John, whose love compelled her to famously miss the Cooper. During her senior season at UNC, Leslie Gaston discovered she is actually a distant cousin to Dorrance.

Geoff Griffin is now Dorrance's stockbroker, and Susan Ellis' father, Bill, was his dentist for years. Carolyn Springer, a.k.a. Ntozake Zola, has since changed her name to N. Zola Solamente and is now a painter and art gallery director in Boston. She has one of her paintings displayed in the Dorrance bedroom. Tracey Bates once found comfort in a Bazooka Joe comic fortune that read, *If at first you don't succeed, you're doing it wrong,* and saved it through her entire UNC career. A decade later, Bates mailed the yellowed comic to Jordan Walker, who regularly pulled it out for psychotherapy throughout her four years. Emily Pickering and Betsy Johnson, still the best of friends, reunite nearly every sum-mer to work a week of UNC soccer camp together. They both bring their kids to attend UNC camps, and at night they smuggle cheap wine into their squalid dorm room and tell stories about doing the same stupid stuff two decades ago.

When Laura Brockington fled UNC for California in the summer of 1979, she can still recall the last words Dorrance told her: "Twenty years from now you're going to look back and appreciate how wonderful it is in Chapel Hill. The grass is always greener." The relationship for which Brockington sacrificed her UNC soccer career lasted a few years, and then after the breakup, she remained in California, where she attended UCLA law school, played club soccer, married, became an attorney, and had a child. After a divorce, Brockington returned to Chapel Hill in 1997 to raise her son, Josh, where she'd grown up.

That fall Brockington met Jock Noyes, who surprised her on their first date by taking her to a UNC women's soccer game without any knowledge of her history in the sport or with the Tar Heel program. It was the first UNC game Brockington had ever seen. Jock, who married Laura in 1998, is an ardent UNC women's soccer fan who attends most Tar Heel home games. Laura, now a painter and a stay-at-home mom, rarely joins him because even after all these years, she still gets restless watching a game and not playing. In October of 2004, Dorrance phoned Brockington for the first time in twenty-five years and invited her to rejoin the UNC women's soccer community at a pregame ceremony honoring her for her contribution to the program. "At first when I left UNC I didn't have much interest in what went on back here," Brockington says. "But a few years later, I saw that the team won a national title and then kept on winning them. I was very happy for Anson, and it really gave me a sense of pride. For years I always hoped that someday Anson would say 'Thank you,' and those two words meant a lot to me, because I helped get the program to a point where a real coach came in with real funding and real training and turned it into a dynasty. These women have what I always wanted growing up. They can play in college and then maybe in the Olympics and the Women's World Cup. Wow! That is really something."

For many years, Dorrance kept his eye out for offers for Bill Palladino to become a head coach at another school. One day in 1992, when the George Mason coaching job became available, Dorrance began to work the phones on Palladino's behalf. Confused by how intensely Dorrance was politicking for him, Palladino walked into Dorrance's office and asked, "Anson, do you want me to leave?"

"No," Dorrance said. "I never want you to leave."

"Good, I don't want to leave."

The exchange lasted all of ten seconds, yet it was one of the most critical moments ever in the time line of UNC soccer. It was a classic male exchange, a most heartfelt and cathartic moment for two men who had known each other for twenty years, yet totally devoid of any visible emotion. It was the moment that said that these two would be coaching together forever.

Palladino has since turned down the chance to be interviewed for more than a dozen other college coaching jobs. Many former UNC players believe that Palladino may be the second best college coach in the country and would have become Dorrance's nemesis in the game had he ever chosen to leave. On the other hand, Bill Prentice believes that Palladino's personality isn't relentless or meticulous enough for him to thrive as a college coach. Palladino has dabbled as a semipro coach and as an assistant to April Heinrichs with the U.S. national team, but he always finds himself longing to come back to UNC, where he was never even a full-time employee until 2005, just a part-timer who supplemented a small UNC salary by running the program's summer soccer camps. The guy who came just a dissertation short of earning his Ph.D. has never regretted fleeing the research lab for the soccer field. Years ago Palladino ran across a quote that he realized suited him and Dorrance perfectly: *Find a job that you would do for free and figure out how to get paid for it.* "People don't leave our program because it's a very enjoyable environment to work in," Palladino says. "It's low-pressure, ironically. Low-maintenance. Low-demand. All these descriptions that are never associated with a high-profile athletic team. It's attributable to Anson's style. If he were a hard-driving, dot the I's cross the T's guy, none of us would still be here."

There is a running joke around UNC soccer that Palladino has always taken his part-time status to heart, but nobody doubts his impact on the program. "Everyone deals with the little hassles Dino causes because we know that he's essential," Sander says. "If he were ever to leave, I don't know if lightning could strike twice."

Says Dorrance: "Dino has his faults, but he'll be my assistant coach as long as he wants to be. He'll always be with me for 1,000 reasons, but mostly because I *like* him."

None of the current coaching staff expresses any desire to leave. That notion has come as a surprise to Chris Ducar, who like Dorrance grew up as a nomad and whose eleven-year stint in Chapel Hill is by far the longest he's lived in one place in his life. "I know this sounds funky and new age, but people don't leave Anson because he really is that positive life force that he's always talking about," Ducar says. "I don't see these people as co-workers. These are the people I want to spend Thanksgivings with, Christmases with."

Tom Sander believes that one of the strengths of the UNC program is its consistency. "It makes the players more comfortable," Sander says. "It makes it feel more like a family, because you know you'll always have the same people to come home to."

Sander is still the program's unsung cog, the glue. Along with his official duties as the program's statistician, travel agent, and equipment manager, Sander picks up garbage around the team bench after road games so that UNC leaves a good impression. He sometimes fetches Dorrance's breakfast on the road. He still washes the uniforms. The guy who began as a student manager has now done the things that nobody else would do for nearly half the existence of the program. Though he is no longer a medical lab rat, Sander is still underpaid enough that he regularly passes on staff lunches because he can only afford to brown-bag it. "It amazes me that Tom is still around," says Ducar of the man who works eighteen inches away from him in their cramped office. "It's unbelievable how hard he works, the hours that he puts in, the thankless things that he does. Whatever Anson's visions are, Tom makes them reality, and I know Anson appreciates him even if he can't pay him what he's worth."

Says Sander: "Every year the girls have asked me if I'm coming back next year, and I've always said, 'Why not?' I just kept thinking I'd do it until something better came along. More than ten years later, that hasn't happened yet."

Delaine Marbry and Dorrance often speculate that having been hired at UNC in the same year, they should depart together as well, though Marbry openly wonders if she's got the stamina to last as long as her boss. In her fifteen years as Dorrance's secretary, Marbry has never been to a UNC practice, has never gone on a road trip, and has attended fewer than ten games. "In all the time I've known Anson, I've never even heard him give a speech, but I think he's the most inspiring person I've ever met," Marbry says. "I've had some of the other secretaries at UNC tell me they could never work for him, but I would never have wanted to work for anybody else."

Of all the UNC soccer staff, it would be easiest for Bill Prentice to bail out. His department absolved him of any responsibility to the program years ago, but it remains a labor of love for him. Most UNC players never know that the guy who pats them on the back when they're vomiting at 5 a.m. on road trips is at the pinnacle of his field, a man who has authored eight textbooks and is listed in *Who's Who In the World.* They have no idea that he doesn't need this job.

But nobody is more invested than Prentice. The only person on the Tar Heel bench who ever looks even remotely anxious about the result of a game, he calms his nerves by chewing on ice, a habit which has actually worn down his teeth. Prentice has worked every home game since he joined the staff, including when he was on sabbatical from UNC in 1991. Every fall when a new group of freshmen arrives and Prentice bonds with them, he tells himself that he will leave his post with the graduation of that class . . . until the next year's freshman class shows up. "Over the years, I've been desperately hanging on to women's soccer as the academic side tries to pull me away," Prentice says. "I certainly could have utilized my time more productively, but developing all these relationships has its rewards. Sure, there are lots of days at soccer practice when I sit there and think, 'What the hell is wrong with you? Why on earth are you still doing this?' But I'd do it all again."

He calls it "a gilded life." Dorrance says he has no regrets, which is a gimme for a man who stubbornly refuses to dwell on the past. But that doesn't stop him from occasionally pondering how the heck he got here. "Sometimes I still wonder, 'Why am I this soccer bum?'" Dorrance says. "'Why did I quit law school?'"

Dorrance has never seriously lamented not taking the final six courses necessary for his law degree. He says he even gained some closure on that chapter of his life a decade ago when his coaching success earned him an invitation to speak to the North Carolina Bar Association. He grinned contentedly and began his speech with the words, "I must be the first law school dropout ever to address this august body . . ."

"I guess we all read Anson wrong," brother Pete says. "People who look at him and see this unfeeling automaton need to understand that he did what everyone in the world would love to do. He could have been a helluva lawyer and made tons of money, but he followed his heart. He made a decision to do something that he loved doing, coaching, and he hasn't looked back."

"Anson still has the same enthusiasm he had the day he started coaching," UNC administrator Beth Miller says. "There's still a little kid in him. I've often asked myself, 'Is he ever going to grow up?' But I've come to realize that this is just him. He *has* grown up."

There are still plenty of signs of the boy inside the man. Dorrance still drums his fingers constantly on his desk or his steering wheel, and he still compulsively fidgets with a ball at his feet whenever there is a stretching break in practice. He is a middle-aged man who looks forward to nothing more in his day than playing an after-school roller hockey game with his friends. "It's still important that I can hit that competition button," Dorrance says. "Isn't that insane? Aren't there things I should be doing that have much greater value? Aren't you supposed to enjoy just sitting on the porch and watching the sunset with your wife and children? When does that maturity kick in?"

When Dorrance is asked about his family, he says, "There have been lots of days when I've asked myself, 'Would I have been a better husband and father if I had invested less time in being a better coach?' I was never part of my daughters' lives when they were kids, which might explain why they're so successful." If wit is a sword, Dorrance is turning it upon himself this time. He knows that in the past he has sacrificed some priceless time with his family in favor of soccer. By necessity, he often indulged in a form of shorthand parenting with a coach's twist. Janet Rayfield recalls one night when she was babysitting for a three-year-old Michelle who was crying and refusing to eat her vegetables, when Anson arrived home, approached his daughter, and calmly said, "Michelle, do you really think it's worth having an emotional meltdown over peas?" Michelle ate her peas.

"I know it would have been a different story for us if he'd have been home more," Michelle says. "Whenever I saw other fathers around all the time saying how they'd do anything for their little pumpkin, I'd wonder, 'Gosh, what is *that* like?' I'm not a daddy's girl. He never thought to give me a big bear hug. He'd write me a letter, and that was his way of showing affection. I appreciate that it's less ritualistic because I feel like it's less contrived, but there were times when I thought, 'Why not set a up a goal-setting meeting with me, for chrissakes?'"

Michelle, who lives in New York City, is a twenty-six-year-old professional rhythm tap dancer, a skill she credits to a combination of the grace of her mother, a longtime dancer, choreographer, and ballet instructor, and the percussion instincts of her father. Natalie, twenty-four, is a 2004 graduate of UNC who visited her father at his office regularly as a student, still works his summer soccer camps, and jokes that she saw more of him during college than she ever did growing up. Anson says it's a testament to his lack of influence on his children that Michelle is a 21st-century bohemian who is her father's ideological counterpoint. Natalie is her mother's daughter in her deep aversion to the chaos that rules her father's life. But both Dorrance daughters admit that beneath the surface their father has exerted some impact on them. Michelle is a cerebral and passionate debater who possesses The Force to challenge her father the way he once challenged Big Pete. Natalie is a supernaturally competitive grinder. While the apprenticeship of fifteen-year-old Donovan is incomplete, he is the spitting image of his father as a teenager in Anson's Villa Saint-Jean yearbook photos. Anson has embraced Donovan as his last chance to mentor his progeny. He named his son Anson Donovan Dorrance, vetoing his mother's request for Albert Anson Dorrance V, because Anson refused to saddle his son with the unenviable choice of Albert or Anson. Anson is drilling everything into Donovan that he missed with his daughters, making him his protégé if not his namesake.

M'Liss has marveled at the changes in her husband as a father from the days when Michelle was born and he'd impatiently ask, "When is she going to do something new?" In recent years he savored his time tucking Donovan into bed, kissing him goodnight, and saying prayers with him. "In the old days he was so busy and his hours were so wacky that sometimes I'd have to sit him down and lecture him, 'Anson, you haven't seen the kids in three days,'" M'Liss says. "He never saw coaching soccer as a sacrifice because he was doing what he wanted to do, but now he realizes that he only experienced his daughters' childhoods as highlights, and he's become more emotionally touched by his kids. He treasures them more."

Dorrance has gained more of an appreciation for his entire family. He is reminded of his own mortality every time he drives east on Interstate 40 out of Chapel Hill and passes the cemetery where his father is buried. In 2001 he watched his mother dying on the operating table at UNC hospital after suffering a stroke. Her vital signs were weak, the lines on the machines she was hooked up to were all moving in the wrong direction, but doctors brought Peggy back from the brink. For all of his life, Anson's bulletproof attitude has been inspired by Peggy, who scooped up the stray bullet that once nearly killed her husband in their living room in Addis Ababa, dubbed it "Pete's bullet," and placed it on a charm bracelet that she wears to this day. Now Anson is taking care of his mother with the help of his brother Pete, a successful local restaurateur, who sometimes volunteers to videotape UNC home games from a scaffold beside Fetzer Field. Soccer games are as close as the Dorrances get to family reunions. Peggy, Pete, M'Liss, Natalie, and Donovan attend almost every home game.

Without so much as a nudge from their father, each of the Dorrance kids naturally migrated to the soccer field themselves. Michelle, a gritty midfielder, started playing Rainbow Soccer and continued with the game through her freshman year at New York University. Natalie, a defender with a mean streak, played some intramural soccer at UNC. Both played varsity soccer at Chapel Hill High, more for social reasons than because of any Gift of Fury. Although Anson never coached them and rarely saw them play, both daughters constantly worried that they would embarrass their father. On the other hand, Donovan is extremely confident in his soccer skills, believing he has inherited his father's athletic pedigree, which is a constant frustration to Anson because his son's work ethic doesn't match his own lofty standard. Anson has been invited to participate in some of his son's soccer practices, and he laughs at the memory of Donovan once asking him to get off the field because he was playing too hard. After one game, Anson gently suggested to Donovan that he move a bit more, try to cover more space. Donovan replied, "Dad, I'm doing what my coach told me. You don't have any idea what you're talking about."

Once upon a time, Dorrance was close to leaving it all behind. Tempted to coach on the other end of the women's soccer universe. At Stanford. In the summer of 1993, Dorrance received a phone call from the Stanford athletic director, Ted Leland, asking if Dorrance had any recommendations for the vacant Cardinal coaching job. Leland was surprised when Dorrance asked if his own name could be included on the list. Dorrance was intrigued by the school's stellar academic reputation and the program's huge budget. The man who built a soccer dynasty in a state that produced few elite players wondered what he could do with a fertile recruiting base right in his backyard. He told his brother Pete that if he took the job at Stanford, the Cardinal would quickly supplant the Tar Heels as the dominant program in the nation and should never lose a game. Then Dorrance told his mother about it, and Peggy said, "If you go to Stanford, I'll stick my head in the oven." It was the second time in Dorrance's life that his mother had made a life-altering decision for him.

Dorrance knew in his heart that he could never leave Chapel Hill, but he was at a career crossroads. What was left to accomplish at UNC? When he thought about where the Tar Heel program should be headed, he recalled Dean Smith's advice that coaching is not about the winning but about the process, and there was always room for improvement in that area. So the man who led the charge for playing a three-front and then high pressure, and then recruiting gifted athletes and turning them into soccer players, is still looking to revolutionize his approach. He is plotting a dynamic four-across midfield that can manhandle teams with its athleticism, or perhaps even adjusting the numbers in his coveted 3-4-3 to better combat opponents' increasingly potent attacks. In 2005 he added six male students to his permanent practice roster to raise the overall skill level in training and even occasionally stopped recording stats for the competitive cauldron to encourage his women to experiment more with their touches. In the last few seasons he even started to show his women a few minutes of pregame videotape, laced with his sarcastic commentary, but always concluding with Tar Heel goals scored in the most recent game to pump them up.

"Here's a man who's enjoyed unbelievable success admitting that he hasn't learned everything," Ducar says. "Each year the program changes, evolves, he's always trying something new. It would be really easy for him to fall into this 'I'm the Man' syndrome and watch the game pass him by. I respect the fact that he always believes there are better ways to do things."

Dorrance has even learned that sometimes he is better off not coaching, teaching by not overteaching the way his UNC writing professor Max Steele once did. No Tar Heel practice ever lasts more than ninety minutes, and many are cut shorter, because Dorrance wants his players to avoid burnout by stopping while they're still enjoying themselves. As a result, few teams play less soccer during a season than the Tar Heels. "Most coaches think they must do everything to prepare perfectly for a game, which salves their consciences, but that's athletics ad nauseum," Dorrance says. "You want your players to be excited about playing, to have some juice, so you have to do something that is very hard for a coach to do, which is stop the meetings, stop the practice, stop the frigging madness. We really don't teach them that much in practice, and we win more games with enthusiasm than anything else, so our construct here is that in order to prepare them to play at their utmost, sometimes we have to coach at our least."

Dorrance confesses that he still has yet to coach a perfect game. Until he does, he will have to keep trying hard. He readily admits that there are still elements of coaching that he has yet to figure out. "I see myself as a chemist," Dorrance says. "This experiment failed. The experiment before that failed. The experiment before that failed. OK, I'll try this now and see if it works. I want to keep getting better as a coach every year. Wherever we are, it's not good enough. I don't think we're anywhere near the human potential."

"Anson keeps going because he can never know everything," Bettina Bernardi says. "The game keeps bringing him back to coaching. Kids keep changing. He always wants to see if he can win another one with a new group of players by fixing this problem and that problem until he's constructed a new team. He still loves outcoaching other coaches."

"I think it's the joy of combat that is still exciting to my dad," daughter Michelle says. "In a championship game, I think he loves that it comes down to one battle. 'Are we ready? Are we going to be the one to live or die?' What that stands for is still important to him, but the actual championships mean nothing. Every trophy he's ever won has collected dust in a basement somewhere."

Dorrance's motto is appropriately optimistic: *Win Forever.* He loves the story of how Michael Jordan stoked his competitive fire by manufacturing some enmity toward an opponent he was about to face, even when none existed. Dorrance is like that, too. He maintains his edge through the animosity he perceives toward his program. "I like the fact that our success really irritates everyone else out there," he says. "That circulates my blood and drives me like you wouldn't believe to keep torturing them. I'll stay up all night if I'm pissing off some other coach because we're so successful. That's secretly one reason why I keep coaching."

However, Dorrance insists that soccer is no longer what keeps him hungry for every new season. That is not where this man's search for meaning leads. He says he now coaches more for the moments of connection, particularly the unscripted moments. He points to the time halfway through an innocuous practice during Raven McDonald's junior season when she walked over to him and said, "I just want to thank you for being my coach." Or when Mia Hamm called him on his cell phone from her honeymoon with four minutes left in the 2003 NCAA final and told him, "Anson, treasure this moment, because you deserve it." Or the story of Courtney Lehmann, a third-string walk-on goalkeeper, who was critically injured in a moped accident during her sophomore year at UNC. Dorrance arrived at the hospital that day just as Lehmann was being rushed into surgery and called out to her to keep fighting. Lehmann later told him that she'd recognized his voice, and it reminded her of his constant affirmations during fitness drills. She thanked him for playing a part in saving her life. Two years later, Dorrance subbed Lehmann into the waning minutes of the 1990 NCAA championship game at striker, and even though she'd never played the position or scored a goal before in her life, damned if Lehmann didn't shank a ball into the back of the UConn net to produce the Tar Heels' final goal, after which player and coach cried on each other's shoulders. "I've always thought that a gift received on your birthday carries less power than one that arrives completely out of the blue," Dorrance says. "Every so often one of my players pops up like an angel reminding me why I do this and makes me think, 'I can coach forever.'"

Dorrance also keeps coaching because he knows he hasn't completely figured out the strange creatures just yet. In 2002 he received a phone call from Anne Remy, who was distraught over not being selected in the WUSA draft that day. Sensing Remy's disappointment, Dorrance interrupted her and promised to phone every league general manager to get her a tryout. Remy grew even more upset and said, "I thought you were supposed to be an expert on women?" Then Remy hung up on him. Dorrance sat in stunned silence for a few seconds before it dawned on him. "I think she just wanted me to listen to her vent," he said. "I am such an idiot."

These are the self-enlightening moments that still fascinate Dorrance. "The hallmark of my evolution has always been making mistakes and trying never to repeat them," Dorrance says. "I swear, is there a better job in the world than this one? I can't imagine a life more richly spent than watching all of these young women change in so many positive ways over four years. This is drama. This is the human condition. This is life."

Dorrance works on most school holidays, and he despises nothing more than vacations. He takes one week of vacation a year to the North Carolina coast, but every day he's away he phones Marbry with a list of things to do. "M'Liss has trained me to go on vacations, but I always think someone is getting ahead of me," he says. "One day off is one day behind everyone else. Two days? A week? Are you kidding me? I don't consider too many things in this job a burden. I've created a cliché out of this, but I think my life is a vacation. It's the vacations that feel like work."

Dorrance still looks forward to preseason two-a-days. He looks forward to every goal-setting conference, every leadership meeting. He even looks forward to the recruiting. He often drives into his office on Sunday nights, the way he used to in his insurance salesman days, to make two hours of phone calls to potential recruits. He says he suffers no burnout because he has already accomplished more as a soccer coach than he could have ever imagined, so the pressure to win is gone. Whatever he pursues from here are goals he sets for himself. "The University of North Carolina should feel extremely blessed to have a coach like

Anson," former Tar Heel wrestling coach Bill Lam says. "And when he wakes up every morning, he's excited about going to work. So he's blessed too."

"I covered Anson for twenty years, and I've never met anyone so content with his position," says reporter Jim Furlong. "I'm convinced that if you told Anson he could switch jobs with any other person on earth, he'd still be the women's soccer coach at the University of North Carolina."

For Anson Dorrance, there is still plenty of ascending to do. He dreams of the day a UNC lineup consisting entirely of players from the state of North Carolina wins a national title. He dreams of the day when he and three of his former players are all coaching in the same Final Four, the one instance when he says he truly wouldn't care who wins. He dreams of the day he coaches the daughter of one of his former players. He dreams of regional day camps and soccer training DVDs, dreams of building a business the way his father once did, so that he might pay his staff a living wage. He dreams of a new soccer stadium and has even had plans drawn up that he leaves on display in the McCaskill conference room so that potential investors can see it in the theater of their mind. He dreams of using the $20,000 he now commands for his corporate speeches to compile a $2 million endowment that will fund the program in perpetuity and generate enough money so that his players can drink whatever they want with their meals on the road. He dreams of the day he bumps into his old history professor John Headley somewhere on campus and thanks him for teaching him how to set a standard all those years ago. He dreams of the day when Debbie Keller steps back into his community to complete the circle again. He dreams of a time when UNC can be as dominant in other sports as it is in women's soccer, and to that end the man who never intended to be a coach would like to mentor the school's other coaches, to become a coach coach. Finally, he dreams of someday having a clear desk so that instead of always catching up with yesterday, he might actually start working on tomorrow.

In many ways, Dorrance is the Little Prince of Antoine de Saint-Exupéry's imagination, this diminutive son of American imperialist oil aristocracy who has spent his life wandering among distant worlds seeking wisdom, preaching for human values, and against all abuses of the human spirit. Whenever Dorrance hears somebody call college the best years of his or her life, he feels sorry for them. He sincerely believes that every year of his life has been better than the year before, and he wants to keep it that way, for however many years he's got left. Most people who meet Dorrance are stunned to learn that he is fifty-five years old, assuming he is ten years younger, something that he attributes at least partly to working with college kids who keep him young. Like a cartoon character, Dorrance doesn't appear to age as years pass, but he admits there are more and more reminders that he is indeed growing older. During a Q & A session after a recent speech at a local elementary school, a young girl stood up and asked Dorrance, "Are any of the players you've coached still alive?" When Elley Jordan, class of '81, participated in a 2001 UNC alumni game, Dorrance overheard Jordan introduce herself to each

324   The Man Watching

of his current players by saying, "I could be your mother." Indeed, some of the Dinosaurs have started to go gray, and even Dorrance himself has some flecks at the temples. Dorrance has occasionally begun to scribble a crib sheet for practices, a sacrifice that he jokingly attributes to "the inevitable onset of dementia." There have been plenty of times on particularly hot days at the roller hockey rink, when Dorrance is playing his seventh consecutive game, when his indefatigable human spirit has become "fatigable" and he's turned to Palladino and said, "I don't know what it takes to have a heart attack, but I know that these conditions are favorable, so get ready to cover the goal."

While the rest of the college soccer coaching world is skewing younger as more and more former players take over programs, Dorrance and Palladino joke about the time they'll be walking up and down the sidelines with canes. They have no idea when they'll stop coaching. They don't ever think about it. If pressed, Dorrance, who has now coached the UNC women for half his life, will talk abstractly about the day fifteen or twenty years from now when he'll leave the program behind and maybe embark on a Mormon mission back to Ethiopia, presumably retiring again when everybody wants him to stay. At that point maybe Palladino will take over for a few years, or Dorrance has said he would feel comfortable deeding the kingdom to Chris Ducar or Susan Ellis. But Dorrance has no plans to walk away anytime soon. "A lot of times I've asked him, 'Can you actually see yourself retired?'" M'Liss says. "I can't see it yet, but I wonder if as he gets older, if he finds that he can no longer compete in soccer or hockey and release that part of him that connects him to athletics, if his involvement in sports will lose its draw to him? Or will his interest increase if he can only experience it vicariously?"

"Anson's got a lot of fight, a lot of vigor, a lot of life left in him for the game, but eventually the question he's going to run into is, 'When will I stop connecting?'" Geoff Griffin says. "Will eighteen-year-old females connect with a sixty-five-year-old guy? Nobody in this sport has really tested that yet."

No one who knows Dorrance can imagine him not coaching the Tar Heels. "I just can't picture Anson watching from the stands," says Teague dormmate Freddie Kiger, who is still friends with Dorrance. "He will have to be like a comet after that long run across the heavens who burns out in one cataclysmic blast, because I just don't see him one day saying, 'OK, that's enough, I'm going to go home and knit socks.'"

"Anson is arrogant enough to coach until he physically can't," Kristine Lilly says. "He's arrogant enough to never stop believing he can coach his team to championships."

"Why would anyone want to leave this community?" Dorrance asks. "We live in a beautiful place. We joke around a lot. We stay fit playing golf and hockey. And we're helping a lot of young people grow up. We may not have our names in lights, but we're successful." *You may never be rich, but you'll lead a rich life.*

Dorrance is keenly aware that in every coaching journey there must be a rise and fall. For guidance about the end of his career, Dorrance as usual has turned to

Dean Smith. He recalls reading an article about Smith when he retired after thirty-six seasons at age sixty-six in 1997. "A reporter asked Dean what career accomplishment he is most proud of," Dorrance recalls. "Dean could have said, 'I am most proud that I won more basketball games than anyone in history,' or 'I won two national championships,' or 'I developed an athlete like Michael Jordan,' or 'I impacted on the lives of so many young men.' He could have said a thousand different things. Instead he said something that only those of us who have coached for a living can understand. Dean said, 'Of all the things I've done, I'm most proud that I retired coaching.' In other words, he coached until he wore his ass out. I can see myself coaching until I drop dead of a heart attack on the sideline."

Dorrance often speaks matter-of-factly about his own death. Gone is that immortal kid who refused his own demise in ROTC at St. Mary's, but Dorrance is a man who hasn't feared death since the day he read his name on the white cross at the American Cemetery in Normandy and experienced the odd sensation that he was looking at his own gravestone. He says when that day comes, he just prays the ending is quick and dignified. Dorrance has always admired the way his father passed away. Suddenly. A violent human implosion. Big Pete never knew what hit him. Anson can only hope to die that well.

He says he wouldn't mind being buried in the old cemetery at the other end of the driveway to Fetzer Field, so that he could honor his grandmother's wish and stay a Tar Heel forever. After sprinting through an entire UNC spring practice in 2002, going nose to nose and kneecap to kneecap with players less than half his age and joking that he could keel over at any second, he gathered his staff and players around him and quoted to them the words he'd like to have engraved onto his headstone, a favorite line from Jack Kerouac's *On The Road*:

> *The only people for me are the mad ones, the ones who are mad to live, mad to talk, mad to be saved, desirous of everything at the same time, the ones who never yawn or say a commonplace thing, but burn, burn, burn like fabulous yellow roman candles exploding like spiders across the stars . . .*

Upon hearing this, Palladino replied, "Anson, that's going to be one big stone."

23 | *Renewal*

Our souls are not hungry for fame, comfort, wealth, or power. Our souls are hungry for meaning, for the sense that we have figured out how to live so that our lives matter, so that the world will be at least a little bit different for our having passed through it.

—Harold Kushner

*A*llllllrightthen, obviously I can sense in this room that we're all still basking in the glow of that great championship victory this past weekend. Bask in it forever. I mean, wasn't that fun? One of the things I absolutely loved about you guys this year is that many of you had amazing seasons relative to last year. I'm unbelievably proud of what a lot of you guys did to become extraordinary, and doesn't it feel good? Doesn't this feel good? I have enjoyed every second since the championship game ended. I'm on Cloud Frigging Nine. I mean I haven't been able to sleep the last two days I feel so damn good. Everyone in my family feels good. Everything I eat tastes good. The sun is brighter. The world all of a sudden has become a better place. My whole life has been transformed because of this past weekend. And it wasn't just that we won. It was the way we won. We beat the shit out of those two teams. It was unbelievable the way we played. You guys worked. You guys fought. You guys were relentless. You won those games with extraordinary heart, effort, technique, artistry, and excitement. Our ultimate satisfaction is when we show the potential of women's soccer, and on the biggest stage the college game has to offer, you guys showed how well women can play. You took the game up a level. You guys set the standard higher for the rest of the country.

The thing that continues to motivate me is that you guys were so frigging awesome in that Final Four, and yet neither opposing coach or any of the players on the teams that you crushed would pay you that compliment. Isn't it tragic that nobody there was gracious enough to genuflect before you and admit that you guys were awesome? In a way that satisfies me even more because that must mean that this is burning them to death. If they don't have the grace to say that you guys are an amazing team, then this must still hurt them right now, and I love that. I absolutely love that. That kind of excites me about next year because you know what I'd like to do next year? The same fucking thing. Basically that starts now. Did you guys enjoy your day off? . . . Good. Next year begins today.

The man delivers this speech before an audience of women. Coach Anson Dorrance conveys this message to a specific team inside a specific locker room during a specific season, but these are words he could have said to begin almost any season in the history of the University of North Carolina women's soccer program, because, like so many of Dorrance's speeches, this one is timeless.

The speech marks the end of the soccer off-season, a transitional respite that is also known as Monday. Every year on that Monday in December, the day after the national championship game, Tar Heel players are encouraged to forget about soccer. Be decadent or, in some cases, *more* decadent. It is revelry tempered only by the unfortunate coincidence that the Monday usually occurs smack in the middle of final exams.

Then comes Tuesday.

On this particular Tuesday morning, the roses representing past championships that Dorrance presented to the team three weeks ago have withered and died; their blackened, shriveled petals strewn across the floor. The seniors who commanded the team to that underappreciated championship two days earlier have vanished, as ephemeral as the roses, their customary places on the meeting room benches emptied, not to be replaced until August by freshmen as yet unknown. *Athletics is about renewal.*

Although only forty-four hours have passed since the championship game ended, there is suddenly a feeling in the room as Dorrance completes his opening remarks that a tide has shifted. Dorrance then pulls out a sheet of paper, and it is officially next season.

This is an extraordinary poem that captures so much of what I believe our program represents and I want to read it to you. It is called "The Man Watching" by Rainer Maria Rilke:

> *I can tell by the way the trees beat, after*
> *So many dull days, on my worried windowpanes*
> *that a storm is coming,*
> *and I hear the far-off fields say things*
> *I can't bear without a friend,*
> *I can't love without a sister.*
>
> *The storm, the shifter of shapes, drives on*
> *across the woods and across time,*
> *and the world looks as if it had no age:*
> *the landscape, like a line in the psalm book,*
> *is seriousness and weight and eternity.*
>
> *What we choose to fight is so tiny!*
> *What fights with us is so great!*
> *If only we would let ourselves be dominated*
> *as things do by some immense storm,*
> *we would become strong too, and not need names.*
>
> *When we win it's with small things,*
> *and the triumph itself makes us small.*

What is extraordinary and eternal
does not want to be bent by us.
I mean the Angel who appeared
to the wrestlers of the Old Testament:
when the wrestlers' sinews
grew long like metal strings,
he felt them under his fingers
like chords of deep music.

Whoever was beaten by this Angel
(who often simply declined to fight)
went away proud and strengthened
and great from that harsh hand,
that kneaded him as if to change his shape.
Winning does not tempt that man.
This is how he grows: by being defeated, decisively,
by constantly greater beings.

The room falls silent. Some of the young women stare up at Dorrance, while some others nervously peek at each other. Dorrance tells his players that the poem epitomizes the UNC program's philosophy that even in the wake of a national championship, there is still room for growth. Keep pushing. Don't quit. Take responsibility. Ascend never-endingly. And if you ever become afraid of failing to become everything you've always dreamed, think about this poem. Dorrance tells them that the way to keep growing is not by winning, but instead by being defeated, decisively, by constantly greater aspirations. The older players, who have heard this poem before, nod in recognition and whisper to the younger ones that they will try to explain it to them later. Dorrance then pulls out a stack of papers and asks each of his players to take one.

So, let me just set the rhythm for what happens now. What we are sharing with you now are your final rankings from the competitive cauldron this season. Some of you are ranked high and some of you aren't, and usually that's reflective of why we've chosen the people who play. Here's what we want you to do. Look at this self-critically and figure out a way to climb. That begins now with your Christmas break. Obviously, take a break completely from the game. Don't touch a soccer ball until we see you again, but don't waste this time. Some of you guys are extraordinarily fit, so don't lose your base. Those of you who aren't fit have never invested in your fitness base in your life. Now is your opportunity. This should not be a break for you, because you've been taking a break your whole frigging life. So make a decision right now that you're going to get fit. If we want to win next year and you want to contribute, it's based on what you do now, how you organize your time, and how you discipline yourself. It's your choice.

This is such a simple yet profound lesson that I learned as a teenager from a brilliant algebra teacher that I had in my sophomore year at my boys' boarding school in Switzerland. I didn't realize it at the time, but this math teacher inspired me and has affected the way I've thought for the rest of my life. On the first day of class he said, "I am giving you a homework assignment and I'll give you one day to do it. You will be graded on this assignment and you can select to do it or not. If you select not to do it, don't worry about it. I'm not going to reprimand you. Just make sure that whatever you do in place of the math homework is something you value more than getting an F on the assignment. Please understand that I don't expect you guys to always turn homework in. If you're having a rollicking good time or you think you're doing something that genuinely has greater value to you than a math assignment, please do it. Over the course of the year, you've got a hundred homework assignments, so it's not going to affect your grade that much if you miss one or two."

We thought that teacher was full of shit, and part of the joy of being at a boys' boarding school is acting like an absolute jackass, so we decided to test him and not do our homework. He never reprimanded any of us, never treated any of us differently if we didn't turn something in. And then one day it dawned on me what he was really trying to teach us. It's a tremendous lesson. How you choose to spend your time every day is going to shape who you are.

So I'm going to make the same suggestion to all of you. I know that some people in this room aspire to be the best, aspire to play on the national team. Others are doing this for social reasons. Keep in mind that I've always felt like you guys have the right to make the choice. I am not going to choose whether this is something you're going to take seriously or not. You guys don't have to be great soccer players. You can do what most ordinary people do. Go to the mall. Sit on the couch eating bonbons. Whatever. My respect for you as a human being has nothing to do with your development as a soccer player, so if you want to dork off all spring, you may lose playing time, but you won't lose my respect. I know from my own experience that not all of you will choose to be extraordinary, and something I've never understood is a coach who gets angry with players who don't choose that path. Hell, being extraordinary is not an easy choice. Not too many people can truly be extraordinary because then that would undermine the definition of what extraordinary is. At North Carolina, excellence is a choice.

Obviously, I would love for all of you guys to select to be absolutely extraordinary at this game, or at least commit yourselves to being as good as you can be. There are enough hours in the rest of the day for you to chase every other dream you have. But to chase this as a dream, to be absolutely the best you can be, is going to take a serious commitment from you. It's not going to be easy. There are going to be days when you don't want to pour anything into this, and as a result on those days, just like with the algebra grade, it can compromise you. It may just be to the tiniest degree, but the margin between the very good and the extraordinary is something incredibly minor like that. So make sure you understand that whatever you decide to do, that you've chosen it. And make sure you understand that it's not what you do in the week or the month before the season begins, it's what you do now.

Trust me, I didn't take the day off yesterday. I couldn't wait to get back to work. I couldn't wait for this meeting today because I have so much frigging energy right now, I have so much juice to bring to bear, and I want to spend it on winning it again next year. I don't know about you guys, but I'm still on this unbelievable high. This for me was incredibly special, and I want you guys to know that. I loved seeing all you guys so happy. Every sacrifice you made in the last year to be where we are right now, in my opinion, was worth it and I'll tell you this— and this is genuine—we may have an even better team this coming year. Isn't that scary? Are you frigging kidding me? It's a new year and we could be even better this year. So that is our challenge. What I want you to remember is that nobody else is celebrating what we did this past weekend. Our opponents are embittered about that victory, and what they would love more than anything else is to pretend like it was an aberration and beat us down next year. So, continue to enjoy this feeling and remember it, because I want us to be back in this room enjoying the same damn thing next year, and that will be based on how hard we work. It was such a pleasure watching us play at our best, and I think we can ascend even higher. So, girls, what do you say? What do you want to do this year? Should we try to win the national championship? All right, let's get to another level. Are you with me? . . .

Postscript

It is still hard to believe that UNC women's soccer won only one national championship in the five seasons during which I reported and wrote this book, by far the most severe championship drought in the program's history. As those seasons passed, I neglected to mention that unfortunate coincidence to anyone in the Tar Heel program for fear they'd stop talking to me.

Naturally, there is a period of withdrawal after spending so much time around a particular subject. I have continued to follow the story of UNC soccer a bit less personally, but with no less interest, in subsequent seasons. Sure enough, the Tar Heels returned to the mountaintop just a couple of months after this book was first published, winning the NCAA championship in 2006. Then they won it all again in 2008 and 2009, each title further cementing my concerns that I had been a jinx. These three championships each represent a distinct ingredient in what makes the program unique.

The 2006 season began with a slumber party. Three weeks before the start of the season, nine UNC freshmen bucked tradition and chose not to split up and stay with upperclassmen during the preseason. Instead they would spend five days and nights nesting together elbow-to-elbow on air mattresses laid out on the floor of the team meeting room at the McCaskill Soccer Center.

The nine rookies ate Teddy Grahams and hugged teddy bears and fretted over how the heck they were going to pass UNC's draconian fitness testing. Every so often a veteran teammate would drop by and remind them that the Tar Heels had missed out on the final four the last two seasons. The freshmen vowed to help get UNC back to where it belonged. On the blackboard one of the squatters scribbled a simple message: *OUR TURN.*

UNC's youngest team ever lost its first game of the season to Texas A&M 1–0 in double overtime in front of an NCAA record crowd in College Station. While the Tar Heels bounced back to win their next eight games, Anson Dorrance still questioned his team's toughness, so at practice on the day before a home game against top-ranked Florida State, he spoke to them about how lions mark their territory in urine and then defend it with their lives. That evening, the Tar Heels gathered at Fetzer Field to "mark their territory" and then proceeded to maul the Seminoles the following night.

During the pregame before Florida State, the Tar Heels met 12-year-old Kelly Muldoon, a UNC fan and soccer player who had been diagnosed with cancer. The Tar Heels decided to dedicate the rest of the season to Kelly, to play for something larger than themselves. The UNC players bombarded

Kelly with "Get Well" e-mails and Kelly's father, Steve, sent weekly updates about her deteriorating condition, imploring the Tar Heels to please, please, please, make it to the College Cup so that, if his daughter lived long enough, she might make the trip to watch her favorite team play one more time. Before every game, the Tar Heels etched a word on their wrist tape: *Fight* or *Strength* or *Hope*. And always the initials *K.M.* UNC did reach the final four and Kelly was there, sitting right behind the Tar Heel bench.

In the NCAA championship match against Notre Dame, one of the Tar Heel freshmen, Casey Nogueira, looped a pass to senior Heather O'Reilly behind the Irish defense and O'Reilly scored UNC's first goal in the 18th minute. Then Nogueira scored what would prove to be the decisive goal on a header off a cross early in the second half.

When the final whistle sounded on UNC's 2–1 victory, the team's 27th straight win, there were seven freshmen on the field for the Tar Heels, all making good on their pledge that it was indeed UNC's turn. Again. Moments later, a photographer approached the North Carolina players huddled around Kelly Muldoon on the field and asked, "Where's the trophy?" The Tar Heels pointed to the young girl in her wheelchair smiling proudly and in unison they responded, "Right there."

UNC's success is really all about what you don't see.

You don't see several Tar Heels huddled together in tears just outside of the UNC locker room after a 3–2 loss to Notre Dame in the third round of 2007 NCAA Tournament, all of them in total disbelief that a UNC team had been knocked out before the College Cup for only the third time ever.

You don't see those same players huddled at the first team meeting before the 2008 season, promising each other never to take winning for granted again.

You don't see Dorrance on the day before the 2008 NCAA semifinal reminding his Tar Heels that UNC is the only team among the final four that has actually lost a game during the season, somehow convincing them that they are "underdogs" and "spoilers," even though he doesn't totally believe it himself.

You don't see the Tar Heel players gather at the end of that last practice before the College Cup, giggling like the schoolgirls that they are and chanting, "Soccer is fun! Soccer is fun! Soccer is fun!"

You don't see Dorrance erasing the tension minutes before the NCAA semifinal against UCLA by reading an email about how Art, the team's genial octogenarian ballboy, defended the Tar Heels against a heckler earlier in the season by saying, "Be quiet! If you can't yell something supportive then shut up!"

You don't see that none of the UNC coaches are around their players for one second on the day after UNC has beaten UCLA 1–0 in the semifinal, so instead the players spend their off-day competing over stuff like who can do the best impersonation of Shrek.

You don't see Dorrance shaking his head incredulously after completing his pregame talk before the NCAA final as his players dance maniacally around the locker room to Lil Wayne and Michael Jackson when they are supposed to be out on the field warming up.

You don't see Dorrance's halftime speech during the final when he simply asks his players, "Who's the better team?" and they respond in unison, "We are!" and suddenly UNC isn't the underdog anymore, they are the clear favorites, despite trailing 1–0 against Notre Dame.

You don't see the cold-blooded confidence in Nogueira's eyes as she walks back out of the locker room, knowing that on this field she has already won two high school state championships and scored the game-clinching goal in the NCAA final two years earlier.

You do see (assuming you're a college soccer fan) Nogueira score two goals in the second half, the first on a rocket free kick in the 52nd minute and the second on a bending shot over the goalkeeper's head with just over two minutes left to play, to defeat the Irish 2–1.

You don't see Dorrance's humility in the postgame press conference, deflecting all of the credit for the victory onto his players by describing his team as playing with "a wonderful sort of joyous anarchy."

You don't see a dozen Tar Heels still hanging out on the field an hour after the final, totally oblivious to the near freezing temperatures, because they don't want to change out of their uniforms.

You don't see the national championship trophy. Nobody does. It is still at the Chapel Hill restaurant where the victory party occurred, left behind when all the joyous anarchy finally ceased.

You don't see Dorrance in his office early the next morning strategizing about how to win it all again and saying, "Basically, what motivates me right now is the pain the other programs go through when we win championships. That kind of suffering is worth its weight in gold. We went in and just destroyed everyone else's hopes and dreams and that was so invigorating for me."

You don't see Art later that day with tears streaming down his cheeks, saying, "You have no idea what this means to me," as he reads the e-mail about him that Dorrance had shared with the team.

You don't see ten UNC players gathering to play pickup soccer that evening because according to one, "we already miss each other."

You don't see that Nogueira is not among them, as she would normally be, because she is sitting at her desk at home writing thirty-seven thank-you notes, one to each of her teammates and coaches, including the last one to Dorrance that reads:

Anson—
    Thanks for an amazing season and thanks for always believing in me and challenging me as a player. You have created such an amazing program that is truly my family and I'm so honored to be a part of it. I have so much respect for

you and the balance that you have perfectly figured out between being serious and having fun. Thank you also for your crazy stories and advice. You are truly an amazing person with an awesome personality and you deserve every achievement you have accomplished.
Casey

During the flight home from Miami on October 25, 2009 the oppressive weight of history was enough for the plane carrying the Tar Heels to lose altitude. UNC had just suffered a 1–0 defeat to the Hurricanes that afternoon after losing in the waning seconds of double overtime to Florida State three days before. The Tar Heels had a total of three losses in the ACC. No UNC team had ever lost more. The Tar Heels had a two-game losing streak. No UNC team had ever lost more. College road trips to Florida are supposed to be a lot more fun.

Dorrance has always believed that one of the key elements to leadership is the capacity to provide hope, and so on the trip back to Chapel Hill he decided he needed to convene what amounted to a father-daughter chat with his players. As the bus from the airport arrived back on the UNC campus just after 11 o'clock that Sunday night, Dorrance stood up in the aisle and calmly addressed his team.

"I can feel the overwhelming pressure that our tradition imposes on you," he said. "Please don't feel like you have to defend that tradition. You don't. All you have to do is achieve your own goals. You are not alone in these losses. Trust me. Most of this is my fault. You know what? Life is difficult sometimes, but we're going to be OK. We're going to get back to work the day after tomorrow and we're going to play with heart and play for each other and we're going to be fine. Let me tell you something. Other teams are so excited about how we've sucked lately. They're talking crap about us, but believe me, not a single one of those teams wants to play the Tar Heels in the NCAA Tournament. It's going to be so much fun to blow up the NCAA bracket. Are you all ready to blow up the NCAA bracket? We're going to win the frigging national championship. Are you with me?"

Two months earlier, at the dawn of the 2009 season, Dorrance had suspected that he might be watching not just the greatest UNC team he'd ever coached, but the greatest women's soccer team he'd ever seen. A season-opening 7–2 demolition of third-ranked UCLA followed two weeks later by a 6–0 victory at second-ranked Notre Dame did nothing to change his mind. Then the Tar Heels lost dynamic midfielder Nikki Washington to a season-ending knee injury, Nogueira lost her goal-scoring touch, Dorrance lent the quarterback of his midfield, Olympic gold medalist Tobin Heath, back to the U.S. national team for a while, and suddenly the Tar Heels' offense fizzled.

Dorrance sensed that UNC could only compete for a national championship on the strength of its suffocating defense, so he challenged his team to shut opponents out. He thought UNC might need to win games 1–0, the most perilous way to approach a soccer game.

After the loss at Miami, the Tar Heels began a streak of eight games—a total of 799 minutes—without allowing a goal. In fact, the only goals scored against UNC the rest of the season were two second-half goals in an already decided 5–2 victory over Wake Forest in the NCAA Tournament quarterfinal. In UNC's last 11 games, the Tar Heels would pitch ten shutouts, including six 1–0 wins, and allow only twenty shots on goal.

In the NCAA semifinal against Notre Dame at Texas A&M's Aggie Soccer Stadium, the Tar Heels won 1–0 on a Nogueira goal in the 83rd minute. Then in the final against undefeated and top-ranked Stanford, UNC held the second-highest scoring team in the nation to a season-low nine shots in another 1–0 victory, completing the only championship season in which UNC won both games in the College Cup by a 1–0 score.

The 2009 national title was UNC's twenty-first in twenty-nine seasons and its twentieth NCAA title, making Dorrance the only coach ever to win twenty NCAA championships in a single sport. Dorrance called it his most challenging coaching season of all time, but also his most satisfying. "I don't think in terms of battles, I think in terms of campaigns," he said. "We're like Napoleon trying to conquer Europe, always trying to expand the empire, and because of my lousy record in recruiting against Stanford, they are like the Prussians. When we vanquish the Prussians, we have a chance to rule the world."

In a program steeped in poetic coincidence, nine Tar Heel seniors had come full circle. They had lost their first game as freshmen at Aggie Soccer Stadium, UNC's first season-opening defeat in twenty-three years. After that game an exhausted and overwhelmed freshman named Whitney Engen lay prone on the field, stared up at Dorrance and asked, "Is every game going to be like this?" After her final UNC game, an exhausted and overwhelmed Engen lay prone in almost the same spot on the very same field, stared up at Dorrance and said, "I wish every game could be like this."

Tim Crothers
January 2010

Appendix

Year	Record	National Tournament	Goals For	Goals Against
1979	10-2-0	No Tournament	78	15
1980	21-5-0	No Tournament	104	21
1981	23-0-0	Champion	172	8
1982	19-2-0	Champion	112	8
1983	19-1-0	Champion	95	11
1984	24-0-1	Champion	120	6
1985	18-2-1	Second Place	98	13
1986	24-0-1	Champion	113	10
1987	23-0-1	Champion	96	2
1988	18-0-3	Champion	58	9
1989	24-0-1	Champion	99	9
1990	20-1-1	Champion	87	12
1991	24-0-0	Champion	101	9
1992	25-0-0	Champion	132	11
1993	23-0-0	Champion	92	15
1994	25-1-1	Champion	114	12
1995	25-1-0	Tied Third Place	108	6
1996	25-1-0	Champion	109	11
1997	27-0-1	Champion	117	8
1998	25-1-0	Second Place	98	7
1999	24-2-0	Champion	91	12
2000	21-3-0	Champion	97	17
2001	24-1-0	Second Place	79	12
2002	21-2-4	Tied Third Place	84	19
2003	27-0-0	Champion	113	11
2004	20-1-2	Third Round	68	14
2005	23-1-1	Quarterfinals	90	15
2006	27-1-0	Champion	81	13
2007	19-4-1	Third Round	56	15
2008	25-1-2	Champion	89	16
2009	23-3-1	Champion	63	12

Overall Record: 696-36-22 (.938)
ACC Regular Season Record: 139-10-4 (.922)

ACC Tournament Record: 57-0-3 (.975)
NCAA Tournament Record 106-7-1 (.934)
Goals For: 3,014
Goals Against: 359
20 ACC Tournament Championships
19 ACC Regular Season Championships
20 NCAA Tournament Championships
1 AIAW Tournament Championship
28 NCAA Tournament Appearances
25 NCAA College Cup Appearances

UNC's Retired Jerseys (National Players of the Year)

April Heinrichs #2
Shannon Higgins #3
Robin Confer #7
Debbie Keller #8
Whitney Engen #9
Tisha Venturini #13
Lorrie Fair #14
Kristine Lilly #15
Yael Averbuch #17

Mia Hamm #19
Heather O'Reilly #20
Cindy Parlow #22
Lindsay Tarpley #25
Staci Wilson #27
Meredith Florance #28
Catherine Reddick #31
Casey Nogueira #54

UNC's All-Time Letter Winners

A
Acquavella, Kristin 1989–91, 1993
Allan, Senga 1982–85
Averbuch, Yael 2005–08
Azzu, Renee 1990

B
Ball, Elizabeth 1999, 2001–02
Ball, Susie 2000–01
Ballinger, Anne 1979–80
Barnes, Brandy 1987
Bartok, Brittani 2008–09
Bates, Tracey 1985–87, 1989
Baucom, Eva 2006
Beatty, Diane 1981–84

Bernardi, Bettina 1985–86
Bialas, Erin 1995
Billings, Chrissy 1980–81
Black, Corinne 2002–05
Blazo, Stacey 1988–91
Bliss, Katherine 1979
Blomgren, Leigh 2001–03
Boneparth, Caroline 2006–09
Boneparth, Pammy 2008
Boobas, Jo 1983–86
Boone, Laura 1987–90
Borgman, Danielle 1998–2001
Boyle, Missy 1992, 1994
Brallier, Robyn 1995–96
Branam, Jenni 1999–2002

Briggs, Leslie 2007–08
Brigman, Megan 2009
Bronze, Lucy 2009
Brooks, Alison 1992–94
Brooks, Amber 2009
Brooks, Katie 2004–07
Burns, Amy 1992–93
Bush, Susan 1999–2002
Byers, Jane 1993–94

C
Caldwell, Shanna 1998
Carbery, Rosemary 1979–80
Carter, Julie 1988–91
Castelloe, Keath 1984–87
Catchings, Toni 1985
Chalupny, Lori 2002–05
Clary, Nancy 1980–81
Cobb, Suzy 1981–84
Coley, Paige 1990–93
Confer, Robin 1994–97
Costa, Johanna 1998–2001
Crow, Dawn 1991–94
Crowley, Liz 1980–81
Current, Molly 1979–81
Currie, Kim 2009

D
Dacey, Sarah 1993–96
Daly, Hannah 2009
Davenport, Shannon 1991–92
Dempsey, Erika 1997–99
Denney, Mikki 1993
DePlatchett, Kristin 1998–2001
Donahue, Tracy 1991–92
Dougherty, Meagan 1990–93
Duffy, Lisa 1984–87
Dunlap, Joan 1983–84

E
Eames, Jenn 1991–94
Early, Caroline 2008
Egan, Danielle 1991–94
Eller, Karli 2003–05

Ellis, Julie 1984
Ellis, Susan 1980–81, 1983–84
Engen, Whitney 2006–09
Enos, Stacey 1982–85
Esposito, Kelly 2005–06
Eubanks, Mary 1989
Eveland, Kristi 2006–09
Everton, Erin 1990
Everton, Holly 1983

F
Fair, Lorrie 1996–99
Falk, Aubrey 1994–97
Felts, Anne 2001–04
Fettig, Nel 1994–97
Finger, Shelley 1991–94
Fletcher, Kendall 2002–05
Florance, Meredith 1997–2000
Fox, Carolyn 1983
Frederick, Betsy 2005–08
Friedman, Nancy 1991–92

G
Gale, Judy 1981
Garrison, Kathy 1979
Gaston, Leslie 1999–2002
Gayle, Robyn 2004–07
Gebauer, Wendy 1985–88
Gegg, Gretchen 1986
Gervais, Sophie 2001–04
Gilbert, Jaime 2004–07
Givan, Rachel 2007–09
Goldberg, Ellen 1979–80
Goulson, Amy 1983–84
Green, Susie 1991–94
Greenberg, Wendy 1981
Gregg, Laurie 1981–82
Griffin, Tyler 2002
Guarnotta, Julie 1986–89
Guess, Elizabeth 2003–06

H
Hackett, Nancy 1998–2000
Haines, Kelly 1979

Hamilton, Linda 1990
Hamm, Mia 1989–90, 1992–93
Hardman, Brynn 2002–05
Harrelson, Lynn 1982
Harris, Ariel 2004–07
Harris, Ashlyn 2006–09
Hawkins, Ali 2006, 2008–09
Hayes, Melissa 2006
Heath, Tobin 2006–09
Hegstad, Birthe 1985–88
Heinrichs, April 1983–86
Henry, Lori 1986–88
Higgins, Shannon 1986–89
Huber, Beth 1981–84
Hurst, Ginger 1980
Huston, Chris 1988–89
Hutton, Leslie 1994–95
Hyatt, Ava 1986–89

J

Jacobs, Cassie 1983
Jakowich, Jill 1990
Jennings, Melissa 1996–97
Johnson, Betsy 1982–85
Johnson, Marianne 1981–82
Johnson, Rye 1994–95
Jones, Courtney 2008–09
Jones, Kasey 1985–86
Jordan, Eleanor 1979–81
Judd, Kerry 1980

K

Kalinoski, Pam 1987–89, 1991
Kamholz, Kalli 1999–2000
Karvelsson, Rakel 1995–98
Keller, Debbie 1993–96
Kelly, Angela 1991–94
Kelly, Kathy 1981–84
Kinney, Jamie 1999–2000
Klas, Ann 1980–81
Klimczak, Katie 2007–09
Klingenberg, Meghan 2007–09
Kluegel, Jena 1998–2001
Kovanen, Dori 1981–82, 1984–85

L

Lancaster, Elizabeth 2003–06
Lawler, Helen 1996–99
Lehmann, Courtney 1988–90
Lewis, Celia 1979
Lilly, Kristine 1989–92
Lincoln, Amy 1995–96
Lippard, Allison 1983
Lockwood, Booie 1987
Long, Allie 2007–08
Lubrano, Maria 2007, 2009
Ludington, Sarah 1988–90
Luft, Tina 1984
Lutz, Katie 2007–09

M

Machin, Amy 1981–84
Marr, Sarah 1980
Marslender, Elizabeth 1995–96
Marslender, Julia 1997–2000
Martens, Beth 1987
Mathias, Merritt 2008–09
Maxwell, Jessica 2003–04, 2006–07
McCartney, Jill 1984–85
McDavid, Sherri 1984–86
McDermott, Marcia 1983–86
McDonald, Jessica 2008–09
McDonald, Raven 1997–2000
McDowell, Mary 2001–04
McDowell, Rebekah 1996–99
McLaughlin, Caroline 1979
McNeill, Annie 1985–86
Mikula, Erin 2007, 2009
Mills, Meg 1980–81
Mitchell, Charlotte 1996–99
Monroe, Kasey 1992–93
Moore, Ashley 2006–09
Moraca, Mandy 2005–08
Morrell, Anne 2001–04
Morrison, Mandy 1997–2000
Mullinix, Siri 1995–98
Munden, Paula 1991
Murphy, Leea 2002–05
Murphy, Tina 1997–2000

N

Nelson, Stacey 1984–85
Nogueira, Casey 2006–09
Noonan, Tracy 1992–95

O

O'Dell, Kathleen 1983–86
O'Reilly, Heather 2003–06
Overgaard, Gretchen 1996–97
Owen, Lisa 1988–89
Ozier, Ellen 1990
Ozier, Mary Ann 1989

P

Parlow, Cindy 1995–98
Parsons, Aja 1984
Pastiglione, Meghan 1997
Patrick, Kim 1999–2000
Pediaditakis, Nicole 1980
Perkins, Jennifer 2003–06
Pfankuch, Emmalie 2008–09
Phillips, Liz 1980–81
Pickering, Emily 1981–84
Poore, Louellen 1988–91
Premji, Ranee 2009
Proost, Merridee 1987–90
Prosser, Anne 1979

R

Ramsey, Alyssa 2000–03
Randolph, Sara 2001–04
Rayfield, Janet 1979–82
Record, Elizabeth 1990
Record, Emily 1990
Reddick, Catherine 2000–03
Remy, Anne 1998–2001
Rice, Emily 1988–90
Rich, Alyssa 2009
Riggs, Ashley 1992–95
Rigley, Donna 1986–88
Roberts, Amy 1993–96
Roberts, Nicole 1996
Roberts, Tiffany 1995–98
Rodenbough, Anna 2005–08

Royal, Pam 1981–82
Rubio, Vanessa 1992, 1994–96

S

Samsot, Katie 1986–87
Sanchez, Keri 1991–94
Santana, Roz 1991–94
Schwoy, Laurie 1996–98, 2000
Scott, Synthia 1980–82
Scruggs, Emily 1979
Serwetnyk, Carrie 1984–87
Sharpe, Leonora 1979–80
Sheppard, Beth 1995–96, 1998–99
Sherow, Anne 1985–88
Simmons, Katie 2000–01
Slocum, Nancy 1983–85
Smith, Jane 2000–02
Smith, Julie 2000
Smith, Mary 1984
Smith, Sterling 2006–2009
Soares, Sasha 1989–92
Springer, Carolyn 1990–93
Steadman, Amy 2003–04
Stoecker, Lindsay 1996–99
Stollmeyer, Suzie 1982
Stumpf, Andrea 1980

T

Tarpley, Lindsay 2002–05
Taylor, Lou 1979–80
Thomas, Caeri 1990
Toll, Vanessa 2005
Tomecka, Maggie 2000–03
Tooly, Lee 1979
Tower, Rita 1989–90, 1992–93
Trojak, Sonja 1992–95
Tucker, Amanda 2007–09

U

Uritus, Meg 1994–95, 1997

V

Venturini, Tisha 1991–94
Vest, Jane 1990–91

W

Walker, Jordan 2000–03
Walker, Lori 1989–91
Wallace, Diane 1980
Washington, Nikki 2006–09
Watley, Carmen 2000–03
Welsh-Loveman, Kristine 2009
Welsh-Loveman, Monica 2007–09
Werden, Carla 1986–89
White, Kacey 2002–05
Whittier, Amy 1997, 1999, 2001
Wiegman, Sarina 1989
Wilson, Staci 1994–97
Winget, Aly 2002–05

Winslow, Laura 2001, 2003–04
Wiren, Tracy 1979–80
Wood, Rachel 2008

Y

Yates, Julie 2004–07
Young, Hilary 2000

Z

Zaccagnini, Jennifer 1990–93
Zarzar, Katie 2003–04
Zeh, Stephanie 1981–82
Zeman, Andrea 1985–88

Acknowledgments

First, I'd like to thank Faye. I don't know her last name, but Faye bestowed upon me 239 precious daily parking passes at the UNC soccer office over a four-year period and, bless her heart, never once asked, "So, when will your book be done?"

Along with Faye, there are many other talented and patient Sherpas who contributed to this book, each of whom deserves something between a gracious thank-you note and a kidney. Skip DeWall at Ann Arbor Media Group passionately embraced this story. Then with the help of Chris Parris-Lamb, it found its way into the caring hands of Rob Kirkpatrick, Margaret Smith, and Bethany Reis at St. Martin's Press.

I am also indebted to my keen-eyed readers, Joe Mustian, Tim Nash, and John Walters. UNC Women's Soccer Hall of Fame curator Tom Sander unearthed much buried treasure and Julie Carter, the program's player archivist, shared some ancient manuscripts not found in the hall. Dr. Bill Prentice spoke to the stranger at practices early on when nobody else would, and UNC administrative assistant Delaine Marbry turned a blind eye to my abuse of her copy machine. UNC media coordinator Dave Lohse answered what must have seemed like a million pointless questions. M'Liss and the rest of the Dorrance family trusted me, someone they must have feared their husband/son/brother/father wouldn't take sufficient time to judge.

I'd also like to thank Jordan Walker, a faithful confidant, and Heather O'Reilly, a timely muse, as well as the 127 other Tar Heels and dozens of other Dorrance acquaintances who gave their valuable time to be interviewed for this book. Dr. John Gelin, who provided me the "tranquil" atmosphere in which to write. My mom and dad, because we all should. And, most importantly, my son, Atticus, whose birth provided me with an immutable deadline, his sister, Sawyer, and their remarkably tolerant mother, Dana, both the sweetest and toughest editor I've ever had.

Finally, many of the more fruitful interviews for this book took place on the golf course, so thank you to Anson Dorrance, Bill Palladino, and Chris Ducar for occasionally permitting me to be the fourth in their foursome. A truly compassionate bunch, shortly after finishing a golf scramble tournament with them a few years back, I was devastated to discover that my wedding band had fallen out of my pocket and was missing somewhere on the back nine. I told Ducar, "Oh no, I lost my wedding ring out there."

Ducar responded, "Really, wow, I lost the long-drive contest by just *two yards*."

Thank you all for your support.

Index